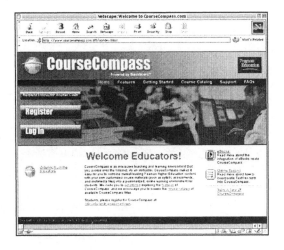

Best-Selling Professional Resources for College Instructors!

As the world's leader in education, Allyn & Bacon understands your interest in continual professional development. From the latest advancements in technology for the classroom to special insights for adjunct professors, these books were written for you! [See the Teaching Tips section at the back of the manual for teaching advice, ideas, and suggestions.]

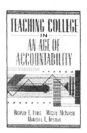    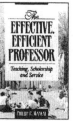 

Instructing and Mentoring the African American College Student: Strategies for Success in Higher Education
Louis B. Gallien, Jr., Regent University and
Marshalita Sims Peterson, Ph.D, Spelman College
©2005 / 0-205-38917-1

**Grant Writing in Higher Education:
A Step-by-Step Guide**
Kenneth Henson, The Citadel
©2004 / 0-205-38919-8

**Using Technology in Learner-Centered Education:
Proven Strategies for Teaching and Learning**
David G. Brown and Gordon McCray, both of Wake Forest University,
Craig Runde, Eckerd College and Heidi Schweizer, Marquette University
©2002 / 0-205-35580-3

**Creating Learning-Centered Courses
for the World Wide Web**
William B. Sanders, University of Hartford
©2001 / 0-205-31513-5

Success Strategies for Adjunct Faculty
Richard Lyons, Faculty Development Associates
©2004 / 0-205-36017-3

**The Effective, Efficient Professor:
Teaching, Scholarship and Service**
Philip C. Wankat, Purdue University
©2002 / 0-205-33711-2

**Emblems of Quality in Higher Education:
Developing and Sustaining High-Quality Programs**
Jennifer Grant Haworth, Loyola University, Chicago and
Clifton F. Conrad, University of Wisconsin, Madison,
©1997 / 0-205-19546-6

Faculty of Color in Academe: Bittersweet Success
Caroline Sotello Viernes Turner, Arizona State University
and Samuel L. Myers Jr., University of Minnesota
©2000 / 0-205-27849-3

An Introduction to Interactive Multimedia
Stephen J. Misovich, Jerome Katrichis, David Demers, William B. Sanders, all of the University of Hartford
©2003 / 0-205-34373-2

**Learner-Centered Assessment on College Campuses:
Shifting the Focus from Teaching to Learning**
Mary E. Huba, Iowa State University and Jann E. Freed,
Central College
©2000 / 0-205-28738-7

**The Online Teaching Guide: A Handbook of Attitudes,
Strategies, and Techniques for the Virtual Classroom**
Ken W. White and Bob H. Weight, both of University of Phoenix
Online Faculty
©2000 / 0-205-29531-2

**The Adjunct Professor's Guide to Success:
Surviving and Thriving in the College Classroom**
Richard Lyons, Faculty Development Associates, Marcella L. Kysilka,
and George E. Pawlas, both of University of Central Florida
©1999 / 0-205-28774-3

**Teaching Tips for College and University
Instructors: A Practical Guide**
David Royse, University of Kentucky
©2001 / 0-205-29839-7

Advice for New Faculty Members
Robert Boice, Emeritus, SUNY Stony Brook
©2000 / 0-205-28159-1

**Writing for Professional Publication:
Keys to Academic and Business Success**
Kenneth Henson, The Citadel
©1999 / 0-205-28313-6

Teaching College in an Age of Accountability
Richard Lyons, Faculty Development Associates, Meggin McIntosh,
University of Nevada - Reno, and Marcella L. Kysilka, University of
Central Florida
©2003 / 0-205-35315-0

Save 20% on any of these resources when you order online...

www.ablongman.com/highered

Instructor's Resource Manual

for

Beebe and Beebe

Public Speaking
An Audience-Centered Approach

Sixth Edition

prepared by

Melinda Morris Villagran
University of Texas at San Antonio

with contributions by

Charles N. Wise

and

Diana K. Ivy

Boston   New York   San Francisco
Mexico City   Montreal   Toronto   London   Madrid   Munich   Paris
Hong Kong   Singapore   Tokyo   Cape Town   Sydney

ISBN   0-205-46230-8

Printed in the United States of America

10 9 8 7 6 5 4 3 2 1   10 09 08 07 06 05

CONTENTS

TEACHING THE PUBLIC SPEAKING COURSE

The Importance of the Public Speaking Course in Your Department

If public speaking in your department is considered the "basic course," then it is probably the most important course in your department--particularly if it is required of all or many students to graduate. Here are some reasons why this course is significant to instructors and students.

1. Public speaking students arrive at your door with expectations that include a desire to improve their **communication competence**. No other skills are so closely tied to a student's personal and professional success as communication skills. Improved public speaking skills can directly affect students' employment and participation in their community.

2. A **department's reputation** is closely tied to the reputation of its basic course. For many people, the introductory public speaking course will be their only contact with your department. Students, faculty, and administrators may come to know your department by the reputation of your basic course.

3. Many colleges and universities have selected the introductory public speaking course as a requirement because they consider **communication skills** to be extremely valuable. Your course may be required by the entire university--as part of the core curriculum or general education components--or it may only be required of certain majors, such as those in Business, Education, Engineering, and Science. This requirement aspect necessitates coordination of expectations that faculty and students have about the course throughout the institution.

4. A fourth reason the public speaking course is significant relates to **generating communication majors**. Some students will become interested in the field and change their majors to communication because of a positive experience in your class. Many departments experience an increase in enrollment directly related to the success of their basic course.

5. Public speaking **instructors learn** about various subjects, about instruction, and about themselves from teaching this class. Listening to speeches helps instructors gain knowledge about a range of topics, as well as fueling their example base for subsequent sections of the course. Also, there is the added benefit of gaining exposure to a cross section of students from the institution, rather than only communication majors.

6. Finally, many if not most students will come to your public speaking course with serious anxiety, yet they must pass the course to graduate. Anyone who teaches public speaking will encounter different manifestations of this problem. For some students, their **communication apprehension** causes great physical and emotional stress. There's the graduating senior who has put off taking the course until his or her last semester; a student who takes the class for the fourth time, trying to simply get through and pass the course; the young person who "loses her or his cookies" before every class; the student who "breaks down" before a speech; and the "phantom student" who disappears weeks at a time because of a debilitating fear of public speaking. For these students, pubic speaking is not just another course. Teachers of such students have responsibilities beyond the typical instructional situation. These students need compassionate, sensitive, patient, and knowledgeable instructors to help them complete the course and experience some success.

Course Standardization

In many institutions, especially larger ones, multiple sections of public speaking are offered each semester or quarter. Standardization becomes a real issue in these contexts, possibly unlike smaller institutions offering only a few sections each term or those in which public speaking is an elective, not a requirement. But no matter the size and profile of the institution, standardization helps ensure that students receive comparable instruction across sections.

Some departments hear complaints about differences between public speaking sections, comments like: "In Dr. Smith's class they only have to give four speeches; why do we have to give five?" "The business department made this course a requirement for all their majors, but from what we hear, sections with lots of business majors have really different assignments from ours." "My teacher has a strict attendance policy, but my roommate's teacher doesn't make a big deal out of missing class." No matter the approach--mass or large lecture sections that rotate across faculty members, multi-sections taught by TAs, or small sections taught by full professors--some form of standardization enables consistency in meeting course goals. It allows students who complete the course to experience similar activities, complete comparable assignments, learn basic content, and meet similar standards. Within the commonality, teachers have latitude for individual creativity. The key is to balance the standardized elements with individuation so that instructors don't feel stifled, but students don't feel compromised.

Standardization is Important Because of......

--the potentially large number of students taking the course.

--the need for consistency across multiple sections, to ensure fairness for students.

--the potentially large number of instructors involved in teaching the course.

--the need for taking advantage of the knowledge of experienced course instructors.

Common Forms of Standardization Include......

--a course director who coordinates instruction.

--required or voluntary training and course meetings for instructors and TAs.

--the use of a common textbook.

--the use of a common workbook with pre-established assignments and evaluation materials.

--standardized departmental exams.

--a departmental syllabus with any or all of the following: standard course descriptions, goals, and objectives; a standard attendance policy; a minimum number of speeches of certain types; standard weights given to speeches versus exams; a uniform schedule for how the course is to progress, including standard testing dates for midterm and final exams.

--a required graduate or undergraduate course that enrolls TAs who teach public speaking.

--the use of an Instructor's Resource Manual.

--standardized speech evaluation forms.

New to Teaching Public Speaking?

New instructors and Teaching Assistants teach the introductory public speaking course. They provide innovative ideas and valuable enthusiasm. If you are new to teaching speech, first -- WELCOME! Many public speaking teachers have unanswered questions, especially when new to teaching itself. Universities may have new teachers; colleges, universities, and community colleges are increasingly utilizing Adjunct (part-time) professors; and all institutions wish to improve the teaching quality in their (Speech) Communication classes. As taught in Communication classes, answers are important, but not nearly so important as *questions*. You and your colleagues might wish to discuss some or all of the questions following. Your author has provoked such discussion; seldom wearies of it; and expects different points of view from experienced and inexperienced colleagues alike (perhaps your institution promotes "Faculty Development" workshops where the Communication faculty could schedule collegial discussion and debate).

1. What are the qualities of an effective public speaking teacher?

2. Where are idea sources for improving my instruction and class management?

3. By which titles and name(s) should students address me?

4. How may I increase my credibility in the classroom?

5. How do I earn the respect of students close to me in age? Far apart in age?

6. How do I respond to student content questions when not certain of the answers? To class procedure questions when not sure of the proper answer?

7. How do I recognize strong communication apprehension in a student? How can I best help with this problem?

8. How can I encourage quiet students to speak up more?

9. How do I handle the occasional "troublemaker," those who disrupt the class, show lack of respect for instructor and classmates?

10. How should I react to student use of classroom profanity or obscenities?

11. What should be my classroom dress code: conservative? liberal? none?

12. How should I react to ethnic slurs, sexism or racism or age discrimination in speeches or class discussions? (and what are school policies for these areas?)

13. What procedures shall I establish to minimize plagiarism and cheating. How shall I react if I do detect either?

14. What types of student personal problems should I respond to, and with what levels of response?

15. Suppose a student showed romantic interest in me. Now what?

16. What types and levels of student misconduct should be reported to my superior?

17. How do I get students to perceive me as "fair?" (feedback, grading, calling on for participation)

18. How do I react to student disappointment, perhaps even anger, about grades on exams and speeches?

19. What should I do if a parent calls about a student's grades? Should I have a witness if I decide to talk? What are my legal rights in this situation?

20. How can classroom speeches be made more like the real world? Do they have to be?

21. How do I describe performance standards in my syllabus, and how do I initially justify the standards orally in the classroom?

22. How do I get students to choose significant speech topics? To want to produce high quality speeches?

23. Is there truly to be "Freedom of Speech" in my classroom? Are any topics "off limits?" If so, which topics? How do I explain my topic limits? If I decide that topics are to be pre-approved, what procedures shall I establish?

24. What attendance policy shall I establish and enforce?

25. How shall I schedule the order of speeches? What if students are absent for a scheduled speech? Not ready?

26. Should my classes meet every scheduled class period? For the entire period? What seems to be the habits of the other instructors?

27. Should I audio record and/or videotape student speeches? Should each student be required to furnish a tape for their recordings? How shall I ensure that students get maximum learning value from the recordings? The honor system? Be required to visit me with their recordings?

28. Should students be welcomed to the podium or speaking area? Applauded after completing a speech?

29. Should instructor feedback after speeches be oral? Written? Both? Immediate? Delayed? Only from instructor, not students?

30. Are time limits for speeches (minimums and maximums) to be enforced? Who should do the timing? How important are time specifications?

31. In a public speaking first course what weights should be given to organization, content, and delivery? What will be my #1 goal (your author chooses "organization")?

32. Shall I use a letter grade system, yielding an average? A total points approach to grading? Shall each assignment be "sink or swim," or should students be allowed to correct assignments? Should points be lost for late work?

33. Are students to be enlisted in a peer evaluation system? What weights should be given to student peer evaluations?

34. How shall I deal with ethical violations in speeches, intentional or unintentional?

35. Must I author my own examinations, or may I use test banks? Are there to be departmental standardized exams?

36. What are the most effective and ethical ways for me to prepare students for my exams? How should I feel about weights between exams and speeches? Are there standard outlines or course syllabi that specify these weights? Do later speeches get heavier weight than later speeches?

37. In the classroom shall I be strongly positive in my approaches to students and their speeches? Balanced between "positive" and "constructive?"

38. Should instructors discuss amongst themselves students' examination scores, speaking performances, and classroom behavior?

39. Should I support some type of end-of-semester competition among my students?

INTRODUCTION

RE-VISIONING TO ACHIEVE SEX AND GENDER EQUITY IN THE PUBLIC SPEAKING CLASSROOM, by Diana K. Ivy, Ph.D.

During the past decade, much has been spoken and written about the increasing multicultural environment in the United States. The process of learning to celebrate cultural uniqueness rather than assimilate or deny it has created a new metaphor. The U.S. is now referred to as a "salad bowl" rather than a "melting pot." In a essay entitled *Public Speaking in the Multicultural Environment*, Devorah A. Lieberman discusses ways that some of these unique cultural dimensions can affect classroom behavior and speeches. The material you are about to read complements Lieberman's information by examining another dimension of cultural diversity we encounter every day in the classroom: sex or gender diversity.

In the view of some researchers, women and men represent significantly different cultural groups, so the communication between them can be viewed as intercultural. Of course, studies based on this assumption tend to be reductionist, and some points in this essay may seem stereotypical or overly generalized to you—as though all women or all men were implied. However, if we explore research, keeping in mind that "it may not work like this for everyone," we can begin to understand what makes men and women unique. Then we can examine how that uniqueness affects communication. For this reason, examining sex and gender issues in the classroom is an excellent way to help students understand and practice the audience-centered approach promoted in the Beebes' text.

Although the new respect for cultural diversity in the U.S. has also heightened respect for sex and gender diversity, our discipline's attitudes and classroom practices have lagged behind. While some instructors work toward the goal of gender equity, many do not, or at least do not find the need to, apply that goal to public speaking courses. In this Introduction, I describe some problems related to sex and gender equity in education and share the results of my own fairly recent "re-visioning," including changes I have implemented in my own courses. As you read this material, please keep in mind that I do not propose these changes as keys to classroom success. Instead, they offer alternative responses to the "call" of diversity, and supplement the array of practical suggestions and approaches detailed throughout this volume. Before I describe these changes, let me explain what is meant by "re-visioning."

Re-visioning Versus Revising

As public speaking instructors, we all work hard to <u>revise</u> our courses so they stay current and meet students' needs. We change the order of content, assign different readings, alter exercises and exams, and require different types of speeches each year. Adjusting a course to be sensitive to sex and gender diversity, however, requires going beyond the revising process to what Sonja Foss and Karen Foss have called <u>re-visioning</u>—viewing the course through a new lens. This process involves re-thinking or questioning assumptions and experimenting with new approaches. The outcomes of re-visioning range from developing a new attitude about what you teach and how you teach it to a full curriculum overhaul.

The first section of this Introduction suggests re-visioned basic approaches for the teaching of audience analysis, organizational patterns, language usage in speeches, and applications of public speaking outside the classroom. I also discuss the selection of sample speeches for classroom viewing and analysis. The second section examines instructional methods—class discussions, classroom management, instructors' use of language, and expectations for student achievement.

Re-visioning the Public Speaking Course

• Audience Analysis Instruction

My classroom instruction on audience analysis used to contain humorous stories about past speeches in which audience analysis was a bit lacking. I would tell of one female student's speech on "how to give yourself a facial," followed by a male student's "how to clean your hunting rifle" speech. I explained to students that, while there was nothing inherently feminine about facials nor inherently masculine about rifles, those topics might tend to appeal more to one sex in the audience than the other. Then, after a brief, somewhat superficial discussion of the relationship between audience analysis and topic selection, I talked about ways that even the most sex-specific speech topic could be developed into an "inclusive" speech. At this point, I felt that my coverage of sex-based audience analysis was sufficient.

However, I soon realized how insufficient this approach really was. In reading research about the tendency for men and women to attend to and process information differently, I realized that I needed to teach students how to go beyond demographic and attitudinal analysis to consider how diversity affects the way people think, listen, and process and respond to information.

I began a re-visioning effort by asking students to pinpoint which approaches to speechmaking enhanced their attentiveness and recall. The female students revealed that they were more attentive to speech topics of an intimate nature, speeches that contained personal references or illustrations and direct appeals to the audience in "you" and "we" language. Because they triggered emotional responses, these speeches heightened their interest and remained in their memory. In contrast, many of my male students found these types of speeches "too personal" and felt they were inappropriate for a public forum such as a classroom with an audience of strangers. These apparent sex-related preferences can help speakers vary their approaches to reach both female and male listeners. In constructing their speeches, students can recognize which approaches will appeal to which segments of the audience. They can then alter their approach to assigned speeches and experiment with what works best to enhance audience attention.

Occasionally students do not respond along these sex-typed lines, but instructors can use these atypical responses as teaching tools. In order to help students avoid making stereotypical assumptions in their audience analyses, it is important to hold frequent discussions of how certain speech purposes, topics, and approaches affect them. I sometimes start off a discussion of this sort with a "Good/Bad" exercise. I simply ask students to tell me about speaking events they have been to or seen on television that they thought were good, versus ones they really disliked. I put the men's responses on one side of the board and the women's responses on the other. The class then looks for overlap, sex-related trends, and other interesting features of the list. A follow-up discussion on what made the speeches memorable—for good and bad reasons—reveals students' preferences and helps them understand the issues involved in audience analysis.

• Instruction on Organizing a Speech

Public Speaking: An Audience-Centered Approach offers an insightful discussion of cultural differences in preferences for organizational patterns. Some interesting findings related to sex and organizational methods have also emerged in recent research. These findings indicate that, in U.S. culture, someone is considered masculine if he or she displays instrumental traits and behaviors, typified by competitiveness, self-assertion (i.e., being one against the world), and an emphasis on objectivity. For such people, verbal messages are explicitly coded, and the primary purpose of communication is to relay content and information, rather than to connect with others. According to this research, men tend to prefer and focus on direct and objective forms of communication. Statements such as "Let's get to the point" or "Say exactly what you mean" reveal their preference for linear thought patterns and corresponding communication behavior.

In contrast, research suggests that women communicate primarily from a motivation to establish and develop relationships. Their expressive orientation includes a concern for cooperativeness, a communal view of self (i.e., being at one with the world), an emphasis on subjectivity, and an expressive sense of emotion. Female students, therefore, may likely be more interested in and sensitive to the relationships between interactants than contrasts in ideas. These students' thoughts and interests do not tend to conform to the linear mold.

As the Beebes' text explains, there are a number of alternate patterns preferred by other cultural groups. Recent research in the U.S. suggests that female speakers prefer a circular or web-like pattern of organizing content. In such a pattern, the speech's central point gives rise to a set of subpoints that connect to one another, like the strands of a spider's web, but then lead back to the original point. To respond to the challenge of sex and gender diversity in their classrooms, public speaking instructors can re-vision the standard linear organizational instructions given in most textbooks. They can also help students explore the assumptions behind various approaches to organizing information to determine if standard patterns actually enhance or inhibit the expression of ideas. A non-value-laden discussion about various methods of translating thought patterns into communication can provide insight into sex and gender differences, as well as other cultural distinctions.

• Language Usage Instruction

"Powerful" and "powerless" are the unfortunate labels that have emerged from research describing men's and women's respective use of language. This research suggests that women and men have different styles for expressing themselves. In some research, women's speech has been labeled helpless and uncertain because of the following characteristics: (1) higher pitch, more pitch variation, and a tendency to use rising intonation (make statements into questions); (2) more tentative forms of expression, including the use of tag questions (e.g., "This is a great party, don't you think?"), disclaimers (e.g., "This is kind of a dumb question, but..."), hedges (e.g., "I feel," "I wonder," "I guess that..."), and compound versus simple requests (e.g., "Won't you please call your mother" rather than "Call your mother"); and (3) more qualifiers, meaning the use of such terms as "very," "so," "vastly," and "really."

Some of this research suggests that women are often "powerless" in mixed-sex conversation. They are less likely than men to introduce a topic for conversation, to attempt to change the topic under discussion, or to interrupt or overlap another interactant. They take fewer and shorter turns at talk and typically wait for recognition or a signal (usually from a male interactant) that it is appropriate to interject. Men's style, according to this research, is "powerful"—exhibiting the reverse of the women's traits.

These power tags, however, seem unfortunate and sexist. Could it be that what this research labels "powerless" communication is actually polite and facilitative, a sensitive style that is responsive to the situation and the needs and styles of the interactants? Could this style be equally effective if used by a male or female speaker? In contrast, the "masculine" style—constantly interrupting, seeking to control the floor, dictating conversational topics, and giving simple requests instead of explaining or softening them—seems unproductive rather than "powerful."

It is important that public speakers examine these styles in the context of audience, purpose, and setting. For example, if a speaker's purpose is to persuade a group of townspeople that a tax increase is needed for educational funding, then a personal, emotional, non-confrontational approach using provisional language may be far more "powerful" than a dominant style that may antagonize the audience.

Again, I've found that asking students to discuss these power labels aids my own re-visioning. Usually such a discussion leads to the posing of different scenarios, imagining how certain styles might accomplish certain speech goals with certain audiences. Videotaped segments from television talk shows illustrating "powerful" and "powerless" styles can also help students analyze linguistic devices that speakers use.

• Teaching Materials: Selecting "Great Speeches" as Models

Traditionally, the videotapes of "great speeches" available to public speaking instructors tend to include mostly <u>men's</u> speeches, such as Martin Luther King's "I Have a Dream" speech, Kennedy's inaugural address, Nixon's resignation, and Jesse Jackson's "Rainbow Coalition" speech. The majority of videotapes overlook Sojourner Truth's "Ain't I a Woman" speech, Shirley Chisholm's speech about the Equal Rights Amendment, Geraldine Ferraro's nomination acceptance, Barbara Jordan's and Ann Richard's addresses to political conventions, and other memorable speeches by female speakers. Naturally, students who view these tapes may form the impression that all of the great speakers are male. Moreover, female students may have a hard time finding role models among these male speakers.

As an alternative to "great speeches," some instructors show videotaped student speeches for critiquing. These tapes may be either "home grown" or produced by publishers or media houses. However, because students will undoubtedly use these speeches as models—even those that are flawed—it is important to screen tapes carefully to ensure that they represent diversified speakers, topics, approaches, and cultural perspectives.

Still other alternatives are available through other media. Some printed sources include transcripts and analyses of historical speeches as well as references for other speeches on videotape and film. Karlyn Kohrs Campbell has edited *Women Public Speakers in the United States: A Bio-Critical Sourcebook*, a two-volume compilation of women's contributions to public dialogue. It explores the oratory of African American women, as well as speakers from a variety of ethnicities and cultural backgrounds. Another source is *Women's Voices in Our Time: Statements by American Leaders*, edited by Victoria DeFrancisco and Marvin Jensen.

• Messages about Public Speaking Applications

How many times have you heard yourself admonish public speaking students that "This will become extremely important when you make presentations in the business world"? We seem to assume that most of our graduating students will eventually make their way in the corporate arena, enabled in part by the public speaking skills developed in our class. Some of them will fit this profile, but for many, the next step will be into something other than corporate America. While the number of women entering and excelling in corporate careers continues to increase steadily, women have not yet achieved equity in the corporate arena. Many women find comfortable, rewarding options elsewhere. Why, then, do we, as instructors, not extol the benefits of effective speechmaking in such areas as the ministry, teaching, non-profit organizations, medically-related organizations, graduate and professional schools, and so forth?

We also tend to ignore or place less value on speaking done outside the purview of one's career. Have you ever thought to say, for example, "This will become extremely important when you address the PTA, the city council, or your Sunday school class"? Instead, the public speaking course seems, as instructor Sonja Foss expresses it, designed "to enable students to achieve success in the corporate world, where the white male is standard and where hierarchy, control over others, and ends over means are valued. To privilege the kind of speaking valued in such a world at the exclusion of others means that public speaking instructors are not teaching, or even recognizing as legitimate, the diverse speaking goals, contexts, and approaches of those whose communicative practices and interests lie outside of it."

The re-visioning required of us here is simple: First, instructors need to assess what they tell students about applications of public speaking skills to find out how broad or narrow their scope is. Second, they should ask students which fields or jobs they expect to go into after receiving their degrees, and in what ways they think they will use their public speaking skills. Doing these kinds of simple reality checks can help us formulate more meaningful messages about why students need a public speaking course and motivate them to learn particular skills.

Re-Visioning Teaching Strategies

• Classroom Discussion and Student Participation

According to instructional scholar Pamela Cooper, college classroom instruction is still strongly affected by a male-majority standard, termed the "dominant intellectual ethos of our time." Recent research has found significant differences in the communication behavior of women and men in college classrooms. There are also differences in the ways professors communicate with male and female students. Some scholars have characterized the college campus as a "chilly climate" for women.

More specifically, research spanning two decades has determined the following: (1) male students engage in classroom discussion more than female students; (2) male students talk for longer periods and take more turns at speaking; (3) men exert more control over the topic of discussion in the classroom; (4) male students interrupt female students much more frequently than vice-versa; (5) men's interruptions of women often introduce trivial or inappropriate comments that bring discussions to an end or change their focus; (6) masculinity is associated with higher amounts of question-asking by students; and (7) most classrooms favor a traditionally masculine approach to learning, one that emphasizes objectivity and competitiveness, and disconfirms a traditionally feminine approach—one that emphasizes cooperation and collaboration.

Whereas most public speaking instructors have no intention of communicating sex bias in their course content or approaches to instruction, many may use an unconscious set of biased assumptions. For example, typically an instructor initiates class discussion by asking a question or a series of questions. Research shows that male students are much more likely to answer such questions, ask one back, or make a comment than female students. This seems to occur even for female-oriented topics such as breast cancer or PMS; the tendency is for male students to offer their opinions or knowledge on the subject before female students do, even if they are outnumbered by female classmates.

As instructors, we have a natural tendency to respond to students who respond to us. But research shows that we are biased in these responses: When female and male students raise their hands simultaneously, male students get called on significantly more often by female and male instructors alike. Apparently, instructors communicate an unspoken assumption that male participation is expected, rewarded, and possibly more highly valued than female participation.

In addition, compelling research shows that instructors exhibit sex bias (most often unpurposefully) by managing their public speaking classrooms according to a masculine standard of competition, rather than a feminine standard of cooperation. Frequently class discussions are fairly orderly events, characterized by one-at-a-time student turn-taking prompted by instructor comments and questions. However, all too frequently instructors allow students to interject comments in order to prove themselves, "top" someone, or compete for the teacher's and other students' attention. When students and instructors interrupt one another, these interruptions typically convey anything but cooperativeness. Sometimes the interruptions are intended to show support or solidarity, but then shows of solidarity among students may actually compete with the instructor's wishes or points of view.

We need to monitor our behaviors when managing class discussions. If a male student cuts off a female student's comment in a discussion, what is your response? How do you respond when female or male students interrupt you? Are your responses any different because of the sex of the interrupter? After finding out that I did not like my own answers to these questions, I began making deliberate re-visioning efforts to balance my attention to female and male students in my courses. In some instances, this meant asking the men to be patient with their responses because I wanted a woman's point of view to emerge first. In all discussions, you can use your awareness of sex-based issues to act as a facilitator. Give everyone a chance to pose a question or raise an issue without the pressure that can build into a competitive environment.

10

Moreover, it is important to consider how a competitive classroom environment affects female students overall. What happens if a portion of the course grade is based on class participation? How might female students' learning be affected by a classroom protocol that doesn't match their experience or value system? Should they be expected to adopt a masculine standard in order to succeed in the class? Should they attempt to alter the protocol? Try doing a re-vision of your classroom management procedures to check for sex bias. Discuss the issue with male and female students; this may foster the kind of teacher-student and student-student communication that actually facilitates learning.

• Expectations of Student Achievement

Studies regarding the effects of sex on a teacher's expectations of student achievement have produced contradictory findings. Research in the 1980s suggested that a student's sex played a role in the formation of a teacher's expectations. Male students were expected by teachers to outperform female students in math, science, and engineering; female students were expected to outperform their male counterparts in English, communication, and education. In many cases, these teacher expectations manifested themselves in classrooms, limiting the potential of both women and men. Similar research in the 1990s, however, found no correlation between student sex, the formation of teacher expectations, and the assessment of student achievement.

Since the research is inconclusive, it is up to us as individual instructors to examine our own assessment practices. Having recently gone through the exercise of trying to detect any trends in my own grading according to the sex of my students, I recommend a re-visioning effort in which instructors (a) track their grading of individual speeches and assignment of final course grades across past and present sections of public speaking; (b) detect any emergent trends according to sex (or race or other aspects of diversity); and (c) analyze and attempt to understand any patterns that surface, given the context of the particular institution and the goals and objectives of your courses.

Finally, when you talk about how you evaluate and grade speeches, do you set a competitive tone of encouraging students to strive to be the "top" speaker? Or do you set a collaborative tone through the use of group exercises and by stressing personal goals, i.e., the hope that each student will do her or his best? Only recently did I become aware of how one of my teaching practices contributed to a competitive tone in my class. As I handed back graded speech critiques to students, I used to announce the top speaker for that round. Until I received a comment on a teaching evaluation saying that the practice created additional anxiety and stress, I never stopped to think about what it might convey to some students, how it might pressure students by creating expectations for future performances.

In addition to reviewing your approach to grading, consider re-visioning how you talk about grades and evaluation with students. While instructors' evaluative approaches and grading practices are typically private, in that they reflect professional decision making, re-visioning this important aspect of your courses is advisable. Even if you choose not to change anything, the re-visioning activity helps you check for biases you may not realize you have. The process has a confirming effect also, in that the end result will be that you feel better about your system of providing feedback and evaluating student achievement.

• Instructors' Use of Language

Although most of us by now are acutely aware of the role inclusive language plays in establishing a classroom climate free from bias, we may still gloss over some of the more insidious forms of sexist language and linguistic practices inherent in the English language. First, we tend to be more lax in speaking than in writing. Research has shown that some instructors still use generic masculine pronouns and terminology in classroom teaching. Instructors pose questions such as the following: "When men rise up together, united in battle, what can possibly stop them?" and "If a student wants to get an 'A' on the upcoming test, what should he do to ensure a good grade?" As instructors, we sometimes forget the effect that such language has on students, especially female students. Research suggests that many women do not feel represented by such terminology, so instructors may be excluding a portion of their students if they use this it. If you are interested in re-visioning on this point, you might try consciously alternating feminine and masculine terms by inserting into your teaching a question such as "If a student makes an 'A' on her first speech, does it naturally follow that she will make an 'A' on all of her class speeches?" Register any student reactions to this change in your behavior.

Second, even instructors who have diligently attempted to rid their oral behavior of exclusive language may be surprised to find a subtle sexist element lurking in the ordering of terms. Many of us tend to use a "masculine-first, feminine-second" pattern when we speak. We speak in "boyfriend-girlfriend," "husband-wife," "bride and groom," and "Mr. and Mrs. So-and-so" terms. Such a pattern may represent a subconscious privileging of the masculine over the feminine. To re-vision this habit, try reversing the pattern. Students notice the difference immediately when an instructor refers in class discussions to "her or his speeches" and "women's and men's communication." Of course, the intention is not to reverse the order every time; doing so would be an equally sexist practice. Instead, the goal is to convey an attitude of sex and gender sensitivity that resonates with other classroom practices.

Concluding Thoughts

It is clear that college classrooms in the United States will increasingly diversify and that we will continue to experience more of a "salad bowl" effect than a "melting pot." Sex and gender diversity is a challenging subset of this phenomenon, and public speaking classrooms represent rich opportunities for questioning long-held assumptions. Most educators recognize that changing attitudes offer an opportunity to explore not only what more can be learned, but how it can best be learned by a multicultural student population. This is the process of re-vision.

We first examine our own biases, then attempt to expose, through creative instruction, students' biases, hoping that learning will be enhanced. As an instructor who constantly seeks to improve my own self-awareness as well as my teaching effectiveness, I encourage you to expand on the re-visioning I have suggested here and to share your insights with others. As our discipline moves into the 21st century, one of the greatest lessons we can teach each other and our students is an awareness of and appreciation for a multicultural society, as well as the ability to more effectively communicate with the women and men in it.

BIBLIOGRAPHY

Beach, W. A., & Dunning, D. G. (1982). Pre-indexing and conversational organization. *Quarterly Journal of Speech, 67,* 170-185.

Bell, R. A., Zahn, C. J., & Hopper, R. (1984). Disclaiming: A test of two competing views. *Communication Quarterly, 32,* 28-36.

Benz, C., Pfeiffer, I., & Newman, I. (1981). Sex role expectations of classroom teachers, grades 1-12. *American Educational Research Journal, 18,* 289-302.

Brooks, V. (1982). Sex differences in student dominance behavior in female and male professors' classrooms. *Sex Roles, 8,* 683-690.

Brophy, J. E. (1985). Interactions of male and female students with male and female teachers. In L. C. Wilkinson & C. B. Marrett (Eds.), *Gender influence in classroom interaction* (pp. 115-142). Orlando, FL: Academic Press.

Cameron, D. (1985). *Feminism and linguistic theory.* New York: St. Martin's Press.

Campbell, K. K. (1991). Hearing women's voices. *Communication Education, 40,* 33-48

Campbell, K. K. (Ed.) (1993). *Women public speakers in the United States, 1800-1925: A bio-critical* sourcebook. Westport, CT: Greenwood.

Cooper, P. J. (1993). Communication and gender in the classroom. In L. P. Arliss & D. J. Borisoff (Eds.), *Women and men communicating: Challenges and changes* (pp. 122-141). Fort Worth, TX: Harcourt Brace Jovanovich.

Cooper, H., & Good, T. (1983). *Pygmalion grows up: Studies in the expectation communication process.* New York: Longman.

DeFrancisco, V. L., & Jensen, M. D. (Eds.) (1994). *Women's voices in our time: Statements by American leaders.* Prospect Heights, IL: Waveland.

Dusek, J. B., & Joseph, G. (1983). The bases of teacher expectancies: A meta-analysis. *Journal of Educational Psychology, 75,* 327-346.

Edelsky, C. (1981). Who's got the floor? *Language in Society, 10,* 383-421.

Fishman, P. M. (1980). Conversational insecurity. In H. Giles, W. P. Robinson, & P. M. Smith (Eds.), *Language: Social psychological perspectives* (pp. 127-132). New York: Pergamon Press.

Foss, K. A. (1992). Revisioning the American public address course. *Women's Studies in Communication, 15,* 66-78.

Foss, S. A. (1992). Revisioning the public speaking course. *Women's Studies in Communication, 15,* 53-65.

Frank, F. W., & Treichler, P. A. (1989). *Language, gender and professional writing: Theoretical approaches and guidelines for non-sexist usage.* New York: Modern Language Association.

Graddol, D., & Swann, J. (1989). *Gender voices.* Cambridge, MA: Basil Blackwell.

Hall, R. M., & Sandler, B. R. (1982). *The classroom climate: A chilly one for women?* Washington, DC: Project on the Status and Education of Women, Association of American Colleges.

Holmes, J. (1990). Hedges and boosters in women's and men's speech. *Language and Communication, 10,* 185-205.

Ivy, D. K., & Backlund, P. (1994). *Exploring genderspeak: Personal effectiveness in gender communication.* New York: McGraw-Hill.

Ivy, D. K., Bullis-Moore, L., Norvell, K., Backlund, P., & Javidi, M. (1995). The lawyer, the baby-sitter, and the student: Inclusive language usage and instruction. *Women and Language, 18,* 13-21.

Kennedy, D. (1992). Review essay: She or he in textbooks? *Women and Language, 15,* 46-49.

Koester, J., & Lustig, M. W. (1991). Communication curricula in the multicultural university. *Communication Education, 40,* 250-254.

Lustig, M. W., & Koester, J. (1993). *Intercultural competence: Interpersonal communication across cultures.* New York: Harper Collins.

McConnell-Ginet, S. (1983). Intonation in a man's world. In B. Thorne, C. Kramarae, & N. Henley (Eds.), *Language, gender, and society* (pp. 69-88). Rowley, MA: Newbury House.

McMillan, J. R., Clifton, A. K., McGrath, D., & Gale, W. S. (1977). Women's language: Uncertainty or interpersonal sensitivity and emotionality? *Sex Roles, 3,* 545-559.

Mulac, A., & Lundell, T. L. (1986). Linguistic contributors to the gender-linked language effect. *Journal of Language and Social Psychology, 5,* 81-101.

Nadler, L. B., & Nadler, M. K. (1990). Perceptions of sex differences in classroom communication. *Women's Studies in Communication, 13,* 46-65.

O'Barr, W. M., & Atkins, B. K. (1980). "Women's language" or "powerless language?" In S. McConnell-Ginet, R. Borker, & N. Furman (Eds.), *Women and language in literature and society* (pp. 93-110). New York: Praeger.

Pearson, J. C., & West, R. (1991). An initial investigation of the effects of gender on student questions in the classroom: Developing a descriptive base. *Communication Education, 40,* 22-32.

Penelope, J. (1990). *Speaking freely: Unlearning the lies of the fathers' tongues.* New York: Pergamon.

Sadker, M., & Sadker, D. (1985, March). Sexism in the schoolroom of the '80's. *Psychology Today,* pp. 54-57.

Sandler, B. R., & Hall, R. M. (1986). *The campus climate revisited: Chilly for women faculty, administrators, and graduate students.* Washington, DC: Project on the Status and Education of Women, Association of American Colleges.

Schrader, D. (1992, November). *Instrumental and expressive orientations to interaction and judgments of communicator acceptability: The effects of interaction goals.* Paper presented at the annual meeting of the

13

Speech Communication Association, Chicago, IL.

Spender, D. (1983). Telling it how it is: Language and gender in the classroom. In M. Mailand (Ed.), *Sex differentiation and schooling* (pp. 98-116). London: Heinemann Educational Books.

Spender, D. (1985). *Man made language* (2nd ed.). London: Routledge & Kegan Paul.

Sternglanz, S. H., & Lyberger-Ficek, S. (1977). Sex differences in student-teacher interactions in the college classroom. *Sex Roles, 3,* 345-352.

Tannen, D. (1990). *You just don't understand.* New York: William Morrow.

Treichler, P. A., & Kramarae, C. (1983). Women's talk in the ivory tower. *Communication Quarterly, 31,* 118-132.

Wood, J. T., & Lenze, L. F. (1991). Strategies to enhance gender sensitivity in communication education. *Communication Education, 40,* 16-21.

Zimmerman, D. H., & West, C. (1975). Sex roles, interruptions, and silences in conversation. In B. Thorne & N. Henley (Eds.), *Language and sex* (pp. 105-129). Rowley, MA: Newbury House.

SAMPLE PUBLIC SPEAKING COURSE SYLLABI & SCHEDULES

Several examples of a course syllabus and schedules are provided for your adaptation. For a 3-credit hour course taught in a 15-week semester system, schedules are included for 3-day a week, 2-day a week, and 1-evening a week classes. A schedule is also provided for a 4-credit hour course taught in a 10-week quarter system.

15-WEEK SEMESTER
3-Day per Week Class, 4 Graded Speeches, 2 Exams, Critique of Outside Speaker Assignment

PUBLIC SPEAKING   Professor:
Section: Office:
Room: Office Hours:
                                                            (Other office visits by appointment.)

COURSE DESCRIPTION: This course is designed to provide both a practical introduction to the fundamental principles of public speaking and a forum for practicing public speaking skills. Through a variety of instructional strategies--discussion, class workshops, readings, lectures, and presentations--you will learn the processes by which effective speeches are conceived, prepared, and delivered.

COURSE OBJECTIVES:
1. to increase your confidence in your public speaking ability.
2. to learn principles of effective public speaking.
3. to reinforce existing speaking skills and identify areas for improvement.
4. to demonstrate effective aspects of speech preparation.
5. to demonstrate effective aspects of speech delivery.
6. to appropriately apply public speaking skills to a variety of speech contexts.

REQUIRED TEXT: The required textbook for this course is *Public Speaking: An Audience-Centered Approach* (6th ed.), by Steven Beebe and Susan Beebe. Students are expected to keep current in the reading of the text, even if chapter material is not directly covered in class. Exams will be drawn primarily from the textbook.

ATTENDANCE/LATE ARRIVAL/EARLY DEPARTURE POLICY: Because this course emphasizes live performance as well as class discussion, attendance at all class sessions is imperative. (You can't do public speaking without a "public.") Attendance will be checked at each class period. PLEASE realize that if you <u>miss class the day</u> you are expected to present a speech, turn in an assignment, or take an exam, you will <u>not be allowed to make up</u> that activity or present the speech on a subsequent date. The grade is a zero. If you do miss a class, it is your responsibility to get the information that was covered from one of your classmates. The following policy will be enforced in this class:

    (1) Your first three absences are without penalty. Use these absences for illness and emergencies which may occur.
    (2) Your fourth absence will lower your final course average by 3 points.
    (3) Each subsequent absence will lower your final course average by 3 points.
    (4) You must attend at least 40 minutes of a 50-minute class to be counted present.

EQUITY STATEMENT: All persons, regardless of gender, age, class, race, religion, physical disability, sexual orientation, etc., shall have equal opportunity without harassment in this course. Any problems with or questions about harassment can be discussed confidentially with your instructor.

PLAGIARISM POLICY: Be forewarned: Plagiarism is grounds for probation and/or suspension from the university. Any student caught cheating on an exam, using (plagiarizing) someone else's speech topic, outline, or notes, or lifting information from sources without citing those sources (another form of plagiarism) **may be given an automatic "F" for the course.** Instructors <u>do</u> compare notes and discuss student speeches. <u>Do not even think about using outline material or an entire speech that is not your own.</u> If you are uncertain about the university's policy on academic misconduct, refer to the Student Code of Conduct in your student handbook. If you are uncertain as to what actions constitute plagiarism in public speaking, ask your instructor.

ASSIGNMENTS & EVALUATION: Each of the following assignments and speech critiquing information are thoroughly detailed in handouts. Information about exam reviews/study guides will be given to the class later in the term.

Critique of Outside Speaker	50 points
Informative Speech	100 points
Impromptu Speech	50 points
Demonstration Speech	100 points
Persuasive Speech	100 points
Midterm Exam	100 points
Final Exam	<u>100 points</u>
	600 points maximum

Your final grade is based on a percentage of 600 points, minus any points for excessive absences.

COURSE SCHEDULE: The tentative schedule that follows details assigned readings, information to be covered during each class session, presentation and exam dates, due dates for assignments--roughly everything you need to know to stay on top of this class. I use the word "tentative" because this schedule might change; however, students will be informed well in advance of any changes in the schedule. <u>Check the schedule **before** you come to every class so that you will be prepared.</u>

****

TENTATIVE MWF CLASS SCHEDULE

Week 1

M   Syllabus Overview & Student Introductions
                     Assignment: Autobiographical Speech
                     Draw for Speaking Positions

W   **DUE: Autobiographical Speeches**
                     Read: Chapter 1 by F

F   **Finish Autobiographical Speeches**
                     Discuss Ch. 1: Introduction to Public Speaking
                     Read: Critique of Outside Speaker Assignment by M

Week 2

M   **Assignment: Critique of an Outside Speaker**
                     Read: Chapter 2 by W

W   Discuss Ch. 2: Overview of the Audience-Centered Speechmaking Process
                     Read: Chapter 3 by F

F	Discuss Ch. 3: Ethics & Free Speech Read: Chapter 4 by M Assignment: Complete Listening Habits Inventory by M

Week 3

M	Discuss Ch. 4: Listening to Speeches Review Critique of Outside Speaker Assignment Read: Chapter 5 by W
W	Discuss Ch. 5: Analyzing Your Audience Read: Chapter 6 by F
F	Discuss Ch. 6: Developing Your Speech Brainstorming for Speech Topics Activity Read: Informative Speech Assignment by M

Week 4

M	**Assignment: Informative Speech** **Draw for Speaking Positions** Read: Chapter 15 by W
W	Discuss Ch. 15: Speaking to Inform Discuss Outline & Bibliography Format Review Informative Speech Assignment Read: Chapter 7 by F
F	Discuss Ch. 7: Gathering Supporting Materials Read: Chapter 8 by M

Week 5

M	Discuss Ch. 8: Supporting Your Speech
W	Informative Speech Workshop
F	**Round 1: Informative Speeches**

Week 6

M	**Round 2: Informative Speeches**
W	**Round 3: Informative Speeches**
F	**Finish Informative Speeches** **DUE: Critique of an Outside Speaker Assignment** Read: Chapter 9 by M

Week 7

M	Discuss Ch. 9: Organizing Your Speech Midterm Exam Review (Chs. 1-9; 15)
W	**Midterm Exam** Read: Chapter 10 by F

F   Discuss Ch. 10: Introducing & Concluding Your Speech
Read: Chapter 11 by M

Week 8

M   Discuss Ch. 11: Outlining Your Speech
Read: Impromptu Speech Assignment by W
Read: Chapter 12 by W

W   Discuss Ch. 12: Using Words Well: Speaker Language & Style
Assignment: Impromptu Speech
Read: Chapter 13 by F

F   Discuss Ch. 13: Delivering Your Speech
Review Impromptu Speech Assignment

Week 9

M   **Round 1: Impromptu Speeches**

W   **Round 2: Impromptu Speeches**

F   **Finish Impromptu Speeches**
Read: Chapter 14 by M
Read: Handout on Effective Use of Audio-Visual Aids by M
Read: Demonstration Speech Assignment by M

Week 10

M   Discuss Ch. 14: Visual Aids
Assignment: Demonstration Speech
Draw for Speaking Positions

W   Demonstration Speech Workshop

F   **Round 1: Demonstration Speeches**

Week 11

M   **Round 2: Demonstration Speeches**

W   **Round 3: Demonstration Speeches**

F   **Finish Demonstration Speeches**
Read: Chapter 16 by M

Week 12

M   Discuss Ch. 16: Principles of Persuasive Speaking
Read: Chapter 17 by W

W   Discuss Ch. 17: Strategies for Speaking Persuasively
Read: Persuasive Speech Assignment by F

F   **Assignment: Persuasive Speech**
        Draw for Speaking Order
        Read: Chapter 18 by M

Week 13
M   Discuss Ch. 18: Speaking on Special Occasions
        Review Persuasive Speech Assignment

W   Persuasive Speech Workshop

F   **Round 1: Persuasive Speeches**

Week 14
M   **Round 2: Persuasive Speeches**

W   **Round 3: Persuasive Speeches**

F   **Finish Persuasive Speeches**
        Read: Chapter 19 by M

Week 15
M   Discuss Ch. 19: Speaking in Small Groups

W   Final Exam Review (Chs. 10-14; 16-19)

FINAL EXAM: _____

****

15-WEEK SEMESTER
2-Day per Week Class, 4 Graded Speeches, 2 Exams, Audience Analysis Assignment

<table>
<tr><td>PUBLIC SPEAKING</td><td>Professor:</td></tr>
<tr><td>Section:</td><td>Office:</td></tr>
<tr><td>Room:</td><td>Office Hours:</td></tr>
<tr><td></td><td>(Other office visits by appointment.)</td></tr>
</table>

COURSE DESCRIPTION: This course is designed to provide both a practical introduction to the fundamental principles of public speaking and a forum for practicing public speaking skills. Through a variety of instructional strategies--discussion, class workshops, readings, lectures, and presentations--you will learn the processes by which effective speeches are conceived, prepared, and delivered.

COURSE OBJECTIVES:
1. to increase your confidence in your public speaking ability.
2. to learn principles of effective public speaking.
3. to reinforce existing speaking skills and identify areas for improvement.
4. to demonstrate effective aspects of speech preparation.
5. to demonstrate effective aspects of speech delivery.
6. to appropriately apply public speaking skills to a variety of speech contexts.

REQUIRED TEXT: The required textbook for this course is *Public Speaking: An Audience-Centered Approach* (5th ed.), by Steven Beebe and Susan Beebe. Students are expected to keep current in the reading of the text, even if chapter material is not directly covered in class. Exams will be drawn primarily from the textbook.

ATTENDANCE/LATE ARRIVAL/EARLY DEPARTURE POLICY: Because this course emphasizes live performance as well as class discussion, attendance at all class sessions is imperative. (You can't do public speaking without a "public.") Attendance will be checked at each class period. PLEASE realize that if you <u>miss class the day</u> you are expected to present a speech, turn in an assignment, or take an exam, you will <u>not be allowed to make up</u> that activity or present the speech on a subsequent date. The grade is a zero. If you do miss a class, it is your responsibility to get the information that was covered from one of your classmates. The following policy will be enforced in this class:

    (1) Your first two absences are without penalty. Use these absences for illness and emergencies which may occur.
    (2) Your third absence will lower your final course average by 4 points.
    (3) Each subsequent absence will lower your final course average by 4 points.
    (4) You must attend at least 65 minutes of a 75-minute class to be counted present.

EQUITY STATEMENT: All persons, regardless of gender, age, class, race, religion, physical disability, sexual orientation, etc., shall have equal opportunity without harassment in this course. Any problems with or questions about harassment can be discussed confidentially with your instructor.

PLAGIARISM POLICY: Be forewarned: Plagiarism is grounds for probation and/or suspension from the university. Any student caught cheating on an exam, using (plagiarizing) someone else's speech topic, outline, or notes, or lifting information from sources without citing those sources (another form of plagiarism) **may be given an automatic "F" for the course.** Instructors <u>do</u> compare notes and discuss student speeches. <u>Do not even think about using outline material or an entire speech that is not your own.</u> If you are uncertain about the university's policy on academic misconduct, refer to the Student Code of Conduct in your student handbook. If you are uncertain as to what actions constitute plagiarism in public speaking, ask your instructor.

ASSIGNMENTS & EVALUATION: Each of the following assignments and speech critiquing information are thoroughly detailed in handouts. Information about exam reviews/study guides will be given to the class later in the term.

Audience Analysis Paper	50 points
Informative Speech	100 points
Impromptu Speech	50 points
Demonstration Speech	100 points
Persuasive Speech	100 points
Midterm Exam	100 points
Final Exam	<u>100 points</u>
	600 points maximum

Your final grade is based on a percentage of 600 points, minus any points for excessive absences.

COURSE SCHEDULE: The tentative schedule that follows details assigned readings, information to be covered during each class session, presentation and exam dates, due dates for assignments--roughly everything you need to know to stay on top of this class. I use the word "tentative" because this schedule might change; however, students will be informed well in advance of any changes in the schedule. <u>Check the schedule **before** you come to every class so that you will be prepared.</u>

****
TENTATIVE TTH CLASS SCHEDULE

Week 1
TU   Syllabus Overview & Student Introductions
                      Assignment: Autobiographical Speech
                      Draw for Speaking Positions
                      Read: Chapter 1 by TH

TH   **DUE: Autobiographical Speeches**
                      Discuss Ch. 1: Introduction to Public Speaking
                      Read: Chapters 2 & 3 by TU

Week 2
TU   **Finish Autobiographical Speeches**
                      Discuss Chs. 2 & 3: Overview of the Process; Ethics & Free Speech
                      Assignment: Complete Listening Habits Inventory by TH
                      Read: Chapters 4 & 5 by TH
                      Read: Audience Analysis Assignment by TH

TH   Discuss Chs. 4 & 5: Listening; Analyzing Your Audience
                      Assignment: Audience Analysis Paper
                      Read: Chapter 6 by TU

Week 3
TU   Discuss Ch. 6: Developing Your Speech
                      Brainstorming for Speech Topics Activity
                      Review Audience Analysis Assignment
                      Read: Chapter 15 by TH
                      Read: Informative Speech Assignment by TH

TH   **DUE: Audience Analysis Papers**
                      Discuss Ch. 15: Speaking to Inform
                      Assignment: Informative Speech
                      Draw for Speaking Positions
                      Read: Chapters 7 & 8 by TU

Week 4
TU   Discuss Chs. 7 & 8: Gathering Supporting Materials; Supporting Your Speech
                      Discuss Outline & Bibliography Format
                      Informative Speech Workshop

TH   **Round 1: Informative Speeches**

Week 5

TU   **Round 2: Informative Speeches**
Read: Chapter 9 by TH

TH   **Finish Informative Speeches**
Discuss Ch. 9: Organizing Your Speech
Midterm Exam Review (Chs. 1-9; 15)

Week 6

TU   **Midterm Exam**
Read: Chapters 10 & 11 by TH

TH   Discuss Chs. 10 & 11: Introducing & Concluding; Outlining Your Speech
Read: Chapter 12 by TU
Read: Impromptu Speech Assignment by TU

Week 7

TU   Discuss Ch. 12: Using Words Well: Speaker Language & Style
Assignment: Impromptu Speech
Read: Chapter 13 by TH

TH   Discuss Ch. 13: Delivering Your Speech
Review Impromptu Speech Assignment

Week 8

TU   **Round 1: Impromptu Speeches**
Read: Chapter 14 by TH
Read: Handout on Effective Use of Audio-Visual Aids by TH

TH   **Finish Impromptu Speeches**
Discuss Ch. 14: Visual Aids
Read: Demonstration Speech Assignment by TU

Week 9

TU   **Assignment: Demonstration Speech**
Draw for Speaking Positions

TH   Demonstration Speech Workshop

Week 10

TU   **Round 1: Demonstration Speeches**

TH   **Round 2: Demonstration Speeches**
Read: Chapter 16 by TU

Week 11

TU   **Finish Demonstration Speeches**
Discuss Ch. 16: Principles of Persuasive Speaking
Read: Chapter 17 by TH

Read: Persuasive Speech Assignment by TH

TH   Discuss Ch. 17: Strategies for Speaking Persuasively
Assignment: Persuasive Speech
Draw for Speaking Order
Read: Chapter 18 by TU

Week 12
TU   Discuss Ch. 18: Speaking on Special Occasions
Review Persuasive Speech Assignment

TH   Persuasive Speech Workshop

Week 13
TU   **Round 1: Persuasive Speeches**

TH   **Round 2: Persuasive Speeches**

Week 14
TU   **Round 3: Persuasive Speeches**

TH   **Finish Persuasive Speeches**
Read: Chapter 19 by TU

Week 15
TU   Discuss Ch. 19: Speaking in Small Groups

TH   Final Exam Review (Chs. 10-14; 16-19)

FINAL EXAM: _____

****

15-WEEK SEMESTER
1-Evening per Week Class, 4 Graded Speeches, 2 Exams, Audience Analysis Assignment

PUBLIC SPEAKING   Professor:
Section: Office:
Room: Office Hours:
                 (Other office visits by appointment.)

COURSE DESCRIPTION: This course is designed to provide both a practical introduction to the fundamental principles of public speaking and a forum for practicing public speaking skills. Through a variety of instructional strategies--discussion, class workshops, readings, lectures, and presentations--you will learn the processes by which effective speeches are conceived, prepared, and delivered.

COURSE OBJECTIVES:
1. to increase your confidence in your public speaking ability.
2. to learn principles of effective public speaking.
3. to reinforce existing speaking skills and identify areas for improvement.
4. to demonstrate effective aspects of speech preparation.
5. to demonstrate effective aspects of speech delivery.
6. to appropriately apply public speaking skills to a variety of speech contexts.

REQUIRED TEXT: The required textbook for this course is *Public Speaking: An Audience-Centered Approach* (5th ed.), by Steven Beebe and Susan Beebe. Students are expected to keep current in the reading of the text, even if chapter material is not directly covered in class. Exams will be drawn primarily from the textbook.

ATTENDANCE/LATE ARRIVAL/EARLY DEPARTURE POLICY: Because this course emphasizes live performance as well as class discussion, attendance at all class sessions is imperative. (You can't do public speaking without a "public.") Attendance will be checked at each class period. PLEASE realize that if you <u>miss class the day</u> you are expected to present a speech, turn in an assignment, or take an exam, you will <u>not be allowed to make up</u> that activity or present the speech on a subsequent date. The grade is a zero. If you do miss a class, it is your responsibility to get the information that was covered from one of your classmates. The following policy will be enforced in this class:

    (1) Your first absence is without penalty. Use this absence for illness and emergencies which may occur.
    (2) Your second absence will lower your final course average by 6 points.
    (3) Each subsequent absence will lower your final course average by 6 points.
    (4) You must attend at least two hours, fifteen minutes of class to be counted present.

EQUITY STATEMENT: All persons, regardless of gender, age, class, race, religion, physical disability, sexual orientation, etc., shall have equal opportunity without harassment in this course. Any problems with or questions about harassment can be discussed confidentially with your instructor.

PLAGIARISM POLICY: Be forewarned: Plagiarism is grounds for probation and/or suspension from the university. Any student caught cheating on an exam, using (plagiarizing) someone else's speech topic, outline, or notes, or lifting information from sources without citing those sources (another form of plagiarism) **may be given an automatic "F" for the course.** Instructors <u>do</u> compare notes and discuss student speeches. <u>Do not even think about using outline material or an entire speech that is not your own.</u> If you are uncertain about the university's policy on academic misconduct, refer to the Student Code of Conduct in your student handbook. If you are uncertain as to what actions constitute plagiarism in public speaking, ask your instructor.

ASSIGNMENTS & EVALUATION: Each of the following assignments and speech critiquing information are thoroughly detailed in handouts. Information about exam reviews/study guides will be given to the class later in the term.

Audience Analysis Paper	50 points
Informative Speech	100 points
Impromptu Speech	50 points
Demonstration Speech	100 points

Persuasive Speech 100 points
Midterm Exam 100 points
Final Exam <u>100 points</u>
600 points maximum

Your final grade is based on a percentage of 600 points, minus any points for excessive absences.

COURSE SCHEDULE: The tentative schedule that follows details assigned readings, information to be covered during each class session, presentation and exam dates, due dates for assignments--roughly everything you need to know to stay on top of this class. I use the word "tentative" because this schedule might change; however, students will be informed well in advance of any changes in schedule. <u>Check the schedule **before** you come to every class so that you will be prepared.</u>

****

TENTATIVE EVENING CLASS SCHEDULE

<u>**Week 1**</u>

Syllabus Overview & Student Introductions
DUE: Autobiographical Speeches
Read: Chapters 1 & 2

<u>**Week 2**</u>

Discuss Chs. 1 & 2: Introduction to Public Speaking; Overview of the Process
Read: Chapters 3 & 4
Read: Audience Analysis Assignment
Assignment: Complete Listening Habits Inventory

<u>**Week 3**</u>

Discuss Chs. 3 & 4: Ethics & Free Speech; Listening
Assignment: Audience Analysis Paper
Read: Chapters 5 & 6

<u>**Week 4**</u>

Discuss Chs. 5 & 6: Analyzing Your Audience; Developing Your Speech
Brainstorming for Speech Topics Activity
Review Audience Analysis Assignment
Read: Chapters 7 & 15
Read: Informative Speech Assignment

<u>**Week 5**</u>

DUE: Audience Analysis Assignment
Discuss Chs. 7 & 15: Gathering Supporting Materials; Speaking to Inform
Assignment: Informative Speech
Draw for Speaking Positions
Discuss Outline & Bibliography Format

<u>**Week 6**</u>

Informative Speeches
Read: Chapters 8 & 9

<u>**Week 7**</u>

Finish Informative Speeches
Discuss Chs. 8 & 9: Supporting Your Speech; Organizing Your Speech
Midterm Exam Review (Chs. 1-9; 15)

Week 8	**Midterm Exam**
	Read: Chapters 10 & 11
	Read: Impromptu Speech Assignment

Week 9	Discuss Chs. 10 & 11: Introducing & Concluding; Outlining Your Speech
	Assignment: Impromptu Speech
	Read: Chapter 12

Week 10	**Impromptu Speeches**
	Discuss Ch. 12: Using Words Well
	Read: Chapters 13 & 14
	Read: Demonstration Speech Assignment
	Read: Handout on Effective Use of Audio-Visual Aids

Week 11	**Finish Impromptu Speeches**
	Discuss Chs. 13 & 14: Delivering Your Speech; Visual Aids
	Assignment: Demonstration Speech
	Draw for Speaking Positions

Week 12	**Demonstration Speeches**
	Read: Chapters 16 & 17

Week 13	**Finish Demonstration Speeches**
	Discuss Chs. 16 & 17: Principles of Persuasive Speaking; Strategies
	Read: Chapters 18 & 19
	Read: Persuasive Speech Assignment

Week 14	Discuss Chs. 18 & 19: Special Occasions; Speaking in Small Groups
	Assignment: Persuasive Speech
	Draw for Speaking Order

Week 15	
	Persuasive Speeches
	Final Exam Review (Chs. 10-14; 16-19)

FINAL EXAM: _____

****

10-WEEK QUARTER SYSTEM, 4-HOUR COURSE
4 Graded Speeches, 2 Exams, Audience Analysis Assignment

****
TENTATIVE CLASS SCHEDULE

Week 1	Syllabus Overview & Student Introductions
	DUE: Autobiographical Speeches
	Discuss Chs. 1 & 2: Introduction to Public Speaking; Overview of the Process

<u>Week 2</u>	Discuss Chs. 3, 4, & 5: Ethics; Listening; Analyzing Your Audience **Assignment: Audience Analysis Paper**
<u>Week 3</u>	**DUE: Audience Analysis Assignment** Discuss Chs. 6, 7, & 15: Developing; Gathering Support; Speaking to Inform Brainstorming for Speech Topics Activity **Assignment: Informative Speech** **Draw for Speaking Positions** Discuss Outline & Bibliography Format
<u>Week 4</u>	**Informative Speeches** Discuss Chs. 8, 9, & 10: Supporting; Organizing; Introducing & Concluding Midterm Exam Review (Chs. 1-10; 15) **Assignment: Impromptu Speech**
<u>Week 5</u>	**Midterm Exam**
<u>Week 6</u>	Impromptu Speeches Discuss Ch. 11: Outlining
<u>Week 7</u>	Discuss Chs. 12, 13, & 14: Using Words Well; Delivery; Visual Aids **Assignment: Demonstration Speech** **Draw for Speaking Positions**
<u>Week 8</u>	**Demonstration Speeches** Discuss Chs. 16 & 17: Principles of Persuasive Speaking; Strategies
<u>Week 9</u>	Discuss Chs. 18 & 19: Special Occasions; Speaking in Small Groups **Assignment: Persuasive Speech** **Draw for Speaking Positions**
<u>Week 10</u>	**Persuasive Speeches** Final Exam Review (Chs. 11-14; 16-19)

FINAL EXAM: _____

****

PUBLIC SPEAKING ASSIGNMENTS

For public speaking instructors who may be making decisions about assignments or who are looking for alternatives to ones they have used in the past, various assignments are provided in this section of the Instructor's Resource Manual. Elaborations and alternative assignments are also included in chapters one and two. Readers probably do not need reminding, but, here goes. <u>Explain all assignments in as many ways as you can.</u> Unfamiliarity with assignments added to initial speech anxiety can easily block understanding of an assignment.

INTRODUCTORY SPEECHES

INTRODUCTORY SPEECH OBJECTIVES MAY INCLUDE:

> to become acquainted with class members
> to practice effective organizational and delivery skills
> to provide speaking experience early in the course
> to practice extemporaneous speaking
> to give the instructor a "first look" at student speakers
> to begin, early on in the course, to help students cope with speech anxiety

TYPES OF INTRODUCTORY SPEECHES

Autobiographical Speech: Typically this speech is not officially graded and is assigned early in the semester, serving as an icebreaker or get-acquainted speech. Students prepare the speech, keeping in mind a structure of introduction, body, and conclusion. You decide whether students should or should not use minimal notes when they deliver the speech. Students introduce themselves to the class by including information about their hometown, year in school, major, and other biographical information they think will be relevant. Additionally, one-half of the students include talk about their proudest moment; the other half talk about their most embarrassing moment. This kind of narrative speech seems less anxiety provoking to students than graded speeches requiring research.

Group Introductory Speech: Form students into small groups (no more than five people per group) and ask each student to introduce her/himself to the group in a creative, interesting, and memorable way. Groups should discuss the similarities and differences among members' introductions. Next, have students create a group introductory speech, of a length you feel appropriate. Each group member should participate in the planning and delivery. While groups should work to establish a group identity, they should also keep in mind that they are composed of individuals, people whose names the rest of the class and the instructor want to remember.

Who Are You, at Your Core? For this introductory speech, students should select an excerpt from a poem, essay, or speech that reflects their values, beliefs, or philosophy of life. Presented as a speech, students provide a brief summary of the author's main point in the excerpt and what kind of connection the student feels to the particular piece of literature, followed by oral reading of the excerpt.

Personal Experience Speech: Students prepare and present a short speech about a recent personal experience they have had. Their goal is to use clear, descriptive language to relate the experience to the class. Instruct students to select a personal experience that had a significant impact on them, such as a great accomplishment, a personal challenge, travel that was especially meaningful, a vivid memory, or a favorite cause. To help them prepare and organize this speech, suggest that students develop answers to the organizing questions of "Who," "What," "When," "Where," and "Why." You might want to explain that students need not feel compelled to reveal something about themselves that they consider to be "high risk," because such an interpretation could be viewed by a student as an unethical demand on your part.

A Classmate's Story: Divide students into pairs, making sure that partners do not know each other prior to this class. Give them ten minutes to interview each other, exchanging humorous or interesting stories about their lives. This story becomes the basis for each student's introduction of his or her partner to the class.

Why I Am in College: A simple form of introductory speech is for students to explain to the class why they are attending college. Speeches may include such points as learning to learn, personal pride, independence, academic major, and career aspirations. Non-traditional students' speeches tend to be quite different, often inspirational.

INFORMATIVE SPEECHES

INFORMATIVE SPEECH OBJECTIVES MAY INCLUDE:

> to inform classmates about a topic or issue
> to use a variety of supporting material
> to effectively organize information
> to develop research and citation skills
> to demonstrate effective use of visual aids

Two aspects of informative speaking should probably be emphasized to students.

(1) Special consideration should be given to <u>analyzing the knowledge and interest levels</u> of audience members. The Beebe and Beebe textbook centers on speaker audience awareness and audience adaptation. Students should be encouraged and given time in class to conduct audience analyses prior to developing and delivering this speech. Audience analyses can take the form of informal question-and-answer sessions, or polling between speakers and classmates. Students may wish to design an anonymous questionnaire to distribute to students for feedback on a potential topic. Be sure to stress to students the benefits of questionnaires, but explain that questionnaires must be brief, that they must be given out on days prior to speechmaking days, and that speakers should incorporate the results of the questionnaires in their speeches. The result should be added speaker credibility in the minds of listeners.

(2) You may find it important to stress to students differences between the speech purposes of informing and persuading. Explain this to students by presenting a hypothetical scenario in which the boss or the chair of an organization asks you to take five minutes at an upcoming meeting to summarize the progress on a certain project. Emphasize the task is "to summarize," not to color the facts, to add evaluative remarks or opinions on the topic, or to try to persuade the audience in any way. However, the supervisor might well have asked you to take a persuasive position, the adopting of the conclusions reached in the project. A horse of a different color, is it not? Differentiating between the two, informing and persuading, is hardly life critical. However, somewhat different skills are involved, and students will probably acquire the skills more quickly if clear on differences between the two speeches.

TYPES OF INFORMATIVE SPEECHES

A Brief Speech of Definition: If you wish strong parameters for your initial informative speaking assignment, you could ask students to develop informative speeches centering on defining a single word or concept, such as "the national debt," "racism," "sexual harassment," or what it means to be "HIV positive." Students should be encouraged to develop visual aids that will assist the audience in understanding the concept. Skillfully used, a definition can illuminate not only a word or concept, but an entire point of view. This author feels that arts of definition are not well taught currently, and that communication teachers can assist in filling the "definition gap."

A Brief Speech of Description: The principal characteristic of this initial informative speech is description. Students should use details arranged to give an overall or dominant impression (i.e., to reveal the distinguishing features of what is described). Explain that this speech is evaluated on whether the description creates a clear, vivid, and detailed picture in the listeners' minds. Stress audience analysis here also because these kinds of speeches are highly dependent on whether the audience is familiar with the subject being described. Description speeches are typically well received by audiences because description lets listeners see, understand, appreciate, and react through the eyes and words of the speaker.

Major Informative Speech. The textbook (chapter fifteen) describes informative speaking as being about ideas, objects, procedures, people, or events. Your students may have choices or, as this author has occasionally decided, all students focus on a single element of the five choices. A major informative speech is described below, along with evaluative approaches and forms. Before that exposition, let us turn to a subject your students will appreciate attention to, finding and choosing informative speaking topics.

One of the first challenges in informative speaking is to find topics that not only interest a speaker, but that will interest audiences. Often, students' first ideas come from things that they are really interested in, but getting them to turn a corner to consider if the audience will be interested may be, at least temporarily, another story. Students should be encouraged to incorporate visual aids into their informative speeches, because visual aids add interest and support to the speaker's words. Listed below are numerous topic ideas you may wish to share with students.

Racism in America	Genetic engineering	Hospice concept
The Internet	Special Olympics	Japanese culture
The plight of the homeless	Solar energy	The dam being built in China
Down's Syndrome	Media-related topics	Illiteracy
Contributions of ancient civilizations	Health care crisis	Vegetarian diets
Child abuse	Alcoholism	Terrorism
Disappearing rain forests	Campus security	Student stress
Suicide	Hurricanes	Financial aid for students
AIDS research	Apartheid	Drive-by shootings
Sexism in music videos	Humor in TV sitcoms	Safer Sex
Rising crime	Electronic library resources	Eating disorders
Nuclear energy	U.S. relations with Russia	The Bosnian war
Gang violence	The lure of soap operas	New relations with Israel
Water conservation	Sleeping disorders and dreaming	Resurgence of Nazism
Militia movement	Acid rain	Recycling
Cholesterol management	Planned Parenthood	Flood plains
Drinking and driving	Nutrition	Toxic waste disposal
Presidential elections	Winning the right to vote	Sexism and equality
The salt mines of Utah	The abortion controversy	History of capital punishment
Weight management	Parent-child communication	Privacy and your computer
Outward Bound	Pornography	Domestic violence
Preservation of whales	My dream vacation	Child safety laws

INFORMATIVE SPEECH ASSIGNMENT

PURPOSE: The primary objective of this informative speech is to inform or teach your audience about a topic of interest. You will get your opportunity to persuade your classmates in a later assignment! You are to share information clearly with your audience so that they receive the information, understand it, and retain it.

If you feel unclear about this assignment in any way, visit your instructor during office hours.

PRESENTATION DATE: _____
[Feel free to visit and talk with instructor about ideas for speech topics, aspects of preparation, etc.]

PROCEDURES:
1. <u>SPEAKER ORDER</u>: You will know at least one week in advance the date that you will present your informative speech and the order of speakers for each day, unless the class decides that order will be determined by volunteers. Order of speaking will not change unless another student is willing to change with you. Please recognize that you are expected to perform <u>on the day that you are assigned or have volunteered for.</u> If you are unprepared or absent, the syllabus policy about absences and lack of preparation will be applied.

2. <u>TIME LIMIT</u>: Four to six minutes. Your speech is expected to not exceed six minutes nor be under four minutes, or your grade will suffer. Time yourself in rehearsal so that you don't go over or under time. If you go over or under time in practice, reduce or add material; don't assume you'll adjust for time problems during the actual presentation.

3. <u>TOPIC SELECTION</u>: Select a topic you find interesting, one you think will interest your audience. Try to think of a new and different topic or add a new twist to a common topic.

4. <u>SUPPORTING MATERIALS</u>: Use your own knowledge of the topic first; then find outside published and/or interview sources to back up your points and enhance your credibility as a speaker. You must include a **minimum of two outside sources of different types** into this informative speech. Only one personal interview will count as a source. Please remember: it is very important that you **cite your sources orally during the speech**, as well as in the bibliography that you turn in with your outline.

5. <u>AUDIENCE ANALYSIS</u>: Speaking effectiveness is greatly dependent upon how well you analyze your audience and adapt your speech to them. Review audience analysis (chapter five in your textbook). Reflect on your class audience, their demographics, their knowledge of and interest in your topic. **The more personal, the more audience-centered the speech, the stronger your effects on your listeners (and your grade).**

6. <u>ORGANIZATION & WRITTEN WORK</u>: Structure your ideas and draft an outline, using supporting material for substance. The speech should have only one overall thesis, with three or four main points. The **typed** outline **you hand in the day you speak** should conform to the format discussed in class. Feel free to discuss that outline with instructor before due day. Also turned in with the outline is a bibliography of all sources used in your speech. For this format, refer to the APA style information provided you or to the *APA Style Manual* (4th ed.) in the reference section of the library. **Bibliographies that do not appear in APA style will not be acceptable.**

7. <u>DELIVERY</u>: This is **NOT** a manuscript speech; thus, **you should not read your speech**. Your notes should contain a brief outline of the speech or key words to cue your memory. **Your best delivery is extemporaneous.**

8. <u>VISUAL AIDS</u>: Visual aids enhance any speech. Unless otherwise specified by instructor you are not required to use them for this first major speech. But, if you do decide to incorporate visual aids into your speech, consult the handout and the textbook chapter on visual aids for tips on preparing and using them. Handling aids poorly can undermine even a well-planned speech.

EVALUATION: Below follows the critique form that will be used to evaluate your informative speech. Examine it carefully, noting the weight of points given to various elements in the presentation. This speaking assignment is worth 100 points or approximately 18% of your final course grade.

INFORMATIVE SPEECH CRITIQUE

NAME _____

DATE _____

TOPIC _____

TOTAL SCORE _____
(100 pts.)

TOTAL TIME _____

I. ORGANIZATION
  A. Introduction:
      1. Gain attention?
      2. Create bond with audience?
      3. Preview main points?
      4. Transition into body?

          _____
          (15 pts.)

  B. Body:
      1. Main points well selected?
      2. Support material appropriate?

          _____
          (15 pts.)

  C. Conclusion:
      1. Transition from body?
      2. Review main points?
      3. Make speech memorable?

          _____
          (15 pts.)

  D. Outline: clearly organized? correct format?
      Bibliography: sources clearly documented? correct format?

          _____
          (5 pts.)

II. CONTENT
  A. Suitable informative topic:
      1. Informative? (fit the assignment)
      2. Reflect audience analysis?

          _____
          (15 pts.)

  B. Knowledge of topic:
      1. Credibility?
      2. Well cited sources?

          _____
          (15 pts.)

III. DELIVERY
  A. Enthusiasm/Vocal variety?

          _____
          (5 pts.)

  B. Eye contact?

          _____
          (5 pts.)

  C. Gestures/Nonverbal delivery?

          _____
          (5 pts.)

  D. Time?

          _____
          (5 pts.)

IV. COMMENTS:

DEMONSTRATION OR AUDIO-VISUAL AID SPEECHES

The purpose of demonstration speeches is to support a topic through the effective use of audio-visual aids and demonstration techniques. Explain to students that while demonstration speeches are primarily informative, they typically contain minor elements of persuasion. This assignment usually takes the form of "how to" instructions. Mild persuasion enters in via appeals to the audience to take up the activity, or to improve upon a process or procedure they already utilize. Refer students to the "Speeches about Procedures" section of chapter fifteen (topics that reflect a process or procedure do work well for this assignment). Explanation of the demonstration speech assignment and a critique form follow.

The following structure will help students organize demonstration speeches:

1. Introduction: Develop an attention-getting opening that will inform your audience of your topic. Provide a clear preview statement, one that enumerates the steps in the process you will demonstrate. Students will find very useful the information in Beebe and Beebe's chapter ten on effective introductions.
2. Transition: Use a statement to move from your introductory remarks to your first main point.
3. Main Points and Supporting Material: Explain, support, and demonstrate your points. Explanations and descriptions should be brief, simple, concrete, and interesting. Weave in your audio-visual aids so the aids are an integral part of the speech.
4. Transition: Use a statement to move from your main points and supporting material to your ending.
5. Conclusion: Summarize or restate your main points or steps. Reviewing the information on effective conclusions in chapter ten, textbook, will be very helpful.

Sometimes students are stumped for demonstration topics. First, remind them of all the things they do in an average day that involve processes or a series of steps. Often, the more ordinary the topic, the better for this speech. Second, refer students to the list of sample topics below to spark topic choices.

Changing a flat tire	Martial arts	Dental care
Scuba equipment	Cake decorating	Cartoon drawing
Setting up an aquarium	Rollerblading	Improving your golf swing
Decorating Easter eggs	Yoga	Recipes
The Heimlich maneuver	Planning dance routines	Basic CPR or infant CPR
The perfect indoor picnic	Ceramics	Bicycle maintenance
Restaurant serving	Tanning hides	How to set a formal table
Magazine layout	Stained glass	Hair styling or cutting
Making holiday ornaments	African art	Repotting plants
Writing the president or a senator	Stretching exercises	Checking your blood pressure
Keyboard versatility	Selecting music for a party	Basic first-aid procedures
Taking a better photograph	Weight training	Origami (art of paper folding)
Floral arrangements	Packing for a trip	Ironing a dress shirt
Simple cooking in the dorm	Registering to vote	Donating blood

About audio-visual aids

Research indicates that the addition of even the simplest audio-visual aid to a speech produces three valuable results: (1) an increase in audience interest and attention; (2) an increase in listener understanding; and (3) an improvement in audience retention of speech ideas over time. Chapter fourteen in Beebe and Beebe is a thorough discussion of types of audio-visual aids, purposes for using them in a speech, and guidelines for their effective use. However, if you would like a digested handout for students, a quick review of information about audio-visual aids follows. Attached is an evaluation form for the demonstration speech assignment. Feel free to adapt this material for your classes.

DEMONSTRATION SPEECH ASSIGNMENT

PURPOSE: The primary objective of this demonstration speech is to **inform via the demonstration of how to do or make something, or by showing how something works.** This speech is about a **process**, a series of steps that can be demonstrated to an audience. You are to share information and demonstrate clearly, such that your audience receives information, understands the information, and retains the information. This assignment is primarily an informative speech, but will most likely have elements of persuasion in it.

PRESENTATION DATE: _____

PROCEDURES:

1. SPEAKER ORDER: You will know at least one week in advance the date that you will present your demonstration speech and the order of speakers for each day, either because of speaker volunteering, instructor assignment, or another form of ordering the speeches. You are expected to perform on the day that you are assigned. If you are unprepared or absent, syllabus policy will determine your next step.

2. TIME LIMIT: four to six minutes. This time frame is the same as for the informative speech; however, it is somewhat more difficult to accomplish because you are actually demonstrating something, not just informing. Accordingly, rehearsal and practice is even more critical, using all your planned materials and timing yourself carefully.

3. TOPIC SELECTION: Select a topic you find interesting, one you think will interest your audience. Be sure to select something that can be **easily demonstrated**. Simple processes make the best topics. However, if a process is complicated, it doesn't necessarily mean it is a poor topic. You may have to group some steps, or simply make reference to them, choosing to demonstrate fully only a portion of the process.

4. SUPPORTING MATERIAL: Use your own knowledge of the topic first. Then, plan to include at least **one published source** to enhance your credibility. This one source **may not be a manual, recipe, or label of instructions.** The source must be a printed source of information that supports your topic. As in the introductory informative speech, **cite your sources orally during the speech**, as well as in the written bibliography you turn in.

5. AUDIENCE ANALYSIS: Focus on things that people can easily make or do, or on activities that the common person is likely to engage in. In other words, complicated processes with multiple steps that require a lot of expense, time, and energy won't go over as well as simple, everyday processes. Repeating from the informative speech, **the more personal and audience-centered the speech, the better the effect on your listeners (and your grade).**

6. ORGANIZATION & WRITTEN WORK: Structure your ideas and draft an outline, using your sources of supporting material for substance. The speech should have only one overall thesis with three or four main points. A typed outline and bibliography are required for this speech just as they were for the informative speech. **Bibliographies that do not appear in APA style will not be acceptable.** If you lost points last time on your written work and don't understand why, please talk to me.

7. DELIVERY: This is **NOT** a manuscript speech, so **you should not read your speech**. Your notes should contain a brief outline of the speech or key words to cue your memory. **Your best delivery is extemporaneous**.

8. AUDIO-VISUAL AIDS: **Audio-visual aids are required for this speech**. Consult the handout and the textbook chapter on visual aids (chapter fourteen) for tips on preparing and using visual aids. Handling aids poorly can undermine the best planned speech. A guiding section concerning appropriate and effective use of audio-visual aids appears on the demonstration speech critique form.

EVALUATION: The following page is the critique form that will be used to evaluate demonstration speeches. Read through it and note the weight of points given to various aspects of the presentation. This speaking assignment is worth 100 points or approximately 18% of your final course grade.

DEMONSTRATION SPEECH CRITIQUE

NAME _____

DATE _____

TOPIC _____

TOTAL SCORE _____
(100 pts.)

TOTAL TIME _____

I. ORGANIZATION
   A. Introduction:
      1. Gain attention?
      2. Create bond with audience?
      3. Preview main points?
      4. Transition into body?

                          _____
                          (10 pts.)

   B. Body:
      1. Main points well selected?
      2. Support material appropriate?

                          _____
                          (10 pts.)

   C. Conclusion:
      1. Transition from body?
      2. Review main points?
      3. Make speech memorable?

                          _____
                          (10 pts.)

   D. Outline: clearly organized? correct format?
       Bibliography: sources clearly documented? correct format?

                          _____
                          (5 pts.)

II. CONTENT
   A. Suitable demonstration topic:
      1. Demonstrative? (fit the assignment)
      2. Reflect audience analysis?

                          _____
                          (15 pts.)

   B. Knowledge of topic:
      1. Credibility?
      2. Well cited sources?

                          _____
                          (15 pts.)

   C. Audio-visual Aids: prepared & used well in the speech?

                          _____
                          (10 pts.)

III. DELIVERY
   A. Enthusiasm/Vocal variety?

                          _____
                          (5 pts.)

   B. Eye contact?

                          _____
                          (5 pts.)

   C. Gestures/Nonverbal delivery?

                          _____
                          (5 pts.)

   D. Handling of audio-visual aids?

                          _____
                          (5 pts.)

   E. Time?

                          _____
                          (5 pts.)

IV. COMMENTS:

Chapter fourteen, textbook, is very strong in describing and prescribing design, construction or selection, and use of visual aids. A handout below supplements, but does not replace chapter fourteen.

AUDIO-VISUAL AIDS

Audio-visual aids consist of any type of supplemental material that effectively and dramatically clarifies your points in a speech. Aids draw attention to certain aspects in your remarks; they also add interest to your speech. Another benefit is that aids often reduce a speaker's nervousness, in that visual aids appear to the speaker to draw some of the audience's attention away from the speaker. Aids also assist with another problem of concern to inexperienced speakers: what to do with my hands!

Types of Audio-Visual Aids:

1. Yourself (dress, movements, etc.)
2. Objects or models of objects (e.g., sports equipment, model cars, model solar system, etc.)
3. Chalkboard for words, addresses, simple diagrams, and the like
4. Pictures
5. Diagrams, charts, and graphs on poster board or flip charts
6. Videotapes
7. Audiocassettes, records, and CDs
8. Other persons or animals
9. Handouts of printed information (brochures, pamphlets, you name it)
10. Maps
11. Overhead transparencies using an overhead projector
12. Computer-generated graphics and materials

Tips for Using Audio-Visual Aids: Although the list above should give ideas for selecting audio-visual aids, most speakers need some pointers on how best to use aids in a speech. The suggestions following should guide you in both your selection and use of audio-visual aids.

1. Make sure that your chart, poster, picture, or object is large enough to be **clearly** seen by everyone in your audience. Don't use a small picture from a magazine or a photograph that you took, unless you enlarge it so that everyone in the room can see it. If an object is quite small, such as a part from a larger object, for example, then a poster depicting a blown-up diagram of the part would be more visual than showing the part itself. Remember--visual aids should be, first and foremost, **visual**.

2. Anything you think about putting on a chalkboard can be done just as easily on a poster prepared ahead of time. Posters are much more visual than a chalkboard. Save the board for something simple, such as an address or key phrase. If you use the board, talk to the audience, not the chalkboard.

3. If possible, conceal your audio-visual aids until you are ready to refer to them. If you display your aids before you speak, some of the impact will be lost.

4. Use aids to control your audience's attention. Remember that audio-visuals **aid** a speaker, **not substitute** for a speaker. When using an overhead projector, for example, turn the projector on only when you want your audience to see your information. When you move on to another point, turn the projector off, or cover your next points so that the audience will focus their attention on you, not on the projection.

5. **Rehearse your speech thoroughly using your audio-visual aids**. Remember that the aids will be more difficult to handle once the nervousness of public speaking sets in. The more familiar you are with your "props," the more you have practiced with them, the smoother your speech will be.

6. Double check your audio-visual aids just before you begin to speak. Are pictures, charts, the lot of them in proper order and secured? Does the projector, VCR, tape deck, **actually work**? Does the tracking on the video player need adjusting so that your videotape picture will be clear? Do you need an extension cord? Do you have chalk? Do you have an easel or other means of positioning a chart or poster?

7. Keep charts and diagrams simple. Use dark markers and **large lettering** to make your charts more visible Remember, it is better to use two or three simple posters than to try to cram everything on one poster. **Take a position across the room from an aid: can you read your own lettering?**

8. If you want to pass out materials to the audience, **make sure that they do not distract from your oral presentation.** If you pass an object or picture around the room or hand out information to your audience at the start of or during your speech, your audience will look at the aid and **not at you**. Moreover, they will not be listening to you. If you really want to distribute a handout, give it out **after** the speech has concluded. Don't incorporate the handout into your conclusion, because you are likely to "water down," weaken the strong conclusion you have so nicely planned. Give your conclusion, then hand out materials. If you are in a situation where an outline or other material must be disseminated for the audience's benefit, or if your audience is taking notes from an overhead you are using, take every opportunity to hold audience attention on your message. You should be the focal point, not the audio-visual aid.

9. Talk about your visual aids, don't just display them or play with them. Placing materials around a room or on display to simply create a mood can be confusing to an audience who expects you to use the materials or make reference to them. For example, if you put your key ideas on a chart or poster, help your audience understand the information in your speech by specifically referring to the chart at appropriate times.

10. Display and indicate the audio-visual aids at the time you talk about them.

11. Talk to the audience, not to your audio-visual aids. Be especially careful not to keep your back to the audience when using the chalkboard or referring to a chart or TV monitor.

12. When using an easel to display a chart or poster, be careful where you position the easel. Make sure that it isn't placed at such an angle as to cut off part of the audience from viewing the aid. You don't want to frustrate your audience by talking about things they can't see.

13. Think twice about using other people in your speech as visual aids. If you need another person to help you demonstrate something, make sure to solicit that person's involvement ahead of time. Surprising someone by asking her or him to volunteer often backfires on a speaker, because the person is put on the spot and may take attention away from the speaker. Occasionally, a helper can foul up a speaker's plan; make sure the person agrees to help and that he or she knows exactly what to do.

14. Think three times before you use an animal as a visual aid for a speech. Late night TV shows wanting a boost in ratings are fond of animal specialty acts, and those shows have experienced weird and dangerous happenings. The unpredictable nature of using animals makes this practice unwise. Please do not use a frightening creature of some sort (like a snake) as a shock or attention-getting technique. This device is an example of poor audience analysis, and, likely as not, may backfire on a speaker.

15. If you use an audiotape, CD, or videotape in your speech, use a planned segment and then turn the device off. Using sounds or images as effects, or to create a mood running through your speech, may be unwise, because it will be more difficult for your audience to hear and concentrate on you. The overall effects may be distracting—the last thing you want your audio-visual aids to accomplish for you.

IMPROMPTU SPEECHES

A portion of public speaking instructors do not assign a round of impromptu speeches for students in introductory classes. Some instructors feel that it unnecessarily "puts students on the spot," that it can undermine a student's progress, especially students who have high levels of speech anxiety. Both points of view can be documented, and perhaps no generalization is valid. This author has found that impromptu speeches that arise in class as the result of experiential exercises are relatively non-threatening. Should you choose to schedule formal impromptu speeches, you may find that later in the semester, after students have gained experience and confidence, may be the proper learning time. With more experience and confidence students are more likely to feel challenged by impromptu speaking, and confident enough to rise to that challenge. This author does urge the obvious: explain this assignment with forethought, tact, and caring.

Providing a Purpose: The rationale for assigning a round of impromptu speeches is to give students an opportunity to practice speaking "off the cuff" or "off of the top of their heads." Most instructors will probably agree that impromptu speaking skills are **a critical skill to develop**--one that helps students communicate effectively and impressively in other classes, and that is invaluable in their professional and community lives.

Dealing with Nervousness: To counteract nervousness students will no doubt feel, it helps to remind them that they do this kind of speaking every day, when they converse with people, when they speak up in classes, when they interview for jobs. Most of the time conversations and the other activities are spontaneous and impromptu, not planned out and rehearsed. Explain to students exactly how the impromptu round will work and give them tips for how to "think quickly on their feet." Refer students to the information on impromptu delivery in chapter thirteen of the textbook.

Ways to Approach the Impromptu Round: Many approaches to this assignment exist and since some work better than others, you may have to use the trial and error method to find an approach that makes you and your students comfortable.

• **Topic Development and Selection:** One way to approach this assignment is to generate many topics and write them on small slips of paper, put them in a large bowl or box, and have students draw for the topic they will speak about. Some instructors take a different approach. Diane Ivy has an unusual approach, and you may consider it. She explains: "I have several pages of topics--both humorous or light-hearted and serious--that I have used for years and update regularly for this assignment. . . . First I write students' names on a legal pad. Then I think about each student, what each has spoken about thus far in the term, what might stretch or challenge the student. Next I refer to my collection of topics and select the most appropriate topic with the student in mind. I explain to the class that this round of speeches is not meant to embarrass anyone or throw them off, but simply to give an opportunity to practice important skills. In case anyone feels put upon or like this is a power play, I allow the class to generate an impromptu topic for me. I speak last on the last day of speeches, and I follow the exact procedure I use for students. (The best difference, however, is that I'm not graded!) Also, I am careful to explain to students **why** I chose a particular topic for them. I explain that if by chance the topic I assign triggers a personal, emotional reaction in them, I want students to tell me before they attempt the speech, and I am very apologetic in that situation. Occasionally, completely by chance, a student will connect with topic a in a way that I could not have anticipated, so I give those students a breather and then offer them a second topic.

• **Running the Impromptu Speaking Rounds:** Because I teach small classes, I can often get through a whole round of impromptu speeches in one class session--which is wholly desirable, for nerves and scheduling purposes. I call students' names in random order, but I sometimes try to alternate between lighter and heavier topics for the sake of the audience. When students' names are called, they go up to the front where I give them their topic and make sure they understand it. Speakers turn their backs to the audience, and the timekeeper gives them 30 seconds to organize their thoughts. I instruct students that in this 30-second period, they should first try to generate two main ideas to discuss, then they should plan an introduction, and then--if time permits--think of a conclusion. After 30 seconds, the timekeeper says "Time" and the speaker turns around and speaks for two to four minutes.

• **Evaluating Impromptu Speeches:** It is a good idea to carefully explain what you are looking for in these speeches, i.e., what you consider to be effective impromptu speaking. You should also thoroughly go over the speech critique form you will use for grading impromptu speeches, making sure students understand how grades will be determined. (Following this general information, an <u>explanation of the impromptu speech assignment</u> and the <u>critique form</u> I currently use in my classes is provided.) I always explain that I am viewing these speeches more globally, meaning that I don't evaluate them in as detailed a fashion I do prepared speeches. I don't expect students to present a polished presentation, but I ask that they try to remember what they've been taught, and try to come up with interesting ideas organized into some semblance of an introduction, body, and conclusion format.

• **Student Reactions to Impromptu Speaking Assignments:** More often than not, students tell me that this was their favorite speech. While it made them energized or nervous, they enjoyed the experience and became more relaxed because they didn't have notes and weren't locked into a pre-set plan. In many cases, students' impromptu delivery is more fluid and audience-centered than in prepared speeches."

Sample Topics: These topics are divided into categories of "Heavy-er" and "Light-er," but you may have a different vision of the depth or seriousness of a topic. A light topic can be interpreted in a serious manner, and vice versa. Topics represent subjects most students can talk about, meaning that they stem from common knowledge and opinion bases.

<u>Heavy-er Topics</u>

What advice will I give my grandchildren?
Assisted suicide: Is it help or murder?
Are the media out of control?
Comforting someone who's terminally ill
What I'll teach my children about racism
AIDS tests as part of college admission packets
Responses to sexual harassment on the job
Do we have too much technology for our own good?
If I were a terrorist's lawyer . . . .
My view on gay rights
Persecution of the elderly
Responsibilities of cigarette manufacturers
What scares me most for future generations is . . . .
Would I consider being a single parent?
Getting people to take safe sex seriously
Effects of TV and movie violence on society
The legalization of drugs: Pros and cons
Animal testing: Science or barbarism?
Could I put my parents in a nursing home?
The single most important advance in society is . . . .

<u>Light-er Topics</u>

Who will be the first female President of the U.S.?
If I could be a man, I'd be . . . .
If I could be a woman, I'd be . . . .
My first love
The problem of puberty
My favorite sport
My least favorite television program
What I fear most about marriage
Do we need a male liberation movement?
The strangest aspect of American culture is . . . .
If I could change one thing about this campus . . . .
What I dislike most about women is . . . .
What I dislike most about men is . . . .
My favorite childhood book
My most embarrassing moment was . . . .
A country I want to visit before I die, and why
The lighter and brighter side of dumpsters
The funniest thing I've seen my parents do
Music videos I have known, and hated
If I won the lottery . . . .

IMPROMPTU SPEECH ASSIGNMENT

PURPOSE: The primary objective of this impromptu speech is to give you practice in thinking "on your feet," organizing ideas quickly, and communicating them as effectively as possible.

PROCEDURES:

1. <u>SPEAKER ORDER</u>: You will **not** know the date nor the order of speakers for impromptu speeches (that's what "impromptu" implies). Students will either volunteer, or the instructor will simply call your name, give you your topic, allow you thirty seconds to prepare, then ask you to speak. Please realize that the days scheduled in your syllabus for impromptu speeches are **the only days these speeches will be possible for a grade. Realize that your name may be called at any time on any day of these speeches.** If you are absent, you cannot make up this assignment.

2. <u>TIME LIMIT</u>: two to four minutes. Your speech should not exceed four minutes nor be under two minutes. Your grade could be reduced. Listen to instructor's explanation of possible penalties.

3. <u>TOPIC SELECTION</u>: Your instructor will assign a topic for you that will challenge or "stretch" you, **not embarrass you.** Use your own knowledge of the topic, try to organize your points as quickly as possible, then communicate those points to your audience clearly and effectively. You choose whether to make the speech informative. The evaluative emphasis is on how well you think on your feet and express yourself.

4. <u>AUDIENCE ANALYSIS</u>: Even in this speech, keep your class audience in mind; gear your presentation to them. Just as in other speaking assignments, **the more personal, audience-centered the speech, the better the effect (and your grade).**

EVALUATION: The following page is the critique form used to evaluate your impromptu speech. Read and note the weight of points given to various aspects of the presentation. This speaking assignment is worth fifty points or approximately 9% of your final course grade. **Don't worry! Instructor expectations are not nearly as high for this speech as for other speeches you prepare and rehearse in advance.** Try to view this assignment as a challenge, a chance to see what you can do as a speaker. It might just actually be fun.

IMPROMPTU SPEECH CRITIQUE

NAME _____   TOTAL SCORE _____
                                                            (50 pts.)
DATE _____

TOPIC _____   TOTAL TIME _____

I. ORGANIZATION

    A. Introduction: _____
                                                            (7 pts.)

    B. Body: _____
                                                            (7 pts.)

    C. Conclusion: _____
                                                            (7 pts.)

II. CONTENT: _____
                                                            (17 pts.)

III. DELIVERY

    A. Enthusiasm/Vocal variety?   _____
                                                            (3 pts.)

    B. Eye contact?   _____
                                                            (3 pts.)

    C. Gestures/Nonverbal delivery?   _____
                                                            (3 pts.)

    D. Time?   _____
                                                            (3 pts.)

IV. COMMENTS:

PERSUASIVE SPEECHES

PERSUASIVE SPEECH OBJECTIVES MAY INCLUDE:

to persuade listeners to change their beliefs, attitudes, values, and behaviors
to modify listeners' attitudes, beliefs, values, and behaviors
to reinforce listeners' pre-existing beliefs, attitudes, values, and behaviors
to move listeners to action
to realize the ethical responsibilities inherent in persuasive speaking

TYPES OF PERSUASIVE SPEECHES

Actuation Speech: The speech to actuate is one in which the audience already agrees with the topic, but the speaker motivates listeners to act. The purpose is, first, to reinforce attitudes, beliefs, and values, and second, to challenge the audience to behave in accordance with their attitudes. "Put Your Money Where Your Mouth Is" expresses the objective quite well. Students should choose interesting, meaningful topics. Remind students or have a class discussion about the power of persuasive speaking and the ethical implications of endorsing certain actions. The best speeches will probably be those in which speakers view the speech as an opportunity to rally a cause or gain support for an important idea.

Argumentative Speech: This approach will choose a controversial topic, a topic which will probably split the audience into sides or subgroups. Students need to be very familiar with chapter seventeen, textbook, in particular the sections which discuss the use of logic and evidence to persuade an audience and how to persuade a receptive, neutral, or hostile audience. Stress to students the importance of audience analysis, perhaps by giving them in-class time to conduct informal attitudinal audience analyses. More logical appeal than emotional appeal is typically present in an argumentative speech.

Inspirational Speech: The purpose of inspirational speaking is to motivate an audience to improve: personally, emotionally, professionally, or spiritually. The speech may be geared toward experiencing greater success, developing attributes that evidence growth as a human being, achieving personal or professional goals, or helping others. Although the inspirational speech is often a "feel good" kind of speech, it is a challenge and it can create audience tension. Encourage thorough audience analyses by inspirational student speakers. More emotional than logical appeal is typically present in this speech.

On pages following are provided rationale, assignment explanation, and evaluation form. You may wish to consider assigning written peer evaluations, to give students experience in critiquing live presentations and to provide more real world information for speakers. You might also wish to assign oral peer critics to speakers, making sure that a person who critiques a speaker is not, in turn, critiqued by that person. A peer critique form which could be used for this persuasive speaking peer criticism assignment and an adapted version for peer feedback follow the assignment description. Following practice with the other speech assignments suggested topics are listed.

Sample Topics

Racism in America	Genetic engineering	Special Olympics
The Internet	Child abuse	AIDS research
Media-related topics	Health care crisis	Welfare reform
Illiteracy	Hurricanes	Sexism in music videos
Safer Sex	Rising crime	Gun legislation
Capital punishment	Gang violence	Water conservation
Militia movement	Recycling	Lowering your cholesterol
Getting regular exercise	Voting	Abortion
Preventing computer theft	Pornography	Domestic violence
Preserving the environment	Children's rights	Affirmative Action
Blood donation	The home HIV test	Assisted suicide/euthanasia

PERSUASIVE SPEECH ASSIGNMENT

PURPOSE: The primary objective of this speech is **to persuade**, either by reinforcing or altering the audience's attitudes, beliefs, values, and behavior, or by suggesting new attitudes, beliefs, or values to your audience.

PROCEDURES:

1. <u>SPEAKER ORDER</u>: You will know at least one week in advance the date you will present your persuasive speech and the order of speakers for each day. As usual, volunteers may be accepted. But, again, recognize that you are expected to perform <u>on the day you are assigned or have volunteered for.</u> If you are unprepared or absent, realize that syllabus policy will control your next step.

2. <u>TIME LIMIT</u>: Five to seven minutes. You must observe time limits or your grade may be adjusted. Time rehearsals carefully, to ensure effective use of your allotted persuasive speaking time. For strongest persuasive impact, plan and rehearse to utilize your full time.

3. <u>TOPIC SELECTION</u>: Select a topic you feel is important, a topic on which you strongly hold an attitude, belief, or value. Consider the audience also in your topic choice. Will your chosen topic allow you to wax persuasive with <u>this</u> audience? Don't dig a hole and pull it in after you: don't choose to speak on why this audience should always consider suicide when confronting problems.

4. <u>SUPPORTING MATERIAL</u>: Use your own knowledge of the topic first, then find published and interview sources to back up your points and enhance your credibility as a speaker. You must include a **minimum of three different sources of at least two source types** in this speech. Only one personal interview will count as a source. Remember, it is imperative that you **cite your sources orally during the speech**, as well as in the bibliography that you turn in with your outline.

5. <u>AUDIENCE ANALYSIS</u>: Speaking effectiveness in persuasion is very dependent on how well you analyze your audience and adapt your speech to them. A personalized, carefully worked-out approach works best when attempting to influence an audience. Consider your audience's pre-existing attitudes, beliefs, and values about your topic. Estimate how much of a change to ask from the audience. **The more personal and audience-centered the speech, the better the effect (and your grade).**

6. <u>ORGANIZATION & WRITTEN WORK</u>: Structure your ideas and draft an outline, using your sources of supporting material for substance. The speech should have only one overall thesis with three or four main points. The **typed** outline **you hand in the day you speak** should conform to the format discussed in class. Also to be turned in with the outline is a bibliography of sources cited in your speech, or considered for the speech. For the format of bibliography, refer to the APA handout provided you, or to the *APA Style Manual* (4th ed.) in the reference section of the library. **Bibliographies that do not appear in APA style will not be acceptable.**

7. <u>DELIVERY</u>: This is **NOT** a manuscript speech. Therefore, **you should not read your speech**. Your notes should contain a brief outline of the speech or key words to cue your memory. **Your best delivery is extemporaneous.**

8. <u>AUDIO-VISUAL AIDS</u>: Audio-visual aids can enhance any speech. You are not required to use them for this speech, but you may wish to use some. If you do decide to incorporate audio-visual aids into your speech, consult the handout and textbook chapter on visual aids for tips on preparing and using them. If you handle aids poorly, it can undermine the best planned speech.

EVALUATION

The following page is the critique form used to evaluate your persuasive speech. Read and note the weight of points given to various aspects of the presentation. This speaking assignment is worth 100 points or approximately 18% of your final course grade.

PERSUASIVE SPEECH CRITIQUE

NAME _____

DATE _____

TOPIC _____

TOTAL SCORE _____
(100 pts.)

TOTAL TIME _____

I. ORGANIZATION
    A. Introduction:
        1. Gain attention?
        2. Create bond with audience?
        3. Preview main points?
        4. Transition into body?

            _____
            (10 pts.)

    B. Body:
        1. Main points well selected?
        2. Support material appropriate?

            _____
            (10 pts.)

    C. Conclusion:
        1. Transition from body?
        2. Review main points?
        3. Make speech memorable?

            _____
            (10 pts.)

    D. Outline: clearly organized? correct format?
        Bibliography: sources clearly documented? correct format?

            _____
            (5 pts.)

II. CONTENT
    A. Suitable persuasive topic:
        1. Persuasive? (fit the assignment)
        2. Reflect audience analysis?

            _____
            (15 pts.)

    B. Knowledge of topic:
        1. Credibility?
        2. Well cited sources?

            _____
            (15 pts.)

    C. Use of Appeals:
        1. Logical reasoning?
        2. Emotional appeal?

            _____
            (15 pts.)

III. DELIVERY
    A. Enthusiasm/Vocal variety?

            _____
            (5 pts.)

    B. Eye contact?

            _____
            (5 pts.)

    C. Gestures/Nonverbal delivery?

            _____
            (5 pts.)

    D. Time?

            _____
            (5 pts.)

IV. COMMENTS:

WRITTEN PEER CRITIQUE: PERSUASIVE SPEECH

CRITIC _____   **TOTAL SCORE** _____

SPEAKER _____

TOPIC _____   **TOTAL TIME** _____

I. ORGANIZATION
   A. Introduction:
      1. Gain attention?
      2. Create bond with audience?
      3. Preview main points?
      4. Transition into body?

                                                            _____
   B. Body: (10 pts.)
      1. Main points well selected?
      2. Support material appropriate?

                                                            _____
   C. Conclusion: (10 pts.)
      1. Transition from body?
      2. Review main points?
      3. Make speech memorable?

                                    _____
   D. Outline: clearly organized? correct format?   (10 pts.)
      Bibliography: sources clearly documented? correct format?

                                    _____
                                    (5 pts.)

II. CONTENT
   A. Suitable persuasive topic:
      1. Persuasive? (fit the assignment)
      2. Reflect audience analysis?

                                    _____
   B. Knowledge of topic: (15 pts.)
      1. Credibility?
      2. Well cited sources?

                                    _____
   C. Use of Appeals: (15 pts.)
      1. Logical reasoning?
      2. Emotional appeal?

                                      _____
                                    (15 pts.)

III. DELIVERY
   A. Enthusiasm/Vocal variety?   _____
                                    (5 pts.)
   B. Eye contact?   _____
                                    (5 pts.)
   C. Gestures/Nonverbal delivery?   _____
                                    (5 pts.)
   D. Time?   _____
                                    (5 pts.)

IV. COMMENTS:

GROUP PRESENTATIONS

Advantages: Some instructors like to give students practice in group presentations, especially because these formats are commonplace in professional and community settings (and in many senior level college courses). One advantage of group speeches is the typical reduction in nervousness compared to individual presentations. Another is the fuller coverage of a topic than one individual can provide.

Disadvantages: One disadvantage reflects the most common problem with group work: a group member "goofs off," and expects other group members to carry her or his weight in the assignment. Another kind of problem and disadvantage arises when one person (or small coalitions within the larger group) dominate the planning and presenting of information. Students must realize that **all members** are required to make presentations, even if the configuration is a group, and **balance** across members is expected.

Considerations: Chapter nineteen in the Beebe and Beebe provides an excellent printed discussion to prepare students for this kind of assignment. After urging students to that reading, discuss with students the purpose(s) of a group presentation. For instance, do you want these speeches to be persuasive? Informative? Perhaps you will wish to be flexible and allow groups or group members to decide their own purposes. Do you expect groups to incorporate audio-visual aids into their presentations? How long should the presentations be? Will there be any question-and-answer periods? If there is a moderator, what is expected of the person in that role and how will he or she be evaluated? How will you evaluate the effectiveness of the assignment--by assigning individual speaker grades or by grading the presentation as a whole? Will you create options for group members whose grades might suffer because of the group, but who performed up to standard? Planning and effectively communicating your expectations and evaluative criteria for this assignment is perhaps even more critical than it is for other speaking assignments. You may wish to select one of the following formats for all groups, or to vary the format among groups.

TYPES OF GROUP PRESENTATIONS

Panel Discussion: This approach is an informative group presentation that does not involve formal individual speeches. Speakers make presentations from notes containing key facts or supporting material. Most often a moderator is appointed or elected by the group with responsibilities that include: (a) introducing the general topic, subtopics, and panelists; (b) monitoring panelists' participation in the presentation;
(c) summarizing individuals' statements; and (d) facilitating the post-presentation question-and-answer session. In this format, it is not as critical as it is in other formats that groups make united decisions or know what other members will present, nor that they be evaluated as a cohesive group.

Symposium: Small groups of four or five speakers should agree first on a general topic, and then the subtopics individual speakers are expected to cover. Each person should research the topic; develop a well-organized, fully supported speech; and deliver that speech in an effective manner. In this format, it is important that members know what each other will present so as to avoid duplication. This type of group presentation also typically involves a moderator whose duties duplicate those of a moderator in a panel discussion.

Forum: This format is suggested as a group way to accomplish an impromptu round of speeches. A forum consists of an audience which directs questions to a group whose members respond to questions with short impromptu speeches. The moderator's primary responsibility is to arouse audience interest in the topic, to elicit audience questions, and, secondarily, to be the traffic cop, directing questions to different speakers.

ALTERNATIVE, NON-SPEAKING ASSIGNMENTS

You may wish to incorporate non-speaking assignments in your course. Typically, these kinds of assignments are not weighted as heavily as speeches in the calculation of final grade. You might consider one non-speaking assignment early in the term, so that students get a grade in the first two or three weeks of class, prior to the first big speech (and, big grade). During this time, you will probably be introducing "nuts and bolts" elements of the speechmaking process and conducting practice, non-graded rounds of speeches. These alternative assignments give instructors a "feel" for how well students are understanding the most important "fastener" of them all, audience analysis and how to become an audience-centered speaker.

Audience Analysis Assignment: Students do not easily understand that the true and best test of a successful speech does not reside in the speaker's perception of the presentation, but in the audience's response to the presentation. Students often think they understand this concept, but they are still affected by years of believing that to be an effective communicator, a speaker focuses on the message, not how a receiver or audience member will take the message. This exercise can help students chip away at the older, less productive way of looking at public speaking. A detailed handout describing the assignment I use for this purpose appears shortly. The gist of the assignment is: students develop an opinion on a controversial topic; next, they are presented with two very different audiences for which they must develop speeches (or parts of speeches) defending their opinions. Instructor informs them their opinion does not change, but the approach, the language used, the kinds of supporting material should be significantly different across the two supposed audiences. You may certainly insert any controversial topic you wish the students to explore (note: students do not actually deliver these speeches; this is a written assignment).

Critique of an Outside Speaker: One of the best ways to improve as a speaker is to do it--time and time again. But, another way certainly is to observe other speakers in action. This assignment formalizes the learning by observation process by requiring that students complete an in-depth report and evaluation of a speaker outside of classrooms. While helping develop students' critical listening and thinking abilities, the assignment also exposes them to models of what and what not to do as a speaker. This assignment probably works best if it is due sometime during the first three weeks to one month of class, because after that time students should not be distracted from working on their own speeches. But, you and your students have to keep your eyes and ears open and alert each other as to possible speaking opportunities on campus and in the local community. A description of this assignment to be handed out to students appears on appears shortly.

Course Portfolio Assignment and Feedback Form: The purpose of the course portfolio assignment is to provide students a means of assessing their own daily work and progress throughout the course. The assignment is designed to assist students in self-evaluation, to give them a structured opportunity for reflection through writing, and to offer instructors insight into students' learning. Students should bring the portfolio to each class and make entries for each class session. Instructors may choose to scan the portfolios periodically, with the first scan coming fairly early in the term. The portfolio is a part of the final grade in the course, but how much it counts is up to you. A sample portfolio feedback form is provided for your adaptation, coming up shortly. One procedural suggestion is to have students purchase three-ring notebooks to contain their coursework (e.g., text assignments, in-class and out-of-class written and discussion assignments, notes, study materials and test results, research for speeches, outlines and bibliographies, and instructor and peer critiques). Students might choose to organize their portfolios into four sections: (1) class activities; (2) text materials/handouts; (3) speech preparation materials (e.g., outlines and bibliographies, audience analyses), research materials, and critique sheets; and (4) testing materials.

AUDIENCE ANALYSIS ASSIGNMENT

SITUATION: Imagine that you have been invited to speak to <u>two very different audiences</u> about the same topic. Your topic is "Gays in the Military."

PROCEDURES:

1. Formulate your own opinion regarding the controversy over gay individuals in the armed forces. Any opinion is acceptable; you just have to formulate and articulate one.

2. Assume that you have been invited to speak about this topic and to explain your particular opinion. Then think about the two audiences described below, in terms of how you would analyze these audiences and change your approach to the speeches accordingly. **Remember, only your approach to your audiences changes, NOT your opinion on the topic.**

3. In a 4 to 5-page paper (typed, double-spaced), demonstrate how you would adapt your approach for these different audiences.

4. You may choose to do a "mini audience analysis," noting some ideas as to demographic and attitudinal audience analysis for each group. Or, you may be more comfortable writing out, in paragraph style, what you perceive each group would be like. You can then do a brief outline of main points for each speech or do it in narrative style (e.g., "At this point in my speech, I would mention that . . .). What you must do is to **be sure to include** an actual excerpt from each speech, so the instructor can see how you would vary the two speeches for the unique audiences. This is a <u>free-flowing assignment</u>, meaning that there is more than one way to do it correctly. <u>The bottom line is to make sure to give the instructor enough copy to show a **significant** difference in two approaches to a speech on the same topic.</u> Think about how your language would change, your style or demeanor, your supporting material (what would carry the most weight with each group).

Audience One: The senior citizens' church school class has invited you to one of their morning classes to offer your perspective on the issue of gays in the military. This church setting can be of any denomination or religion you prefer, as specific or as general as you want to make it.

Audience Two: The Intrafraternity Council and Campus Panhellenic (organizations that oversee fraternities and sororities on college campuses) have asked you to speak to a sorority pledge class at one of their evening meetings. They want to hear your perspective on the issue of gays in the military.

Remember!! The opinion you will express concerning gays in the military **does not change for the two speeches**. Whatever your opinion, you must decide how to best present **that opinion** to these two very different audiences.

EVALUATION: This paper is due on the date noted in your syllabus. **No late papers will be accepted.** Please put a cover sheet on your paper with your name on it and staple it.This paper is worth 50 points or approximately 9% of your final grade.

GUIDELINES FOR CRITIQUE OF OUTSIDE SPEECH ASSIGNMENT

PURPOSE: One way to become a more effective public speaker is to be an audience member, observing other speakers, and noting and critiquing their strengths and weaknesses. Observation allows you to adopt some of the observed more effective behaviors into your own performances (as well as to avoid some of their "bad habits"). The purpose of this assignment is to provide an exercise in which students observe and critique a public speech.

INSTRUCTIONS: Using the two-page form that follows, critique a **LIVE** speaking event. Try to attend a meeting, or rally in which a person or persons will be speaking to an audience. A minister's sermon, a politician's speech, or a presentation at a professional meeting will all serve this assignment effectively. **However, here are some things that will NOT work**: (1) You cannot use a speech presented by a classmate in your public speaking class; (2) you cannot critique an informal presentation, such as one in which the leader of a group speaks to that group and group members interact, ask questions, offer comments (the informality and give-and-take with the audience make this format unacceptable for this assignment) (3) you cannot use an instructor's lecture in another class you're taking as data for this assignment.

If there appears to be no way you can critique a live speech, then you may as a last resort use a speech that is from a mediated source. The media center of the library has several speeches on videotape, laserdisc, and CDRom. (The collection includes "classic" speeches, such as Martin Luther King's "I Have a Dream" speech, Barbara Jordan's keynote address to the Democratic convention, JFK's "Ask Not . . ." inaugural address, and other timeless speeches) You cannot check out these materials; you must view them (and complete your critique) in the library. If a national figure happens to make a speech that is televised (such as on CNN or C-Span), you may use that speech for your critique. **However, please realize that you will automatically have a grade deduction for not using a live speech for this assignment.** Critiquing a speech from a videotape is not regarded the same as critiquing a live presentation. For this fifty-point assignment, grades for critiques of non-live speeches will start at a B (or forty-four points instead of fifty).

Type your responses to the items on the 2-page form that follows in the spaces provided. If you wish, you may want to enter this form on your computer, along with your responses to the various items. If you do this, however, please try to conform to the space constraints I have indicated on the form. Lengthy critiques will likely hurt, not help, your grade. This assignment is due on or before the date noted in your class syllabus. I will not accept late critiques.

EVALUATION: This assignment will be graded on appropriateness of speaker selection, depth of insight in critiquing elements of the speaker's performance, appropriate application of course terms to speaking event, and clarity of written style. This assignment is worth fifty points, or approximately 9% of your final course grade.

CRITIQUE OF OUTSIDE SPEECH

STUDENT'S NAME: _____

1. Name & Title/Position of the Speaker:

2. Subject of the speech:

3. Occasion for speech, including sponsoring group:

4. Place, time, & date of speech. (If you have flyers or handouts, attach them to this critique.)

5. Purpose of speech, as you understood it. (If possible, go up after the speech & ask the speaker what her or his purpose was.)

6. Describe the type of introductory and concluding devices the speaker used. Discuss why these devices were effective or ineffective.

7. Who was the audience? Discuss the way the speaker adapted to the specific audience. If the speech was not well-adapted to the audience, comment on this & suggest ways to improve.

8. Critique the speaker's organization of ideas, including the use of connective devices (e.g., signposts, internal summaries, previews, reviews, transitions).

9. Critique the speaker's use of support materials (e.g., examples, statistics, testimony) & sources.

10. Describe the speaker's use of language. Was it appropriate for the audience? Why or why not? What elements of the speaker's language stood out to you?

11. Describe the speaker's delivery, including vocal & bodily delivery, eye contact, timing, etc. Was it effective? Why or why not? Were there any physical constraints on his/her delivery?

12. What general or specific suggestions for improvement might you offer the speaker?

COURSE PORTFOLIO FEEDBACK FORM

Instructions to Students: Insert this feedback sheet as the first page of your course portfolio and leave it there throughout the course. Save this sheet as a record of your progress.

1. DATES COLLECTED: _____   _____   _____

2. ORGANIZATION BY SECTIONS:

    A. Class activities and lecture notes (self-analyses of progress; ideas, essays, course suggestions; responses to assignments in class; activity applications, exercises; etc.)

    B. Responses to textbook (summaries or notes based on readings; responses to chapter objectives, critical thinking questions, ethical questions, and suggested activities)

    C. Speech materials (research materials; drafts of outlines; bibliographies; audience analyses; speaker notes; instructor and peer critique sheets; etc.)

    D. Testing materials (study notes; study guides or handouts; test results; etc.)

3. EVIDENCE OF IMPROVED PUBLIC SPEAKING COMPETENCE:

   _____   _____   _____

4. ABILITY TO ANALYZE, EVALUATE, & PROBLEM SOLVE:

   _____   _____   _____

5. APPROPRIATE WORK FOR THIS COLLEGE LEVEL:

   _____   _____   _____

6. NO CHANGES NEEDED; KEEP UP THE QUALITY WORK:

   _____   _____   _____

7. NEED MORE ENTRIES, HIGHER QUALITY, A MORE SERIOUS EFFORT:

   _____   _____   _____

8. INADEQUATE; IF THIS IS A GENUINE EFFORT, MAKE AN APPOINTMENT WITH ME SOON.

   _____   _____   _____

9. GRADE:

   _____   _____   _____

10. INSTRUCTOR INITIALS:

   _____   _____   _____

GIVING FEEDBACK TO STUDENTS

Many public speaking teachers believe that providing feedback to students is the most challenging aspect of this course, because public speaking is often personal and ego-involving. Students are more used to risking themselves by turning in papers or taking exams, but standing up and sharing yourself in front of a group is a daunting, risky activity. Thus, it is important to have a carefully planned system of grading that is clearly explained to students, orally the first day of class and at points throughout the class, and in writing in your syllabus. Here are some aspects of feedback and grading you might consider.

Giving Constructive Feedback to Speakers

Healthy differences exist among teachers about feedback to students, as well as healthy agreements. This author's strongly-felt opinions about feedback follow, stated rather strongly. Go there with him, please. Effective feedback should suggest alternatives, be specific, be behavior-centered, and be as immediate as possible. Positive comments should be strong, balanced by positive suggestions for improvement. Students know what they need to do to improve; their improvement is best driven by reinforcement of what they already do well.

- Give descriptive feedback. Vague and general feedback leads students to feelings you are avoiding them. Additionally, without specificity, students may not comprehend your suggestions for improvement. College students are not children, but a principle of developmental psychology should guide our feedback. **Focus on behavior, not the behavior** (which will be received by the students as nicely impersonal, but caring). As one western religion puts it, "Hate the sin; not the sinner!" Describe the events and development of the speech, not the implied intellectual and personality shortcomings of the student.

- Give students "Space" in your feedback. Feedback that offers students apparent choices in solving their presentational difficulties will be well-received. "You might consider this, or that, or these" is, to this author, effective instructional feedback.

- Consider use of peer feedback. Public speaking instructors here and there involve students in peer feedback and, occasionally, in grade evaluations. Examples of peer input forms appear in later sections of this IRM. Peer input can have favorable consequences, such as (1) deeper involvement by students as listeners; (2) valuable training for students in evaluating the communication of others; (3) student development of tact and sensitivity in sharing observations and judgments with colleagues; and (4) in addition to trained criticism by instructor, student speakers receive "real world" comments from peers. If you use peer critiques, it is important to thoroughly explain to students the nature of their task. A discussion of what students view as destructive, versus constructive, feedback can prove beneficial. Go over your feedback format with students. Some instructors prefer students to complete the same form that teachers use for critiquing; others prefer a more informal means, such as simply taking notes during the presentation. Sample feedback forms for instructors' and peers' use appear on following pages. Also, explain to students what weight their feedback will carry--if their comments will be taken into account when you grade a speaker, or if they are to assign a grade that will be considered or actually averaged with yours. Decide if you wish to give the peer critic a grade for his or her involvement in the evaluation process and explain that decision to students. Finally, it is not a good idea to assign student critics in pairs, meaning that student critics should not be assigned to the same speakers who will critique them when they speak. Makes sense, does it not?

This author includes two special types of feedback you might wish to consider. The first type of special feedback occurs during oral exercises. During speeches, the instructor develops (over several rounds of speeches) a series of signals to the speaker. Students appear to have found the idea and the specific signals acceptable and usable. Raise Volume: instructor cups hands to ears. Slow Down: instructor extends palm and moves it toward the floor. Get more involved; get more excited: the military signal for advancing, or action, arm and index finger pointing at sky, rotating finger in tight circle. Increase contact with audience: arm extended mid-body, moving arm and down-pointing palm in a left-to-right slow sweep of the audience. You're going great! The clenched fist arm pump associated with the "YESSSSSS!" verbalization.

The second type of special feedback is given by students to students (and, occasionally, and usually with humor, to the instructor) involves 8 ½ x 11 colored pages given to students with syllabii. Each student receives five pages, with one large number appearing on each page. The numbers are 6, 7, 8, 9, 10 (the Olympic "10," eh?) The first response to a completed speech is always <u>applause</u>. The second response is students holding up their feedback cards displaying the evaluation number each student feels the speech warranted. A variation of the speech-ending evaluation is for the instructor to ask two students in different parts of the room to be the "Designated Hitters" for the day. Those students will, when the spirit moves them, display a number to the speaker to indicate "how it's going right now." This procedure also encourages the instructor to follow through with the task indicated several paragraphs above, to take time to train students as effective critics.

This author has a great deal of trust in students as evaluators and judges. He considers his proper classroom role to be that of coach, in suggesting sequences of improvements to students. See his article: "That Old Time Religion: The Intramural Speech Tournament is Alive and Well in El Paso." *Texas Speech Communication Journal.* Summer, 1999.

NOTES ABOUT GRADING

This author and instructor has truly never known another instructor who was publicly and privately always comfortable with his or her grading system and individual grades. Over a period of years, this instructor determined to follow certain pieces of advice about, and principles of, grading. These guidelines, shall we call them, have served him reasonably well.

You Can't Win Them All. Rational students are not always rational, any more than you and this author are always rational. Around grading time is a perfect time for a formerly content, relatively passive student to erupt in righteous anger. Your best bet (not necessarily a winner, either) is to have described the graded element (exam, speech, other) very clearly, to have retained careful copies where paper is involved, and to have recorded speeches. You probably won't change the student's mind, but perhaps the student will desist instead of persisting. The administrators above you, where the student might invite himself or herself next, are all-too-human; it is easier for them to seek compromise than to buck your student, inasmuch as you answer to the administrator and the student does not.

Maybe You Can't Give "A" for Effort, But You'd Better Give. The subject being taught is not English composition, where both student and instructor are closeted and instructors can and do flunk up to 40% of their students. The public speaking student's ego is up front and personal in our game. That ego deserves special positive attention in interpersonal communication classes. This instructor has never given a failing final grade to a student who conscientiously attempted all speeches assigned and all examinations given. He has, devoutly and in secret, hoped that a student or two would decide to drop the course voluntarily. He has never, to his recollection, ever heard a speech teacher say they did give such a student an "F." This paragraph is coming, by the way, from a teacher regarded by students and colleagues as <u>strict</u>.

Don't Try to Swim Upstream. An old politician's saying has it that "You can't serve in office unless you get elected (and reelected)." Similarly, to become a silver-haired, much beloved by students instructor you must be re-appointed or tenured. In the minds of others who evaluate you resides, and understandably so, a **normal grading curve.** Don't give all high grades, and don't give all low grades. In this author's institution, during annual evaluation sessions with administrators, certain statistical data are shared, and rightfully so: where stand you on retention of students vis-à-vis institutional averages? what does your grade distribution look like, compared to averages? how often have your students complained to your supervisors? what do students say about your grade system and grading on student evaluations of instruction?

Don't Despair. To this instructor it appears perfectly possible to remain within departmental and institutional grading norms and still demand excellence from students. The key is: <u>support.</u> Aim high and push your students to the same aim. However, the more you ask from students, the more you had better be prepared to give, emotionally and chronologically.

All the World's But a Stage, and the People Merely Players On It. Develop a fair grading system and confidently stand by it. Administer the system fairly and insist you have done so. Listen to student complaints with confidence, answer complaints confidently, admit occasional malfeasance (but not too often).

QUESTIONS FOR ANALYZING AND EVALUATING A SPEECH

SPEAKER:

LISTENER:

DATE: TIME: PURPOSE:

TOPIC:

1. Is the message understandable?

2. Is the purpose clear and appropriate?

3. Is the topic appropriate to the purpose?

4. Is the central idea clear?

5. Are the main ideas clear and related?

6. Are the supporting materials interesting, varied, and appropriate?

7. Is the overall organization effective?

8. Is there effective audience analysis and adaptation?

9. Is the speaker ethical?

10. Is the overall delivery effective?

11. Does the speech achieve the desired effect?

12. Suggestions for improvement:

WRITTEN SPEECH EVALUATION FORM

Student: _____   **Assignment:** _____

Time: _____   **Grade:** _____

Use check or 'x' marks, or insert a number or letter grade in the blanks preceding the major headings.

_____ Choice of Topic
    Appropriate to speaker, audience, occasion
    Appropriate to assignment and time limit

_____ Introduction
    Gains attention
    Introduces the subject
    Builds credibility
    Motivates audience to listen
    Previews main ideas

_____ Organization of Body
    Clear and easy to follow
    Appropriate to the topic
    Effective use of signposts

_____ Supporting Materials
    Variety of types
    Logical proof
    Emotional appeals
    Effective use of audio-visual aids

_____ Content
    Innovation and depth of ideas
    Adequate research support for ideas
    Effective citations of sources

_____ Conclusion
    Reviews main ideas
    Makes speech memorable
    Motivates audience to respond
    Provides closure

_____ Bodily Delivery
    Facial expressions
    Eye contact
    Gestures and movement

_____ Vocal Delivery
    Quality, rate, and volume
    Articulation and pronunciation

_____ Language
    Clarity, simplicity, vividness, and
        concreteness
    Use of unbiased language

_____ Written Work
    Outline
    Bibliography

_____ Overall Effectiveness of Presentation

SPEECHMAKING PROCESS FEEDBACK

Speaker Name:

Listener Name:

Assignment:

Selected appropriate topic?

Narrowed topic well?

Developed central idea effectively?

Communicated main ideas clearly?

Supported ideas well?

Organized speech coherently?

Rehearsed speech effectively?

Delivered speech effectively?

General Suggestions:

GROUP DISCUSSION FEEDBACK FORM

Assignment: **Date:**   **Topic:**

Group Name & Members' Names:

Showed knowledge of subject?

Asked appropriate questions of each other?

Made relevant comments?

Led discussion effectively?

Examined ideas rationally?

Selected and cited sources appropriately?

Demonstrated independent research and thinking?

Kept an open mind?

Examined various sides of the issue?

Facilitated question-and-answer session effectively?

Answered important questions effectively?

Demonstrated effective problem solving skills?

General Suggestions:

CHAPTER ONE: Speaking with Confidence

Chapter-at-a-Glance

Detailed Outline	Instructor Resources	Supplements	Professor Notes
Why Study Public Speaking? (p. 2) • Empowerment • Employment	**Learning Objective 1:** Explain importance of public speaking **Annotated Chapter Outline (ACO): 1-1**	**The Value of Public Speaking:** ABLongman Transparency # T-1 **Getting Started:** ABLongman Public Speaking Video Segment	
Public Speaking and Conversation (p. 3) • More planned • More formal • Defined roles	**Learning Objective 2:** Describe how public speaking differs from conversation **ACO:** 1-2 through 1-11	**Digital Media Archive (DMAC)** T09I01, T01I01 **Models of Communication** ABLongman Transparency #T-5, T-6, & T-7	
The Communication Process (p. 5) *Communication as action* • Source • Message • Channels • Receiver • Noise *Communication as interaction* (p. 6) • Feedback • Context *Communication as transaction* (p. 7)	**Learning Objective 3:** Explain the components and processes of a model of communication **ACO:** 1-12 through 1-15	**DMAC #** T01I02, T01I03 **DMAC #**T01I06, T01I04, T01I07	
Rich Heritage of Public Speaking (p. 7) • Rhetoric • Great Speakers: Martin Luther King	**Learning Objective 4:** Discuss the history of public speaking **ACO:** 1-16, 1-17, 1-18	**Audience Demographics** http://wps.ablongman.com/ab_public _speaking_2/0,9651,1593257- .00.html	
Public Speaking and Diversity (p. 10)	**Learning Objective 5:** Explain how to effectively speak to diverse audience **ACO:** 1-19, 1-20	**Speech Preparation Workbook** Demographic Analysis (p. 2)	
Improving Your Confidence as a Speaker (p. 11) **Understanding Your Nervousness** (p. 11)	**Learning Objective 6:** Describe why speakers feel nervous **ACO:** 1-21	**Accept Your Nervousness:** http://wps.ablongman.com/ab_public _speaking_2/0,9651,1593283-- 1593287,00.html **Overcoming Speech Anxiety** Allyn and Bacon Transparency #T-3	

Detailed Outline	Instructor Resources	Supplements	Professor Notes
Building Your Confidence (p. 13) • Don't procrastinate • Know your audience • Select appropriate topic • Be prepared **Develop and Deliver a Well-Organized Speech** (p. 14) • Know introduction and conclusion • Re-create the speech environment when you practice • Use deep breathing techniques • Channel nervous energies • Visualize your success • Give yourself a pep talk • Focus on message, not fears • Look for listener support • Seek out speaking opportunities	**Learning Objective 7:** Techniques to become a more confident speaker ACO 1-22		

LEARNING OBJECTIVES

1. Students will be able to explain why it is important to study public speaking.

2. Students will be able to explain how public speaking differs from casual conversation.

3. Students will be able to sketch and explain a model illustrating the components and process of communication.

4. Students will be able to discuss in brief the history of public speaking.

5. Students will be able to explain how becoming an audience-centered public speaker can help one speak effectively to diverse audiences.

6. Students will be able to describe why speakers sometimes feel nervous about speaking in public.

7. Students will learn several techniques to become more competent speakers.

CHAPTER OUTLINE

I.   Studying public speaking is important for two reasons.

    A. Effective public speaking empowers the speaker in a variety of situations.

    B. Effective public speaking can bring the jobs we really want.

II.   Public speaking differs from conversation in three ways.

    A. Public speaking is more planned than conversation.

    B. Public speaking is more formal than conversation.

    C. In public speaking, the roles of speaker and audience are more clearly defined.

III.   Communication is a process of action, interaction, and transaction.

    A. Basic models show five components of the communication process.

        1. The speaker is a *source* of information and ideas for an audience.

        2. A *message*, in public speaking, is the <u>speech</u> itself.

        3. The *channels,* through which messages are transmitted, are primarily <u>visual</u> and <u>auditory</u>.

        4. The *receiver* of the speaker's information and ideas is the individual audience member.

        5. *Noise* is anything that interferes with the communication of a message.

            a. Noise may be <u>external</u>, or physical noise.

            b. Noise may also be <u>internal</u>, or within listeners, from either physiological or psychological causes.

    B. Communication is interactive.

        1. Interactive, circular models replaced the basic linear models.

        2. Such models added two elements to our understanding of communication.

            a. Audiences are not passive, but provide responses for speakers to see and hear—these responses are called *feedback.*

        b.   Speakers and audiences are affected by the particulars of their total situation, or *context.*

   C. Communication is properly viewed as a transaction.

       1. Linear models of communication did not account for the simultaneous nature of communication.

       2. Speakers and audience constantly send and receive verbal and nonverbal messages in context.

IV.   As students of public speaking you will participate in thousands of years of tradition.

   A. The study of rhetoric is ancient. See Appendix A for a more thorough discussion of rhetoric.

   B. Martin Luther King's "I Have a Dream" is one of the great speeches in history.

V.   Public speaking education continues to add theory in this century, especially in the area of public speaking and diversity.

   A. The gender, ethnicity, and culture of both speaker and audience are increasingly viewed as critical to the analysis of speech effects and results.

   B. To be effective, public speakers need to understand, affirm, and adapt to diverse audiences.

   C. As with our predecessors, the AUDIENCE must be the focus of successful speaking.

   D. Our task is to understand, affirm, and adapt to the requirements of increasingly diverse audiences.

VII.   Improving your confidence as a speaker means understanding the sources of nervousness and learning skills to combat it.

   A. Understanding nervousness means exploring psychological and physiological changes that occur while giving a speech.

   B. As a speaker, building confidence is the result of planning your speech.

       1. Before your speech, don't procrastinate, learn about your audience, select a topic with which you are familiar, be prepared, rehearse, channel nervousness, and breathe to help you relax.

       2. Thinking about your speech in advance means visualizing success and giving yourself a mental pep talk.

3. As you speak, you should try to connect your message with your audience and look for positive feedback from the audience.

4. After you speak, you should focus on successes rather than criticisms.

REVIEW GUIDE

1-1. Can you list three differences between casual conversation and public speaking?

1-2. What are the five typical elements (parts) found in a linear communication model?

1-3. Can you define and explain feedback in human communication?

1-4. Can you describe context and its probable effects on one of your classroom speeches?

1-5. Why should communication be labeled as "transactional"? Does it mean anything to your classroom speeches?

1-6. How is communication a transaction involving feedback and context?

1-7 What is your definition of diversity?

1-8 Are you part of this concept we call diversity? As an audience member, has your diversity affected your responses to a speaker?

1-9 How can you deal with nervousness as a speaker?

1-10. What specific techniques can you use prior to, during, and after a speech to deal with nervousness?

ANNOTATED CHAPTER OUTLINE (ACO)

A. *Public Speaking is a Unique Communication Format*

1-1. Teaching Strategy

Public speaking students have a very common fear of the act. Consequently, students have "cognitive dissonance" (on the one hand, they have an understanding of the need for public speaking study and practice and, on the other, they are reluctant to approach the activity). Introduce the concept of cognitive dissonance (Chapter 16). Previewing Chapter 2, show the students their way out of this particular cognitive dissonance, emphasizing the fifth way in which dissonance is overcome. Stress the textbook arguments: society will call on us to speak because our oral skills brought us to societal notice.

1-2. **Background Information**

Define the words "intentional," "roles," and "formal." Using these criteria, contrast a speech you have given with a recent conversation you had.

1-3. **Background Information**

Discuss differences between public speaking and other communication forms. Make it real for students; create a hypothetical conversation and then ask three volunteers to convert the conversation into a speaker's monologue. Ask students what would happen if differences among communication forms were ignored. For example, would everyday conversation sound appropriate? Would it seem right for audiences to constantly interrupt, ask questions, or make comments?

1-4. **Classroom Activity.***prep*

Achieving class **cohesion** is an immediate and continuing requirement to help combat speech anxiety. Students need warm, friendly, supportive, and enthusiastic classmates as audiences. Cohesion is promoted when students in the class know one another, so taking time as a group to learn each others' names is a worthwhile strategy. Try these exercises to help:

1. On the first day, divide the class into small equal groups. Give them five minutes to memorize the names of all of their group's members. Next, one group at a time, designate one member to call out the names of all members, including themselves. Name callers will do well. Next, have one-half of each group move clockwise to the next group and repeat the exercise. Next, have the group halves that did not move before move counterclockwise to the next group and, again, repeat the exercise.

2. During the second class, form two concentric circles, with students facing each other at about three feet. Play a bit of your favorite "traveling music" while the students move sidewise to rotate the circles in opposite directions. Stop the music. Students facing each other must now introduce themselves using their complete names. Start the music and the circle movement again. Continue as appropriate, assuring maximum number of "confrontations."

OR

Assign students to design, construct, and wear a nametag to class, meeting two requirements: both their first and last names must be on the nametags, and the nametags must communicate something quite important about the wearers. Nametags will be worn, "until everybody in the class knows everybody else by both names!" (Require the students to wear the tags each class day, and do expect the tags to be worn for many class days.) Within the first one-third of the course, take part of a session with students individually up-front to explain what they are communicating with their nametag. This activity can be done in one class period or spread out over several days to invite informal conversation at the beginning of each class session.

1-5. **Class Activity.***prep*

Complete the "Get Acquainted" student survey. Collecting the information will acquaint instructor and students and also provide contact information. Ask students to complete data between the first and second class meetings. In class, students will pair off and discuss responses to the survey. Students could introduce their partners to all classmates, commenting on interesting responses. Feel free to edit, adapt, or extend the survey. Encourage (but do not require) students to exchange surveys with each other (at your Department's budget expense, if possible).

1-6. **Class Activity.***prep*

Complete the "Communication Behavior Questionnaire." Responses will introduce students to the theme of the Beebe and Beebe textbook, audience-centered public speaking. Additionally, the responses serve as audience analysis data for student speakers. Again, feel free to edit, adapt, or extend the survey. Plan to provide all students with this "demographic analysis," being certain that information is kept anonymous. As the instructions suggest, you might find it advantageous to share general information from the questionnaires. Your responses to student questions on this form will probably be quite welcome.

1-7. **Background Information**

Students will find the following article relevant and interesting: Edgerton Kendall, K. (1974). "Do Real People Ever Give Speeches?" *Central States Speech Journal,* 25, 233-235.

1-8. **Class Activity.***prep*

Consider a first speech often called, "What's My Name?" Objectives for introductory speeches are typically for students and instructor to become acquainted with each other. Many instructors choose not to evaluate and grade beginning efforts. To this author, however, even first efforts deserve careful attention from instructors. In his classes the first speech requires research and preparation, and is evaluated as "Complete" (on to the next speech), or "Incomplete" (must be consulted on with instructor, fixed, and delivered again, typically outside the classroom and during office hours). Either first speech approach, relatively unprepared or relatively prepared, will probably produce good results. Introductory speeches have objectives other than acquaintance, including initial practice of organizational and delivery skills, speaking experience early on, practice in the "extemporaneous" method of delivery, to give anxious students an opportunity for early success, and to allow instructor first impressions of a particular class needs. Your author requires sustained applause as students approach to speak, and even louder responses when students finish speaking. To him, clapping, whistles, catcalls, and even foot-stomping are highly productive means of immediately reducing student speech apprehension. The author provides very positive oral feedback and limited written feedback immediately following each presentation. The "What's My Name?" initial speech fits in well with attempts to stimulate immediate class cohesion.

Talking about oneself is relatively non-anxiety-provoking. Talking about one's names is ego involving. The combination of the two promotes excellent first speeches. A minimum time of two minutes works well, with students often going on for five minutes. The specific purpose for all is: "I want my audience to remember me by both names FOREVER!" Preview important future research methods by assigning students to interview themselves and others (especially family) about their names. Ask them also to conduct formal research (library; Internet) into the etymology of their names. Encourage students to plan a number of memory assists, such as repetition, association, others' reactions to their names, and nicknames. With strong positive feedback from instructor, and loud, enthusiastic responses from audience, this speech can get a class off to a bang-up start.

1-9. Teaching Strategy

If you have not already done so, consider building a videotape library of your former students presenting speeches, especially the "Names" first speech. Students feel comfortable seeing others "just like themselves" demonstrating an assignment. This author remembers that imitation was an integral part of Roman rhetorical education. This speech is further described in Chapter 2 of this IRM. You might also choose to personally model this assignment, as well as those that follow.

1-10. Writing Suggestion.*prep*

Assign two written essays on the topic of "My Favorite Animal." In one essay, students should use language and style appropriate for casual conversation with a friend. In the other, they should use language and style appropriate for a formal public speech to a large group. They select one of the following contexts for the second essay: a fund-raiser for the American Society for the Prevention of Cruelty to Animals, an animal rights activist group, or a meeting of the Board of Directors for the zoo.

1-11. Writing Suggestion.*prep*

Ask students to write a one-page essay explaining their goals for the class. What do they believe they already do well in public speaking? What do they hope to do better by the end of the course? Encourage them to write about their behavior goals, as well as their attitude goals. Ask them to identify both short-term and long-term goals for their public speaking future. Return essays at the end of course, for students to evaluate their progress toward self-stated goals.

B. *Viewing Communication as a Process Helps Formulate an Audience-Centered Approach*

1-12. Teaching Strategy

ENCOURAGE STUDENTS TO USE FULL SENTENCE ANSWERS IN ALL ANSWERS IN CLASS. DO NOT ACCEPT SINGLE WORD OR FRAGMENTARY ANSWERS. This author has found it to be good policy all around; to him, current glumness about students' critical thinking ability, if justified, could certainly relate to instructor permissiveness as they accept incomplete oral answers.)

1-13. Teaching Strategy

Define the word "process," first using a dictionary, then a thesaurus, and finally an example other than speech communication (try your own work experience). Share with students that "process" is not easy to understand and apply, but is quite important to true understanding of public speaking. To illustrate lack of process thinking, tell them of speaker-centered approaches (e.g., elocution, declamation) versus today's conversational audience-centered approach.

1-14. Teaching Strategy

Interact with students to the tune of the question, "what are models?" Accept a number of answers and examples. Explain the linear model concept with transparencies. State the main advantage of linear models (simplicity of understanding and learning) and the big disadvantage ("static" understanding versus "process" thinking). Briefly explain the five typical components of linear model communication: source, message; channels, receiver, noise. Develop the feedback concept by analogy with furnace and thermostat. The thermostat tells furnace when to burn or rest, just as audiences may tell the speaker when to start and stop, when to expand, when to change topics, and when the speaker is doing well. Use your classroom experiences to illustrate how student (audience) feedback altered the behavior of the speaker (instructor). Make the *context* variable meaningful by contrasting instruction in a middle school classroom versus college instruction in the same subject. Add an example where a speaker argues for a strong Social Security system, first to a group of teenagers and second to an audience of "Gray Panthers."

1-15. Class Activity.*prep*

There are various representations of models of communication. Using the textbook's models as a basis, have students visually present an analogy of the communication process by drawing a picture. They should label the parts and be prepared to explain the analogy to their classmates. For example, in drawing a computer model of communication one might compare the source to the computer operator, compare encoding to the keyboard and mouse, decoding to information on the screen or a print-out, and so on.

C. *Public Speaking has a Rich Heritage of Many Thousands of Years*

1-16. Teaching Strategy

Discuss the "I have a dream" speech with students. How do these words affect our ideas about diversity today? How is the speech historical? What about this passage: "I have a dream that . . . one day right there in Alabama, little black boys and black girls will be able to join hands with little white boys and white girls as sisters and brothers"?

1-17. Class Activity

Demonstrate the practices of declamation and elocution using material from Chapter 13 in Beebe and Beebe (the section on nonverbal aspects of delivery will work well). Show the materials to students via transparency as you speak. Giving it your best shot, "elocute" the material! Then, contrast by delivering the material in our modern style. For a perfect model of elocution, see John Caradine as a last century politician and elocutionist in the Jimmy Stewart/John Wayne/Lee Marvin film, *The Man Who Shot Liberty Valance.*

1-18. Class Activity

Lead the class in a discussion of speeches that have changed public awareness, attitudes, and willingness to take action. Ask students about speeches observed on television or on campus. Ask them why they remembered such speeches. Give students practice in critical analysis of speechmaking by probing a bit, not settling for vague reactions (i.e., "it was very moving"). Discovering what made a speech moving, motivating, or especially informative will help students understand the textbook's main point that public speaking is a unique communication tool.

D. *Public Speaking Must Deal With Diversity in Audiences*

1-19. Class Activity

Ask each audience member to write down three or four words that describe who they are in terms of their identity. The words might reflect their family's heritage, their gender, culture, or religion. For example, one student might describe herself as, "Buddhist; Chinese-American; woman." After the students have written their own descriptions, ask each person to read what he or she has written. Discus how this audience is diverse, and how other audiences might be similar to or different from this audience. How might an audience in a different setting be different? How about another region of our country, or another country? How should a speaker adapt to that?

1-20. Background Information

Explain that adapting to diversity is a natural development of public speaking (Rhetorical) theory, inasmuch as public speaking is measured by its effects in and on audiences. Do, however, briefly review social and political pressures toward achieving societal equity in a nation of diversity.

1-21 Writing Suggestion.*prep*

To help students identify their on nervous tendencies related to public speaking, ask them to write a paragraph about the worst public speaking experience they ever had. Then ask them to rewrite the story with a more positive outcome by imagining a different audience, location, or topic. What could they change in the story to make themselves feel more comfortable? For example, a student might rewrite the story so the entire audience was comprised of their best friends or their family. Discuss the rewritten stories to help students understand how to use visualization to "imagine" the best scenario while they are speaking.

1-22 Teaching Strategy

Repetition helps students become more confident speakers. Be sure to assign several ungraded, small, speaking opportunities that lead up to any major graded assignment.

PUBLIC SPEAKING STUDENT SURVEY

<u>Instructions:</u> Please provide desired information to acquaint yourself to instructor (and classmates, if you consent). Contact with instructor may be necessary.

Name:_____**Phone(s)**_____ _____

Mailing Address_____

E-Mail Address_____

Year in School_____**Probable Major**_____**Minor**_____

Had a Public Speaking Course Before?   **Yes**_____   **No**_____

If Yes, where?   High School_____   **College**_____   **Other**_____

Some persons experience communication apprehension (stage fright, anxiety) when thinking of public speaking. Which statement below best expresses the way you feel now about yourself and public speaking? (Check only one statement, please)

_____**I really have no public speaking apprehension.**

_____**I have less public speaking apprehension than most people I know.**

_____**I think I have average public speaking apprehension.**

_____**I have more public speaking apprehension than most people.**

_____**I have much more public speaking apprehension than most people.**

Would you care to express concerns or ask questions about the course? If so, please write them below. (I will share and respond to your concerns and those of other students during a class, without revealing names.)

_____

_____

_____

_____

COMMUNICATION BEHAVIOR QUESTIONNAIRE

Instructions: Below are a variety of communication situations. Please estimate the frequency of the situations for you, by entering an appropriate code letter from the group below:

**A=Daily   B=Once or twice a week   C=Every two weeks
D=Every month or two   E=seldom, or never**

HOW OFTEN DO YOU:

_____1. Attend a campus or community speech?

_____2. Attend a campus (or local) event, festival, or program?

_____3. Attend a live concert?

_____4. Attend a religious service?

_____5. Attend a movie?

_____6. Read campus newspaper?

_____7. Read local newspaper?

_____8. Read national newspaper?

_____9. Read a news magazine

_____10. Read a general interest, sports, or other magazine?

_____11. Read a novel?

_____12. Read college textbook, or other scholarly materials?

_____13. Read news on the internet?

_____14. Listened to CDs?

_____15. Listen to radio music?

_____16. Listen to talk radio?

_____17. Listen to religious or political information on the radio?

_____18. Listen to self-improvement tapes?

_____19. Watch music videos?

_____20. Watch shows on the internet?

_____21. Watch rented videos?

_____22. Watch a speech on TV?

_____23. Watch TV news and information programming?

_____24. Watch "infomercials"?

_____25. Watch television sports?

_____26. Watch TV comedy, drama, or TV entertainment?

_____27. Speak face-to-face with people?

_____28. Speak to a boss, supervisor, or professor?

_____29. Speak on telephone?

_____30. Speak to a small group?

_____31. Speak to a large group?

_____32. Speak to family members and friends?

_____33. Write a letter to family members or friends?

_____34. Write a paper for a class?

_____35. Write a business letter?

_____36. Write a creative essay or other piece?

_____37. Correspond through instant messaging?

CIRCLE ONE CHOICE:

38. Which do you do most often?

    A. Attend to

    B. Read
    C. Listen

    D. Watch

    E. Speak

    F. Write

39. Which do you enjoy most?

    A. Attending

    B. Reading

    C. Listening

    D. Watching

    E. Speaking

    F. Writing

40. In which area do you feel you need most improvement?

    A. Attending

    B. Reading

    C. Listening

    D. Watching

    E. Speaking

    F. Writing

ONLINE TEACHING PLAN

Preview Activity: Create a list-serve for your class that includes your email address and all student email addresses. Send a test email using the list that outlines your email policies including rules for sending email to the class and information about how long students should wait for a response. Setting up a return-time guideline up front will help you manage overly anxious students who expect immediate responses. Ask each student to respond to your email to ensure they are receiving your messages.

Teaching Activities: These activities are especially important at the beginning of the semester. Take time to go through each website and explore its content for students to use throughout the semester.

1. Demonstrate accessing the Companion Website for the text at:
http://www.abacon.com/beebepub/index.htm

2. The Speaker's Homepage can be found at:
http://www.abacon.com/beebepub/homepage/shchapter1.htm
Access each major heading and point out the subcategories for each major heading.

3. Also, check out the Allyn and Bacon Public Speaking Website at:
www.ablongman.com/pubspeak
Specific sections on this site are entitled *assess, analyze, research, organize, deliver, and discern.* Urge students to use the companion websites often as the semester progresses. You may also want to include the website addresses in your syllabus.

Review Activity: Now that students are briefly introduced to the public speaking course, introduce them to the Internet Public Library. This website is an excellent resource for finding speech topics and information. The address is: http://www.ipl.org/

CHAPTER TWO:
The Audience-Centered Speechmaking Process

Chapter-at-a-Glance

Detailed Outline	Instructor Resources	Supplements	Professor Notes
An Audience-Centered Speechmaking Model (p. 24) **Consider the Audience** (p. 25) **Select and Narrow Topic** (p. 26) • Who is the audience? • What is the occasion? • What are my interests, talents, experiences? **Determine Your Purpose** (p. 27) **Develop Your Central Idea** (p. 29) **Generate Main Ideas** (p. 29) • Are there logical divisions? • Are there reasons the idea is true? **Gather Verbal and Visual Supporting Materials** (p. 30) **Organize Your Speech** (p. 32) **Rehearse Your Speech** (p. 34)	**Learning Objective 1:** Explain why it is important to be audience-centered **Annotated Chapter Outline (ACO)** **ACO:** 1-1 **Learning Objective 2:** Select and narrow topic **ACO:** 1-2 **Learning Objective 3:** Differentiate between general and specific speech purpose **ACO:** 1-3 **Learning Objective 4:** Develop a sentence that captures central idea **ACO:** 1-4 and 1-5 **Learning Objective 5:** Three strategies for generating main ideas **ACO:** 1-6 **Learning Objective 6:** Describe types of supporting material **ACO:** 1-7 **Learning Objective 7:** Develop speech with three main parts **ACO:** 1-8 **Learning Objective 8:** Identify successful rehearsal strategies **ACO:** 1-9 and 1-10	**Allyn and Bacon Public Speaking Website** http://wps.ablongman.com/ab_public_speaking_2/0,9651,1593249-,00.html **PowerPoint Chapter 2** **The Value of Public Speaking** Allyn and Bacon Transparency # T-2	

Detailed Outline	Instructor Resources	Supplements	Professor Notes
Speaker's Homepage (p. 35) **Deliver Your Speech** (p. 36) **Sample Speech** (p. 36)	**Learning Objective 9:** Describe essential elements of delivery **ACO:** 1-11 through 1-13	http://www.ablongman.com/pubspeak/	

LEARNING OBJECTIVES

1. Students will be able to consider your audience

2. Students will be able to select and narrow an appropriate topic for a speech.

3. Students will be able to differentiate between a general speech purpose and specific speech purpose.

4. Students will be able to develop a sentence that captures the central idea of a speech.

5. Students will be able to identify three strategies for generating the main idea for a speech.

6. Students will be able to describe several types of supporting material that could be used to support speech ideas.

7. Students will be able to develop a speech with three main organizational parts- the introduction, the body, and the conclusion

8. Students will be able to identify successful strategies for rehearsing a speech.

9. Students will be able to describe the essential elements of effective speech delivery.

CHAPTER OUTLINE

I.   An audience-centered speechmaking model offers an overview to get you started and some good tips for becoming a confident speaker.

    A.   Consider the audience.

        1. Learn as much as you can about your audiences.

        2. Anticipate your audiences' reactions.

        3. Focus on connecting to listeners rather than on your own fear.

    B.   Select and narrow your topic.

        1. Who is the audience?

        2. What is the occasion?

        3. What are my interests, talents, experiences?

    C.   Determine your purpose.

        1. Three general purposes are to inform, to persuade, and to entertain.

            a. To inform is to teach, define, illustrate, clarify, or elaborate a topic.

            b. To persuade is to seek change or reinforce beliefs, values, or behavior.

            c. To entertain is to use stories, examples, or illustrations.

        2. A specific purpose tells what you want listeners to do or feel.

            a. A specific purpose asks, "What's the point?"

            b. A specific purpose lets the audience know the direction of the speech.

    D.   Develop your central idea.

        1. A central idea is the essence of your speech; a one-sentence summary.

        2. Central ideas are clear, concise, precise full sentences.

    E.   Generate main ideas.

        1. Does the main idea have logical divisions?

        2. Can you think of several reasons the idea is true?

        3. Can you support your idea with a series of steps?

F.   Gather visual and verbal supporting materials.

    1.   Facts, examples, and quotations amplify, clarify, and provide evidence.

    2.   Supporting materials should be personal, concrete, and appealing to your listeners

G.   Organize your speeches (disposition).

    1.   A clearly structured speech helps you to feel in control.

    2.   Your speech will have three major divisions: introduction, body, and conclusion.

    3.   Use traditional forms of outlining to complete your organization.

    4.   Learn from sample speeches and outlines provided on the website.

H.   Rehearse your speech.

    1.   Practice until comfortable, but without memorizing content.

    2.   Always practice by speaking out loud.

    3.   Visualize an audience, even to the degree of having eye contact with them!

    4.   Whenever possible, use the style to which your audience is accustomed.

I.   Deliver your speech.

    1.   Observe your audience just prior to approaching to speak.

    2.   Are last minute adaptations called for?

    3.   Make a confident approach to the speaking area, both mentally and bodily.

REVIEW GUIDE

2-1.   Why is being audience-centered so important to your speechmaking?

2-2.   Why is knowledge of audience diversity critically important to effective speechmaking?

2-3.   Why is topic narrowing often necessary, and what questions will help you narrow topics?

2-4.   What are the three general purposes from which you may choose? What are the objectives of each purpose?

2-5.   What is your specific purpose? What is its function in speeches?

2-6.   What is your central idea? How is it related to your specific purpose and main points?

2-7.   What are objectives for using visual and verbal supporting materials?

2-8.   Where and how can you learn to better use online sources to find supporting materials?

2-9.   What forms of outlining will help you organize your speech?

2-10.   How will you know when it is time to stop practicing?

2-11.   What might you see or hear in your audience that would suggest making last-minute changes to your speechmaking plan?

2-12   What are the essential elements of effective speech delivery?

ANNOTATED CHAPTER OUTLINE

2-1. Teaching Strategy

Explain the concept of audience-centered speechmaking as the most important principle in the textbook. Define the concepts of human beliefs, attitudes, values, and needs. Explain how each concept contributes to audience responses to you and your speechmaking. Analyze the audience-centered model of speechmaking, showing how audience characteristics can affect each step in the model. Draw your examples from sample speeches in the textbook or from historical speeches on the Internet, which can be found at:
http://curry.edschool.virginia.edu/go/multicultural/sites/hisspeeches.html

2-2. Class Activity (2)

Lead a class discussion on what it means to be an audience-centered public speaker, as explained in the textbook. Discuss possible reasons for the authors' selection of this approach. Why is each step in the speechmaking process keyed to the audience? In what ways does an audience-centered speech differ from a non-audience-centered speech? Try to get the class to generate as many examples as they can of non-audience-centered approaches, topics, introductions and conclusions, and delivery styles, and then contrast these with audience-centered alternatives. Make a list of topics that would NOT be appropriate and discuss your reasoning.

2-3. Teaching Strategy

Explain the concept of General Purpose and its usefulness to speechmaking planning. Define "specific purpose" and show the interrelationships of general purpose and specific purpose. Emphasize the controlling role of specific purpose for initial research, final research, invention, and disposition. Refer students to Suggested Activity #1 at the end of the chapter. Complete the activity together in class.

2-4. Teaching Strategy

Define the concept of "central idea." Explain a central idea as both the essence and the summary of a speech. Emphasize that central ideas emerge from initial research and then function as guides for final research. Examine and analyze the textbook's examples of well-done central ideas.

2-5. Class Activity

Divide students into groups. Ask each group to simultaneously compose a one-point central idea on a topic you announce (for example: "Sex"). Emphasize that good central ideas are clear, concise, precise, full sentences. Ask each group to write its work on the chalkboard. Analyze the examples (humor will be appreciated). Be generous with praise for effective work. Repeat the exercise for two-point and three-point central ideas.

2-6. Teaching Strategy

Define "main ideas" (or "points"). Use the textbook's examples to show how a good central idea divides into logical main ideas (show an example of a "one-point speech," in which the central idea contains only a single point). Use questions from the chapter outline (II, E, 2) to demonstrate to students how central ideas divide into logical main points. Demonstrate that the actual number of main points in a speech is determined by such factors as speech time limits and depth of information to be shared.

2-7. Teaching Strategy

Explore the word "support" in the context of writing and speaking. Identify and define a short list of supporting materials, dividing them into verbal and visual materials. Include at least examples, definitions, and quotations. Illustrate the use of supporting materials in the textbook and on the internet.

2-8. Teaching Strategy

Using analogy, motivate students to appreciate and improve structure in their speeches. For example, building a home requires a foundation, framing, and a roof. Using speech outlines from Chapter 2, show that outlines promote the building and checking of structure in a speech. Briefly discuss the purposes of an introduction (to gain the attention and goodwill of audiences); the body (to develop and support the central idea); and the conclusion (to summarize, perhaps to motivate, and certainly to leave a "good taste" in the audience).

2-9. Class Activity

In 1967 Barbra Streisand received a death threat just before giving a concert to a New York City audience of 135,000 people. She "went blank" and forgot the words to a song early in the program. The incident caused a continual stage fright problem that lasted for many years. Ask students to think about (or write about) what they would do if they suddenly "went blank" in a speech—either in class or at some other event. How would they recover or regain composure at that moment? What might be the effect on their self-confidence? Their views of themselves as public speakers? Students should also discuss the role effective rehearsal and good speaker's notes play in combating nervousness when speaking publicly. This essay is not meant to increase students' anxiety, but to encourage them to confront it, think about it, and plan a course of action to help counteract it if it happens.

2-10. **Class Activity**

There is safety in numbers. Students may well open up in a group communication situation. Assign students to bring a small object to class (do not yield to student questions about the objects—the activity is more fun that way). Divide students into two lines, facing each other at a distance of six to eight feet, displaying their objects to the other line. Tell students they are to "sell" their objects to students in the other line, loudly and simultaneously. Allow a minute for the sales and several minutes for tension release and laughter to result from the exercise. Cruise the lines during the sales pitches, encouraging those who need it. As a variation, suggest a closer approach to the other line of students. Conclude the exercise by complimenting as many "stars" as you can.

2-11. **Class Activity**

Divide students in groups. Each group is to select two members to act out a skit devised by the group. Using the class as an audience, speaker #1 from each group will present a speech introduction that shows a poor audience-centered approach. However, the #2 speaker from each group will give an introduction which nicely shows the audience-centered approach at work. Groups will have devised in their skits the content and techniques to be used by their speakers. At the conclusion of speeches, have groups vote by show of hands which group did best (not voting on their own group). Encourage loud verbal and non-verbal support for voting choices. Offer profuse compliments for all groups and speakers. Lead a Socratic analysis of the speeches. Be specific in guiding the class to recognize effective and not-so-effective audience-centered work by the speakers. Demonstrate how the audience-centered approaches could have been made even stronger.

2-12. **Class Activity**

Ask for four volunteers without telling why you need them. You might ask for the "Four Strongest Egos" in the class, or the "Four Most Intelligent," or the "Four Most Attractive." Charge them with demonstrating a "confident approach to the speaking area." Give them time to individually think about it, but provide little instruction (they will do well in their demonstrations). Require the rest of the class to applaud loudly as each volunteer demonstrates their approach. Analyze the performances.

2-13. **Class Activity**

Divide students in groups. Direct each group to individually recall its "Good Instructor" experiences, especially the classroom lecturing behaviors of the instructors they describe. After group interactions lead a class discussion of rhetorical devices used by the good instructors in their delivery of course content. How did those instructors gain and hold attention? Good will? What types of supporting materials did those instructors favor? Were visual supporting materials used often and well?

ONLINE TEACHING PLAN

Preview Activity: View the website entitled, "Public Speaking: How to Relax for Your Talk" at http://www.public-speaking.org/public-speaking-relax-article.htm. Students should perform each of the simple preparation activities, practicing them in preparation for their first speech. So go ahead, shake your hands and legs, and pretend to chew a very tough steak! These simple techniques may help you relax when you actually give a speech.

Teaching Activity: Toastmasters is a large organization offering lifelong continuing training in public speaking. Review the article at http://www.toastmasters.org/pdfs/debatable.pdf to begin a discussion about the importance of effective speechmaking. Ask students to respond to the article.

Teaching Activity: Demonstrate the process of accessing Allyn and Bacon's Digital Media Archive. Discuss the relative benefits of the digital archive for students.

Review Activity: Students should review the "stage fright strategies" website at http://www.public-speaking.org/public-speaking-stagefright-article.htm. Print a copy to review just prior to the first speech.

CHAPTER THREE: Ethics and Free Speech

Chapter-at-a-Glance

Detailed Outline	Instructor Resources	Supplements	Professor Notes
Ethics Defined (p. 42) Beliefs, values, and moral principles by which we determine what is right or wrong	**Learning Objective 1:** Define ethics **Annotated Chapter Outline** **ACO:** 3-1 through 3-4	**Speakers Homepage, Chapter 3:** http://www.abacon.com/bee bepub/homepage/ shchapter3.htm	
Speaking Freely (p. 43) • History of Legislative and Court Protection of Free Speech • "Speech acts" protected by First Amendment	**Learning Objective 2:** Explain the relationship between ethics and free speech **ACO:** 3-5 through 3-9		
Speaking Ethically (p. 45) • Have clear, responsible goals • Use sound evidence and reasoning • Be sensitive to and tolerant of differences • Be honest • Avoid plagiarism	**Learning Objective 3:** Five criteria for ethical public speaking **ACO:** 3-10, 3-11, and 3-12 **Learning Objective 4:** Learn to avoid plagiarism **ACO:** 3-13 through 3-17	**Speakers Code of Ethics:** http://www.nsahouston.org/ code_of_ethics/index.html **Plagiarism:** Allyn and Bacon Transparency #T-27 **Academic Integrity:** ABLongman's *New Public Speaking Teachers Guide* p. 47	
Listening Ethically (p. 51) • Communicate your expectations and feedback • Be sensitive to and tolerant of differences **Listening critically** (p. 52)	**Learning Objective 5:** List and explain three criteria for ethical listening **ACO:** 3-18 and 3-19		

LEARNING OBJECTIVES

1.   Students will be able to define "ethics."

2.   Students will be able to explain the relationship between ethics and free speech.

3.   Students will be able to list and explain five criteria for ethical public speaking.

4.   Students will be able to discuss how to avoid plagiarism.

5.   Students will be able to list and explain three criteria for ethical listening.

CHAPTER OUTLINE

I.   Ethics are the beliefs, values, and moral principles by which we determine what is right and what is wrong.

    A.   Refusing to cheat on exams; not calling in sick when healthy; the property owner who does not overstate storm damage: all are examples of ethical choices.

    B.   Cloning, stem cell research, and drug testing for doctors; attorneys debating whether to publicly advertise; political debates over social reform and fiscal responsibility; again, all are decisions based on ethical choices.

II.   Ethical considerations and choices also affect public speaking.

    A.   Our country has a twin heritage: guaranteed free speech, and the protection of free speech by law.

    B.   The <u>privilege</u> of free speech, however, carries with it the <u>responsibility of ethical speaking</u>.

        1. Your speech goal, arguments, and evidence must take into account morals, values, and beliefs of your audience.

        2. Ethical public speaking is inherently audience-centered.

III.   Unfortunately for ethical public speaking, ethics are not hard and fast objective rules.

    A.   Ethical decisions are affected by individual values, cultural norms, and religious beliefs, preventing the use of universal principles for making those decisions.

    B.   This chapter does offer principles and guidelines for ethical speaking choices drawn from contemporary North American social norms and legal doctrine.

IV. Since the First Amendment was ratified, state legislatures, colleges and universities, the American Civil Liberties Union, and federal courts have sought to define (and redefine) the original concept of "freedom of speech."

    A. The federal government has occasionally attempted to restrict free speech.

        1. Congress passed the Sedition Act to limit speaking against the government.

        2. During World War I, the Supreme Court tried to restrict speech that appeared to present a "clear and present danger" to the nation.

        3. In 1940 Congress declared it illegal to advocate "the violent overthrow of the government" (a move aimed at Nazi sympathizers in this country).

    B. History reveals more efforts to protect free speech than to restrict it.

        1. Concerned citizens formed the ACLU (American Civil Liberties Union), working towards organized lobbying for free speech (1920).

        2. Courts and lawmakers argued that only by <u>protecting</u> free speech to unpopular lengths could the free speech rights of minorities and the disenfranchised truly be <u>preserved</u>.

        3. The Supreme Court narrowed the legal definition of "slander" (false speech that harms another), by requiring that actual <u>malice</u> be shown before a judgment can be gotten (1964).

        4. Also in 1964, the Berkeley Free Speech movement (University of California-Berkeley) permanently changed the political climate of American college campuses.

            a. Outspoken student activists demonstrating primarily against the Vietnam war and related matters conducted sometimes violent demonstrations.

            b. The courts ultimately held that occupation of college classrooms and administrators' offices were legitimate exercises of free speech.

        5. The Supreme Court, continuing to protect free speech, has ruled against punishing the burners of U.S. flags (1989), and against restricting obscenity on the internet (1996).

        6. Oprah Winfrey (1998) successfully defended her television utterance about mad cow disease and not eating hamburgers (beef) when sued by Texas cattlemen for "driving down the price of beef."

        7. After the September 11, 2001 terrorist attacks, the Patriot Act sparked new debate over balance between national security, free speech, and patriotism

V. As definitions of free speech expand, the requirements for ethical public speaking become more critical.

    A. Ethical speaking requires that speakers have a clear, responsible goal.

        1. Your ethically responsible goal should be made clear to your audience in order to give them choices.

        2. Socially irresponsible speech includes brainwashing, as in Adolph Hitler's speeches inciting the German people to genocide; and as in Chinese speeches exhorting Chinese citizens to reveal the whereabouts of student leaders of the 1989 uprising in Tiananmen Square.

        3. Law and ethics of free speech may conflict since the protection of broad, free speech includes both ethical and unethical speech.

    B. Socially responsible, ethical speakers use critical thinking skills (analysis, evaluation) to formulate arguments and draw their conclusions.

        1. Unethical speakers substitute false claims and manipulation of evidence instead of logic such as Senator Joseph McCarthy (Wisconsin, 1950s) who conducted a Communist "witch hunt" by exaggerating and distorting the truth.

        2. Both media sound bites and highly staged Presidential debates have come under fire for shallow use of evidence and argument.

        3. Ethical use of evidence requires speakers to share all evidence with the audience, even evidence that is potentially damaging to your cause

    C. Ethical speaking requires that speakers be sensitive to and tolerant of differences.

        1. Senator Bill Bradley has described this dimension of ethical speaking as "tolerance, curiosity, civility—precisely the qualities we need to live side by side in mutual respect."

        2. Sensitivity and tolerance is increasingly labeled as "accommodation."

        3. Sensitivity and tolerance, or accommodation, suggests avoidance of language that might be interpreted as biased, or offensive.

        4. Chapter 12 elaborates on words and phrases that may be unintentionally offensive, and that are to be avoided.

    D. Ethical speakers must try to be honest.

        1. Knowingly offering false or misleading information to an audience is an ethical violation.

2. In 2003, President Bush and his staff accepted responsibility for using evidence based on discredited intelligence reports, and President Clinton's 1998 troubles stemmed from using false and misleading statements, particularly in relation to his denial of sexual relations with Monica Lewinsky.

VI. A most serious aspect of ethical speaking is the avoidance of <u>plagiarism,</u> which warrants here a separate treatment.

    A. Plagiarism is typically and properly defined as: presenting the words and ideas of others without crediting them (to their proper authors).

    B. Plagiarism may be punished, sometimes severely.

        1. Most colleges impose stiff penalties on students who plagiarize.

        2. Senator Joseph Biden plagiarized the words of a foreign speaker and was forced out of a Presidential race.

        3. Hamilton College (New York) President Eugene Tobin and a school board president in North Carolina plagiarized in convocation speeches and paid the price with their reputations and careers

    C. Do your own work.

        1. Plagiarizing others does not provide you with new skills.

        2. Avoid turning someone else's speech into your own.

        3. You should even avoid a friend's extensive editing; your speech may turn into your friend's speech.

    D. Acknowledge your sources.

        1. Credit direct quotations, statistics, non-original visual materials.

        2. Credit the opinions and assertions of others, even if you paraphrase rather than quote directly.

        3. In speaking, make sure the audience hears the credits; usually the date and author are sufficient information for an oral citation.

        4. Expect your instructors to require written credits (bibliographies).

VII. Listen ethically.

    A. Communicate your expectations and feedback to speakers.

        1. Know what information and ideas you want to get out of the communication transaction.

2. Expect a coherent, organized, and competently-delivered presentation.

3. Communicate your objectives by reacting to speaker's message and delivery.

B. Be sensitive to and tolerant of speakers whose messages and deliveries reflect different ethnicities and cultures.

C. Listen critically.

1. Listening critically means holding a speaker to ethical speaking responsibilities.

   a. Is the speaker presenting both sides of an issue?

   b. Is the speaker disclosing the available information?

   c. Communicate your approval or disapproval through nonverbal feedback.

2. If the speaker's message troubled you, check afterward for possible misunderstanding, or confer with others, and seek a forum for expressing your dissent.

3. Do not, yourself, resort to unethical messages and tactics while seeking to express your opinions and beliefs about others' messages.

REVIEW GUIDE

3-1. Define "ethics."

3-2. In what ways do ethics and ethical choices affect public speaking?

3-3. Are the principles of ethical public speaking hard and fast, objective rules?

3-4. What factors affect ethical choices in public speaking?

3-5. Briefly describe the legislative and legal efforts to define and delimit freedom of speech.

3-6. As free speech has been expanded, what have been the effects upon ethical speaking?

3-7. What are the requirements for ethical speaking as audiences continue to diversify?

3-8. State a classical definition of "plagiarism."

3-9. Is plagiarism formally and informally punished in our society? In our colleges?

3-10. In what ways may a speaker intentionally (or even unintentionally) commit plagiarism?

3-11. How may a student speaker avoid even the appearance of plagiarism?

3-12.   What are the requirements for "listening ethically" to speakers?

3-13.   What are ethical actions to take when you disagree with a speaker's views and points?

ANNOTATED CHAPTER OUTLINE

A. *Introduction to Ethical Public Speaking*

3-1. Teaching Strategy

Define ethics; give a series of prepared examples of ethical choices. Textbook examples are instructive, but personal and student examples will be closer and more meaningful. Ask students for short examples of their own ethical dilemmas (and ethical choices they expect to confront in the future).

3-2. Class Activity

Direct students to give between-class thought to these ethical propositions. Ask students to come prepared with opinions and defenses of their opinions.

   a.   Should students who know themselves to be HIV positive play in pick-up basketball games?

   b.   You are aware that a close friend has successfully "Aced" an examination by cheating. Do you tell, or not tell?

   c.   You have received information that your instructor, who authored the textbook you are required to buy, committed acts of plagiarism in writing the book. Were the author's actions ethical or unethical?

Divide students into small groups and ask them to discuss one of the propositions. Direct each group to select one member to report on the group's deliberations. Allow a 15 to 20 minute discussion. As each group reports, allow the class to agree, disagree, and question the group. When the exercise has maximized, provide an overall summary. Ask students what options they suggest for resolving their feelings about a proposition. For example, should the "acing" friend be required to retake the exam?

3-3. Teaching Strategy

Lead a student discussion of ethics in politics. If you have access to videotapes from the last presidential election, scan the various speaking formats ("sound bites;" full speeches, and variations), issues, and candidates. Discuss both candidates and the journalists who followed them. What are the candidate's and the journalist's ethical responsibilities to our society? How do we, as a mass audience, determine whether political figures are ethical?

3-4. **Class Activity**

Have students watch commercials surrounding specific events on television. For example, they might monitor TV advertisements surrounding sporting events, late night programming (especially soap operas!), daytime programming (soap operas, again!), or cartoons on Saturday mornings. Ask them to evaluate the ethics of commercials. Are some target audiences (for specific programs) treated less ethically by advertisers than others? If so, why?

B. *Speaking Freely*

3-5. **Teaching Strategy**

Briefly trace the history of "free speech" in the United States, beginning with its constitutional basis. Share with students the most famous statements about free speech: the French philosopher, Voltaire, "I may disagree with what you have to say, but I shall defend to my death your right to say it," and, a Supreme Court Justice, "Freedom of speech does not extend to a right to shout 'fire' in a crowded theatre." Argue very correctly that freedoms bring with them responsibilities. Freedom of speech must be balanced by responsible, or ethical, speaking. Although some may feel that ethical speaking proceeds from principles set in stone, most feel that rules are not hard and fast. Ethical public speaking decisions are affected by individual values, cultural norms, and religious beliefs. To quote a famous literary character, "What is a poor fellow to do?" Another Supreme Court justice may have offered perspective when he wrote, "It is possible to know pornography when you see it." Perhaps ethical choices in public speaking are easier to make than would seem apparent.

3-6. **Class Activity**

Ask students to wear "wild message" T-shirts to class (be ready for some raunchy messages). Use the ready-to-wear messages as a basis for a free-wheeling discussion on freedom of speech. Remind students of the difficult balance between freedom of speech and responsibility of (ethical) speech. See if students can reach consensus on the T-shirts.

3-7. **Class Activity**

This author's Director of Forensics colleague and his students once conducted a strong creative publicity and recruiting drive for the "squad." Among other posters, they had a widely-distributed model that reported "Debaters Do It Orally." An enraged college Public Relations Director had all those signs taken down and destroyed. A lively brouhaha ensued. What are your students' opinions (ask after they have stopped laughing)?

3-8. **Class Activity**

Ask students for examples of free speech violations from either high school or college. In what ways did a speaker violate freedom of speech? What should the speaker have done differently? How did listeners react to the violation?

3-9. **Class Activity**

The purpose of this activity is to further students' understanding of the concept of free speech and how it functions to protect society. Announce that a certain day is "Flashback to the '60s Day." Ask students to wear or bring to class clothing from that era, posters and other forms of art reflective of the time, or anything else they (or their parents) can find dating back to the 1960s. The "show and tell" session may last half a period, but be certain to save time for an in-depth discussion of how the First Amendment right of free speech was treated in that time period.

C. *Speaking Ethically*

3-10. **Class Activity**

Divide students into groups, with instructions to consider between classes a speech topic you provide. Direct them to list individually both ethical and unethical approaches to their topic. In a subsequent class, allow group discussion. This exercise will permit students to clarify the ethical need for clear, responsible goals. Have each group make a short report of its discussion and conclusion.

3-11. **Class Activity.*prep***

The Book of Questions: The purpose of this exercise is to prompt students to evaluate their use of ethics in public speaking. Obtain a copy of G. Stock's *The Book of Questions: Business and Ethics* (Workman Publishing, New York). Select various questions that seem most appropriate for this course. Use the questions in one or more ways. Students can write essays answering the questions, each student can give a mini-speech on the question, small groups can discuss the questions, or the instructor can organize a game of "Truth or Dare" using the questions.

3-12. **Teaching Strategy**

Share verbatim with students the requirements of ethical speaking found in this IRM chapter three, Outline V, A, 1 through V, D, 2. Tell students to follow these guidelines until they discover for themselves a better analysis of ethical speaking. The analysis therein will serve them well.

3-13. **Teaching Strategy**

Introduce the plagiarism topic by recounting the tragic experience of Senator Joseph Biden. Dramatize your presentation; it will serve you well in this unit of ethics. A front-runner for the Democratic presidential nomination, Biden erred in a public speech by appropriating, without crediting, words of another orator (a former British Labor Minister). A sharp reporter found Biden out and, despite Biden's protestations of innocent intent, the senator was forced to leave a race he may well have won.

3-14. Teaching Strategy

Plagiarism is a hot topic with many students. No doubt some will have gotten into trouble for plagiarism at some point in their educational careers. An honest, open discussion of plagiarism early in a speech course is advisable. Students tend to view plagiarism in a restricted sense, typically relating it to the practice of lifting materials from published sources and using it in papers as if it were their own work. They tend to be unaware of plagiarism that occurs in live events (such as public speeches); or when students collaborate on projects and produce one work for two grades; or when they share outlines, notes, or full speeches and use them in public speaking classes. A discussion of the many forms of plagiarism may help instructors avoid, or at least reduce, this problem and keep students out of "hot water!"

3-15. Teaching Strategy

If you feel it warranted, as this author has at times, share with students portions of the plagiarism section found in their "Code of Student Conduct." If you are personally aware of them, or have other reliable information, share with students some examples of "Crime and Punishment" (of plagiarism) in their college. Treat the examples as tragic, as happenings that may have been avoided by study of plagiarism, as their class is now doing.

Bring prepared examples of famous-saying paraphrases. For example: "You should not depend on your country to take care of you; you should instead help care for your country." Is this a paraphrase you need not credit, or is it (if you don't credit it) a plagiarism of John F. Kennedy? Ask students what they think of this and other examples you have brought. Tell students how lucky they are to have an intelligent roommate. Even more fortunately, the roommate has had two courses in public speaking. If the roommate helps you extensively in researching, gathering materials, disposing your materials, and coaching your delivery, are you required to credit your roommate? Or, will any amount of crediting validate the ethics of what you have done? What do your students think of this example?

3-16. Class Activity

This activity should prompt students to consider the lack of ethics involved in plagiarism. Assign five students to find an interesting magazine or newspaper article, outline it, and present it as a speech in class, without citing the source of the information. Although the activity may illuminate students who had not previously thought about it, discussion should help students understand and avoid this kind of plagiarism. Some questions to stimulate students' thinking include:

1. What does a student learn about public speaking when she or he gives a speech that is simply an oral summary of a magazine or newspaper article?
2. What does that do to the ethical climate of the classroom? Of the institution?
3. What is your school's official policy regarding plagiarism? What are the potential consequences?
4. As a listener, how can you identify a speech that is plagiarized?
5. What might be the consequences of plagiarizing a speech presented to a professional or community group?

3-17. **Teaching Strategy**

Share verbatim with students IRM Chapter 3 Outline, VI, A through VI, D.

D. *Listening Ethically*

3-18. **Teaching Strategy**

Students will be somewhat skeptical when you tell them to "listen ethically." You will have to admit the concept is a bit of a stretch. But, listeners are not required to uncritically accept messages. If speakers can be <u>active</u> plagiarizers, then listeners can be <u>passively</u> unethical both during and after an unethical speech by not protesting to the speaker and others. Now, you inform students, the other side of the coin has emerged. Just as speakers must be audience-centered, <u>audiences must be speaker-centered</u>! A process is a process. As speakers must be a part of the audience in order to be effective, so must audience members be a "part of the speaker." And no more tellingly so than in the case of audience members assisting speakers in ethical presentation. There is a <u>responsibility</u> for audiences to provide verbal and nonverbal feedback that encourages speakers toward ethical presentation. Share verbatim the materials from IRM Chapter 3, VI, A through C, 3.

3-19. **Class Activity**

Beginning public speakers often omit oral citations or rush them in presentations. This activity helps students understand the importance of clearly citing sources; it also gives them practice in oral citation. Present aloud to your class several examples of citations that could be used in a speech, but include errors, such as the omission of information, incorrectly placed citations in the speech, and so on. Ask students to "jump on" your errors and explain how to correct the errors.

ONLINE TEACHING PLAN

Preview Activity: Students should view the National Speaker's Association Speakers Code of Ethics at http://www.nsahouston.org/code_of_ethics/index.html. Ask them to review each major element of ethics in public speaking and ask them to write a brief action plan to accomplish each of the eight articles of the code.

Teaching Activity: View the web site entitled, "Speak Freely, Act Responsibly" at: http://pageturners.com/CDA/. Write a brief response paper discussing how publishing on the Internet presents a variety of issues related to free speech. How is Internet speech different and similar to public speaking? How does the Speakers Code of Ethics relate to free speech on the Internet?

Review Activity: View the Speakers Homepage for chapter 3 at: http://www.abacon.com/beebepub/homepage/shchapter3.htm

CHAPTER FOUR: Listening to Speeches

Chapter-at-a-Glance

Detailed Outline	Instructor Resources	Supplements	Professor Notes
Four Stages of Listening (p.58) • Select • Attend • Understand • Remember	**Annotated Chapter Outline (ACO):** 4-1, 4-2 **Learning Objective 1:** Identify the stages in the listening process **ACO:** 4-3, 4-4,	**How Your Audience Listens:** ABLongman Transparency #T-8 **Digital Media Archive (DMAC)** T02I01, T02I02, T02I04, T02I05	
Barriers to Effective Listening (p. 58) • Information overload • Personal concerns • Outside distractions • Prejudice • Wasting speech rate and thought rate differences • Receiver Apprehension	**Learning Objective 2:** List and describe barriers to effective listening **ACO:** 4-5 through 4-10	**ABLongman Public Speaking Video Segment:** Listening **DMAC** T02I03, T02I07, T02I08, T02I09	
Becoming a Better Listener (p. 62) • Adapt to the speaker's delivery • Listen with eyes as well as ears • Monitor emotional reactions • Avoid jumping to conclusions • Be a selfish listener • Listen for major ideas • Identify your listening goal - pleasure - empathy - evaluation - information • Practice listening • Understand your listening style - people -oriented - action-oriented - content oriented - time-oriented	**Learning Objective 3:** Discuss strategies to become a better listener **ACO:** 4-11, 4-12, 4-13 **ACO:** 4-14 **ACO:** 4-15 **ACO:** 4-16	**DMAC** T02I10 **DMAC** T02I13	
Becoming an Active Listener (p. 67) • Become an active listener (re-sort, rephrase, repeat)	**ACO:** 4-17	**DMAC** T02I11, T02I12 **Enough Information:** ABLongman Transparency #T-96	

Detailed Outline	Instructor Resources	Supplements	Professor Notes
Improving Your Note-Taking Skills (p. 69) • Prepare to take notes • Determine necessity for note-taking • Determine type of notes needed • Make notes meaningful	**Learning Objective 4:** Strategies for improving note-taking skills **ACO:** 4-18 through 4-20	**DMAC** T08I01, T08I02	
Listening and Critical Thinking (p. 70) • Separate facts from inferences • Evaluate quality of evidence • Evaluate underlying logic and reasoning	**Learning Objective 5:** Discuss the relationship between listening and critical thinking **ACO:** 4-21, 4-22	**DMAC** T08I11	
Analyzing and Evaluating Speeches (p. 72) • Understanding criteria for evaluating speeches • Message should be effective • Message should be ethical • Identify and analyze rhetorical strategies (goal, organization, role, tone, audience, techniques)	**Learning Objective 6:** Criteria for evaluating speeches **ACO:** 4-23, 4-24	**DMAC** T02I06	
Giving Feedback to Others (p. 76) • Be descriptive • Be specific • Begin and end feedback with positive comments • Be constructive • Be sensitive (use "I" to reflect that feedback is personal)	**ACO:** 4-25, 4-26		
Giving Feedback to Yourself (p. 78) • Look for and reinforce your speaking skills and abilities • Evaluate your effectiveness in *this* speaking situation • Identify areas for improvement	**ACO:** 4-27		

LEARNING OBJECTIVES

1.   Students will be able to identify stages in the listening process.

2.   Students will be able to list and describe five barriers to effective listening.

3.   Students will be able to discuss strategies for becoming a better listener.

4.   Students will be able to identify strategies for improving note-taking skills.

5.   Students will be able to discuss the relationship between listening and critical thinking.

6.   Students will be able to use criteria for evaluating speeches.

CHAPTER OUTLINE

I.   Evidence suggests our listening skills can and need to be improved.

    A.   Recall of a message twenty-four hours later drops to 50%.

    B.   Recall at forty-eight hours is only 2.5%.

    C.   A psychology professor found interesting data about his student listeners' thoughts at the moment he fired a blank shot in the classroom.

        1. 20% were pursuing erotic thoughts or sexual fantasies.

        2. 20% were reminiscing about something.

        3. 20% were worrying or thinking about lunch.

        4. 8% were pursuing religious thoughts.

        5. 20% of students reported listening to the professor.

        6. 12% were able to recall the professor's words when the gun was fired.

II.   Barriers to effective listening exist.

    A.   Barriers are created when we skip one or all of the four stages of listening.

        1. The first stage is to <u>Select</u>.

            a. We cannot attend to all incoming stimuli.

             b. We can choose what we select.

      2. The second stage is to <u>Attend</u>, a sequel to selecting.

             a. Our average attention span is eight seconds.

             b. As speakers we must capture and hold our audiences' attention.

      3. A third stage in listening is to <u>Understand</u>.

             a. Understanding is the process of making sense of the world by assigning meaning to the stimuli we select and attend to.

             b. A speaker assists audience understanding by using ideas and words within the audience's knowledge.

      4. The fourth and final stage is to <u>Remember</u>.

             a. A class test is a test of both knowledge and listening skills.

B.   The first barrier is <u>Information Overload</u>.

      1. Occasionally we select too much information to remember, causing us to "tune the speaker out."

      2. Speakers can overcome this barrier by balancing new information and supporting material, pacing the flow of information, and by using redundancy effectively.

C.   A second barrier is <u>Personal Concerns.</u>

      1. As audience members, our own thoughts compete for our attention.

      2. As speakers, employ "wakeup messages," utilizing body movements, voice, and special messages such as, "Now listen carefully because this will affect your grade."

      3. As a listener, monitor yourself for competing thoughts and discipline yourself to listen.

D.   <u>Outside Distractions</u> are a third listening barrier.

      1. Most of us do not listen well when external noise (Chapter 1) is interfering with listening.

      2. As a speaker, try to reduce or eliminate distractions in the physical environment prior to speaking.

3. When listening, try moving to another seat, or, perhaps, even assisting speaker in controlling the speaking environment.

E. Prejudice (from the verb "prejudge") is a significant fourth barrier to listening.

1. Social and political beliefs sometimes interfere with listening.

2. We can, unfortunately, negatively prejudge a speech topic.

3. A speaker's appearance (e.g., gender, dress, voice, body) may cause dismissal of ideas as inconsequential, or irrelevant.

4. A speaker's appearance, or ethnic and other apparent memberships, may have a reverse effect: "positive prejudices" may lead to acceptance and belief when not warranted.

5. Public speakers may counteract, or at least minimize prejudice with several techniques.

   a. Grab audience attention strongly, from the word go.

   b. Focus on listeners' interests, needs, hopes, and wishes.

   c. With hostile audiences, try to use arguments and evidence credible to that audience.

   d. Minimize strong emotional appeals; maximize careful language, sound reasoning, and convincing evidence.

   e. As listener, guard against *too quickly* deciding that a speaker is or is not credible, deserving trust or distrust.

F. Another barrier to effective listening is Wasting Speech Rate and Thought Rate Differences.

1. We have the ability to process words much faster than needed.

   a. An average speaker's rate of speech is 125 words per minute.

   b. We are able to process at least 700 words per minute, perhaps even as many as 1200 WPM.

2. Speakers should build in redundancy, be well organized, and make major ideas clear in order to counter this.

G.   The final barrier, <u>receiver apprehension,</u> is a fear of misunderstanding or misinterpreting the spoken messages of others.

    1. Apprehension can be overcome by including redundant messages in speeches.

    2. Apprehension can also be overcome by providing listeners with a clear organizational structure, including internal summaries and presentation aids.

III.   Becoming a better listener

A.   Adapt to the speaker's delivery.

B.   Listen with your eyes, as well as your ears.

    1. An expert estimates that 93% of emotional meaning is conveyed by speaker's nonverbal clues.

    2. Facial expressions communicate an emotion; a speaker's posture and gestures can reveal the intensity of the emotion.

    3. Difficulty with speaker's vocalization should be minimized by getting close enough to see the speaker's mouth.

C.   Monitor your emotional reaction.

    1. Strong emotions can affect effective listening.

        a. Differing cultural backgrounds, religious convictions, and political views cause listeners to react strongly to certain sensitive words.

        b. Cursing and obscene language are red flags for some listeners.

    2. How can strong emotions affecting listening be held in check?

        a. <u>Recognize</u> when your emotional state is affecting rational thoughts.

        b. <u>Use the skill of self-talk</u> to calm yourself down.

D.   Avoid jumping to conclusions.

    1. Give a speaker time to develop and support main points before you make positive or negative decisions.

    2. Mental criticism of speaker style or message causes decline in listening efficiency.

B.   Be a selfish listener (find ways to connect and benefit from the information you are receiving).

C.   Listen for major ideas.

    1.   Poor listeners concentrate on such facts as names and dates.

    2.   Good listeners retain major ideas and principles, and summarize mentally the major ideas that specific facts support.

    3.   Be alert for speaker previews and summaries of main ideas.

D.   Identify your listening goal (which helps our focus in listening).

    1.   Almost half our daily communication occurs through listening.

    2.   We are always influenced by one or more of four listening goals.

        a.   Listen for pleasure.

        b.   Listen to empathize with others.

        c.   Listen to evaluate (requiring the greatest focus).

        d.   Listen for information.

E.   Practice listening.

    1.   Listening is not an automatic skill.

    2.   Learning to listen effectively, as any skill, requires proper instruction and evaluated practice (at least self-evaluation).

F.   Understand your listening style.

    1.   There are four different preferences for listening, or making sense out of spoken messages:

        a.   <u>People-Oriented Listeners</u> are comfortable listening to people's feelings and emotions.

        b.   <u>Action-Oriented Listeners</u> like information that is well organized, brief, accurate, and doesn't stray from the main ideas with digressions or long stories.

        c.   <u>Content-Oriented Listeners</u> prefer to listen to complex information that is laced with facts and details.

       d. <u>Time-Oriented Listeners</u> like messages to be presented in a short period of time.

    2. If you know your listening style, you can better adapt your listening to speakers who are speaking in your preferred style.

G.   Become an <u>active</u> listener.

    1. An active listener exercises self-discipline to remain alert.

    2. An active listener "re-sorts" points not well organized by the speaker.

    3. An active listener "rephrases" and summarizes the speaker's ideas and supporting materials.

    4. An active listener periodically mentally repeats key ideas to be remembered.

IV.   Improve your note-taking skills.

A.   Effective listening plus effective note-taking equals effective remembering.

B.   Four procedures can greatly improve your note-taking skills:

    1. <u>Prepare</u>: bring tools (paper; pen; pencil) to every class, lecture, or meeting.

    2. <u>Determine whether you need to take notes.</u>

    3. <u>Decide on the type of notes needed</u> (full outline? main ideas? key words?).

    4. <u>Make your notes meaningful.</u>

V.   Effective listening and critical thinking

A.   <u>Critical listening</u> is the process of listening to evaluate the quality, appropriateness, value, and importance of information.

B.   <u>Critical thinking</u> is a mental process of making judgments about conclusions presented by what you see, hear, and read.

C.   Separate facts from inferences.

    1. Facts are either true by acceptable observation or by expert testimony.

    2. Inferences are conclusions based on partial information or evaluations not directly observed or verified by authority.

3. Identifying facts can lead to correct decisions; resting on, or misidentifying inferences as facts may lead to faulty decisions.

D. Evaluate the quality of evidence.

   1. Evidence consists of facts, examples, opinions, and statistics that a speakers uses to support conclusions.

   2. It is important to question the credibility of evidence and conclusions that are drawn from weak or faulty evidence.

E. Evaluate the underlying logic and reasoning.

   1. Logic is a formal system of rules applied to reach a conclusion.

   2. Reasoning is the process of drawing a conclusion from evidence within the logical framework of the arguments.

F. By learning how messages are constructed you will improve your critical listening and thinking skills.

VI. You can analyze and evaluate speeches you hear and deliver by using methods and standards to determine effectiveness and appropriateness.

A. Understanding criteria for evaluating speeches:

   1. Evaluation of speeches should proceed from criteria (standards of judgment).

   2. Any criteria for evaluating speeches should come from two goals: any speech should be both ethical and effective.

B. The message should be effective.

   1. There should be common understanding of the message between the speaker and the audience.

   2. The message should achieve the speakers intended purpose (to inform, persuade, or entertain).

C. The message should be ethical.

   1. A speech may be effective, but if it uses unethical means then it is not appropriate.

   2. An ethical speech tells the truth, gives credit for words and ideas where credit is due, doesn't plagiarize, and is sensitive to its audience.

D.   Identifying and analyzing rhetorical strategies can help you create better speeches, become more aware of how messages influence your behavior, and determine whether messages are worthy of your support.

    1.   Consider the overall <u>goal</u> or purpose of the message.

    2.   Consider how the <u>organizational structure</u> contributes to the message.

    3.   Consider the <u>role</u> that the speaker plays in relationship to the message and the audience.

    4.   Consider the overall <u>tone</u> of the message and how it is created.

    5.   Consider the intended and present <u>audience</u> of the message.

    6.   Consider which <u>techniques</u> the speaker uses to achieve the speech goals.

VII.   Giving feedback to others

A.   In your class, giving feedback will be labeled "speech criticism," meaning "to judge, or discuss."

B.   The six rhetorical strategies can be a framework for your evaluation of others' speeches.

C.   Six principles of criticism will help you give more effective speech evaluations.

    1.   Be <u>descriptive</u> (description, as opposed to a list of your likes and dislikes).

    2.   Be <u>specific</u> (avoid general, vague comments).

    3.   Begin and end feedback with <u>positive</u> comments.

    4.   Be <u>constructive</u> (give speakers suggestions or alternatives for improvement).

    5.   Be <u>sensitive</u> by using "I think" statements rather than "you are" statements.

    6.   Be <u>realistic</u> by providing usable information, rather than noting things a speaker cannot control or correct (improvement suggestions for future speeches).

D.   The goal of feedback is to offer descriptive and specific information that helps a speaker build confidence and skill.

VIII.   Giving feedback to yourself

A.   *You* are your own best critic.

    1.   As you rehearse, self-talk about choices in that speech to date.

2. After speaking, debrief yourself as to your "virtues" in public speaking, as well as improvements needed.

B.   Follow three principles to enhance your self-critiquing skills.

1. Look for and reinforce your skills and speaking abilities.

2. Evaluate your effectiveness based on your specific speaking situation and audience.

3. Identify one or two areas for improvement.

REVIEW GUIDE

4-1.   Can listening skills be improved?

4-2.   What are interesting statistics about listening habits?

4-3.   What are four stages in the process of listening?

4-4.   The Beebes name eight speaker behaviors for maintaining audience attention. Can you list them?

4-5.   In listening, how do you define the stage called "Understanding"?

4-6.   Can you list and describe the two types of memory?

4-7.   Can you list six barriers to effective listening?

4-8.   The textbook offers eight suggestions for becoming a better listener. Can you list and describe each of the eight?

4-9.   List the Beebes' suggestions for improving note-taking.

4-10. Can you list six principles of giving feedback to others (speech criticism)?

4-11. What two things can you do to improve your own speaking (give feedback to yourself)?

4-12. What three principles will enhance your self-critiquing skills?

ANNOTATED CHAPTER OUTLINE

A. *Listening Can Be Improved*

4-1. **Teaching Strategy**

Ask students if they have had a course, or even just a unit in "listening" (chances are they have not). Argue that listening is a combined mental and motor skill that, as with any other skill, requires knowledge of theory, techniques, and guided criticized practice. Ask students to faithfully read the text material, listen carefully to your chapter lecture, and attempt to measure themselves as they listen to you and their classmates. Relate listening back to Chapter 1, where all of communication was presented as a <u>process</u>. Point out that listening itself is a process, involving four simultaneous and interactive stages. Review the stages. Connect effective listening to the theme of the course— audience-centered public speaking. Remind students that in our democratic form of government we have two responsibilities: to speak up and out effectively on societal issues and to, as audiences, be informed or persuaded through effective listening.

4-2. **Related Reading**

For more extensive information on listening time versus speaking time, students might benefit from reading this source: Barker, L. et al. (1980). "An investigation of proportional time spent in various communication activities by college students." <u>Journal of Applied Communication Research,</u> <u>8,</u> 101-109.

B. *Barriers to Effective Listening*

4-3. **Writing Suggestions**

Assign students a one page essay in which they describe a listening situation within the last day. They should identify, by using appropriate labels from the text, elements within the listening process, including:
  A. Selecting from internal and external sources
  B. Attending to a specific message
  C. Understanding the message, making sense out of what is heard
  D. Remembering the message

4-4. **Class Activity**

<u>The purpose of this activity is to increase students' understanding of differences between</u> <u>effective and ineffective listening.</u> Show videotaped excerpts from films or television that depict characters talking and listening, because interpersonal examples work well to start a discussion (and they are easier to find than mediated examples of public speaking that show audience reactions). As students view the excerpts, have them jot down general descriptions of the kind of listening portrayed, at what points listening broke down, what prompted the poor listening, and how the speaker responded when the receiver stopped listening. When students discuss the importance of listening in interpersonal situations, they can move the discussion further (to the public speaking context).

4-5. Teaching Strategy

Review the barriers to effective listening. Use inductive lecturing; call for personal student examples of each barrier "at work."

4-6. Class Activity

In a discussion or essay, ask students to talk about the six main barriers to listening described in the text. Ask them to explain which barrier they believe affects them the most, as well as ways they have tried to overcome the barrier. Generating specific examples of barriers that emerged in recent listening experiences can be very beneficial.

4-7. Background Information

Related to the listening barrier of prejudice is the notion that accomplishments of great female orators in history have tended to be ignored or overlooked. For some background on women's rhetoric and the problem of making women's voices heard, see Vonnegut, K. S. (1992). "Listening for women's voices: Revisioning courses in American public address." Communication Education, 41, 26-39.

4-8. Teaching Strategy

Mention to your students that the "winners" of televised political debates are generally chosen on the basis of nonverbal factors, according to numerous polls conducted shortly after the debates have aired. Persons polled mention delivery variables, such as facial expressions, gestures, perceived confidence, and self-esteem as criteria for determining who was the best debater. Ask the class why viewers tend to focus on delivery and not content or organization. What, if anything, can be done to reduce this focus on a speaker's presentational style? Is "style over substance" acceptable in this situation?

4-9. Class Activity

Brainstorm with your class a list of red-flag words that could raise a listening barrier. Obscene, racist, or sexist (or other forms of "politically incorrect") language are obvious sources; however, focus on words or concepts that are more subtle. Think of alternative words to substitute for the listed emotionally-loaded words.

4-10. Teaching Strategy

Share with students your personal knowledge or that based on a review of literature about the listening habits of top managers and executives (they are universally stated to be "excellent listeners"). Tell students again about the excellent opportunities they have in this class (they can improve both as senders and receivers).

C. *Becoming a Better Listener*

4-11. Related Reading

For excellent suggested activities to enhance students' active listening skills, see Judith L. McPeak's article in the Spring, 1994 The Speech Communication Teacher, pp.15-16.

4-12. Class Activity

Analyze nine suggestions for becoming a better listener. Remind students that just by attempting to follow suggestions they are becoming more involved in their listening habits. Ask students to recall the "best listener" in their life experience. Ask how they felt, or feel, toward that person. Was effective listening a basis for their feelings? Did that person carry out quite well a particular suggestion they made? Ask students, "Are your evaluations of listening importance changing because of this unit of study?"

4-13. Class Activity

Before an appropriate class ask students to complete the inventory that follows the Annotated Chapter Outline (see page 113). In the subsequent class, divide into groups and share as time permits.

4-14. Class Activity

After putting students into groups, have them explore ways that they tend to "jump to conclusions" when someone is speaking. They should generate a list of topics that push certain buttons or that are regarded as immediate turn-offs. In class discussion, have each group present their topics and explain why members jump to conclusions when they hear these topics introduced.

4-15. Writing Suggestion

If your students are currently keeping a daily log of communication exchanges, ask them to focus specifically on their role as listeners for specified days. If they are not keeping journals, they can be introduced to the activity in correspondence with this chapter. Ask them to record their daily listening purposes and what their listening goals were. Determine a simple format like this one:

7:00 - 8:00 am	Pleasure: listening to a CD while getting ready for class
8:00 - 8:30 am	Empathy: listening to my roommate's financial problems
9:00 - 10:00 am	Learning: listening to a geology lecture and trying to overcome distractions in order to take good notes
8:00 - 9:30 pm	Critical Listening: listening to the president's remarks at a televised gathering and trying to decide whether or not I agree with points

4-16. **Class Activity**

The purpose is for students to use question-asking behavior to increase listening skills in a classroom situation. Require students to plan two questions to ask an instructor during a lecture or discussion in another class. After asking the questions, have students write a summary of the situation, using the following questions:

1. What were the questions you planned to ask?
2. What questions did you actually ask?
3. What was the classroom atmosphere like?
4. What was your purpose in asking the questions? (Besides to fulfill this assignment!)
5. How did asking questions affect your listening in the situation?
6. What were the results of your question-asking?

If time permits ask selected students to briefly summarize their written notes.

4-17. **Teaching Strategy**

Do an excellent oral interpretation of the "Table of Good and Poor Listening" (Beebes, page 68). Your time will be well spent, since the table really "tells it like it is." As was said in the 1970s, "let it all hang out" in your presentation.

D. *Improving Your Note Taking Skills*

4-18. **Teaching Strategy**

Remind students that educational literature long ago explored the relationship between note-taking skills and course grades. Ask the students what they think (they will tell you that good note-takers get better grades, and probably learn much more from their classes). Ask students for specific personal experiences with good or poor note taking. Review the four suggestions for improving note-taking skills, especially the fourth: "Making Notes Meaningful."

4-19. **Related Reading**

For further discussion of the correlation between note-taking and effective listening, see Welland, A., and Kingsbury, S. J. (1979). "Immediate and delayed recall of lecture material as a function of note taking." Journal of Education Research, 72, 228-230.

4-20. **Class Activity**

The purpose is to increase students' skill in taking notes. Give students samples of effective and ineffective note-taking. First, ask if they can tell which set of notes are poor and which are even poorer. Engage students in a discussion of what makes the poorest notes ineffective, and then generate ways in which these notes could be improved.

E. *Listening and Critical Thinking*

4-21. **Class Activity**

Try to make critical thinking" quite important in your students' minds. Using several dictionaries (hopefully theirs), explore the two words most descriptive of critical thinking: <u>Analysis</u> and <u>Synthesis.</u> Explain that critical thinking is necessary to all that humans are, but especially for making correct decisions of many kinds. Define "facts" and "inferences." Distinguish carefully, using humorous examples from students' life and times.

4-22. **Background Information**

For some background on critical thinking, as well as activities that will encourage critical thinking and listening in your students, refer to Carol Beal's article in the spring 1994 newsletter, "<u>The Speech Communication Teacher,</u>" entitled, "Challenging Your Convictions: Critical Thinking Speech Activities for Secondary Students."

F. *Analyzing and Evaluating Speeches*

4-23. **Teaching Strategy**

Remind students (from Chapter 3) of the importance of public speaking (oratory) in our history and government. Connect that importance to a necessity for excellent <u>criticism</u> of public speaking. Ask students for their feelings on the point you are making about speechmaking and speech criticism. Briefly share with them your favorite example of historical speech criticism serving a vital role in our society (your author dearly loves analyzing Henry Grady's "New South" speech).

4-24. **Teaching Strategy**

Briefly define three criteria for evaluating speeches. Refer to your example of historical rhetorical criticism above. Share how a rhetorical critic applies the criteria to a selected speech.

4-25. **Teaching Strategy**

Share a transparency with the six suggestions for giving feedback to others. Tell students you plan to "practice what you preach" to the best of your ability as you give them feedback for their speeches. Tell them what you will ask from them as peer feedback following speeches. Explain why each suggestion is important, practical, and helpful to students.

4-26. Teaching Strategy

Discuss the importance of feedback to a speaker, in terms of the six supplemental suggestions. Ask students to think about what forms of feedback they would like to receive, first, from their instructor, and second, from classmates. What kinds of feedback are constructive, as compared to destructive? How open are students to classmates' suggestions as to ways to improve? An honest discussion like this can help set some parameters regarding students' responses to each others' speeches during the term.

4-27. Teaching Strategy

Remind students that they are their own best critics (Least threatening! Most supportive! Most congratulatory! Least analytical!). Seriously however, tell them they are in an excellent position to help themselves to speech improvement, more than the instructor or classmates. Review, emphasize, and point out the Beebes' suggestions for "Giving Feedback to Yourself." Offer yourself as an example: review one of your own speeches in the light of the three suggestions.

QUESTIONING BEHAVIOR INVENTORY

(developed by Joan E. Aitken and Michael Neer)

Instructions: There are no right or wrong answers, only opinions. Consider your question-asking behaviors by answering the items below.

1. How often do you ask questions in a typical college course?

    1. A few times each class meeting
    2. Once a class meeting
    3. Once a week
    4. A couple of times a month
    5. A few times a course
    6. Seldom or never

2. Do you think that students, in general, should ask:

    1. More questions than they do now?
    2. Fewer questions than they do now?
    3. About the same number of questions as they do now?

3. In general, would you like to:

    1. Ask more questions in class than you do now?
    2. Ask fewer questions in class than you do now?
    3. Continue about the same?

4. Of whom are you most likely to ask a question in class?

    1. A female instructor
    2. A male instructor
    3. I never noticed a difference based on an instructor's sex.

5. Who is most likely to ask you a question in class?

    1. A female instructor
    2. A male instructor
    3. I never noticed a difference based on an instructor's sex.
    4. None of my instructors ask me questions.

6. How many of your college courses have included a large amount of time in class discussion (at least 30% of class time)?

    1. None of my courses
    2. 10%
    3. 25%
    4. 50%
    5. More than 50%

7. What percentage of course instruction do you think should involve class discussion?

    1. No discussion
    2. 10% of class time
    3. 25%
    4. 50%
    5. More than 50%

8. Do you think that instructors, in general, should:

    1. Limit questions asked by certain students?
    2. Encourage questioning by a larger variety of students?
    3. Continue questioning a about the same rate?

9. In comparing a lecture-oriented course to a highly discussion-oriented course (where discussion occurs 30% or more of the time), when do you learn best?

    1. In the lecture course
    2. In the discussion course
    3. In a course using a combination of the two
    4. It makes no difference.

10. In considering the questions asked by other students, how much of the time do you find their questions to be valuable?

    1. Nearly always (90% or more)
    2. Usually (60-80%)
    3. Often (40-50%)
    4. Sometimes (20-30%)
    5. Seldom or never (less than 10%)

11. When <u>other students ask questions</u> in class, which behavior is most typical of you?

    1. Paying attention and listening attentively
    2. Becoming irritated or impatient
    3. Thinking of questions I will ask
    4. Thinking of my own questions (even though I may not ask them aloud)
    5. Daydreaming, doodling, or doing unrelated work.
    6. Focusing on my class notes, course reading, or other course-related material
    7. Talking to other students

12. When students ask questions in class, how <u>long do you want question-asking to last</u> before the instructor returns to her or his lecture?

    1. 0 minutes (disregard question and return immediately)
    2. 1-2 minutes
    3. 3-5 minutes
    4. 6-10 minutes
    5. 11-15 minutes
    6. 16-30 minutes
    7. Prefer discussion to returning to lecture

13. Imagine a class situation where you could ask any question of an instructor because he or she encourages questions on all types of topics. About which one of the following topics would you most like to raise questions?

    1. Specific course content
    2. The instructor's personal life
    3. Controversy surrounding celebrities (entertainment, social, or political figures)
    4. Current news-making events
    5. Television shows and movies recently seen
    6. Problems with the economy
    7. Controversial issues being discussed on a local, state, or national level
    8. International events
    9. Ethical issues (such as steroid use by athletes, misconduct by political figures)
    10. Campus-related issues

14. In which situation do you most often ask questions of an instructor?

    1. In the classroom, before class starts or after it ends
    2. During regular class meetings
    3. In the classroom during lecture or discussion breaks
    4. In the hallway before or after class
    5. In the instructor's office
    6. By giving a written question in class
    7. By leaving a written message in the instructor's mailbox
    8. By sending a written message on e-mail
    9. By telephone
    10. I never ask instructors questions.

15. Think about instructors who taught you more than one course. When you have the same instructor for two courses, what is nature of your questioning?

    1. I ask more questions in the second course with an instructor.
    2. I ask fewer questions in the second course.
    3. I ask different kinds of questions in the second course.
    4. I ask about the same kind and number of questions in each course.

16. Based on your answers above, how involved do you think you are in the listening process in a typical college classroom situation?

    1. Little or no involvement
    2. Limited involvement
    3. Fair involvement
    4. Good involvement
    5. Excellent involvement

17. How can you use your question-asking behavior to improve your listening in classroom situations?

ONLINE TEACHING PLAN

Preview activity: Begin your discussion of listening by asking students to consider how they listen in traditional classrooms. How does "listening" change when class material is presented online? View the web site entitled "Listening Skills" to consider the role of listening in traditional classrooms. The web address is: http://www.d.umn.edu/student/loon/acad/strat/ss_listening.html

Teaching activity: "Listening with your face" is the process of offering active feedback to the speaker. Review the web site entitled, "Listening Skills" at: http://www.casaa-resources.net/resources/sourcebook/acquiring-leadership-skills/listening-skills.html (This is not the same site described in the preview activity).

Review activity: Remind students to review the companion web site for this chapter of the text at: http://cwabacon.pearsoned.com/bookbind/pubbooks/beebe_ab/chapter4/deluxe.html. Students should complete the multiple choice and true/false questions as a review of all concepts from the chapter.

CHAPTER FIVE: Analyzing Your Audience

Chapter-at-a-Glance

Detailed Outline	Instructor Resources	Supplements	Professor Notes
Becoming an audience-centered speaker (p. 84) • Gather information about your audience • Analyze your audience • Adapt to your audience	**Learning Objective 1:** Discuss the importance of audience analysis **Annotated Chapter Outline (ACO):** 5-1 through 5-4	**Know the Audience:** ABLongman Transparency # T-13 **Speech Preparation Workbook** (SPW) pp. 1-13 **Digital Media Archive for Communication** (DMAC) T09I05, T09I06	
Gather Information About Your Audience (p. 85) • Gathering information informally • Gathering information formally	**Learning Objective 2:** Describe formal and informal methods of audience analysis ACO: 5-5 through 5-11	**Demography and Population Studies Website:** http://demography.anu.edu.au/VirtualLibrary/	
Demographic Audience Analysis (p. 90) • Age • Gender distribution • Sexual orientation • Culture, ethnicity, and race • Group memberships • Socio-economic status	**Learning Objective 3:** Explain how to gather demographics about your audience. ACO: 5-12 ACO: 5-13 through 5-15	**Know the Audiences Culture:** ABLongman Transparency #T-15	
Adapting to diverse listeners (p. 94) • Focus on a target audience • Use diverse strategies • Identify common values • Rely on visual materials	ACO: 5-16 through 5-21 ACO: 5-22 ACO: 5-23	**DMAC** T04I05, T12I06	
Psychological audience analysis (p. 97) • Analyze attitudes, beliefs, and values • Analyze attitudes toward a speech topic • Your speech class as the audience	ACO: 5-24, 5-25	**Know the Audience: Psychology/Attitudes** ABLongman Transparency #T-14 **Know What Motivates Your Audience** ABLongman Transparency #T-16	

Detailed Outline	Instructor Resources	Supplements	Professor Notes
• Analyze audience attitudes toward you, the speaker	**ACO:** 5-26, 5-27		
Situational audience analysis (p. 100) • Time • Size • Location • Occasion	**ACO:** 5-28 **ACO:** 5-12, 5-29 **ACO:** 5-30, 5-31	**Know the Setting** ABLongman Transparency # T-19	
Adapting to Your Audience as You Speak (p. 104) • Identify nonverbal audience cues • Eye contact • Facial expressions • Movement • Nonverbal responsiveness • Verbal Responsiveness • Observe audience facial expressions • Look for restless movement • Check out amount of nonverbal responsiveness • Assess audience verbal responsiveness	**ACO:** 5-32, 5-33, 5-34 **Learning Objective 4:** Identify methods of assessing and adapting to your audience's reaction to your speech **ACO:** 5-35 through 5-40	**DMAC** T03I07, T03I08, T03I09 **Methods of Audience Analysis** ABLongman Transparency # T-17 **Example of Audience** Questionnaire ABLongman Transparecy # T-18	
Responding to nonverbal cues (p. 105) • List eleven ways to respond if your audience seems inattentive or bored • List twelve ways to respond if your audience seems confused and doesn't understand • List five ways to respond if your audience disagrees with your message		**SPW** pp. 83-85 **ABLongman Public Speaking Video Segment:** Audience Analysis **Responding to Messages** http://homepages.ius.edu/Groups/BLI/BLI%5CNonverbal%20Elements%20of%20Interaction.htm	

Detailed Outline	Instructor Resources	Supplements	Professor Notes
Strategies For Customizing Your Message to Your Audience (p. 108) • Appropriately use audience members' names • Talk about the place where you are speaking • Talk about a significant event that occurred on the date of your speech • Refer to people who belong to a group or organization • Relate information directly to your listeners **Analyzing Your Audience AFTER You Speak** (p. 109) • Audience nonverbal and verbal responses • Survey responses • Behavioral responses	**Learning Objective 5:** Identify methods of assessing the audience after your speech **ACO:** 5-41, 5-42		

LEARNING OBJECTIVES

1. Students will be able to describe informal and formal methods of analyzing speech audiences.

2. Students will be able to discuss the importance of audience analysis.

3. Students will be able to explain gathering demographic, attitudinal, and environmental information about audiences and speaking occasions.

4. Students will be able to identify methods of assessing and adapting to audience reactions to their speeches while in progress.

5. Students will be able to identify methods of assessing audience reactions after concluding their speeches

CHAPTER OUTLINE

I. Become an audience-centered speaker.

    A. Audiences are collections of individuals, each with a unique point of view.

    B. Audience-centered public speaking requires you to find out as much as you can about the audience as individuals.

        1. Gather information about your audience's needs and background.

        2. Analyze the information to determine the audience's psychological profile.

        3. Adapt the message and delivery by ethically using the information gathered.

    C. Gather information informally by making observations and asking questions.

        1. Gather demographic information about age, race, gender, sexual orientation, educational level, and ideological or religious views.

        2. Ask questions of either audience members or people who know about the audience.

    D. Gather information formally by developing a survey or questionnaire.

        1. Decide what you need to learn about your audience in relation to the topic and speaking occasion.

        2. Ask either open-ended or closed-ended questions to gather information about audience members' attitudes, beliefs, and values

        3. Test the questions on a small group to make sure they are clear and encourage meaningful answers.

    E. Analyze information about your audience.

        1. <u>Audience analysis</u> is the process of examining information about the listeners you expect to hear your speech and adapting your message to this information.

        2. Consider three questions when analyzing the information you've gathered about an audience.

            a. How are audience members similar to each other?

            b. How are audience members different from each other?

            c. Based on these similarities and differences, how can I establish common ground with the audience?

F. Adapt to your audience

1. <u>Audience adaptation</u> is the process of ethically using information you've gathered to help your message be clearly understood and to achieve your speaking objective.

2. Adjust topic, purpose, central idea, main ideas, supporting materials, organization, and speech delivery in order to encourage the audience to listen to your ideas.

3. Being audience-centered does not mean you tell audiences only what they want to hear or fabricate information to please the audience.

4. Even if they are not persuaded, the goal is to make an audience go away feeling at least thoughtful, rather than offended or hostile.

II. Analyze Your Audience Before You Speak.

A. DEMOGRAPHIC ANALYSIS. Identify demographics in the audience.

1. <u>Age</u>: Use caution in generalizing from only one factor (such as age) which types of humor, examples, illustrations, and other supporting materials would be appropriate.

2. <u>Gender:</u> A key question is, "What is the ratio of females to males?"

a. Speakers must attempt to select topics and development that appear acceptable and interesting to both sexes.

b. Speakers must attempt to avoid sexist language or remarks.

c. Try to use inclusive language (that draws all audience members into an idea or its development).

d. Despite gender differences, little evidence supports the possibility of different responses to, say, persuasion.

e. The genders may be equally emotional and empathic (sensitive), suggesting care in making sweeping generalizations based on gender.

3. <u>Sexual orientation</u>: Be sensitive to issues and attitudes about sexual orientation in order to enhance understanding rather that create "noise" that interferes with listening.

a. Monitor language choices and use appropriate humor and illustrations.

b. Inappropriate choices of stories, illustrations, and humor may result in lowered perceptions of your credibility.

4. <u>Culture, ethnicity, and race</u>: Each of these aspects of a person's being influences the way an audience perceives a message, and requires adaptation by speakers.

a. Speakers must avoid "ethnocentrism," the belief that one culture is somehow superior to another.

b. An audience need not have international students to be a culturally diverse audience; most audiences represent subcultures, with many traditions represented.

c. Researchers present cultural differences in four major ways, which can provide clues for speaker adaptation to diverse audiences.

   1) *Individualistic and collectivistic cultures.* Some cultures place emphasis on individual achievement (Great Britain; United States; Belgium; Denmark), while others value group, or collective achievement (Japan; Taiwan; Venezuela).

   2) *High-Context and Low-Context Cultures.* High-Context cultures place high importance on contextual factors such as tone of voice, gestures, facial expressions, and movement (Arabs; Japan; Southern Europe); Low-Context cultures place a high value on words, and expect detailed and explicit information from a speaker (Switzerland; United States; Australia).

   3) *Tolerance of Uncertainty and Need for Certainty.* Great Britain and Indonesia have considerable tolerance for uncertainty, while Russia, Japan, and Costa Rica are more comfortable with vagueness.

   4) *High-Power and Low-Power Cultures* (refers to ability to influence or control others). Some cultures prefer clearly-defined lines of authority and responsibility, including the Philippines, Mexico, and France; other cultures are more comfortable with blurred lines of authority and titles, such as Austria, Israel, and Norway.

5. <u>Group membership:</u> Audience group memberships will influence speaker choices.

   a. Religious groups — Be sensitive to the fact that that some members of the audience will not share your religious beliefs and religious beliefs are often held with great intensity.

   b. Political groups — Knowing whether a significant portion of your audience are involved in groups such as Young Republicans, Young Democrats, or environmental groups can help you address political topics.

   c. Work groups — Determine common beliefs, values, and abbreviations or acronyms shared by members of professional organizations.

   d. Social groups — You can adapt your topic or (if you share the interest) establish common ground with audience members that enjoy a common activity.

e. Service groups (Lion's Club; Kiwanis) — will respond well to a speaker who praises community service and improvement of communities.

6. <u>Socioeconomic status</u>: Be mindful of a person's perceived importance and influence based on factors such as income, occupation, and education level.

7. Adapt to diverse listeners by considering demographic and psychological differences as well as ethnic and cultural differences.

   a. Choose to focus on a target audience that you most want to influence while not alienating the rest of your listeners.

   b. Choose a variety of strategies that reflect the diversity of your audience such as different types of supporting materials, stories both logical and emotional support, or a visual outline of key ideas.

   c. Identify common values (such as peace, prosperity, or family) to help you find a foothold so that the audience will at least listen to your ideas if there are real differences between you and your audience

B. A PSYCHOLOGICAL AUDIENCE ANALYSIS explores audience attitudes and possible reactions to topic, purpose, and speaker. It also probes beliefs and values which may affect intensities of attitudes.

   1. Audience attitudes, beliefs, and values influence audience reactions.

      a. *Attitudes* reflect a person's likes and dislikes for persons, objects, places, and events.

      b. *Beliefs* reflect what we hold to be true or false, and underlie attitudes.

      c. *Values* determine our choices of right and wrong and are more deeply ingrained that attitudes or beliefs.

   2. Analyzing attitudes toward the topic

      a. Audiences may be analyzed along three dimensions: interested–disinterested; favorable–unfavorable; captive–voluntary.

      b. Determine whether the audience members are <u>interested</u> or <u>uninterested</u> in your speech topic.

      c. Determine whether audience members are <u>favorable</u>, <u>unfavorable</u>, <u>neutral</u>, or <u>apathetic</u> towards your speech topic.

   3. Consider your speech class as an audience

      a. The speech class is a *captive* audience rather than a *voluntary* audience because they are required to be present.

       b. You should make a speech for a captive audience as interesting and effective as one designed for a voluntary audience.

    4. Analyzing attitudes toward you, the speaker

       a. The more credible the audience perceives you, as the speaker, to be, the more likely they are to be interested in and supportive of your message.

       b. *Credibility* is the degree to which you are perceived to be trustworthy, knowledgeable, and interesting.

C.   SITUATIONAL ANALYSIS considers the time and place of your speech, size of the audience, and speaking occasion.

    1. Time is important because skilled public speakers are mindful of the time limit for the speech, and the placement of the speech in the overall time of a program.

    2. The size of the audience has a direct effect on your speaking style and audience expectations.

    3. The location for your speech is fairly constant if you are speaking to a public speaking class, but other speeches require research on the physical arrangement of the setting.

    4. The occasion reveals the reason the audience has gathered and helps predict demographic and psychological characteristics of the audience.

    5. Environmental analysis proceeds from ten questions to be asked, with answers to be accepted and adapted to, or changes made.

       a. How many people are expected to attend the speech?

       b. How will the audience seating be arranged?

       c. How close will I be to the audience?

       d. Will I speak from a lectern?

       e. Will I be expected to use a microphone?

       f. What time of day will I be speaking?

       g. What will be the room lighting? Will the audience seating area be darkened beyond a lighted stage?

       h. Will I have adequate equipment for my visual aids?

       i. Will there be noise or distractions outside the speaking area?

        j.   Where will I appear on the program?

        k.   Will there be noise or distractions outside the room?

    6. A well-prepared speaker adapts the message to both audience and speaking environment.

III.   Adapting to Your Audience As You Speak.

    A.   Identify and react to nonverbal cues from your audience.

        1. Estimate amount of audience eye contact, which may indicate audience interest or disinterest.

        2. Observe audience facial expressions, which can signal daydreaming and other attention barriers.

        3. Look for restless movement in the audience, often directly revealing loss of interest.

        4. Check out nonverbal responsiveness, such as head nodding, clapping, and reacting to speaker suggestions; without these signs, your audience lacks interest and support.

        5. Note amounts of verbal responsiveness, which can suggest interest and attention (also agreement or disagreement).

    B.   Responding to nonverbal audience cues - it is not enough to just observe them.

        1. If your audience seems inattentive or bored:

           a.   Tell a story, humorous if appropriate.

           b.   Use a striking example — a personal example, if possible.

           c.   Make direct references to audience, by names if possible, asking for participation by show of hands and answering questions.

           d.   Pick up the pace of your delivery; do still use dramatic pauses, however.

           e.   Remind your audience why your message should be interesting to them.

           f.   DO eliminate some planned abstract facts and statistics!

        2. If your audience seems confused and does not understand your point:

           a.   Try phrasing your information in another way; if possible use a visual aid (chalkboard; flip chart).

          b. Slow your speaking rate if you have been speaking too rapidly; build-in more redundancy.

          c. Repeat, for clarity, your overall organization.

          d. Ask an audience member for feedback to identify the unclear message (perhaps ask that person to summarize the key point you are making).

      3. If your audience seems to be disagreeing with your message:

          a. Rely less on anecdotes and more on factual data; provide additional data and evidence to make your point.

          b. Present facts and data visually (e.g., chalkboard; overhead or other projections; flip chart).

          c. If you do not have the data or answers demanded, tell audience you *will* provide more information post-speech by mail, telephone, or e-mail.

          d. Remind audience of your credibility, background, and credentials.

  C. Strategies for customizing your message to your audience

      1. Audiences prefer messages that are adapted to them rather than feeling like they are hearing a "canned" message.

      2. Appropriately use audience members' names without embarrassing them.

      3. Specifically talk about the town, city, or community where you are speaking.

      4. Talk about a specific event that happened on the date you speak to give your message a feeling of immediacy.

      5. Refer to a recent news event that you can connect to the central idea of your talk.

      6. Make references to people who belong to a group or organization that are honestly positive.

      7. Relate information directly to your audience by applying facts, statistics, and examples to people in your audience.

IV. Analyze Your Audience <u>After</u> You Speak.

  A. Always review the audience's positive or negative response to your speech so that you can make your next speech (and the next, and the next) <u>better</u>!

  B. Use four methods of post-speech analysis, or survey:

1. Measure *nonverbal responses*, such as the intensity of applause (remembering that diversity may conceal an actual enthusiastic evaluation).

2. Cumulate audience *verbal responses*, seeking both general and specific comments, especially on your most important main points.

3. Use questionnaires again for *survey responses*.

    a. Comparing prespeech and postspeech attitudes can provide a speech effectiveness measurement.

    b. As a "post-test," your survey may indicate the clarity of your informing.

4. Note *behavioral responses* especially closely.

    a. Did you want them to vote in an upcoming election? Did they do it?

    b. Listener <u>actions</u> are the best indicator of speech success

REVIEW GUIDE

5-1. What is the Beebe and Beebe definition of "audience adaptation"?

5-2. How many of the key questions about the audience-centered approach can you recall?

5-3. What is the proper relationship between learning more about audiences and telling them what they want to hear?

5-4. List as many of the typical questions asked in a demographic analysis as you can.

5-5. What are current generalizations about the "persuadibility" of the genders?

5-6. Name the four dichotomies used in the text to describe differences among cultures.

5-7. What is "ethnocentrism," and what negative effects might its display have on speaker effectiveness?

5-8. The Beebes suggest two speaker techniques which may produce "universal messages" to diverse audiences. What are the techniques?

5-9. Is there any truth to the old saying that, "Speakers should not talk about religion, politics, and sex"?

5-10. What are attitudes, beliefs, and values? What are their interrelationships?

5-11. Describe speaker credibility and its relationship with speech effectiveness.

5-12.   What are the ten Beebe questions used in situational audience analysis?

5-13.   What are the differences between, advantages, and disadvantages of *informal* and *formal* audience analysis?

5-14.   Distinguish between open-ended and close-ended survey questions.

5-15.   List four common problems in designing effective survey questions.

5-16.   What nonverbal cues from your audience relate to interest, support, and agreement?

5-17.   What speaker strategies or techniques should be used when an audience seems inattentive or bored?

5-18.   What speaker strategies or techniques may help an audience grasp a point when they seem confused?

5-19.   What four methods of post-speech analysis are recommended by the Beebes?

ANNOTATED CHAPTER OUTLINE

A. *Become an Audience-Centered Speaker*

5-1. Teaching Strategy

Reinforce audience-centered philosophy. Refer to IRM Chapters 1 and 2. Remind students that audiences are groups and will display many instances of collective behavior (draw upon your experiences and courses in sociology and social psychology). Stress, however, that audiences are collections of individuals who will react as individuals more often than as members of a group. A need for information is therefore a need for *individual* information. Review key questions guiding the audience-centered approach. Draw examples for each question's importance from your rhetorical analysis knowledge. Do share with students that audience analysis is not for "toadying" or "pandering" to audiences. Analysis permits easier audience acceptance of your information, logic, arguments, evidence, and ethical position.

5-2. Background Information

For an excellent, concise introduction to audience analysis, show this film: *The Topic and the Audience,* Films for the Humanities, P.O. Box 2053, Princeton, NJ, 08543; color; 15 minutes.

5-3. Class Activity

Ask the Director of Forensics to provide a speaker; both the director and the speaker should know the purpose of this activity. Either "persuasive" or "informative" speaking will serve. After the speech (much applause going up and sitting down, please) students should question the speaker (gently, please) about his or her sources of information about the audience. What did the speaker think, before the speech, about audience attitudes toward the topic, speaker, and occasion? What would the speaker like to have known about the audience prior to coming to speak? After the speaker departs, lead students in a discussion of the "Good News" and the "Bad News" about speaker–audience adaptation success. Tell students briefly about debate and forensics, and invite them to visit you or the director for further information.

5-4. Class Activity

The purpose of this activity is to help students better understand the notion of matching a message to an audience. Each student should bring one advertisement from a magazine or newspaper to class. As each student shows her or his ad, the rest of the class should determine the ad's target audience. Ask them to discuss these questions: What messages in the advertisement are conveyed? What elements of the advertisement are most closely linked to the target audience? If the advertisement was redirected to appeal to a very different target audience, what elements would need to change?

B. *Gather Information About Your Audience*

5-5. Class Activity

Ask students to imagine that their high school alma mater has a special week when administrators and teachers ask graduates to talk to juniors and seniors about the colleges they are attending. As they answer the questions below (either in writing or class discussion), students should imagine that they have been asked to speak at the high school as part of the program.

1. How should you formally and informally analyze this high school audience?
2. Why should you analyze this audience before you speak?
3. How will you gather demographic, attitudinal, and environmental information about your high school audience?
4. How can you gather information about the speaking occasion?
5. How will you assess and respond to audience reactions during your speech?
6. How will you assess audience reactions after you have finished speaking?

5-6. Background Information

Nielsen and Arbitron conduct audience analyses on various groups to determine television viewing habits. Ask interested students or small groups to do a project centering on these research firms. Have students determine how the firms go about defining their populations and samples, designing surveys, and collecting and analyzing survey responses. Students should investigate the kinds of decisions that are made based on survey results and how something like "Sweeps Week" can make or break a television series. Answers to these questions should relate to audience analysis, extending students' in-class activities to the real world.

5-7. **Class Activity**

Describe real or hypothetical examples of "informal" and "formal" acquisition of knowledge about an audience. Caution students to be wary of generalizing from data, at least in order to avoid sweeping generalizations upon which to base speaker strategies. Remind students that nobody can "win 'em all." Review with students "open-ended" and "closed-ended" questions, sharing the advantages and disadvantages of each form. Briefly review the four common problems in designing questionnaires.

5-8. **Class Activity**

In advance, prepare a standard deck of 52 cards, plus a joker. On each side of each card attach a typed-out demographic question. Do include some humorous questions, even if slightly irrelevant to the task. Shuffle the cards. Ask a student you have been wanting to get involved to cut the deck. Divide students into four- or five-person groups and scatter them about the room. Deal a card to all group members; the student who draws the joker gets to make up a question and put it to the instructor! Within each group, instruct students to take turns asking their question (one card side or the other) of the other group members. Cruise the groups, offering assistance and commentary. After an allotted time, choose a student in each group to stand and report the acquired information.

5-9. **Class Activity**

Assign all students the topic of "fair grades." Students are to review what they discovered about their group members; to think about what points they might try to make in a speech on the assigned topic to their group; and what kinds of arguments they believe their group would accept. In a subsequent period, instruct the groups to debrief each other. Again, cruise the groups, offering assistance and commentary. After an allotted time, ask one student in each group to report on the group's discussions. If rapport is good in the class, challenge a student strongly on one of their conclusions about speaker strategy (label the conclusion, perhaps, as an unwarranted generalization).

5-10. **Group Activity**

Prepare ten questions on five note cards. On the same topic, include one open-ended question and one close-ended question. The questions should be humorous, even titillating (if you are comfortable with it). For example: Topic = "Who is the Weaker Sex?"

- Open-ended: Why is your sex the stronger sex?

- Close-ended: Have you ever mud-wrestled a member of the other sex?

- Call on a student not previously alerted to distinguish which question is which. Repeat for each set of questions for which you have time. Allow time for the wisecracks, snickers, and bellows which will accompany the exercise (also expect each student to acquire good understanding of the two question forms).

5-11. **Class Activity**

Between classes assign students to develop six questions each, including three open-ended questions and three close-ended questions. Questions may be demographic, attitudinal, or both, and should aimed at their classmates. Ask students to make six copies of their questions. On the assigned day, divide students in small groups. Instruct them to consider all questions and come up with a joint group questionnaire. Ask each group to produce a finished copy of the joint product; you will distribute copies from each group to all students.

C. Demographic Audience Analysis

5-12. **Class Activity**

This exercise will help student speakers discover the demographics of the classmates to whom they will be speaking throughout the term. Instruct students not to put their names on the questionnaires.

CLASS DEMOGRAPHIC AUDIENCE ANALYSIS QUESTIONNAIRE

Instructions: Please do not place your name on this questionnaire. Please answer briefly in the space provided.

1. Age:
2. Sex:
3. Culture, Nationality, Ethnicity, and/or Race:
4. Religion:
5. Hometown and State:
6. Marital Status:
7. Major:
8. Hours Enrolled in this Term:
9. Current Employment:
10. Membership in Organizations, Clubs, & Groups:
11. Favorite Leisure Time Activities (e.g., sports, hobbies):

5-13. **Classroom Activity**

Place a list of potential speech topics on the board or on handouts. Have students indicate whether they think the topic is more of a "woman's topic" or a "man's topic" and to explain their designations. "Giving Yourself a Facial," "Cleaning Your Hunting Rifle," and "Mammograms as Lifesavers" are examples of topics that could be used for this exercise. A class discussion about why we tend connect certain topics to one sex or the other may prove insightful. Then, select a few class-designated, single-sex topics and discuss ways in which those topics could be presented to appeal to members of both sexes.

5-14. **Teaching Strategy**

Summarize current conclusions about "persuadibility" among genders. Suggest that time-consuming efforts to develop gender-related persuasive approaches may not have been productive (no "different strokes for different folks"?). Perhaps "one size fits all" is the appropriate approach, at least with respect to gender.

5-15. **Related Reading**

For excellent sources about gender-related issues in communication education, see (1) Thomas, D. (1991). "Rethinking pedagogy in public speaking and American public address: A feminist alternative." Women's Studies in Communication, 14, 42-57, and (2) Wood, J. T., and Lenze, L. F. (1991). "Strategies to enhance gender sensitivity in communication education." Communication Education, 40. 16-21.

5-16. **Teaching Strategy**

International students on your campus are a valuable resource. If you have international students, ask them to offer some insights as to how U.S. culture varies from their home cultures. If you do not have international students in your class, invite some to sit in on a class discussion. Ask them to discuss their expectations when attending a public presentation. They will probably talk about delivery factors first, but organizational and content factors may also be mentioned.

5-17. **Teaching Strategy**

Discuss the importance of being culturally aware of your audience. What does it mean to be culturally sensitive? How does a speaker reflect that sensitivity in a speech? When audience members sense that a speaker is aware of cultural dimensions, customs, and sensitivities, they are usually much more receptive to that speaker than to one who ignores the cultural diversity of today's world community.

5-18. **Background Information**

Cultural and ethnic diversity has a profound effect on public speaking classrooms. Staying "culturally current" is no easy task. However, essays in Gonzalez, Houston, and Chen's (1994) *Our voices: Essays in culture, ethnicity, and communication* (Roxbury Publishers) offer excellent insight into issues surrounding diversity.

5-19. **Class Activity**

Break students into small groups for this exercise in cultural sensitivity. Each group should be assigned one of the cultural classifications identified in the culture description section of this chapter. Provide lists of speech topics for each group and ask them to determine how members of distinct cultural groups would respond to these topics. For example, for the speech topic, "Communication Skills for Successful Job Interviewing," how would members of an individualistic culture compare with members of a collectivistic culture? How would members from a high-context culture versus a low-context culture respond to a speech demonstrating various shots in basketball? The following culture descriptions and speech topics can be used nicely in this activity.

Individualistic/Collectivistic
- My Proudest Moment in Elementary School
- Fostering Teamwork in the Corporate World

High-Context/Low-Context
- Stretching Exercises
- How I Maintain a 4.0 GPA

Tolerance of Uncertainty/Need for Certainty
- A Step-By-Step Process of Car Maintenance
- Expressions of Family Loyalty

High-Power/Low-Power
- Separation of Church and State
- The Peace Corps

5-20. **Class Activity**

To the extent possible, divide students into diverse groups; use gender, ethnic memberships, cultures and sub-cultures — do not forget the "Jocks" and the "Nerds." Assign the topic, "The Melting Pot is a Great Idea" (you may have to explain). Assign groups a fifteen minute oral discussion. Cruise the groups, making certain the group stays at or below the boiling point. After concluding discussion, ask two group members in each group to debrief the discussion. In your summary, relate exercise happenings to ethnocentrism and attitudinal analysis.

5-21. **Teaching Strategy**

The United States may be moving away from the "Melting Pot" (in language and culture) to ethnic bilingualism and multiculture. Speakers are increasingly pressured to recognize and respond to the change. Even speaker appearance of ethnocentrism may jeopardize success. Review the four-way classifications of culture in the Outline or Beebe and Beebe pages 86, 87. As you review the scheme, ask students frequently for personal examples of these cultural differences. Suggest to students that reading about differences, talking to others about differences, and experimenting in personal communication will all be pluses for diverse audience speech preparation.

5-22. **Class Activity**

Students should take out their wallets or billfolds and show others in the group what cards they carry. On a sheet of paper, students will list all of the organizations to which group members belong. Then, groups should discuss questions such as: what are the implications of organizational affiliations, regarding audience analysis and adaptation? For example, if one person has a Sam's Club membership card, does that imply that the individual is frugal? A careful shopper? A wholesaler? What benefits can a speaker derive from knowing organizational affiliations of audience members?

5-23. **Class Activity,** *prep*

Students are probably accustomed to being "preached at" with respect to cultural and ethnic sensitivity. Divide into small groups. Ask students to give serious thought to the question, "How should the President on the United States approach a national TV speech in which he strongly urges cultural, ethnic, and religious sensitivity?" Ask students to apply suggestions found thus far in Beebe and Beebe as they make their recommendations.

D. Psychological Audience Analysis

5-24. **Class Activity**

To reinforce the differences between attitudes, beliefs, and values, orally give students a few examples of each, challenging students to distinguish between the examples. A few examples might be: aerobic exercise is crucial to good health (belief); song lyrics should be labeled regarding adult content and language (attitude); our environment should be a clean, non-toxic, and aesthetically pleasing resource for all generations (value).

5-25. **Class Activity**

Class Attitudinal Audience Analysis Questionnaire: <u>The purpose of this survey is to help student speakers discover attitudes of classmates they will be speaking to throughout the term.</u> Instruct students not to put their names on the questionnaires. Computer-scanned response forms allow you to easily summarize student responses for the class.

CLASS ATTITUDINAL AUDIENCE ANALYSIS QUESTIONNAIRE

Instructions: Please do not provide your name on this questionnaire. Indicate your opinion on the following topics by entering, in the blanks in front of the items, the number that corresponds to your answer. Use this scale:

1 = Strongly Agree   2 = Agree 3 = Neutral or Don't Know   4 = Disagree   5 = Strongly Disagree

_____ 1. The answer to the drug abuse problem is partly in legalizing drug use.

_____ 2. Water-way gambling and state lotteries are good solutions to some governmental economic problems.

_____ 3. The most important objective for any government is peace.

_____ 4. Laws that limit cigarette smoking infringe on people's rights.

_____ 5. In general, I support current state government policies.

_____ 6. In general, I support current federal government policies.

_____ 7. I am looking forward to increased cultural and ethnic diversity predicted for the United States' workforce.

_____ 8. Animal rights groups are fanatics who interfere with economic and scientific progress.

_____ 9. People who are gravely ill or in pain should have the right to die (including by suicide and euthanasia).

_____ 10. A woman has a right to an abortion.

_____ 11. Family values in the United States have deteriorated to a crisis point.

_____ 12. One of the most important issues facing us is the preservation of the planet.

_____ 13. College students are more bigoted and prejudiced than college students twenty years ago.

_____ 14. People who are gay or lesbian should be allowed into the military without recrimination.

_____ 15. For too long the United States has practiced a policy of military intervention and destruction of other cultures.

_____ 16. Women deserve equal rights to men.

_____ 17. I favor more legislation restricting gun usage in the U.S.

_____ 18. The current trends in the United States are too liberal.

_____ 19. Prayer and religious teaching are needed in schools.

_____ 20. I believe that Affirmative Action is still an important and necessary program in the U.S.

_____ 21. Citizens should be more patriotic toward their countries.

_____ 22. I am in favor of capital punishment.

_____ 23. Mass media in the U.S. contains too much sex, violence, and denigration of people.

_____ 24. Pornography is destructive.

_____ 25. One of the most crucial issues of our time is human rights.

5-26. **Class Activity**

Pair students. Instruct them to compare their attitudes on three topics: capital punishment; abortion; and U.S. military interventions. Students should also establish intensities of their attitudes; i.e., Strongly Against, Moderately Against, Somewhat Against, or In Favor Of. After getting the matrix of their attitudes, instruct students to consider this question: "Is there a relationship between the intensity of an attitude and techniques a speaker must use to change the intensity of that attitude?" (Explain the question clearly to students.)

5-27. **Teaching Strategy**

Using both textbook and dictionary definitions, compare and contrast the concepts of ATTITUDE, BELIEF, and VALUE. Point out the interrelationships of the three concepts. Draw from personal experience to illustrate each concept has affected your choices in responding to speeches, advertising, and (if you are comfortable with it) religious experiences.

5-28. **Teaching Strategy**

Review the continua of "Interest–Disinterest," and "Favorable–Unfavorable." Share with students that knowing where listeners are on each continuum can enable a speaker to be much more effective. For example, when audience interest is flagging, a speaker must make impromptu changes in language and delivery to spur interest. If audiences are highly favorable to speaker information or position, a speaker will make certain choices (which will be quite different choices when an audience is highly unfavorable). Beebe and Beebe chapters sixteen and seventeen will elaborate these points.

5-29. **Teaching Strategy**

Review the concepts of "captive" audiences and "voluntary" audiences. Tell students that to you the differences are purely intellectual (if you agree with this author). You want students to give "real" speeches to their "real" classmates, who are live, breathing humans with all the needs, wants, and passions thereof.

5-30. **Teaching Strategy**

What are some ways to increase speaker credibility besides mentioning personal experience with a topic? How can a speaker earn the respect of an audience? What makes an audience trust a speaker? What kinds of things can be done to achieve a friendly reaction from an audience? What factors can weaken speaker credibility? Discuss these questions with your class.

5-31. **Class Activity**

Share briefly with students the classical concepts of *Ethos*, *Logos*, and *Pathos*. Using "credibility" as the modern synonym for ethos, preview for students the importance of speaker credibility to speaker success. Note that Beebe and Beebe Chapters 10 and 17 will each expand on the credibility factor. With students working in small groups, assign an oral discussion of credibility. Instruct each student to think of the most credible person they have known, and to contribute reasons they feel that way to group discussion. At the end of discussion ask one member in each group to choose from all the contributions in their group those factors which influence the credibility of a public speaker <u>new to his or her audience</u>.

E. Situational Audience Analysis

5-32. Class Activity

Have students perform an environmental analysis of the classroom in which they will be delivering their speeches. Use the ten questions (Outline, II, C, 5, a-k) as a guide. Discuss the available options that students have in making major or minor changes in their speaking environment. What barriers need to be overcome? How can problems be solved?

5-33. Teaching Strategy

If you have any personal or acquaintance "horror stories" about a speaker's failure to address environmental audience analysis tell those stories now! (This author has his own favorites!) Review with students the ten aspects of environmental analysis (Outline, II, C, 5, a-k).

5-34. Group Activity

Divide students into groups. Instruct them to recall serious errors made by speakers (especially their instructors!) in arranging, or failing to arrange the environment for their presentations. Ask one student in each group to report the group's recollections.

F. Adapting to Your Audience As You Speak

5-35. Class Activity

Ask students to interview an instructor about the importance of identifying verbal cues coming from their students during classroom lectures or discussions. What do the cues tell them about course content, about themselves and about their students, and should they adapt?

5-36. Teaching Strategy

Ask students to list, first, the characteristics of a good teacher. The responses will probably be communication oriented. How does the competent professor present ideas effectively? In what specific ways is the instructor's delivery effective? How does the instructor respond to student verbal and nonverbal feedback in the classroom? Then have students list characteristics of poor teachers. What specific behaviors seem to make the difference?

5-37. Teaching Strategy

What cultural factors have the potential to affect nonverbal responses from an audience? If the speaker is from a different culture than the audience members, how will the speaker gauge audience feedback? How will the speaker formulate an appropriate response to this feedback? Since cultural diversity has such potential to affect the public speaking context, a discussion of these questions is appropriate.

5-38. Teaching Strategy

Share verbatim the Chapter 5 Outline material from the section "Adapting to Your Audience as You Speak" (found under Roman numeral V). This author considers the material to be an excellent hands-on approach. As he tells his own students, "Use these ideas until you find or figure out something better!"

5-39. Class Activity

Divide students into groups of four, seated two opposite two at a distance of about four feet. Have one member of one twosome begin telling an interesting story, while the opposite two do their best to show disinterest nonverbally. Give each of the four a chance to experience disinterest. Good laughs will occur. Call on several students to express their feelings when being shown disinterest. Ask several other students to recall what advice the textbook gives to speakers facing some disinterest in the audience.

5-40. Class Activity

Ask students to interview an instructor about the importance of identifying nonverbal cues given by their students during classroom lectures or discussion. What do the cues tell those instructors about course content, about themselves, and about their students? How do they adapt? Students might also ask instructors to relate the strangest or most humorous experience they have had with student feedback in a classroom. How did they react?

E. Analyzing Your Audience After You Speak

5-41. Teaching Strategy

We are doubtless all accustomed to "debriefing" ourselves after a performance or test. You will have already have shared with students the interrelationships among theory, guided practice, and critical evaluation. Review the four methods of post-speech criticism, focusing primarily (this author agrees with the Beebes) on the fourth method, *behavioral response.*

5-42. Teaching Strategy

Lead students in a brief discussion of paper and pencil surveys versus observation of people. Ask which is more reliable: surveys or observing behavior? They will probably tell you that "Actions speak louder than words." Challenge them to substantiate their claim that nonverbal behavior always means one thing, while words can have many meanings. After all, actors are paid millions of dollars to lie to us with nonverbal behavior.

ONLINE TEACHING PLAN

Preview activity: Try to complete the multiple choice and true/false activities for this chapter at: http://cwabacon.pearsoned.com/bookbind/pubbooks/beebe_ab/chapter5/deluxe.html. After reading the chapter and completing course activities related to audience analysis, go back and retake the online quizzes to assess how much you have learned!

Teaching Activity: Conduct your own psychographic analysis of your class by accessing an interactive exercise on the ABLongman web site at: http://wps.ablongman.com/ab_public_speaking_2/0,9651,1593257-,00.html.

Teaching Activity: Determining the general political ideology of audience members is one part of audience analysis. Go to the web site entitled, "Where Do You Fit" at http://www.people-press.org/fit/fit.htm. Use the political typology on this web site to help you explore where your own political ideas fit in the American landscape.

Review Activity: View the web site entitled "Ten Tips to Preparing a Super Speech" at: http://www.selfgrowth.com/articles/Allen10.html. How does the information presented on this web page complement and/or differ from Beebe and Beebe's approach to public speaking?

CHAPTER SIX: Developing Your Speech

Chapter-at-a-Glance

Detailed Outline	Instructor Resources	Supplements	Professor Notes
Select and Narrow Your Topic (p.117)	**Learning Objective #1:** Select the topic appropriately	**The Speech Making Process:** Allyn and Bacon Transparency #T-20	
Guidelines for Selecting a Topic (p.117) • Consider the audience • Consider the occasion • Consider yourself	**Annotated Chapter Outline (ACO):** 6-1, 6-2, and 6-3	**Choose a Topic:** Allyn and Bacon Transparency #T-21 **Speech Topic Idea Generator:** http://www.lib.odu.edu/libassist/idea/index.php	
Strategies for Selecting a Topic (p.119) • Brainstorming • Listening and reading for topic ideas • Scanning Web directories	**ACO:** 6-4 through 6-11	**Speech Preparation Workbook** (SPW) pp. 14-21 **Digital Media Archive for Communication** (DMAC) T09I08, T09I09 **Get Topic Feedback:** Allyn and Bacon Transparency #T-25	
Narrowing the Topic (p. 122) • Descending size method	**Learning Objective #2:** Narrow the topic for the occasion **(ACO)** 6-12, 6-13	**DMAC** T09I11 **SPW** pp. 14-18 **DMAC** T09I12	
Determine Your Purpose (p.123)		**Narrow the Topic:** Allyn and Bacon Transparency #T-23	
Three General Purposes (p. 123) • Speaking to inform • Speaking to persuade • Speaking to entertain		**Quick Guide to the Internet**, pp. 6-16 **DMAC** T09I13, T09I14, T09I15	
Formulating Specific Purpose (p.125) • Use precise language • Limit to single idea • Be sure central idea meets the interests, expectations, and levels of knowledge of your audience • Use the specific purpose to guide research	**Learning Objective #3:** Write a specific purpose statement **ACO:** 6-14 through 6-16 **ACO:** 6-17	**DMAC** T12I01 **SPW** p. 19	

Detailed Outline	Instructor Resources	Supplements	Professor Notes
Develop Your Central Idea (p.127) • Use a complete declarative sentence • Use specific language • Focus on a single idea • Center the idea around the audience		**Develop Central Idea's Focus:** Allyn and Bacon Transparency #T-24	
Generate and Preview Your Main Ideas (p.131) • Finding logical divisions • Establishing reasons • Tracing specific steps • Preview your main ideas	**Learning Objective #4:** Explain ways of generating main ideas from the central idea **ACO:** 6-18 through 6-20	**Generate a Main Idea:** Allyn and Bacon Transparency #T-22	
	Learning Objective #5: Develop a blueprint for a speech **ACO:** 6-21	**SPW** p. 20	
	Learning Objective #6: Complete speaking assignment s in four steps **ACO:** 6-22	**DMAC** T11I14	

LEARNING OBJECTIVES

1. Students will able to select a topic for a classroom speech that is appropriate to the audience, the occasion, and self.

2. Students will be able to narrow a topic so that it can be thoroughly discussed within the time limits allotted for a specific assignment.

3. Students will be able to write an audience-centered specific purpose statement for an assigned topic.

4. Students will be able to explain three ways of generating main ideas from a central idea.

5. Students will be able to develop a blueprint for a speech by combining the central idea and a preview of the main ideas.

6. Students will be able to apply to a speaking assignment the four steps for getting from a blank sheet of paper to a plan for the speech.

CHAPTER OUTLINE

I.   Take the First Steps in Preparing a Speech.

    A.   Select and narrow topic.

    B.   Determine your purpose.

    C.   Develop your central idea.

    D.   Generate your main ideas.

II.   Select and Narrow your Topic.

    A.   Use three guidelines for selecting a topic.

        1. Consider the audience.

           a. Choose topic relevant to the interests and expectations of the audience.

           b. Take into account the current knowledge of audience about topic.

           c. Choose an important topic.

        2. Consider the occasion.

           a. Topics should be appropriate to the occasion.

           b. Topics should fit both audience and occasion.

        3. Consider yourself.

           a. Choose topics that reflect your personal concerns and convictions.

           b. Choose topics that incorporate your personal experiences.

           c. Do not neglect topics about which you would like to learn more.

    B.   Use strategies for selecting a topic.

        1. Use "brainstorming."

        2. Listen and read to discover topic ideas.

        3. Scan Web directories to acquire topic suggestions.

    C.   Narrow the topic.

        1. Try the method of "descending size," choosing a progressively smaller descriptor.

           a. "Music" as a topic can be reduced in size to "Folk Music."

           b. If "Folk Music" is still too broad, narrow it to "Irish Folk Music."

           c. If necessary, continue down the size continuum to "Irish Folk Music in the United States."

           d. Finally, perhaps, you might speak on "The Success of the Irish Folk dance show 'Riverdance' in Their United States Tours."

III. Determine Speech Purpose.

    A.   Three "general purposes" include almost all speeches.

B.   A very common general purpose is "Speaking to Inform."

    1.   Informative speakers give information; they teach.

    2.   Most college lectures are informative.

C.   Another common general purpose is "Speaking to Persuade."

    1.   Persuasive speakers may offer information, but they seek to change or reinforce audience convictions, or to secure audience actions.

    2.   A representative from MADD (Mothers Against Drunk Driving) will surely ask you to refrain from drinking and driving, and to urge those around you to do the same.

D.   The final general purpose is "Speaking to Entertain."

    1.   An entertaining speaker tries to get an audience to relax, smile, perhaps laugh, and generally enjoy themselves.

    2.   Storyteller Garrison Keillor spins tales of "Lake Woebegone."

E.   From general purpose comes "specific purpose."

    1.   Specific purpose is defined as, "The response you want from your audience after completing the speech."

    2.   Specific purpose will normally be stated, such as, "At the end of my speech, the audience will be able to use an online periodical index." (informative speech)

    3.   A variation might be, "At the end of my speech the audience will be able to explain why the United States should adopt a plan of national health insurance." (persuasive speech)

    4.   Follow three simple rules to formulate good specific purposes (which must be written as "behavioral" statements, to identify responses wanted):

       a.   Use precise language.

       b.   Limit specific purpose to a single idea.

       c.   Be sure your specific purpose meets the interests, expectations, and levels of knowledge of your audience.

    5.   Use specific purpose to guide your research and the selection of your supporting material.

IV.   Develop Your Central Idea (also called "thesis").

A.   Central ideas should be audience-centered.

B.   A central idea is a one-sentence summary of the speech.

C.   An acceptable central idea meets four criteria:

    1.   It is a complete, declarative, single sentence.

    2.   It uses direct, specific language.

    3.   It must express only a single idea.

    4.   It should be audience-centered.

D.   A central idea divides the speech into "main ideas." (also known as "points")

V.   Generate and Preview Your Main Ideas.

    A.   Generate your main ideas by following one of three procedures.

        1. Find *logical divisions*, such as a speech on the benefits of a liberal arts education ("Job Opportunities," "Appreciation of Culture," and "Concern for Humankind").

        2. Establish *reasons for the truth of the central idea* — for example, arguing that "Marriage is an Endangered Institution" because: (a) there are fewer marriages each year; (b) there are more "live-in" arrangements; and (c) there is an increasing divorce rate.

        3. *Trace specific steps*, as in a chronological progression or stages in a process.

    B.   Having generated *main ideas*, include them directly in your central idea to provide your audience with a clear PREVIEW (a "blueprint" for the entire speech).

        1. For example, the central idea, "owning a gun does not guarantee your personal safety" can become "guns are rarely reached in time of need" and "the risk of accidental shooting is increased."

REVIEW GUIDE

6-1.   List the first four steps in preparing a speech.

6-2.   What are three suggested guidelines for preparing a speech?

6-3.   List three strategies for finding and selecting a topic.

6-4.   What are the two Beebe and Beebe suggestions for narrowing a topic?

6-5.   List the three classical "general purposes."

6-6.   Define "specific purpose."

6-7.   Recall three simple rules to formulate good specific purposes.

6-8.   Define "central idea."

6-9.   List four criteria for producing effective central ideas.

6-10. Recall three methods of dividing central ideas into "main ideas."

6-11. Explain the "blueprint" concept.

ANNOTATED CHAPTER OUTLINE

A. *Guidelines for Selecting Your Topic*

6-1. Teaching Strategy

This author habitually leads off tough discussions with the statement, "Please don't feel put-down by what I'm going to talk about." In this case, he is going to tell students why they are probably experiencing difficulty in selecting topics. Most of the students are passively resisting the speaking assignment itself. Such resistance, of course, is not praiseworthy, whereas "I just can't find a topic" seems intellectually justified. A level higher in this resistance is, "I can't find a *good* topic." Communicate to students that you "feel their pain," but they need to recognize the actual source of their delays. Invite the students to visit you one-on-one to explore their personal "concerns, convictions, and topics you wish to learn more about." Share with them the classic statement about topics: "There are no boring topics, only boring (and unprepared) speakers." Admit to students that class concern with topics is a bit artificial: "In real life topics are often laid on you. As a supervisor, you will talk about 'improving organization in the assembly process.' As a minister or church worker, your topics are quite likely to be religious. As a teacher, you will choose topics related to the objectives of your classes. But this class is learning and practicing, and appropriate student-chosen topics are the 'order of the day.'" Emphasize again the theme of the class — audience-centered choices, always. Consider the audience when choosing topics. What are the interests and expectations? The current knowledge of your topic? Topics important to this audience?

6-2. Teaching Strategy

Ask students to give examples of appropriate and inappropriate topics for the following speech occasions: dedication of a Persian Gulf War veteran's memorial; a funeral; a university commencement ceremony; a "roast;" a new city hall groundbreaking ceremony; an awards dinner.

6-3. Class Activity

Ask students to imagine themselves as a commencement speaker for a high school graduating class in the year 2010. In a brief essay or in-class discussion, students should generate three general speech topics with corresponding specific purpose statements that would be appropriate for that audience, the occasion, and themselves as speakers.

B. Strategies for Selecting a Topic

6-4. Teaching Strategy

Students are likely to delay in selecting topics. Their delays emerge from multiple reasons. An exercise this author finds useful (and the students find amusing) is to call a cooperative student up front as a subject for informative speaking topic-finding. Tell students, "We are surrounded by topics!" Compliment the student's hairdo, and ask, "I wonder when the first barber (or beautician) went to work"; in other words, what is the history of barbering? Remark on the student's shoes; ask, "What is the history of footwear in human history?" Note jewelry, and ask: "What jewelry habits did ancient Egyptians have?" If apparent, ask "Is that a wedding ring?" If so, suggest a topic concerning the beginning of marriage as we know it. What you are doing is increasing student sensitivity to the obvious — topics are, indeed, all around us. Other topic-inducing leads are tattoos, fad clothing, facial hair, and backpacks.

6-5. Class Activity

As a variation of the brainstorming technique mentioned in the text, use several headings or categories to help students structure their topic ideas. The following categories may prove useful: People and Places; Hobbies; Activities/Sports; Travel/Locations; Pet Peeves; Media; Current Events; "Hot" Topics; Campus Facts/Issues. Some of these categories lend themselves more readily to informative, demonstrative, or persuasive speech purposes.

6-6. Class Activity

Divide students into groups. Briefly review the "brainstorming" process. Instruct students to build lists of one-word topics. Brainstormed topics must be suggested from the classroom environment. Set a time limit; cruise the groups offering encouragement and praise. When time expires, determine the "score" (which group had the longest list?). Applaud that group. Encourage students to "jump on" these suggested topics for upcoming speech assignments.

6-7. Class Activity

To generate as many potential topics as possible, have the class brainstorm for ideas that they would like to hear about during the term. Record these ideas on the chalkboard; after you have listed thirty or forty, group them into categories. See if there are students who are willing to take on some of the suggested topics for a subsequent speech. A variety of topic ideas will likely be generated.

6-8. Teaching Strategy.

Bruce Gronbeck has suggested that students give speeches on the "Issues that Divide People." What are those issues? Lead a discussion to determine what students think are "the hot issues of the day," resulting, hopefully, in class speeches given on some of the topics.

6-9. **Teaching Strategy**

Bring to class a daily newspaper, a current weekly newsmagazine, and the most recent campus newspaper. Leaf through each and have students list the revealed topic areas. This process will demonstrate to students that a wealth of ideas can easily be obtained from readily available sources.

6-10. **Related Reading**

For further ideas on generating speech topics, see Susan Diffy's essay entitled, "Using Magazines to Stimulate Topic Choices for Speeches," in the Summer, 1987 issue of <u>The Speech Communication Teacher</u>, pp. 2-3.

6-11. **Teaching Strategy**

Show the class various award-winning newspapers (preferably ones that your campus library carries), such as the *New York Times*, the *Chicago Tribune*, and the *Los Angeles Times*, as examples of excellent sources for timely topics. Highlight the major sections of the papers, such as News, Arts and Leisure, Business, Magazine, Sports, and Travel. Explain how each section may lead students to interesting topics for varying speech purposes.

C. Narrowing the Topic

6-12. **Teaching Strategy**

Bring to class carefully worked out examples of the two methods of narrowing topics. Preparation is more desirable than chalkboard recreations. Use an overhead transparency. Making a step-by-step presentation of the examples is a good idea.

6-13. **Class Activity**

Call the roll, and, as you do, force students to adopt an informative speech topic, which you record (some students will be hesitant — tell them you will return to them). Be sure each has a topic. In a subsequent class, divide into groups. Instruct each group to assist each member in narrowing their topic choice to a width suitable for a 5-8 minute speech to inform. Cruise the groups, guiding, leading, praising, and correcting. Direct students to place, by groups, their results on chalkboards. Lead a brief discussion of several topics, acknowledging good work, as well as making improvements where needed.

D. Determine Your Purpose

6-14. Teaching Strategy

Review the three most common general purposes. Ask students to explore their dictionaries and thesauruses with you. What are the differences between the words "general" and "specific"? Tell students that the specific purpose is the most important part of their planning (outline). Specific purpose is the absolute essence of audience-centered approaches to conceiving, planning, and delivering speeches in this modern age. A specific purpose first guides research and selection of materials, and then serves as constant reminder of the only true measure of your success: getting the desired response(s) from your audience. Review the three rules suggested for constructing effective specific purposes.

6-15. Teaching Strategy

Discuss with students the three general speech purposes described in the text. Students should understand that the categories — to inform, to persuade, and to entertain — are not discrete divisions. Overlapping frequently occurs. For example, a speaker wants to persuade an audience to read all labels on food purchased at the supermarket. First, she or he will need to inform the audience of the importance of reading labels (e.g., potentially harmful preservatives, artificial ingredients and dyes, flavor enhancers, fat calories). Then, the speaker could work in an element of entertainment, by telling a humorous story about trying to decipher the complicated labels now appearing on food products. Therefore, even though the overall general purpose is to persuade, the other two purposes are also involved.

6-16. Teaching Strategy

Ask students to monitor all or part of one of the following TV programs: *CSI, 60 Minutes, Trading Spaces, American Idol, Scrubs, ER*. Ask students to apply the general purpose concept to the programs: Is *Scrubs* speaking to entertain? Is *60 Minutes* speaking to inform? Is *American Idol* speaking to entertain? Students should quickly grasp that general purposes are interrelated. Should students then ask whether general purpose is an important concept or not, reply that thinking from general to specific is always useful. Add that life is interrelated, and that effective critical thinkers proceed from that knowledge.

6-17. Class Activity

The purpose is for students to practice narrowing topics and writing behavioral specific purpose statements. This activity can be done individually (with a partial or whole list of topics), in dyads, as small groups, or as an entire class discussion. First, review with students the information in chapter six of the text. Then, hand out the list of speech topics; explain that they are to narrow each topic and write a behavioral specific purpose statement for each. You wish to come back to this activity in a later chapter to link it to audience adaptation, conducting research, and other developmental aspects. Below is a list of topics in a format that works for this assignment.

PRACTICE IN NARROWING TOPICS AND WRITING BEHAVIORAL SPECIFIC PURPOSES

Instructions: Take each general speech topic and narrow it to something usable for a five minute informative speech. Then write behavioral specific purpose statements for each topic.

ASTRONOMY
Narrowed Topic:

Behavioral Specific Purpose Statement:

DANCING
Narrowed Topic:

Behavioral Specific Purpose Statement:

DINOSAURS
Narrowed Topic:

Behavioral Specific Purpose Statement:

ETHNIC FOODS
Narrowed Topic:

Behavioral Specific Purpose Statement:

GAMBLING
Narrowed Topic:

Behavioral Specific Purpose Statement:

TRADE IMBALANCES WITH FOREIGN COUNTRIES
Narrowed Topic:

Behavioral Specific Purpose Statement:

HAITIAN REFUGEES
Narrowed Topic:

Behavioral Specific Purpose Statement:

LEARNING DISABILITIES
Narrowed Topic:

Behavioral Specific Purpose Statement:

THE LIFE OF A PHYSICALLY-DISABLED PERSON
Narrowed Topic:

Behavioral Specific Purpose Statement:

MALNOURISHED AMERICANS
Narrowed Topic:

Behavioral Specific Purpose Statement:

SEXIST LANGUAGE
Narrowed Topic:

Behavioral Specific Purpose Statement:

ZOOKEEPERS
Narrowed Topic:

Behavioral Specific Purpose Statement:

6-18. **Teaching Strategy**

Explain the relationship between specific purpose and central idea. Specific purposes specify speech <u>outcomes</u>; central ideas guide and organize speech <u>content</u>. Emphasize two "laws" of central ideas: MUST BE AUDIENCE-CENTERED; MUST BE A SINGLE SENTENCE SUMMARIZING THE SPEECH. Review the four helpful criteria for constructing central ideas.

6-19. **Class Activity**

Divide students into three- or four-member groups. Give each group five general topics and ask them to collectively devise a purpose statement and a central idea for each topic. This procedure will help them to distinguish clearly between the two planning elements. Compare the results from each group. Sample topics could include: Gays in the Military; Violence in Films; Current Status of Race Relations in the U. S.

6-20. **Group Activity**

Divide students into groups. Remind them that effective central ideas are precise, concise, clear, and complete single sentences (at least on paper). Issue a topic, such as "teachers." Direct groups to compose <u>single-point</u> central ideas and place their results on chalkboards. A student-generated example might be: "Teachers are dedicated." Lead a class discussion of each group effort. Is a group example truly one-point? Is it a complete sentence? (Don't be surprised if not — just help make it so.) Is the sentence clear, concise, precise? Repeat the exercise, if desired, for two- and three-point central ideas. Examples for the topics "effective students" and "premarital sexual activity" could include, "Effective students have good note taking and study habits," and "Premarital sexual activity can produce sexually-transmitted diseases, unwanted pregnancies, and career interruptions."

D. *Generate Your Main Ideas*

6-21. **Teaching Strategy**

Bring to class a visual aid showing three examples of generating main points from simple central ideas. Although students will find "steps" to be the easier approach, your prepared examples will facilitate quick grasp of "divisions" and "reasons."

6-22. **Class Activity**

<u>The purpose of this activity is to give students added experience in developing potential speech topics, with the benefit of classmates as collaborators.</u> To illustrate the entire process of developing a speech as described in Chapter 6, work through each of the following steps with the class, using a hypothetical speech topic. This activity could take an entire class session (depending on how much discussion students generate).

Step 1: Brainstorm for potential topics with your students, but be sure to remind them that brainstorming does not include evaluating. Encourage free association and building on the ideas of others. Ask a student to record topic suggestions on the chalkboard. Limit this to ten minutes.

Step 2: Take a vote in class on the five most popular topics.

Step 3: Discuss the appropriateness of each of the five selected potential topics by using the three guidelines given in the text (consider the audience; consider the occasion; consider yourself). After a brief discussion, take another vote to determine the winning topic.

Step 4: Lead the class through the process of narrowing the surviving topic to be manageable for a five-minute speech.

Step 5: Ask students to formulate a general purpose (to inform, to persuade, or to entertain) for the topic and then move on to stating a specific purpose. In order to devise the specific purpose, a behavioral objective should be developed. Ask the class to decide what the audience should be able to do, feel, believe, or accomplish at the end of the speech.

Step 6: Students need to carefully word the specific purpose statement. Does the statement of purpose meet these three tests?
- Is the language precise enough?
- Is the purpose written as a single idea?
- Does the purpose meet the needs, interests, expectations, and level of knowledge of the audience?

Allow the class to make any adjustments pertaining to the specific purpose statement at this time.

Step 7: Students next need to develop a central idea for the speech. After formulating central idea, test it against these guidelines:
- Is the central idea a declarative statement?
- Is the central idea a complete sentence?
- Does the central idea use specific language?
- Is the central idea a single idea?
- Does the central idea reflect a consideration of the audience? The occasion? The speaker?

Step 8: The final step is to generate main ideas. As a guide to determining main points, use the following questions:
- Does the central idea have logical divisions?
- Are there reasons why the central idea is true?
- Can steps or a chronological progression support the central idea?

Follow-up: After the activity, summarize for the class what took place. Remind students the group began with nothing and followed a perfect approach to speech planning, be it for the classroom or the real world.

Public Speaking:
An Audience-Centered Approach

ONLINE TEACHING PLAN

Preview Activity: View the web site entitled "The Idea Generator" to begin thinking about speech topics to use during this class. Students should make a list of 5-10 topics that they find interesting. The web site address is: http://www.lib.odu.edu/libassist/idea/index.php.

Teaching Activity: Review the web site entitled Informative Speech Topics at http://www.tcnj.edu/~rhetoric/topics.html, and choose five speech topics that are interesting or appropriate for your own assignment. Demonstrate how the topic could be developed to create a general purpose and specific purpose. Ask students to choose a topic and develop a general purpose and specific purpose on their own.

Teaching Activity: Use the textbook companion web site to help generate and research topics for upcoming speeches. View the web site at http://www.abacon.com/pubspeak/research/search.html. Using this web site as a beginning point to surfing the Internet for topic ideas helps students by offering a list of topical suggestions. Students should be able to use this site as a gateway to the Internet to help find appropriate topics for class speeches.

Review Activity: Use any of the speech topics generated from the above assignments to practice generating and previewing the main idea of a speech. Practicing this with students will enable them to apply concepts from the chapter to actual speech production.

CHAPTER SEVEN:
Gathering Supporting Material

Chapter-at-a-Glance

Detailed Outline	Instructor Resources	Supplements	Professor Notes
Personal knowledge and experience (p.140)	**Learning Objective #1:** List five potential sources of supporting material **Annotated Chapter Outline (ACO):** 7-1, 7-2	**Preparing for Group Presentations:** Allyn and Bacon Transparency #T-78	
The Internet (p.140) • Worldwide Web • Directories and search engines • Evaluating Web sources	**Learning Objective #2** Discuss the resources on the World Wide Web **ACO:** 7-3 through 7-6 **Learning Objective #3** Explain six criteria for evaluating websites	**Digital Media Archive for Communication** (DMAC) T10I04 **Speech Preparation Workbook** (SPW) pp. 22-31 *Quick Guide to the Internet*	
Library Resources (p.145) • Books • Periodicals • Full-text databases • Newspaper • Reference resources • Government documents • Special services	**Learning Objective #4** List seven types of library resources **ACO:** 7-7 through 7-10		
Interviews (p.151) • Determining purpose of interviews • Setting up interviews • Planning interviews • Conducting interviews • Following up the interview	**Learning Objective #5** Plan and conduct an effective interview **ACO:** 7-11 through 7-15 ACO 7-16, 7-17	**DMAC** T10I05 through T10I14	
Resources from special interest groups and organizations (p. 155)	**ACO:** 7-18	SPW pp. 24-25	
Research Strategies (p.155) • Develop a preliminary bibliography • Locate resources • Consider the potential usefulness of resources • Take notes • Identify possible visual aid	**Learning Objective #6** Explain record keeping on information resources **ACO:** 7-19 through 7-23,	SPW pp. 28-29	

LEARNING OBJECTIVES

1. Students will be able to list five potential sources of supporting material for a speech.

2. Students will be able to discuss the variety of sources available on the World Wide Web.

3. Students will be able to explain five criteria for evaluating websites.

4. Students will be able to list seven types of library resources.

5. Students will be able to conduct an effective interview.

6. Students will be able to explain what items of information a researcher should record to document resources.

CHAPTER OUTLINE

I. Supporting materials can be drawn from five broad sources.

    A. A first source of supporting material is *personal knowledge* and *experience*.

        1. You are your own best source!

        2. Using personal illustrations, explanations, definitions will increase credibility with audiences.

    B. A second source of supporting material is the *Internet.*

        1. The Internet today is a vast collection of computers accessible to millions of world citizens.

        2. The World Wide Web delivers information to your computer as text, graphics, and audio and moving visual images.

        3. Individual Web pages are hyperlinked (each is linked to many other pages, forming the "Web").

        4. The Web is accessed via web directories and search engines.

            a. Web DIRECTORIES can guide Web access, by setting up categories and subcategories.

                (1) Popular directories include Argus Clearinghouse and Yahoo!

            b. Web SEARCH ENGINES are a second access method.

                (1) Search engines work in a fashion similar to electronic library card catalogues.

                (2) Popular search engines include Alta Vista, Lycos, and Google.

5. As with all sources, Web resources should be evaluated.

    a. Lack of legal, financial, or editorial restrictions on the Web presents a challenge to researchers.

    b. Five criteria can assist in validating web resources:

        (1) Is the source <u>accountable</u>?

        (2) How <u>accurate</u> are the sources of facts, and have they been validated?

        (3) Is the information presented in an <u>objective</u> manner?

        (4) How <u>current</u> is the information?

        (5) Is the presentation of information <u>diversity</u>-sensitive?

        (6) Although not strictly an issue of validation, the <u>usability</u> of a site is a factor.

C. A third source of supporting material is the typical *library.*

1. Books are a library's prime asset, kept in stacks, and indexed mechanically and electronically by card catalogues.

2. Another large library holding is periodicals: general interest magazines and professional journals indexed by mechanical and electronic methods.

3. Full-text databases, such as Lexis/Nexis and CARL Uncover, provide simultaneous recovery of index and text.

4. Libraries traditionally hold the most up-to-date paper sources of information, newspapers.

5. All major libraries contain reference resources, such as encyclopedias, dictionaries, directories, atlases, almanacs, yearbooks, books of quotations, and biographical dictionaries.

6. Many libraries are official government document repositories, offering such researcher-useful documents as *The American Statistics Index.*

7. Most libraries offer special services, such as interlibrary loan and reciprocal borrowing privileges.

D. A fourth type of supporting material is the information gathered from *interviews.*

1. Having determined that answers are not available in stored materials, researchers may find interviews efficacious.

2. Four stages are required for good interviews.

    a. Determine the <u>purpose</u> of the interview: what do you want to find out, and from whom?

    b. <u>Set up</u> the interview, using common courtesy to secure appointments and permissions to record.

3. Interviews should be <u>well-planned</u>.

   a. Gather background information.

   b. Plan specific questions.

   c. Plan question sequences.

   d. Plan a recording strategy.

4. Conduct the interview.

   a. Be on your mark. (Dress properly and have everything needed.)

   b. Get set. (Arrive on time and brief the interviewee.)

   c. Go! (Maintain time limits, and be sure to thank the interviewee.)

5. Follow up the interview.

E. The fifth and final source of supporting material is *resources from special-interest groups and organizations*.

   1. Business and industrial groups, non-profit organizations, and other professional societies produce pamphlets, books, fact sheets, etc., about an extraordinarily wide variety of subjects.

   2. Find others through the <u>Encyclopedia of Associations</u> and the <u>Directory of Nonprofit Organizations</u>.

II. Acquisition of supporting materials requires good research strategies.

A. Develop a preliminary bibliography, as a "Menu of Possibilities."

B. Design a system to keep track of resources.

   1. For books, record authors' names, book titles, publishers and dates, library call numbers.

   2. For government publications, pamphlets, newsletters, fact sheets and others, record titles, authors, publishers, dates and page numbers.

   3. Documentation forms for websites are still evolving; the "addresses" are certainly critical.

   4. For a ten-minute speech, plan to include ten or twelve bibliographical items, of which three or four may be very useful to the speech.

C. Locate your resources.

   1. Books will typically be found in libraries.

      a. Determine identifying information (call numbers).

      b. In a "closed stack" library, librarians or assistants will procure books.

      c. In an "open stack" library, you find books by means of location guides.

   2. Library periodicals (once you determine the library subscriptions) may be found in a special shelving area or in the "stacks."

3. Newspapers are generally housed in a special library area.

4. Government documents will be kept in a particular section arranged according to the "Superintendent of Documents" classification scheme.

5. Reference materials are universally in the "reference section."

D. Consider the potential usefulness of resources.

1. Devise an informal "rank ordering" of your resources before committing to final step.

2. A numbering or lettering system may indicate your ordering of potential usefulness of material.

E. Take notes.

1. Once you have located, previewed, and ranked your resources, you are ready to begin more careful reading and note taking.

2. Do not create extra work; have on hand a speech notebook, floppy disk, and note cards.

3. Generally plan to isolate important items on separate note cards or in specific word-processing files.

4. Indicate sources in notes, including quotation marks and other methods to clearly indicate when and where to credit later.

F. Be sure to identify and preserve potentially valuable visual aids.

REVIEW GUIDE

7-1.   Can you list five broad sources of supporting materials?

7-2.   Make a summary statement about the Internet as a source of supporting material.

7-3.   Group the material found on the Internet in three ways.

7-4.   What does it mean when we say that Web pages are "hyperlinked"?

7-5.   Name the two broad methods of accessing information on the Internet.

7-6.   Why should communication teachers be concerned about web materials and source documentation?

7-7.   List five criteria for evaluating (documenting) web resources that your students may utilize.

7-8.   List the seven types of supporting resources held in a typical library.

7-9.   What four stages are useful in gathering supporting material by interviews?

7-10.   What types of material are available from special-interest groups and organizations?

7-11.   List six elements in a well-designed research strategy.

7-12.   What is the status of materials documentation from the web?

7-13.   Approximately how many bibliography items should you expect from a student preparing a ten-minute speech?

7-14.   What are effective ways to take notes so that you can properly credit sources?

ANNOTATED CHAPTER OUTLINE

A. *Personal Knowledge and Experience: You are Your Own Best Source*

7-1. Teaching Strategy

Discuss with students how important it is to survey personal experiences and knowledge as a part of the research process. Selecting a speech topic and main points are strongly aided by personal data. Students do not always realize the value of their own knowledge and experiences, and the experiences of those around them. Encourage students to discuss their speech topic with a knowledgeable friend or family member.

7-2. Teaching Strategy

Students typically choose a speech topic based on their own knowledge and experiences. Discuss with your class the value of working personal knowledge and experience in as one simple source of information. Remind them that speaker credibility may be increased by adding a personal anecdote or story into a speech. In what ways will an audience perceive a speaker as an authority on a topic when personal experiences are mentioned?

B. *The Internet is a New and Exciting Source for Supporting Material*

7-3. Teaching Strategy

Students sometimes have more knowledge or expertise with using the Internet than their instructor. If this is the case in your class, enlist the help of students to demonstrate effective sources of information in the Internet, or ask knowledgeable students to do a "demonstration speech" for the rest of the class on using Internet sources.

7-4. **Teaching Strategy**

Lead a discussion of the ethical dilemmas posed by electronic resources and data. How *do* we accurately document Internet sources?

7-5. **Class Activity**

Hold a class session in the computer lab to orient your students to supporting material available in your library. Which search engines are most appropriate for your assignments? Which Internet sites do you recommend for students looking for support for their speeches? From which sites should students stay away? Why?

7-6. **Teaching Strategy**

Consider communicating with your students via e-mail, in place of traditional communication forms (in class course information and performance feedback, other items). Ask some colleagues in various departments if they would mind being interviewed via e-mail by one of your students as an expert witness for that student's speech. Match student to colleague and provide e-mail addresses. In a much later class, debrief the experiment for its values to this research unit. Use the opportunity to review correct citations of interview notes.

C. *Traditional Library Resources Provide Excellent Supporting Material*

7-7. **Background Information**

This film introduces a library's role in aiding public speakers: *Speakers and the Library*. Films for the Humanities, P.O. Box 2053, Princeton, N.J. 08543; color, 15 minutes.

7-8. **Class Activity**

Public speaking teachers traditionally arrange for a tour of the college library. Library personnel will probably encourage you to ask for specific highlights in the tour. Ask if the library has a checklist for tours and use it as a guide (make deletions and additions, as desired). Are there specific communication journals students can only access in hard copy in the library? Which journals can be accessed online?

7-9. **Class Activity**

Create a "My Best Source" list on your WebCT or Blackboard site for students to leave web addresses for good public speaking web sites. Be sure to check the list each semester to make sure the links are still working.

7-10. **Class Activity**

The purpose of this activity is for students to familiarize themselves with the campus library. Take time to set up and organize a scavenger hunt at your campus library, making certain to inform library personnel of the activity. You can create lists of specific electronic resources, traditional types of materials discussed in the text, and unique sources housed in your library. Find specific enough information to list so that students must locate the exact item in question. The size of your class, time constraints, and library limitations will determine the due date for this assignment. Some examples include the following:

1. Where, in specific, are dissertation abstracts stored?
2. Provide bibliographic information for an article from CD-ROM on a prominent societal issue.
3. How do you apply for an interlibrary loan, and how long does it typically take for someone to receive those materials?
4. What is the color of the bound volumes of ERIC Resources in Education?
5. Print out a copy of a homepage on the World Wide Web.
6. Locate bibliographic information on a book published in the 1920s.
7. On what shelf are the current issues of *Vital Speeches of the Day*?
8. Where do you find this year's issues of the *Journal of Experimental Psychology*?

D. *Interviewing Others and Experts is a Sure Source of Supporting Material*

7-11. **Background Information**

Require students to watch or videotape a television broadcast interview (e.g., CNN's *Live with Larry King*, CBS' *60 Minutes*, ABC's *Nightline*). Using textbook strategies on interviewing as a guide, have students analyze and critique the exchanges between and among the interview participants.

7-12. **Class Activity**

Provide the following example to students as a way to prompt their thinking about source material: "The company Ralph works for is going to meet with several representatives from Mexico about the possibility of building a plant there. Four representatives from Mexico will be at the meeting where Ralph will present the plans. What are four ways that Ralph should conduct research to learn about Mexican culture and communication in order to increase the effectiveness of his message?"

7-13. **Class Activity**

Give students three scenarios in which they will play "Interviewer." Ask them to develop five open questions they will ask during hypothetical interviews. Ask them to plan questions in sequence, as the text recommends, and to be able to justify their sequence. Suggest these hypothetical interview scenarios: the campus health director about eating disorders among students; the academic vice-president about campus grading policies; and a local Red Cross representative about the organization's responses to crises. Lead a discussion of effectiveness in the questions volunteered by students in a subsequent session.

7.14. Teaching Strategy

Engage students in a discussion of the pros and cons of telephone interviewing. If only a few questions need to be asked, the phone can be an effective form of making contact. This type of interviewing is convenient, but also has drawbacks. Advantages: saves time and is valuable for rechecking information. Disadvantages: rapport is more difficult to build than in live interviews, sidestepping a question is easier, and nonverbal communication elements are missing.

7-15. Class Activity

Ask four students to volunteer for mock telephone interviewing sessions. Two students will prepare as interviewers, and the other two as interviewees. The interview topic will be "Sex and Violence on TV." The interviewee will be a network "Vice President for Programming," and the interviewers will play Mike Wallace or Diane Sawyer. On the chosen day have the first interviewer and interviewee take up positions somewhat separated in front of the class. Have each simulate a telephone with a thumb to the ear, and a pinky to the mouth—tell them to "ham it up," but to otherwise play it straight. After an appropriate time have the second pair do it. Be sure the interviewer conspicuously takes notes. Debrief extensively with students. Take this opportunity to discuss telephone speech skills, as well as commenting on the information search. Praise the students for volunteering and enlivening the unit.

7-16. Teaching Strategy

Lead a class discussion on types of questions not to ask an interviewee. As examples:

- Avoid overly vague questions, such as, "Do you think racism is on the rise?"
- Reduce leading questions, such as, "Don't you agree that feminism is being overdone?"
- Hostile questions can end the effectiveness of an interview. Consider, "Why has your department continued archaic practices that should have been discarded years ago?" Or, "Why do so many students cheat on examinations?"

7-17. Class Activity

The purpose of this activity is to give students experience in interviewing so they understand better how interview information can be relevant to a speech. With the exception of nontraditional older students, most of your students have probably done little, if any, interviewing. Covering this chapter in the Beebes' text offers you an opportunity to give students practice in the roles of both interviewer and interviewee. Pair students, give each pair a hypothetical speech topic, and request that they plan (independently or as a team) a series of questions for interviewing an authority on the subject. Then, in class, assign each the identity of either interviewer or interviewee (or both if you have time) and role play the interview. Granted, one student will not be an authority, but that student should attempt to answer interviewer questions as best as possible. Have classmates take notes on the role playing for later class discussion.

E. *Special Interest Groups and Organizations Provide Supporting Material*

7-18. Class Activity

Assign students to ask parents, supervisors, friends, doctors, dentists, attorneys for names of organizations to which they belong, with addresses or telephone numbers of the organizations. Direct students to inquire among sources that look interesting or promising to a topic they are thinking of. You might suggest to students that you would enjoy seeing a bibliography card or two produced from this exercise.

F. *Definite Research Strategies Produce Effective Supporting Material*

7.19. Teaching Strategy
Ask your students to bring in a bibliography or a "Works Cited" page from one of their last major writing assignments. Ask them to discuss the entries. How were they initially located? How valuable was each source? How was material used in the paper? Which sources were the easiest to access? Which were the most difficult and why? You may also want to discuss the difference between citing sources in a written bibliography and citing them orally in a speech, as a form of review of information from other chapters.

7-20. Teaching Strategy

Explain to students the importance of correct bibliographical form. Some of your students may not be aware of the common stylistic formats (APA, MLA, Turabian, and the Chicago style sheet). Also, students may not understand why instructors insist upon conformance to a style

7-21. Writing Suggestion

Prepare a written handout on correct bibliographic form. Then give students a written sample bibliography that includes examples of incorrectly cited sources. The students' task is to correct the examples so that they conform to the bibliographic style you assign.

7-22. Class Activity

Allow students to use electronically derived sources as part of bibliographies. Give them practice at documenting and taking notes from these kinds of sources, as well as traditional ones.

7-23. Class Activity

Ask students to bring in a copy of a recent bibliography page from a paper they wrote, omitting their name from the page. Compile several examples and ask students to critique them. How are they the same? How are they different? Give one bibliography to each group and ask them to correct errors in grammar and style.

ONLINE TEACHING PLAN

Preview Activity: The Internet is a wonderful resource for gathering supporting material. Discuss your own ideas about where to find credible sources on the Internet, and which types of sites students should avoid. If you have access to the Internet in your classroom, show some examples of good and bad web sites.

Teaching Activity: Students should conduct an online interview with an expert on their topic. Ask each student to prepare a list of questions for the interview and then report on the expert's responses to the questions. Experts might include professors on campus, personal friends or acquaintances who have experience related to the speech topic, or individuals who participate in chat rooms on the speech topic.

Teaching Activity: Students should visit the APA style website at http://www.apastyle.org and review the style tips section. Lead an online discussion of how APA is similar or different from other writing styles students might be familiar with, such as MLA.

Review Activity: Students should tentatively choose a speech topic and visit 3-5 websites that might be used to find supporting information for their speech. They should then capture an image (either print it or save it as a file) and explain how the image could be transformed into a visual aid for their speech.

Chapter-at-a-Glance

Detailed Outline	Instructor Resources	Supplements	Professor Notes
	Learning Objective #1: Explain the importance of supportive material **Annotated Chapter Outline (ACO):** 8-1, 8-2, 8-3	**Digital Media Archive for Communication** (DMAC) T10I01, T10I02, T10I03 **Speech Preparation Workbook** (SPW) pp. 32-39	
Illustrations (p.168) • Brief illustrations • Hypothetical illustrations • Using illustrations effectively	**Learning Objective #2**: List six main types of supporting material **ACO:** 8-4 through 8-7	**Types of supporting material:** Allyn and Bacon Transparencies #T-28, #T-29	
Descriptions and explanations (p.171) **Definitions** (p.173) **Analogies** (p.175) • Literal analogies • Figurative analogies • Using analogies effectively **Statistics** (p. 176) • Using statistics as support • Using statistics effectively **Opinions** (p.181) • Expert testimony • Lay testimony • Literary quotations • Using opinions effectively	**Learning Objective #3**: Explain at least one guideline for each of the six types **ACO:** 8-8 through 8-10 **ACO:** 8-11 through 8-15	**Sources of support material:** Allyn and Bacon Transparencies #T-30, #T-31 **Resources for Supporting Your Speech:** http://www.cdc.gov/ http://www.census.gov/ http://www.gallup.com/	
Selecting the Best Supporting Material (p. 183)	**Learning Objective #4** Explain six criteria for choosing supporting material **ACO:** 8-16 through 8-22		

LEARNING OBJECTIVES

1.   Students will be able to explain the importance of supporting material to a speech.

2.   Students will be able to explain the six main types of supporting material.

3.   Students will be able to explain at least one guideline for using each of the six types of supporting material.

4.   Students will be able to list and explain six criteria for determining which supporting material to use in a speech.

CHAPTER OUTLINE

I.   Without appropriate, compelling, and effective supporting material, speeches will not be effective.

II.   Effective supporting material falls into seven categories.

    A.   The first category of supporting material is *Illustrations*.

        1.   Illustrations are, at heart, stories—and everybody loves stories.

        2.   Illustrations may be <u>brief</u>, no more than a sentence or two.

        3.   Illustrations may also be <u>extended</u>, resembling a story.

        4.   <u>Hypothetical illustrations</u> may be brief or extended (stories about events that <u>might</u> happen).

        5.   Develop five skills of using illustrations effectively.

            a.   Be certain your illustrations are directly relevant to the idea or point to be supported.

            b.   The illustrations you choose should represent a trend.

            c.   Make your illustrations vivid and specific.

            d.   Use illustrations with which your listeners can identify.

            e.   Remember that the best illustrations are personal ones.

B.   A second category of supporting material is *Descriptions and Explanations.*

    1. To describe is to produce <u>word pictures</u> — detailed sensory information that allows an audience mentally to see, hear, smell, touch, or taste the object of your description.

    2. Explanations clarify <u>how something is done</u> or <u>why it exists in its past or present form</u>.

    3. Use descriptions and explanations effectively.

      a. Keep your descriptions and explanations brief.

      b. Use language that is as specific and concrete as possible.

      c. Avoid too much description and explanation.

C.   A third category of supporting material is *definitions*.

    1. Definitions provide audiences with answers to questions about which, where, how much, how many, and what kind.

    2. Define when necessary by <u>classification</u>, placing a term in the general class, group, or family to which it belongs, or give <u>operational definitions</u>, explaining how a word or phrase "works."

    3. Use definitions more effectively in your speeches.

      a. Use definitions only when needed.

      b. Be certain your definition is understandable.

      c. Be certain your definition and use of the term throughout a speech are consistent.

D.   A fourth category of supporting material is *analogies*.

    1. Analogies assist audience understanding of the unfamiliar (ideas; things; situations).

    2. Analogies may be <u>literal,</u> expressing comparisons between similar things.

    3. Analogies may be <u>figurative</u>, expressing dissimilar but audience-striking comparisons.

    4. Use analogies effectively.

      a. Be certain the two things you compare in a literal analogy are very similar.

b. The essential similarity between the two objects of a figurative analogy should be readily apparent.

E. *Statistics* are a fifth category of supporting material.

1. Just as three or four examples may be more effective than one example, a statistic representing hundreds or thousands of individuals may be more persuasive still.

2. Statistics can help a speaker express the <u>magnitude of a problem</u>.

3. Five principles of using statistics in speeches are important to speech planners.

   a. Use <u>reliable sources</u>, citing reputable, authoritative, and unbiased sources.

   b. <u>Interpret</u> statistics accurately.

   c. Make your statistics <u>understandable and memorable</u>.

   d. <u>Round off numbers</u> whenever you can do so without distorting or falsifying the statistic.

   e. Use <u>visual aids</u> to present your statistics.

F. The sixth category of supporting material is *opinions*.

1. <u>Expert testimony</u>, the testimony of a recognized authority can add weight to your arguments.

2. <u>Lay testimony</u>, although not as authoritative as expert testimony, can stir an audience's emotions.

3. Make a point truly memorable with a <u>literary quotation</u>.

4. Use opinions effectively.

   a. Be certain that your "expert" is an expert.

   b. Identify your sources.

   c. Cite unbiased sources.

   d. Cite opinions that are representative of prevailing opinion.

   e. Quote your sources accurately.

   f. Use literary quotations sparingly.

III.   Select the best supporting material.

    A.   How can a researcher decide what, of a large amount, should be used in <u>this</u> speech?

    B.   Six criteria can assist in filtering supporting material.

        1.   "<u>Bigger is Better</u>" — go for the gold; the larger the numbers the more convincing your statistic, for example.

        2.   <u>Proximity</u> — the best supporting material is that which is the most relevant to your listeners ("closest to home;" "hits home").

        3.   <u>Concreteness</u> — discuss principles with concrete examples and specific statistics, not boring abstractions.

        4.   <u>Variety</u> — a mix of supporting material is highly desirable ("variety is the spice of life").

        5.   <u>Humor</u> — audiences normally appreciate a touch of humor ("You can't get enough of that wonderful stuff").

        6.   <u>Suitability</u> — supporting material should be considered suitable (acceptable, desirable) to you, your speech, the occasion and, of course, <u>the audience</u>.

REVIEW GUIDE

8-1.   Can you list the seven categories of supporting material (six, if description and explanation are combined)?

8-2.   What is the essence of illustrations?

8-3.   List five skills essential to using illustrations effectively.

8-4.   How do descriptions and explanations work? In other words, what is done for the audience?

8-5.   Can you list three principles for using descriptions and explanations effectively?

8-6.   What two types of definition are favored in the textbook?

8-7.   How can definitions be most effectively used in speeches?

8-8.   What are the two basic types of analogies?

8-9.   What cautions are in order for each type of analogy?

8-10.   Why are statistics useful to a speaker?

8-11.   List five important principles for effective speaker use of statistics.

8-12.   Describe two basic opinion types.

8-13.   List, and elaborate on, six pieces of advice for effective opinion usage.

8-14.   List and elaborate on six principles for good selection of supporting material from a larger supply than can be used.

ANNOTATED CHAPTER OUTLINE

A. *A Wealth of Supporting Material Includes Illustrations, Descriptions and Explanations, Definitions, Analogies, Statistics, and Opinion*

8-1. Teaching Strategy

Students sometimes view supporting materials as necessary evils rather than as tools to greatly enhance their speeches. They may end up using the most accessible sources (like a magazine to which they subscribe) rather than the best sources. Discuss this problem with students.

8-2. Background Information

Haven't you always heard that, "Bad luck comes in threes"? That, "The third time is the charm"? The series of examples given in the text's section on brief illustrations shows "The Rule of Three." Three instances strengthen more than just one, and three short sets of independent statistics in strong agreement are almost unbeatable. Indeed, journalists call it the "triadic structure."

8-3. Teaching Strategy

Explore with students the meanings and usages of the word "support." Joke with them about the function of "support" in human clothing (if comfortable with such discussion). Have students apply the discussion to the words "supporting material." Ask students to summarize what other instructors have said about the necessity for support (many writing teachers call support "details"). Dazzle them with your footwork: argue your case for effective use of supporting material by using (and previewing) all seven forms of support material explicated in the textbook:

- "Supporting materials are a must: allow me to illustrate."

- "Let me describe a speaker who failed to use accurate supporting material."

- "Listen to this explanation of the class penalties for using insufficient supporting materials in speeches."

- "Together we have defined 'support,' which gives us a good leg up in this unit." (Ask students to analyze the "Leg" analogy.)

- "What about an <u>analogy</u> to support my arguments?" (Using poor supporting material in a speech is like making an omelet without meat, cheese, salt, pepper, and other spices.)

- "Four out of five beginning speech students can strongly profit from this unit on supporting material (which includes, of course, <u>statistics</u>)."

- "Theodore Sorenson, John F. Kennedy's chief speech writer, once declared 'the proof of the pudding is in the eating.'" (He meant that striking speech phrases are necessary, but audiences need the substance of details and support.)

Since this author would have assigned the chapter prior to these topics, he would be inclined toward a short pop test on supporting material categories after the preceding mini-lecture. In addition to other goals, a pop test can indicate the importance an instructor attaches to a subject.

8-4. Class Activity

Break students into groups of three (naturally!) and give each person a sample speech topic. Have students create hypothetical illustrations that could be used as introductory devices for speeches on those topics. Then ask each student to deliver the illustration to the other two students and receive their raucous feedback (you may have to look it up!)

8-5 Class Activity

Nien is an international student from Vietnam. A campus group asked Nien to make a brief presentation about Vietnam at their upcoming meeting. Ask students to generate examples of support Nien could use that would interest and involve her audience. What types of support might bore the audience? Besides enhancing audience interest, why is supporting material important in speeches?

8-6. Class Activity

Break students into groups of three and give each person a sample speech topic. (Refer to Appendix B, textbook, for speech topic ideas.) Have students create hypothetical illustrations that could be used as introductory devices for a speech on those topics. Then, ask each student to deliver the illustration to the other two and receive their feedback.

8-7. Teaching Strategy

Remind students that illustrations are stories. Children love stories. What about adults? Remind students of the circus ringmaster's opening spiel: "Ladies and gentlemen! Children of all ages!" Indeed, all audiences will respond to well-chosen illustrations, short or long.

8-8. **Class Activity**

Divide the class into groups. Ask each student to tell a story to the other two. The listeners are to critique the stories and offer suggestions for achieving more impact. Stories can be personal anecdotes, jokes, or observations having an emotional dimension. Suggestions for improvement could include making the story more concise or climactic, using more gestures and facial expressions, varying vocal inflections, strategically placing pauses, and so on.

8-9. **Class Activity**

Use a speech from *Vital Speeches of the Day*, or from the Internet for the class. Ask students to identify definitions the speaker used, and whether or not definitions were used effectively according to the text's guidelines. Next, ask students to examine the speaker's use of analogies, both literal and figurative. How were they used in the speech and were they effective? If no analogies were used, at what points could analogies have been inserted to enhance the speech?

8-10. **Class Activity**

Issue students the five terms below. Direct them between classes to (a) look up each term in at least two dictionaries; and (b) construct personal "operational definitions" for each term. Several classes later, when you are calling roll, ask a number of students to provide both dictionary definitions and operational definitions. The suggested words are: reverberate, redundant, retching, reeling, and recanting.

8-11. **Teaching Strategy**

Use a computer or overhead to project a selection from *Vital Speeches*. Ask students first to identify the speaker's use of <u>definition</u>. Ask how well the speaker did with definition, according to textbook guidelines. Secondly, ask students to spot the use of analogies, and how effective the use was. If really rolling, extend the exercise to other supporting material forms.

8-12. **Class Activity**

Assign students to develop figurative analogies for the following instances. Remind them of the value of humor in supporting ideas. Call on students over a period of several classes, when you need a class to get "loosened up." Use these situations.

- A dishonest sales person is. . .
- A procrastinating student is. . .
- The Dallas Cowboys are. . .
- This city is. . .

Start them off with this example: "A boring instructor is like a well that has run dry." (The instructor has no knowledge to share, the well no water to give.)

8-13. Teaching Strategy

Statistics are used to clarify or supplement information and to give ideas persuasive power. Ask students to bring examples of statistics to class. Where are statistics most often used? In addition to evaluating sources, why is it critical for a speaker to refer to the source of a statistic during her or his speech? Students should come up with several reasons, first, from a speaker's point of view and, second, from an audience perspective. What is an audience member likely to think when a statistic is unsubstantiated, when there is no accompanying date and source? What happens when a speaker overwhelms an audience with too many statistics? How can statistics enhance and detract from a speaker's credibility?

8-14. Class Activity

Ask students to thoroughly review the "Six Suggestions for Using Opinion Effectively." Assign students to find, whether in life around them, on TV, or in reading, at least one flagrant violation of a suggestion (they should look up the word "flagrant"). In a subsequent session, ask volunteers to share their "horrible examples."

8-15. Class Activity

Instruct students to bring examples of statistics (downloaded from the Internet would be just dandy). Pick an example or two to analyze, utilizing the effective use of statistics textbook guidelines. Ask students: "Is it critical for a speaker to identify sources of statistics? Why or why not? What is an audience member likely to think when it is realized a speaker is lax in sourcing and crediting statistics? What happens when a speaker 'overwhelms' an audience with numbers? How can a speaker's use of statistics add to credibility? Subtract from credibility?"

8-16. Teaching Strategy

Using the six suggestions included in the textbook as guidelines, discuss what could happen if each of the hints for using opinions effectively were not followed. In other words, what if the authority had unknown credentials or weak credibility? What happens when one fails to identify the source of an opinion? What damage is done, if any, when a biased source is quoted? Why should a speaker take extra care to quote sources accurately?

8-17. Teaching Strategy

Use one of the sample speech manuscripts provided in the textbook for analysis and discussion. Ask students to study the assigned speech intensely. In the subsequent class analyze the speech in terms of supporting material. The following suggestions can guide you and your students through the analysis.

1. Identify the types of supporting materials used in the speech.
2. Judge the effectiveness of at least ten of the supports used.
3. What kinds of illustrations are used?
4. Are the illustrations relevant and interesting?
5. How are explanations and descriptions employed?
6. If definitions are used, how effective are they?
7. If analogies are used, are the comparisons valid?
8. Do the statistics cited adhere to guidelines in the book?
9. Evaluate how well the supporting materials, as a whole, are integrated into the speech.
10. What suggestions would you make to the speaker?

8-18. Class Activity

The purpose of this activity is to increase students' ability to listen for and identify supporting materials when they are used in a speech. Select a videotaped speech to show in class. Select one from the Beebes' text, your library or media services department, or from among sample speeches included in your collection of past student speeches. Have students use the form below to structure the way they listen and attend to the speaker's supporting materials. Then, hold a discussion about their reactions to the speech and about effective use of supporting materials.

FEEDBACK FOCUSED ON SUPPORTING MATERIALS

Speaker's Name: Listener's Name:

<u>Instructions:</u> Check all types of supporting materials you heard in the videotaped speech. Then, evaluate the speaker's use of textbook principles that guide the effective selection and use of support in a speech.

Illustrations:

_____ Brief illustration	_____ Relevant	_____ Personal
_____ Extended illustration	_____ Specific	_____ Represents a trend
_____ Hypothetical illustration	_____ Vivid	_____ Listeners can identify with

Explanations and Descriptions:

_____ Explaining how	_____ Kept brief	_____ Avoidance of overkill
_____ Explaining why	_____ Specific and concrete	
_____ Describing	_____ Use of effective word pictures	

Definitions:

_____ Definition by classification	_____ Used when needed	_____ Understandable
_____ Operational definition	_____ Consistent use	

Analogies:

_____ Literal analogy	_____ Comparison of similar things
_____ Figurative analogy	_____ Comparison readily apparent

Statistics:

_____ Numerical data	_____ Used reliable sources	_____ Interpreted accurately
_____ Graph	_____ Effective visual aid	_____ Understandable
_____ Memorable	_____ Rounded numbers	

Opinions:

_____ Expert testimony	_____ Identified sources	_____ Cited unbiased sources
_____ Literary quotations	_____ Used sparingly	
_____ Cited representative opinion	_____ Authority an expert on subject	

General Effectiveness:

_____ Recency	_____ Significance	_____ Proximity

8-19. Class Activity

As an ungraded assignment ask students to prepare a 1-2 minute speech. Assign half the class the topic of "my most embarrassing moment," and the other half "my proudest moment." Call for speeches in a subsequent class. Take good notes about students' use of supporting material, and comment extensively after the speech round is completed. Praise good use of good supporting material to high heaven; leave off the accusations for now!

B. *Speakers Will Find the Internet an Excellent Source of Supporting Material*

8-20. Class Activity

The purposes are to give students practice at selecting and inserting supporting materials into a speech and to initiate students' electronic research skills Using "The Hunt" information below, ask students to determine what forms of supporting material could be used for each of the topics. Or, you may prefer to extend the exercise into a two-day experience. If so, meet your class in the electronic library for the first day of this exercise. Cut the topics below into strips (one idea per strip), shuffle them, and ask each student to draw one. Students will present brief speeches on their topics during a subsequent class session. The speeches should contain two forms of supporting material that students find on the Internet.

THE HUNT FOR SUPPORTING MATERIALS

1. Malnourished people around the world

2. Public speaking as a valuable course to take

3. Better informed consumers

4. Cardiovascular fitness for health and longevity

5. Flooding from hurricanes in Florida

6. The President's job performance

7. Swimming as a pastime and lifetime sport

8. Cost of a college education

9. Osama Bin Laden

10. The national debt

11. The need for more campus security

12. The health care crisis in America

13. Gang violence

14. Koby Bryant's basketball career

15. Preservation of tropical rain forests

16. Learning a foreign language

17. Recycling

18. President's White House performance

C. *Speakers Must Select the Best Supporting Material*

8-22. **Class Activity**

<u>This exercise will test students' abilities in two ways: how well they have discovered sources for supporting material and how well they can apply the six criteria for selecting the best supporting material.</u> Divide the students into small groups. Allow a week for preparation. Assign this proposition:

Resolved: that this house favors capital punishment.

Inform students that if speeches were to be given, the audience would be the Faculty Senate of the College. Groups may take an affirmative or negative position. They are to find six pieces of supporting material. Each piece is to be judged against one of the six criteria. Instructor or instructor designates will make final decisions. All evidence will be on index cards, to be placed in containers marked for each criterion. Judges will examine the evidence (supporting material) one container (criterion) at a time. The "winning" piece of supporting material gets ten points and the runner-up five points. Considering the nature of the game and the work required, instructor may wish to give several meaningful awards.

ONLINE TEACHING PLAN

Preview activity: Either display the Internet in class or ask students to go to the Speakers Homepage prior to class at: http://wps.ablongman.com/ab_beebe_pubspeak_5/0,4313,124074-,00.html. Look at several of the web sites listed and discuss which types of information might be found at each site. List sample speech topics that students might choose to use these sites to find supporting material.

Teaching activity: Go to the Gallup Organization website and find relevant statistics for your speech topics. If students do not have a current speech topic selected, ask them to choose a current event from the newspaper and find meaningful data about the topic of the article. The Gallup website can be accessed at: http://www.gallup.com/

Review activity: Review the types of support material discussed in this chapter. Students should work together to create a list of websites they are familiar with that might be used to find supporting material. Post the final list for the entire class to utilize.

CHAPTER NINE: Organizing Your Speech

Chapter-at-a-Glance

Detailed Outline	Instructor Resources	Supplements	Professor Notes
Organizing Main Ideas (p. 187) • Chronologically • Topically • Spatially • Cause and Effect • Problem-Solution	**Learning Objective #1:** List and describe five patterns for organizing the main ideas of a speech **Annotated Chapter Outline (ACO):** 9-1 through 9-3 and 9-9 through 9-11 **ACO:** 9-4 through 9-8 and 9-12 through 9-14	**Organizational Patterns: Example Speech Topics:** Allyn and Bacon Transparencies #T-32, T-33 **Speech Preparation Workbook (SPW)** pp. 40-46 **Digital Media Archive for Communication (DMAC)** T11I01-T11I07	
Acknowledging cultural differences in organization (p. 195)	**Learning Objective #2:** Explain how organizational strategies can vary according to culture **ACO:** 9-15 through 9-18	**Selecting support material:** Allyn and Bacon Transparencies #T-69, T-70	
Subdividing Main Ideas (p. 196)	**Learning Objective #3:** List patterns of organization applicable to subpoints **ACO:** 9-19, 9-20		
Integrating Supporting Materials (p. 197) • State the point • Cite the source of supporting material • Present the supporting material • Explain how the supporting material substantiates or develops the point	**Learning Objective #4:** Describe how to integrate supporting material into a speech **ACO** 9-21, 9-22	SPW pp. 45-46 SPW p. 47	
Organizing Your Supporting Material (p. 198) • Primacy or recency • Specificity • Complexity • "Soft" to "hard" evidence	**Learning Objective #5:** List and explain four organizational strategies specifically adapted to supporting material **ACO:** 9-23 through 9-31	**DMAC** T11I10	

Detailed Outline	Instructor Resources	Supplements	Professor Notes
Developing Signposts (p. 201) • Transitions • Previews • Summaries	**Learning Objective #6:** List and define three types of verbal and nonverbal signposts		
Supplementing Signposts with Presentation Aids (p. 205)	**Learning Objective #7:** Explain how visual aids can supplement signposts		

LEARNING OBJECTIVES

1. Students will be able to list and describe five patterns for organizing the main ideas of a speech.

2. Students will be able to explain how organizational strategies can vary according to culture.

3. Students will be able to list patterns of organization applicable to subpoints.

4. Students will be able to describe how to integrate supporting material into a speech.

5. Students will be able to list and explain four organizational strategies specifically adapted to supporting material.

6. Students will be able to list and define three types of verbal and nonverbal signposts.

7. Students will be able to explain how visual aids can supplement signposts.

CHAPTER OUTLINE

I. Central ideas divide into *Main Ideas,* which may be organized according to five organizational patterns.

    A. Chronological Organization is organization by time; that is, your steps are ordered according to when each occurred or should occur.

    B. If your speech has natural divisions, your speech can often be organized Topically.

    C. When you say, "As you enter the room, the table is to your right, the easy chair to your left, and the kitchen door straight ahead," you are organizing your ideas Spatially.

D.   A speech organized to show <u>Cause and Effect</u> may first identify a situation and then discuss the effects that result from it (cause–effect).

E.   If you want to emphasize how best to *solve* the problem, you will probably use a <u>Problem-and-Solution</u> pattern of organization.

II.   In speech planning, speakers should acknowledge and adjust for cultural differences in organization.

A.   U.S. speakers tend to be more linear and direct.

B.   Semitic speakers support main points by pursuing tangents that might seem off-target to many U.S. speakers.

C.   Asians may only allude to a main point through a circuitous route of illustration and parable.

III.   Just as a speaker's central idea divides into main points, so must main points divide into <u>Subpoints</u>.

A.   If a main point is organized chronologically, subpoints will carry out the chronology.

        1. If a main idea were, "I. Gather your supplies," the subpoints would become the listing of supplies.

        2. You may add, regroup, or eliminate subpoints at any stage in the preparation process, as you consider the needs, interests, and expectations of your audience.

B.   Multiple drafts indicate that a speaker is working and reworking ideas to improve the product and make it the best that it can be.

IV.   After central idea, main points, and subpoints, the speech must be "fleshed out" by <u>Integrating Your Supporting Material</u>.

A.   Begin integrating supporting material by organizing your research cards in the order you organized the speech.

B.   Place each supporting-material card behind the appropriate main-idea or subpoint card, resulting in a complete speech plan on note cards.

C.   Once logically placed in the speech, supporting material must be orally integrated through four speech steps.

        1. State the point.

        2. Cite the source.

3. Present the supporting material.

4. Explain how the supporting material substantiates or develops the point.

D. A final issue in integration of supporting materials concerns the <u>order of presenting</u> material grouped with a main point, which may be decided by one or more of four strategies.

   1. *Primacy–Recency*: One item of supporting material may be more current or dramatic than the others; use it first.

   2. *Specificity*: If supporting material varies from specific to general,use the specific first and the general last (audience gets the point quickly from the short, specific material; then receives proof through the longer, general support).

   3. *Complexity*: Arrange materials supporting the point or subpoint from the simplest to the most complex.

   4. *"Soft" to "Hard" Evidence*: Descriptions and explanations, for example, are "soft" and should be used first; factual examples and statistics are "hard" and should hit the audience last and strongly.

V. A "note card" plan is not a speaking plan; a speech plan and delivery must utilize three types of <u>signposts</u>.

A. *Transition* signposts may be verbal or nonverbal.

   1. Verbal transitions are words and phrases that get a speaker "from one place [in the speech] to another."

   2. Many things, ranging from a change in facial expression, a pause, an altered vocal pitch or speaking rate, or a movement, may indicate a speaker transition.

B. Two types of *previews* provide signposts for speakers.

   1. An <u>initial</u> preview tells audiences something is coming.

   2. An <u>internal</u> preview allows audiences to catch up, as the speaker provides previews within or among lengthy points.

C. Initial previews are succeeded by internal previews, and both are capped by two types of *summaries*.

   1. <u>Internal summaries </u>are often used in conjunction with internal previews: "Here's where we are, and here's where we are going."

    2. A <u>final summary</u> ("tell them what you've told them") is the opposite of, or complement to, the initial preview statement.

D.   Signposts must at times be supplemented with *visual aids.*

REVIEW GUIDE

9-1.   What are the five patterns of organization for writing and speaking (at least in our Western culture)?

9-2.   What different styles of organization are used by speakers in some different cultures?

9-3.   With operational definitions, specify the essence of each of the five patterns.

9-4.   How do subpoints flow from main points?

9-5.   List four steps in oral integration of supporting material in a speech.

9-6.   What four strategies may be employed to decide the order in which you present your supporting material?

9-7.   What are three types of signposts in public speaking?

9-8.   Operationally describe each type of signpost.

9-9   What is the difference between internal previews and internal summaries?

9-10.   Why should signposts occasionally be reinforced with visual aids?

ANNOTATED CHAPTER OUTLINE

9-1. Teaching Strategy

We should not assume that students know how to use illustrations, statistics, or testimony in speeches, or how to cite sources of supporting material. A class discussion of how to work these materials <u>smoothly</u> into a speech will be beneficial for students.

9-2. Teaching Strategy

Why is organization even more critical in effective speechmaking than in essay writing? Point out to students that the reader is in control while reading an essay, free to go back and reread or pause to ponder a thought. The speaker, on the other hand, is in control during a speech. The audience has to listen intently and does not have the advantage the reader has. The message, therefore, must be easy to follow since it is a "one-time-only" experience. The more tightly organized a speech is, the easier it is for the audience to follow.

9-3. Teaching Strategy

It is not likely your students will have the skills in *organizing* speech that you might wish them to already have. You have the opportunity to help them acquire those missing skills. Begin with an evaluation of students' present organizational skills. The concepts and principles of this chapter could serve as an evaluation guide. Ask selected students to operationally define "central idea," "main points," "subpoints," "subordination," and "supporting material." See how much they remember about patterns of organization (hopefully from their writing classes). Ask them how to get from central idea to main point to subpoints. Once you assess this information, you can more easily adapt your lesson plan to your students' needs.

9-4. Teaching Strategy

Create five groups and give each group one organizational pattern. Ask them to draw a picture of the pattern without using words. Each group should present their picture.

9-5. Teaching Strategy

Prepare two 4 minute speeches you will give to students. Consider these topics: "Why Teachers Do Not Touch Their Students" (serious, humorous, or both), and "The Requirements for Completing a Masters Degree." Prepare both speeches adequately. However, be sure that your first speech "wanders" all over and around the central idea. Make a full-sentence outline for the second speech (strongly organized) and display it as a projection accompanying the speech. Leave the outline displayed. Allow a bit of time for student questions (or guffaws). Lead a probing discussion about the quality of *organization* in the two presentations. Try to relate student comments and your responses to theory in this textbook chapter. End with an observation that the displayed outline facilitated the discussion.

9-6. Teaching Strategy

Ask students to volunteer a personal triumph or skill mastery. It is likely you will hear stories about such topics as football, art, or writing. Ask the volunteers whether their skill mastery was the result of organized study and practice. Most likely, they will agree that it was an organized and time-consuming process. Then ask whether their teachers and coaches worked on a haphazard basis, or whether they used an organized approach. Then ask the class in a general sense whether they all agree that organization is required for most winning efforts? Effective public speaking is no different. It requires organized practice and planning.

9-7. Teaching Strategy

Ask a volunteer to tell a story about their childhood. After they have finished, involve the class in a discussion of how the story was organized, and how the speaker might have used a different organizational pattern to tell the same story.

9-8. Class Activity

Ask students to remember or find a brief joke (on the Internet or in *Reader's Digest*) or humorous anecdote that is clearly organized according to one of the organizational patterns of the chapter. Have each student relate their joke or anecdote to a small group and ask the other students to correctly identify the organizational pattern. After the groups finish, ask each group to present one of its findings to the class.

9-9. Class Activity

Students should consider how they typically organize everyday activities so they can transfer that skill to organizing speeches. Students should categorize and organize the following "To Do" lists in ways that seems logical to them. Then discuss in class (or in small groups).

Trip "To Do" List	School "To Do" List
Pack	Study for tomorrow's math exam
Get cash	Finish book report for English
Take "Snowball" to the vet	Schedule a time for my parents to visit
Wash car	Call Joe about the day I missed Spanish
Get snacks, drinks, and ice for the road	Clean my room
Buy maps	Go to the library for info on speech topic
Pay bills	Attend a meeting of my major's club
Pick up dry cleaning	Re-read history chapters I skimmed
Do laundry	Work out
Call Brooke about newspapers and mail	Average my grades in biology
Get gas	Call Don to set up racquetball match
Clean out trash in car	Start drafting an outline
Get traveler's checks	Meet Nancy for dinner tonight
Call Mom about where I'll be	Read Stephen King's latest book
Get tapes and CDs for the drive	Return messages people sent on e-mail

9-10. Class Activity

After completing this activity, students should realize the ways in which organization comes naturally to them. Place several items in a paper bag. Anything can be used, but the activity works best if there are similar kinds of items or if students can easily place items into categories. For example, take paper clips of various types, pens of varying colors, different-sized rubber bands, etc., from your office. Give the bag to a student volunteer and tell him or her to "do something with the contents of this bag." (You may want to add the phrase, "that does NOT inflict harm on anyone.") Responses from students typically include: grouping similar items in categories on their desks (your objective); constructing something (so don't give tape or glue as an object); and giving items away to classmates. If your first volunteer doesn't categorize objects, give them to someone else, and so on. Someone <u>always</u> categorizes them. Then, ask the class to describe what that person has done with the objects and why. This activity demonstrates our human tendency to immediately want to make sense of things by examining and categorizing — an excellent introduction to the concept of organizing a speech.

9-11. **Class Activity**

Thia activity allows students to practice using organizational patterns in group problem-solving. Using the list of periods and developments below for a speech about "Life on a Prehistoric Planet," ask small groups of students to use chronological order to plot a prehistoric time line. Other groups will use topical patterns organized around eras, periods, and animals (descending order of specificity). [This activity is adapted from information in the *1984 World Book Encyclopedia*, World Book, Inc., Chicago.]

Amphibians began during the mid-Paleozoic period.	Reptiles began more than 225 million years ago.
Dinosaurs lived during the Mesozoic period.	Fishes began during the mid-Paleozoic
The Jurassic period began 180 million years ago.	The Paleozoic era began 600 million years ago.
Humanlike apes lived more than 5 million years ago.	The Cretaceous period was in the Mesozoic era.
The first horse lived in the early Cenozoic era.	Mammals appeared during the Cenozoic era.
Eras include Cenozoic, Mesozoic, and Paleozoic.	The first people lived about 2 million years ago.
Periods include Cretaceous, Jurassic, and Mesozoic.	The Paleolithic period or Old Stone Age was a period of primitive human beings that lasted from about 3 million to 12,000 years ago

9-12. **Class Activity**

Ask students to choose memorable speeches from film or television. Each student should watch the chosen speech and write a brief summary of its organizational pattern. How did they identify the patterns and the main points? What were the obvious characteristics of each speech pattern? Present the film clips in class.

9-13. **Teaching Strategy**

Prepare a projection of the following as examples of the cause–effect organizational pattern:

- "Smoking and the Risks of Cancer"
- "The Relationship Between Television Violence and Increases in Crime."
- "Obesity and Heart Disease"
- "The Benefits of a High-Fiber Diet"

Ask students, "Should a speech on each topic begin with the cause or the effect?" You may also extend this exercise with similar preparations for the other organizational patterns.

9-14. **Class Activity**

Have students brainstorm major points for the following spatially ordered topics: key locations on the campus; the chambers of the human heart; or major points of interest in your city.

B. *Cultural Differences Exist with Respect to Organizing Discourse*

9-15. **Teaching Strategy**

Explain to students that in Western culture, our minds are generally trained to respond to five patterns. Review Chapter Outline material I, A-E. Prepare examples of each pattern on projections. Make the examples relevant to student (audience) interests, needs, and expectations. Example of cause and effect: "Excellence in finding and using good supporting material leads to improved grades in writing and speaking classes."

9-16. **Teaching Strategy**

Ask students to close their eyes and keep them tightly closed. Ask them to imagine an alien planet on which there are no straight lines. After eyes are opened, ask for reports. What did they see? They will not, of course, be able to describe without involving straight lines. Tell them they might have the same trouble listening to a speaker from another culture, when that speaker does not follow Western ways of "getting from here to there." Reinforce the lessons of Chapters 1 and 2 about becoming sensitive to and tolerant of cultural differences. <u>Draw a lesson from the alien planet exercise, that we see and absorb more when familiar patterns of organization are employed by writers and speakers.</u>

9-17. **Teaching Strategy**

Discuss elements of culture, including such co-cultural aspects as sex/gender, age, socioeconomic status, region within the U.S., ethnicity, and sexual orientation — all of which may need to be taken into account when organizing a speech. How do cultural elements affect organizational patterns? Why might some organizational patterns be more effective with certain cultural groups than others?

9-18. **Class Activity**

If you have some strong cultural differences represented in the class, ask volunteers to prepare a four -minute speech to be delivered in full ethnic dress. Assign volunteers the same topic: "The Importance of Family in my Culture." Ask volunteers to demonstrate how speakers in their culture speak in public. After the speeches, discuss the similarities and differences among the group of speakers. How did they organize their speeches? How could they change their organizational patterns?

C. *Main Ideas Must Often be Subdivided*

9-19. **Teaching Strategy**

Have the class brainstorm main points for the following topics, requiring a chronological pattern: "The Developing Popularity of Tejano Music," "College Registration Procedures," and "The Evolution of Instant Messaging."

9-20. **Class Activity**

Divide students into small groups. Using the topic of "Family Traditions at Holidays," have students generate two or three main points. Next, have groups generate several subtopics and sub-subtopics. As groups complete the task, have them place their examples on chalkboards. Lead a critical but laudatory discussion. Reinforce the truism, "An outline allows you to test the logic of what you have prepared." You will have examples of non-logical subordination of points. Take advantage of the opportunity to correct those examples.

E. *Supporting Material May be Integrated with Main Ideas and Subpoints in a Four-Step Procedure*

9-21. **Teaching Strategy**

Analyzing a speech within a feature film is an effective alternative to using political or student speeches. For excellent resources for the use of feature films as teaching devices in communication courses, see Proctor, R. F. (1995). "Teaching Communication Courses with Feature Films: A Second Look." *Communication Education, 44*, 154, and the three articles which follow.

9-22. **Teaching Strategy**

Explain the material in Chapter Outline IV, A-D, 4. Prepare and deliver an excellent example of the four steps in orally integrating supporting material. Use this suggested point, if you like: "College students frequently fail to register and vote."

D. *To Determine Use Order of Supporting Material Use the Five Traditional Patterns of Organization or One or More of Four Classic Strategies*

9-23. **Background Information**

For more information on primacy and recency in persuasive speaking, see Bostrom, R. (1983). *Persuasion*. Englewood Cliffs, N.J.: Prentice Hall [pp. 177-178]. To ensure students' understanding of these important concepts, have them prepare a five-minute oral report accompanied by a written abstract on the body of research conducted on primacy/recency. Because the research on this subject is extensive, students should focus on the most recent studies and the most significant findings.

9-24. **Class Activity**

Find or invent eight pieces of supporting material supporting one point. The pieces are to illustrate choosing the order of use of supporting material (chapter Outline, IV, D, 1-4). Prepare materials on note cards and projections, with good style and form. Two note cards should represent "Primacy–Recency," with one card more current and dramatic than the other. Ask students to choose the order in which these materials should appear. You get the idea; complete the exercise, which will give students practice in criticizing note cards and in learning the four strategies.

9-25. **Teaching Strategy**

Have students analyze an Appendix D speech specifically for supporting material. Did the speaker use an organizational strategy specifically adapted to the supporting materials? Did the speaker use primacy–recency, specificity, soft-to-hard, or complexity strategies?

9-26. **Class Activity**

Break students into small groups and ask them to brainstorm for potential speech topics that lend themselves to a topical organizational pattern. Then have students isolate the three best topics that emerged from their discussions, and brainstorm for major divisions of each topic. Finally, engage the class in a discussion of why order of arrangement is important in a speech, keeping in mind the principles of primacy and recency.

F. *Effective Speakers Need to Develop Signpost Language*

9-27. **Writing Suggestion**

Provide students with a handout that represents the supposed third page in a five-page essay. Ask students to provide a written internal summary for the third page and an initial preview for the supposed fourth page. In a subsequent class, ask several students to emote their written work to the class.

9-28. **Teaching Strategy**

Discuss ways in which internal and initial preview statements differ. What do previews do for listener comprehension? What ways do they also benefit the speaker?

9-29. **Teaching Strategy**

Point out to students that listeners often rely on ending signals for preparation for disengagement. Often, these cues can signal an audience to listen more carefully for final pieces of information. Encourage students to develop effective ending signals instead of the usual "Finally," and "In conclusion…"

9-30. Class Activity

Transitions into final summaries are often weak or ineffective. Ending transitions, however, are very important, as speakers ask for final concentrated attention. Prepare three one-page, full-sentence outlines and distribute to students. In a subsequent class divide students into groups and ask them to compose one- or two-sentence final summary transitions. Have each group share its best with the class.

9-31. Class Activity

This exercise will permit review of "Listening" as well as giving students intense practice in transitions, previews, and summaries. Develop an outline to the structure below:

Central Idea: (three main points)

I.   (first main point)
    A.   (first subpoint)
    B.   (second subpoint)
    C.   (third subpoint)

II.
    A.
    B.
    C.

III.
    A.
    B.
    C.

Conclusion

    A.   (Summary)
    B.   (Appeal)

Prepare at least twenty-eight slips of paper, corresponding to twenty-eight sentences that are parts of a familiar story or nursery rhyme. Ask students to read their sentences aloud and then order themselves into the outline above. Each student should logically fit into the outline. Ask one additional student to serve as the scribe to write out the completed outline in the spaces above.

ONLINE TEACHING PLAN

Preview activity: Review the section of the chapter that discusses organizational patterns of speeches. Give students a fictitious speech topic and ask them to generate a brief summary of how a speech on this topic might be constructed using a chronological, topical, spatial, cause and effect, or problem–solution organization. After students submit their examples to the instructor, post them on the class bulletin board (such as Blackboard or WebCT) or class chat room. Encourage students to print the examples for use in constructing their own speeches.

Teaching activity: Students should search the Internet to find examples of concepts from the chapter including: primacy, specificity, complexity, and "soft" to "hard" evidence. Look specifically at websites that sell products or services to find examples. Print out examples, or submit web addresses to the instructor with an indication of which concept is exemplified in the submitted website.

Teaching activity: Log on to http://www.historychannel.com/speeches/ and select a radio broadcast version of a famous speech. Play the speech in class for students. Ask them to listen for its main points and it organizational pattern. Discuss their findings after you listen to the speech.

Review activity: Students should practice writing a verbal signpost for an upcoming speech and submit it to the instructor. Post the sample signposts for the rest of the class and ask for suggestions about how the speaker might integrate supporting material into his or her speech.

CHAPTER TEN: Introducing and Concluding Your Speech

Chapter-at-a-Glance

Detailed Outline	Instructor Resources	Supplements	Professor Notes
Purposes of Introductions (p. 212) • Get the audience's attention • Introduce the subject • Give the audience a reason to listen • Establish your credibility • Preview your main ideas	**Learning Objective #1:** Discuss the importance of conclusions and introductions **Learning Objective #2:** Explain five purposes of an introduction **Annotated Chapter Outline (ACO):** 10-1 through 10-4, 10-14 and 10-15 **ACO:** 10-9 **ACO:** 10-10 through 10-13	**Functions of Introductions:** Allyn and Bacon Transparency T-37 **Additional Functions of Introductions:** Allyn and Bacon Transparency #T-38	
Effective Introductions (p. 216) • Illustrations • Startling facts • Quotations • Humor • Questions • References to history • References to recent events • Personal references • References to the occasion • References to preceding speeches	**Learning Objective #3:** List and describe ten methods of introducing a speech **ACO:** 10-5 through 10-8, 10-16 through 10-23	**Types of Introductions:** Allyn and Bacon Transparencies #T-39-T-40 **Digital Media Archive for Communication** (DMAC) T11I08, T11I09 **Speech Preparation Workbook** (SPW) pp. 58-68	
Speaker's Homepage (p. 222) **Four Purposes of Conclusions** (p. 2293) • Summarize • Reemphasize the central idea • Motivate the audience • Provide closure	**Learning Objective #4:** Explain the four purposes of a conclusion **ACO:** 10-24 through 10-29	**Functions of conclusions:** Allyn and Bacon Transparency #T-41	
Effective Conclusions: Four Methods (p. 225) • Same methods as in introductions • References to the introduction • Inspirational appeals or challenges Appeals to action Great Speakers: Patrick Henry	**Learning Objective #5:** List and describe four methods of concluding a speech **ACO:** 10-31 through 10-38 **ACO** 10-39	**Types of conclusions:** Allyn and Bacon Transparency #T-42, T-43	

LEARNING OBJECTIVES

1. Students will be able to discuss why introductions and conclusions are important to the overall success of a speech.

2. Students will be able to explain the five purposes of the introduction to a speech.

3. Students will be able to list and describe ten methods of introducing a speech.

4. Students will be able to explain the four purposes of the conclusion to a speech.

5. Students will be able to list and describe four methods of concluding a speech.

CHAPTER OUTLINE

I. Speech introductions may be said to have five purposes.

   A. Introductions get the audience's attention.

   B. Introductions introduce the subject.

   C. Introductions also give the audience a reason to listen.

   D. Introductions will establish your credibility.

   E. Introductions allow you to preview your main ideas.

II. For effective introductions, utilize one or more of ten introduction methods (note that these methods are not mutually exclusive; one method may be two at once).

   A. *Illustrations*, especially personal illustrations (includes *anecdotes*), are inherently interesting to audiences (get their attention).

   B. *Startling facts and statistics* will invariably catch audience attention as well as motivate them to listen further.

   C. *Quotations*, especially famous quotations, allow you to express things more authoritatively, comprehensibly, and memorably than perhaps you might have said.

   D. *Humor,* handled well, can be a wonderful attention-getter.

   E. Use audience-involving *questions* to open a speech — rhetorical questions (the   kind to which you do not expect vocal answers) or questions you ask with the expectation of an audience answer.

F. Referring, including *references to historical events,* also get an audience involved, by asking them to remember interesting, perhaps personal happenings.

G. If your topic is timely, a *reference to recent events* is interesting to the audience, and may increase your <u>credibility</u> with them.

H. Speakers are typically interesting to an audience, and *personal references* enhance <u>bonding</u> between speaker and audience.

I. *References to the occasion* may endear speaker to audience, as speaker indicates deference to matters important to an audience.

J. *References to preceding speakers* may rescue you when the preceding speaker speaks on your topic or uses your planned supporting material! (This also allows the speaker to "call back" audience warmth developed by that speaker.)

III. Speaker's Homepage

IV. Effective conclusions serve one or more of four purposes.

A. Effective conclusions *summarize the speech* (Golden Rule of Public Speaking: "Tell'em what you're going to tell them; tell them; and then tell them what they have been told!")

B. Effective conclusions *reemphasize the central idea in a memorable way.*

C. Effective conclusions *motivate your audience to respond,* to "deliver" the audience response you first specified in your Specific Purpose (Chapter 6).

D. Speeches need to sound finished; hence, an effective conclusion *provides closure.*

V. Effective conclusions may employ one or more of four methods.

A. Effective conclusions may *reemploy methods also used in introductions.*

B. Effective conclusions may reinforce the conclusion purpose "closure" by *references back to the introduction,* which tie together beginning and end.

C. Effective conclusions <u>climax</u> a speech with dramatic *inspirational appeals or challenges.*

D. Finally, effective conclusions call once again for the Specific Purpose: *appeals for action.*

REVIEW GUIDE

10-1.   List and elaborate the importance of five speech introduction purposes.

10-2.   Give one example each of the ten introduction methods, beginning with illustrations.

10-3.   Have you memorized the "Golden Rule of Public Speaking"?

10-4.   How are the methods of concluding speeches related to the "Rule of Three"?

10-5.   List and explain four effective conclusion purposes.

10-6.   List and explain four methods of conclusion.

10-7.   Is "humor" always appropriate? Why or why not?

10-8.   How often should startling facts and statistics be employed by speakers?

10-9.   Need an audience be familiar with speaker's quotations? Why, or why not?

ANNOTATED CHAPTER OUTLINE

A. *Speech Introductions Should Accomplish Five Purposes*

10-1. Teaching Strategy

Students may be familiar with writing introductions and conclusions for essays and research papers, but have limited experience developing these components for oral communication purposes. Talk with your class about the importance of having an effective beginning and ending to their speeches. Too often speakers leave the introduction and, especially, the conclusion to "inspirations of the moment" or "divine intervention." Usually, these inspirations or interventions don't come, and a speaker may begin and end quite poorly, thus undermining her or his credibility and good ideas in the body of the speech. Students need to realize that all five purposes of introductions and all four purposes of conclusions should be accomplished within a speech.

10-2. Teaching Strategy

The teaching strategy above dealt with the importance of the first purpose of introductions: getting audience attention. Move to the second of the five purposes, introducing the subject. Remind students of the "Rule of Three," that we humans appear to remember something better when we hear it at least thrice. By introducing the subject, that's once. When the central idea is stated, that's twice. As main points are developed, that's thrice. For good measure, throw in the final summary; now the audience has a fighting chance to remember speaker subject and interpretation.

10-3. **Teaching Strategy**

You can point a shotgun at your audience and you <u>will</u> have their attention! But they also need a reason to listen (the third listed purpose of introductions). Strong reasons for an audience member to listen include the "biggies" — desires to survive and reproduce, which a speaker should employ whenever possible. Consider the strength displayed in this one: "I am here to tell you how to extend your active life by ten years." A speaker can similarly offer reasons to listen based on an audience's needs for air, shelter, rest, water, and food (physical drives).

10-4. **Class Activity**

Assign students to prepare to deliver an introduction to the topic, "Premarital Sex," to run no more than one minute long. On a subsequent class day have the class remain in the hall. Invite a speaker in to give just you their introduction and then to be seated (the procedure prevents students from simply "copycatting" the assignment). Lead a discussion of good things in the performances. Indicate generally how improvements could be made. If things went well with the introductions, you might choose to repeat the assignment with conclusions on the same topic.

10-5. **Teaching Strategy**

The film *Patton* opens with actor George C. Scott delivering a classic speech as if given by General George Patton. Show the film clip (but do tell students about mild obscenities and profanities, so that those who may want to do so can opt out for a few minutes). Ask viewing students to make notes about Patton's use of techniques for getting his audience's attention. Focus a post-film class discussion on who the audience was, ways in which the character gained attention, and why the introduction to his remarks was effective.

10-6. **Class Activity**

Beginning speakers often overlook the importance of a "Dyn-O-Mite!" introduction. They run out of steam in the planning process, or feel they will exceed time limits for the speech. The exercise suggested here should help such speakers realize the significance of introductions, and offers them practice in preparing and delivering "cool" introductions. Have students prepare brief introductions to speeches they are planning to present. After preparation time, divide students into groups, scatter them around the room, and have each member deliver a planned introduction. Allow time for debriefing.

10-7. **Teaching Strategy**

Ask students to watch, or to tape for later viewing, daytime television hosts. How do the celebrities gain attention in their opening monologues or other activities? How do their introductions appeal to both the in-house audience and the TV audience? Did they use techniques from this chapter? Shows hosts to consider include Ellen DeGeneres, Oprah Winfrey, Jerry Springer, Montel Williams, and Regis and Kelly.

10-8. Class Activity

Direct students to prepare an attention exercise for the next class. Tell them they must get the attention of the audience <u>without saying a word</u>! Suggest gestures, facial expressions, platform movements, visual aids, weird postures — anything goes. Students will express mild unwillingness and apprehension, but what else is new in public speaking class? Tell them to think about what a speaker they are going to be with <u>both</u> nonverbal and verbal skills in their introductions. Consider giving out awards to the best performers.

10-9. Class Activity

Have small groups of students determine how they could establish listening motivation during introductions for the following speech topics:

- Maintaining an exercise program
- Recycling
- Volunteering for a community agency
- Making your voice heard by writing letters to companies

10-10. Teaching Strategy

Review with students the concept of credibility, which has now appeared in three textbook chapters. You won't waste anybody's time if you once again look it up in both dictionaries and the textbook. The fourth purpose of introductions is to establish or reinforce speaker credibility. Suggest to students these possible elements of establishing speaker credibility in introductions:
- Use warm personal references
- Call audience members by name when possible
- Use "common ground" — speak of "we," "us," "our values," or "our goals"
- Speak casually, but authoritatively of your qualifications to address the subject
- Use some careful namedropping (your associations with persons knowledgeable on your topic)

10-11. Class Activity

Ask students to think about additional ways in which a speaker could use introductions to increase personal credibility with an audience. In a subsequent session, ask students for their thinking and, as needed, add your own thoughts:

- Consider expressing <u>gratitude</u> to the audience for their time and attention (everybody likes to be thanked, and has, at least temporarily, warm feelings for the "thanker").
- Why not <u>compliment</u> the audience (sincerely, of course)? Many things in the audience will allow you to do it in good conscience. Everybody likes deserved compliments and the complimenter. Try "Thank you very much for attending and listening today. It means a lot to me."

10-12. **Background Information**

The following article reviews much of the body of research about speaker credibility: McCroskey, J.C., and T.J. Young (1981). "Ethos and Credibility: the Construct and Its Measurement after Three Decades." *Central States Speech Journal 32,* 24-34.

10-13. **Teaching Strategy**

Dealing with the final purpose of introductions, preview main ideas and reinforce the importance of all types of previews (Chapter 9:Signposts).

B. *Ten Strategies Can Produce Effective Introductions*

10-14. **Teaching Strategy**

Share with students that merely having someone's attention does not necessarily guarantee a favorable response from them. However, without attention there will be no listening, and, without listening, no favorable response. An audience's attention, therefore, becomes indispensable, does it not? A famous quotation has it that "If something is worth doing, it is worth doing well." In the case of attention, it *must* be done well. Remind students that securing audience attention is not enough; attention must be held throughout a speech. Review the ten introduction methods from chapter outline, II, A-J.

10-15. **Teaching Strategy**

Share with students again that getting and holding audience attention is the one inescapable task in effective public speaking. It must follow, as night follows day, that *techniques* for taking your audiences' attention prisoner should be <u>learned, practiced, mastered</u>. It is suggested that you review, verbatim, the techniques from Outline, II, A-J and follow that review with fine, fine audience-grabbing examples of each technique. Some examples are next, and feel free to use any or all.

- <u>Illustration</u> (anecdote): To illustrate a point that college students are not unwilling to get involved in important issues, tell the story of the four Kent State University students who were killed on their campus while expressing their opposition to the Vietnam War.

- <u>Startling Facts and Statistics</u>: To make a point about the importance of "thinking the unthinkable," share with students that current medical research suggests achievement of physical immortality for humans within the next fifty years of medical advancements.

- <u>Quotation</u>: To support the idea that firm foundations are needed for world peace, remind your audience not to "build their houses on shifting sand."

- <u>Humor</u>: For a point about teachers who are overly fond of themselves, combine humor and quotation with: "Those who can, do; those who can't, teach!"

- Questions: For a speech on "Exercising," open the introduction with a series of questions to the audience: "Do you want to feel better physically? Have more endurance? Have fewer illnesses? Maintain a healthy weight? Glow with that healthy look? Live longer? Appropriate and regular exercise is the answer to those questions for us all."

- Reference to historical events: Since your audience is probably twentyish, to make a point about cruelty of man toward man, refer back to the "ethnic cleansing" of Kosovo ethnic Albanians by Serbs. Or, choose to remind them of the events portrayed in that tragically excellent film, *Schindler's List.*

- Reference to recent events: Again taking into account some audience demographics (Chapter 5), refer your students to the baseball homerun heroics of Sammy Sosa and Mark McGuire (by way of illustrating how much Americans value their sports heroes).

- Personal references: Use humor to disclose information about yourself and your own experiences. This helps students view you as a real person, not just an instructor.

- References to the occasion:. What will you say to your students on the last day of class? What every teacher will say: "Did you think we would ever reach this day?"

- Reference to preceding speaker:. When Henry Grady delivered the famous "New South" speech in post-Civil War Atlanta, the speaker before him was General William Tecumseh Sherman, who was known as the "Slash and Burn" traveler through the Confederacy. Grady, to defuse audience hero worship for Sherman, to get the audience laughing a bit, and to draw attention to his theme of reconciliation, referred gently to Sherman as a man "a bit careless with matches!"

10-16. Teaching Strategy

Televise the Patton speech again, this time showing only the introduction. Ask students to note the introductory devices used by George C. Scott in the role of General Patton. Class discussion can focus on who the character's audience was, ways in which the character gained attention, and why the introduction to his remarks was effective.

10-17. Class Activity

This exercise is designed to allow students to connect examples of speech introductions to purposes and methods explained in the text. Make handouts for students of the following complete speech introductions. [This exercise can be adapted for speech conclusions.]

Introduction #1: Criminal Arrest: After being arrested and forced to stand in the pouring rain, Oscar Wilde said, "If this is how Queen Victoria treats her convicts she doesn't deserve to have any." Not many of you, or at least I hope not many of you at this seminar, are familiar with the process one follows in a criminal arrest. My objective today is to tell you the various steps in the pre-trial process, including the suspect's arrest, the initial court appearance, and the arraignment.

Introduction #2: Ozone Destruction:

Picture it — the year 2030. It's early in the morning and you go out to get the morning paper. When you return to the house, you notice a blemish on your hand from the sun. This is what life might be like in only a few years. Although it's an exaggeration to us now, it could be a sad reality in the near future.

This summer seems unusually hot and humid, the reason being that our planetary sunscreen — the ozone layer — is being destroyed. All of us in this room have heard about the ozone layer, but what is it really? Is it only helpful or can it be harmful as well? When did we first become concerned about the depletion of the ozone layer? Is it a real problem or just media hype? Can the damage be corrected? These are questions I will address today in my speech about an environmental phenomenon known as the ozone layer.

Introduction #3: Rain Forests:

"Its lands are high, there are in it very many sierras and very lofty mountains.... All are most beautiful, of a thousand shapes, all are accessible and filled with trees of a thousand kinds and tall, so that they seem to touch the sky. I am told that they never lose their foliage, and this I can believe, for I saw them as green and lovely as they are in Spain in May...."

This was a description of the rain forests of South America that Christopher Columbus told to the Queen and King of Spain. It is the first written account of a rain forest, but sadly this description no longer applies today, as the rain forests are rapidly vanishing from our planet. When I listened to classmates' speeches this week, I realized that many of us hold an enormous amount of concern about our environment and our planet's problems. The plight of the rain forest is surely one of the most important facing us today, because it affects everyone.

Students should analyze the effectiveness of each introduction by addressing these questions:

1. What types or methods of introduction did each speaker use?

2. Were all the purposes of introductions achieved in each example?

3. Identify the central idea and preview statement in each introduction.

4. Was each introduction effective? Why or why not?

5. What improvements should be made, if any?

In example #1, the methods include a quotation, references to the occasion and topic, and a preview statement. In example #2, the methods include a brief hypothetical illustration, a reference to the topic, rhetorical questions, and a preview statement. In example #3, the methods include a quotation, and references to the topic, to preceding speeches, and to recent events.

10-18. Teaching Strategy

Ask students to attend a public speech of their choice at school or within the community, and take notes, paying particular attention to the introduction and its effect on the audience. Have students make 3-5 minute presentations of their critiques. This is a good time to briefly review the listening skills presented in chapter four.

10-19. Writing Suggestion

Ask students to write introductions for the following speech topics. In a subsequent class meeting, students can discuss the effectiveness of each introduction:

- learning a second language
- animal testing for medical and cosmetic purposes
- history lessons taught through feature film
- medical testing on death row inmates
- performance art
- the success of the Fox television network
- the impact of e-mail on corporate communication

While emphasizing that the topic of a speech should always be clearly stated in the introduction, warn students to avoid beginning their speech with the trite, "Today, I'd like to talk to you about..." or "The topic of my speech is...." These overused openings lack the curiosity-provoking dimension requisite for effective introductions.

10-20. Teaching Strategy

Lead a discussion about pitfalls to avoid when planning an illustration for an introduction. Some illustration pitfalls are:

- Too lengthy. The audience will find a long story tedious. Get to the point quickly.
- Too involved. Too many details and characters can cause listener confusion.
- Too emotional. Tugging on the heartstrings is fine, but gut-wrenching emotion may make an audience uncomfortable.
- Too vague. Absence of concrete details leaves the audience unaffected. Be specific with people, places, and events. Let the audience know whether the illustration is real or hypothetical.
- Too tangential. Tie the illustration to the topic of the speech. Don't use an illustration or humorous anecdote merely for the purpose of loosening up the audience.

10-21. **Class Activity**

Divide into groups. Assign each team a statistic to criticize. Here are some of the author's favorites:

- Camel cigarette ad, circa 1940: "Three uut of four doctors smoke Camels"

- Tobacco Growers Association, circa 1960: "75% of studies show no connection between smoking cigarettes and health problems."

- U.S. Department of Labor press release: "The unemployment rate for the nation is at an all-time low."

10-22. **Teaching Strategy**

Demonstrate alternative ways to present statistics in an introduction. Instead of merely stating "One in five people will experience. . .," consider these suggestions:

- Use dramatic visual aids, such as vivid charts or graphs that make you see and feel a statistic, not just hear it.
- Change a statistic that says "30%" into "Three out of every ten persons. . ." (People mean more to audiences than abstract percentages).
- Use statistics that appear to involve this audience. "The Department of Labor says that one-half of us will change jobs four times during our careers."
- Actually "count off" audience members. For example, if a speaker walked in front or among an audience of thirty and asked nine people to stand up, then the statistic "three in ten" would become quite humanized and very real to the audience.

10-23. **Class Activity**

Students should practice building an introduction and conclusion from a quotation. Speakers often use quotations in introductions or conclusions. Below are several quotations from Carolyn Warner's book, *The Last Word*, published by Prentice Hall in 1992. You can copy the quotations onto slips of paper and have students select them for development into introductions or conclusions. This can be done in class or as an outside activity. Sample quotations include the following:

> "My grandfather once told me that there were two kinds of people: those who do the work and those who take the credit. He told me to try to be in the first group; there was much less competition."
>
> Indira Gandhi, Prime Minister of India.

> "Our struggle today is not to have a female Einstein get appointed as an assistant professor. It is for a woman schlemiel to get as quickly promoted as a male schlemiel."
>
> Bella Abzug, feminist, New York State congresswoman

"If you want a place in the sun, you have to put up with a few blisters."

Abigail Van Buren, columnist.

"When we escaped from Cuba, all we could carry was our education."

Alicia Coro, Cuban-American educator and government official.

"The only thing that makes life possible is permanent, intolerable uncertainty; not knowing what comes next."

Ursala K. LeGuin, science fiction writer.

"Every now and then, when you're on stage, you hear the best sound a player can hear. It's a sound you can't get in a movie or in television. It is the sound of a wonderful, deep silence that means you've hit them where they live."

Actress Shelley Winters.

10-24. Teaching Strategy

Speakers often overlook the necessity to "try out" their humor on others before the actual audience hears it. The military calls it a "dry run." Ask students what comedians call it when audiences for unknown reasons fail to respond (comedians say "I died out there!"). No one wants to create a "deafening silence" in their classroom. Try out your humor — on your dogs, on your cats, on other humans. "Try it before you buy it."

10-25. Teaching Strategy

Mention to students the importance of technique when asking rhetorical questions. Tell them to pause briefly after each question and reestablish eye contact with their listeners. This will further stimulate the audience's involvement with the speaker and message.

10-26. Teaching Strategy

Referring to previous speakers is almost always unplanned, a spontaneous adjustment made by speakers. When student speakers do it you will feel a rush of satisfaction with yourself and your chosen teaching strategies. To refer to previous speakers in impromptu fashion means your speakers are gaining strongly in self-confidence. Also, the speaker's image of self-confidence will be stronger in the minds of the audience. Everybody wins: the speaker, with confidence; you, the teacher, with personal reinforcement; and the audience, who always feel better when they perceive a speaker is self-confident.

C. *Effective Speech Conclusions Should Accomplish, In Order, Four Purposes*

10-27. Teaching Strategy

"To everything there is a purpose." Especially speech conclusions. Review the four purposes in the Outline, IV, A-D. Note that a good conclusion repeats the central idea for at least the third time (as a preview statement; as the main points are developed, and in the conclusion).

10-28. Class Activity

This exercise will help <u>students recognize introductory and concluding devices and to understand what makes these aspects of a speech successful.</u> Hand out written scenarios to students working in small groups. The scenarios should briefly describe an excerpt from a successful speaking event or a disastrous one. The key element differentiating good from bad scenarios should be the speaker's introduction or conclusion. Have groups discuss each scenario, label the devices the speaker used to begin or end the speech, and isolate what made the introduction or conclusion successful or disastrous. Group members should offer alternatives for the "disastrous" speeches. Sample scenarios include the following:

Libby was running late to a banquet in which she was the spotlight speaker. She didn't get time to eat with everyone and barely made it into her seat before she was introduced to the audience and expected to speak. When she began her speech, she offered an extensive apology for being late, attempting to explain in a humorous way how she fought traffic to get to the event. Because she was rattled, the story ran long and was disjointed. Finally, Libby made a rather abrupt shift into her first main point.

Miguel spoke to dorm residents about stress and depression leading to suicide. He gave current statistics on the rising rate of suicides among college-aged persons and offered useful suggestions for spotting depression in yourself and your friends, so as to prevent someone's suicide attempt or back away from the thought yourself. After his summary of points, Miguel told a moving story about his brother's suicide attempt — how he pulled him from the "clutches of death." His last line in the speech was: "Life <u>really is</u> precious, no matter how bad it seems in one moment, one day, one year. I know, and my brother knows, that the sun really does come up again in the morning, and it can be an incredible day." The chills and applause in the audience gave testament to the success of Miguel's presentation.

10-29. Class Activity

Call for three volunteers and meet them after class. Ask them to be "Stooges," cooperating with you in teaching a lesson to the class. Have two of the three find or recall a not-well-known short story. They will tell <u>almost</u> their entire story, stopping at a most dramatic point short of an ending. Start innocently applauding the incomplete tales. Students probably won't join you, and may look at you strangely. The third student should tell from science fiction the "World's Shortest Short Story" (here it is: "The last human in the world was seated at a table in the little cabin. There came a knock at the door.")

Be ready for some intense frustration and perhaps more than a little miffing. However, do share with students at the end that they will never again be puzzled by the word "closure!" Do remind them that closure is the most important function of good conclusions. Apologize (a little) for your "deception."

D. *Four Methods, or a Combination of Methods, Will Produce Effective Conclusions*

10-31. Teaching Strategy

Review the four methods of effective conclusions and the outcomes expected from those methods. Tell them why nine of ten people who try to get rich through direct sales fail to do so because they can't directly ask for a sale. A successful conclusion, however, must do just that — ask for the sale, the giving of the specific purpose response the speaker has been seeking. Good conclusions hand an audience the contract and the pen and make them want to sign on the dotted line.

10-32. Class Activity

Procure a student-written speech (from your files, a colleague's collection, or the textbook). Distribute copies to all students, minus the conclusion. Direct all students to write a one-minute conclusion to the speech. In the subsequent class, divide into groups. Instruct each group to decide upon a conclusion, one way or another. After conferences, each team is to send one member to deliver their conclusion. Let the class vote on a "winner." Seize the occasion to review the methods suggested by the textbook.

10-33. Class Activity

The purpose of this activity is to sharpen students' abilities to critique speeches, as well as to reinforce textbook information about introductions and conclusions. Using both famous and ordinary sample speeches on videotape, ask students to listen and take note of speakers' introductions and conclusions. (The best way to do this activity is to use a series of speech introductions and conclusions, in an edited fashion, but that may not be possible due to equipment and time constraints.) Students should write which type of device each speaker used to begin and end her or his speech. Discuss with students their responses, their assessments of the effectiveness of introductions and conclusions, and why some speakers were better than others.

10-34. Teaching Strategy

Ask students to think about "pitfalls" in the use of illustrations. In a subsequent class ask for their thoughts about the pitfalls. Press them gently for their own thinking, and then feed in slowly your own ideas:

- Being too lengthy
- Getting too involved
- Becoming too emotional (a little bit never hurt anybody)
- Ending up vague
- Taking tangents; going in the ditch

10-35. Teaching Strategy

Advise students how to get maximum gain from their use of rhetorical questions. Suggest pauses and reiterate the importance of at least attempting eye contact after such a question. The nonverbal reinforcement will, of course, also maximize the audience involvement with the speaker, question, and message.

10-36. Class Activity

Ask for six volunteers to "emote" this Chapter Outline as a review. Direct them to divide the outline sentence by sentence (one student could do this by marking names consecutively by sentences, and giving you the marked script to copy for all six and yourself). During an appropriate subsequent class, stage the "Up Front Readers Theatre," so to speak. Be prepared to fill in for absentees. Give strong thanks to the volunteers and praise excellent work.

10-37. Class Activity

Ask students to design concluding inspirational appeals or challenges for speeches on the following topics; have them present conclusions in a subsequent class.

- Volunteering to Answer Phones at a Suicide Hot Line
- Donating Blood
- The Peace Corps
- Showing Your Patriotism
- Habitat for Humanity
- Save the Rain Forests Campaigns
- Volunteering at the Local Women's Shelter

10-38. Teaching Strategy

Ask students to give reasons why the introduction and conclusion to a speech are such critical components of the entire message. In what ways are first and last impressions crucial to a speaker's credibility? Brainstorm for some well known beginnings and endings and discuss why they are so memorable. Examples could include the opening of Charles Dickens' *A Tale of Two Cities;* the ending of Martin Luther King, Jr.'s "I Have a Dream" speech ("Free at last..."); the opening of two *Star Trek* television episodes (your author is a *Star Trek* devotee); and the introduction and conclusion to Jonathon Edward's "Sinners in the Hands of an Angry God."

10-39. Class Activity

Divide students into groups. Assign all an intensive review of the entire chapter. In a subsequent class, crank up a quiz game between two groups. Use the Chapter Outline as a source of content questions. Ask five questions and get five answers if you can. The "losing" team must sit and be replaced by a "Challenger" group. Continue until review of chapter is complete. Tell the last winning tean they win the grand prize. When they ask what it is, tell them you don't know. When they ask you where it is, tell them you don't know. When they ask you why you don't know, tell them you don't know!

ONLINE TEACHING PLAN

Preview activity: Using appropriate material in the introduction and conclusion of a speech involves preparation, and a real assessment of students' skills and abilities as a speaker. Review the online article entitled, *Rule of Three Multiplies Speech Humor,* found at:
http://austin.bizjournals.com/austin/stories/1999/11/01/smallb3.html

This article helps introduce the idea that humor in speeches should be appropriate. It gives students information about types of humor to use, when to use humor based on the audience, and how to place humor in the context of a speech.

Teaching activity: Students often make the mistake of focusing only on how they will begin their speech without completely considering exactly how they will conclude their speech. Stress the importance of a well-planned conclusion by asking students to create concluding statements for speeches on a list of topics. Review the website on famous quotations at http://www.tpub.com/Quotes/. Students should select three quotations from this database and write three possible conclusions for speeches using these quotes. Students should submit the quotes along with their fictitious speech conclusions.

Review activity: Students should anonymously submit their proposed introduction and conclusion for an upcoming speech to the instructor. Send each proposed intro and conclusion to another student to solicit constructive feedback and suggestions. Once all the intros and conclusions have been sent back to the instructor, forward each student his or her own intro and conclusion, along with the suggestions from their classmate. Be sure to read the critique before sending it on to the student to make sure it is constructive and accurate.

CHAPTER ELEVEN: Outlining and Editing Your Speech

Chapter-at-a-Glance

Detailed Outline	Instructor Resources	Supplements	Professor Notes
Developing a Preparation Outline (p. 234) • Write in complete sentences • Use standard outline form and numbering • Use subdivisions • Indent properly • Add blueprint, key signposts, introduction, conclusion	**Learning Objective #1:** Describe the purposes of the preparation outline and the delivery outline **Learning Objective #2:** Identify and explain guidelines for developing these outlines **Annotated Chapter Outline (ACO):** 11-1, 11-2	**Types of outlines:** Allyn and Bacon Transparency #T-34 **Example of a preparation outline:** Allyn and Bacon Transparency #T-35	
Sample Preparation Outline (p. 238) **Editing your speech** (p. 240) • Review your specific purpose • Consider your audience • Simply say it	**Learning Objective #3:** Demonstrate standard outline form **ACO:** 11-3 through 11-5	**Speech Preparation Workbook** pp. 49-57 **Digital Media Archive for Communication (DMAC)** T11I11, T11I12, T11I13, T11I14	
Developing a Delivery Outline (p. 242) • Make outline brief • Include introduction and conclusion • Include supporting material and signposts • Do not include purpose statement in outline • Use standard outline form	**Learning Objective #4:** Prepare the preparation outline and the delivery outline **ACO:** 11-6 through 11-8 **ACO** 11-9 through 11-17 **Learning Objective #5** Edit a speech	**Example of a Speaker Outline:** Allyn and Bacon Transparency #T-36	
Sample Delivery Outline and Speaking Notes (p.244) • Develop from delivery outline • Include delivery cues and reminders • Speaking Notes	**Learning Objective #6** Deliver a speech from speaking notes **ACO** 11-18, 11-19	DMAC T11I15	

LEARNING OBJECTIVES

1.   Students will be able to describe the purposes of a preparation outline and a delivery outline.

2.   Students will be able to identify and explain guidelines for preparing a preparation outline and a delivery outline.

3.   Students will be able to demonstrate standard outline form.

4.   Students will be able to prepare a preparation outline and a delivery outline for a speech being worked on.

5.   Students will be able to edit a speech.

6.   Students will be able to deliver a speech from speaking notes.

CHAPTER OUTLINE

I.   The first stage is developing a preparation outline.

   A.   Most speakers develop a preparation outline that includes all major features.

   1. A preparation outline includes main ideas, subpoints, and supporting material.

   2. A preparation outline may also include specific purpose, introduction, blueprint, conclusion, and signposts.

   B.   Preparation outlines may begin with "mapping," (aka "clustering") technique.

   C.   Final goal of a preparation outline is to produce a plan that allows you to judge the unity and coherence of your speech, to see how well the parts fit together.

   D.   Three suggestions will produce an acceptable preparation outline.

   1. Write your preparation outline in complete sentences, like those you will use when delivering your speech.

   2. Use standard outline form.

   a. Use standard outline numbering.

   b. Use at least two subdivisions, if any, for each point.

   c. Indent main ideas, points, subpoints, and supporting materials properly.

      d. Write and label your specific purpose at the top of your preparation outline.

      e. Add the blueprint, key signposts, and an introduction and conclusion to your outline.

      f. Examine and follow the sample preparation outline on textbook pages 244-245.

  3. Use completed preparation outline to analyze and possibly revise speech, guided by five analysis questions.

      a. Does the speech as outlined fulfill the purpose you have specified?

      b. Are the main ideas logical extensions (natural divisions, reasons, or steps) of the central idea?

      c. Do the signposts enhance the comfortable flow of each idea into the next?

      d. Does each subpoint provide support for the points under which it falls?

      e. Is your outline form correct?

II.   Speaker's Homepage is found in the textbook, page 247, with helpful exercises for outlining.

III.   The second stage is developing a delivery outline.

    A.   A delivery outline is to be accomplished after completion of preparation outline and preliminary rehearsals.

    B.   Follow six steps to a good delivery outline.

     1. Make the outline as brief as possible, and write in single words or short phrases rather than complete sentences.

     2. Include the introduction and conclusion in much shortened form.

     3. Include supporting material and signposts.

     4. Do not include your purpose statement in your delivery outline.

     5. Use standard outline form so that you can easily find the exact point or piece of supporting material you are seeking when you look down at your notes.

     6. Examine and follow the sample delivery outline found in textbook, pages 248-249.

IV.   The final stage is developing speaker notes.

     A.   Speakers who have difficulty in handling the outline in paper form transfer delivery outlines to note cards.

     B.   Alternatives to delivery outlines include "maps," or a combination of words, pictures, and symbols.

     C.   A final addition to speaker notes is delivery cues and reminders, such as "Louder" (here), "Pause," or "Move in front of the podium."

REVIEW GUIDE

11-1.   What is the purpose of a preparation outline?

11-2.   List the contents (features) of a preparation outline.

11-3.   What are two special techniques for beginning preparation outlines?

11-4.   What is the final goal of a preparation outline?

11-5.   List three suggestions for producing an acceptable preparation outline.

11-6.   What is the purpose of a delivery outline?

11-7.   List and discuss six steps to producing a good delivery outline.

11-8.   What is the relationship between speaker notes and preparation and delivery outlines?

11-9.   What are two alternatives to outlines that may translate into workable speaker notes?

11-10. Why should delivery cues (and reminders) appear in speaker notes?

ANNOTATED CHAPTER OUTLINE

A. *In Speechmaking Outlining a Preparation Outline is a Desirable First Step*

11-1. Teaching Strategy

Ask your students "What would we look like if we had no skeleton?" After the tittering and laughing has died away, gently push students for answers. Answers will come slowly, but finally be quite imaginative. Ask students if they have seen Steve McQueen's first film starring role. At least one student will have seen the film, *The Blob*. Describe the blob as best you can, and then apply its description to a speech without an outline. Characterize outlines as the skeletons of speeches, not as pretty as the speech (body) itself, but absolutely essential (actually, medical students, artists, and your author consider human skeletons to be functionally and aesthetically beautiful). Make your point with prepared projections, side by side, of a full-sentence outline segment and the speech paragraphs that flow from the outline segments. Mention the Boy Scout motto, "Be prepared," then apply the motto to research, planning, underlining, and preparing to deliver a speech. Appeal to students' pride in self-accomplishment. Tell them that all effective and admired writers and speakers proceed from outlining, even if their outlining skills are so well-developed the process is mostly mental. Discuss with students the advantages of using the outline formats described in the chapter, as opposed to writing a word-for-word speech manuscript. Although students often believe that manuscripted speeches provide a necessary crutch, outlines are preferable. Outlines are considerably less time-consuming to formulate and allow for greater review of specific speech elements. Speaking notes are much more easily abstracted from an outline than from a manuscript.

11-2. Teaching Strategy

Ask students to list ways that outlining has helped them with other projects. Typical responses might include: summarizing chapters in a textbook; writing a research paper, reviewing for a major exam, preparing directions to a location. Point out to students that outlines are, down deep, LISTS. Most people make lists all the time: shopping lists, party invitation lists, lists of chores for the day. Lists (outlines) are handy organizing devices, especially for speechmaking. Emphasize to students that outlines allow a speaker to accomplish many tasks, compared with limitations of a word-for-word manuscript. Some advantages are: (1) speakers can make alterations more easily than in a manuscript; (2) outlines clearly show whether all main ideas have been equally supported; and (3) speakers can easily check whether they have a variety of supporting material.

11-3. Teaching Strategy
Review and redefinition of the major parts of a speech (and speech outline) are probably due: (also consider review of "Blueprint" and "Signposts")
- General Purpose
- Specific Purpose
- Central Idea
- Main Points
- Subpoints
- Subsubpoints
- Final Summary

11-4. **Teaching Strategy**

Review the format of "standard outlines." Killing at least two birds with one stone, use the sample "Preparation Outline" on textbook pages 242-244 as your visual aid. Patiently, perhaps exasperatingly so from students' viewpoint, explain the scheme: Roman Numeral to Capital Letter to Arabic Numeral to Lower Case Letter, and, if need be, to (1) and little i. If you have good samples of previous students' outlines, this is a good place to project them as further examples of correct outlining. This author has examples where errors occurred. With permission of the student authors who erred, the author conducts a critical analysis of errors and corrections to the flawed outlines. Include in the outline some of the most common mistakes the text discusses, e.g., errors in parallelism, indentation, subdivision, capitalization, and missing purpose statements, central ideas, or key transitions. Ask students to correct the mistakes in the outline and discuss their corrections. Correcting errors is an effective activity to do for bibliographies, as well, if you require students to turn in a written bibliography (in an assigned format) along with their outlines. A complete, detailed discussion of the two basic types of outlines is often useful for students. Your students have probably outlined before, but may not be aware of the finer points of proper outline form. Some students will not have drafted outlines for speech-preparing and speechmaking purposes. Discuss with the class the purposes of the preparation and delivery outlines, differentiating aspects, and basics of outline form.

11-5. **Teaching Strategy**

Ask students to stand. Ask them to repeat the following phrase after you: "I, _____ _____, do solemnly acknowledge that the OUTLINE IS THE ONLY WAY TO ADEQUATELY TEST THE LOGIC OF MY SPEECHMAKING PLANNING, and I pledge never again to prepare a written report or a public speech without proper outlining."

B. *A Natural and Normal Development from a Preparation Outline is the Delivery Outline*

11-6. **Teaching Strategy**

Using visual materials from textbook page 239, demonstrate the Mapping technique of arranging ideas.

11-7. **Teaching Strategy**

Share with students this central idea: "Our college has three major advantages over other institutions: small class size, superior instructors, and lots of green grass." By way of review ask students the organizational pattern of the central idea. After a few false starts some will give a correct answer, topical. Casually ask students to evaluate the statement of central idea. A student will quickly discover a problem. The first two topics derived from the central idea are logically connected, but the two are not logically connected to the third element, lots of green grass. You might consider repeating the exercise with samples from the other four organizational patterns shown below (Chapter 9).

- "Instructor careers pass through three stages; Early, Middle, and Retarded." (chronological)
- "Our campus is divided into three areas: North, South, and Technological." (spatial)
- "Unwanted pregnancies are caused by passion, unprotected sex, and abstinence." (cause–effect)
- "Our polluted drinking water can only be cleansed by reducing water use." (problem–solution)

Remind students the final goal of a preparation outline (indeed, any form of outline) is to allow you to judge the logic, unity, and coherence of the planned speech — to see how well the parts fit together.

11-8. **Teaching Strategy**

A major, major point in this chapter is <u>logical connection of parts</u> (of the speech outline and speech). Your students will not have had a formal course in argumentation and debate, i.e., they have yet to be trained in formal logic. Although equipped with various skill levels in recognizing logical faults, they may disappoint you in identifying logical "departures." If at all humanly possible videotape an appropriate segment of the older "Burns and Allen Show." Gracie Burns' comic shtick was the "non sequitur" (it does not follow; one thing does not follow another). Nobody did it better than Gracie, and nobody did the bemused and helpless listener as could George. Your students will quickly grasp the logical problem, which may assist them in spotting other types of logical problems.

11-9. **Class Activity**

Assign students to intensely read Dr. Martin Luther King's "I Have a Dream" speech (Appendix D, textbook). Direct each student to "rough out" a full sentence outline of that speech. In a subsequent class, divide students into groups to compare their outlines. Then project your own outline and allow students to compare it with their own. Seize the opportunity to briefly detail the historical importance of this speech.

11-10. **Class Activity**

In preparation for an upcoming round of speeches, ask students to bring to class a written statement of a potential speech topic. For that topic students are also to bring statements of at least three main points in the suggested topic and supporting materials they have gathered. Pair students and swap papers. Have each student attempt the "mapping" technique with their unfamiliar material. Encourage students to make suggestions to each other about organizational choices.

11-11. **Class Activity**

Assign students a very <u>narrow</u> topic:
- Benefits of having pets, or
- Relaxing techniques, or
- How to sew on a button, or
- My least favorite television commercial, or
- Why CD's are superior to albums or tapes

Each student is to prepare and bring to a subsequent class both types of outline: preparation and delivery. In pairs, direct them to compare both their outlines. Collect the outlines; choose "winners" and prepare projections for a later class.

11-12. **Class Activity**

Photocopy the textbook sample preparation outline and the sample delivery outline. Remove the identifying labels at the top of the samples. Prepare projections. Without comment other than, "This is outline sample one," and "This is outline sample two," project the outlines. Then, drop the bomb. Ask students which type (preparation or delivery) was sample #1, and which type was sample #2? After the guessing game (just joking; you have very sharp, well-read, always-prepared students!) direct students to turn to the textbook pages where both outlines are discussed. Turning to textbook pages as needed, lead a discussion on how to tell the difference between the two.

11-13. **Teaching Strategy**

You might wish to review the topic of "Parallelism." The concept means using similar sentence structure within each outline category. If that definition confuses them, show this example:
1. First main point: "Athletes are devoted to this school."
2. Second main point: "Athletes are loyal to this school."
3. Third main point: "Athletes are generous to this school."

Note the parallelism created by the continuous use of "athletes" and "school," as well as the parallelism of athlete feelings and actions. Share with students that parallelism creates a "rhythm" of words that makes them easier to follow and also creates "redundancy," does it not? (Chapter 4)

11-14. **Class Activity**

Divide students into groups. Tell them they're going to produce a communal full-sentence outline on the topic, "Why Some College Students Drink to Excess." In addition to a valuable outlining training exercise, you say, they will also demonstrate who the smartest groups are around here. Each group must perform a stated task, placing the result appropriately on the chalkboard. Below are the group tasks in order.

Group One:	State General Purpose
Group Two:	State Specific Purpose
Group Three:	Use *illustration* in the introduction
Group Four:	Use *startling facts and statistics* in the introduction
Group Five:	Use *humor* in the introduction
Group Six:	State a three-point central idea(prepare to reuse groups)
Group Seven:	State the first main point (or next group)
Next Group:	State the first subpoint
Next Group:	State the second subpoint (and so on, until the "Body" is complete)
Next Group:	Write stupendous, humongous transition to final summary (Chapter 9)
Next Group:	State final summary
Last Group:	Make inspirational appeal

Lead class in a critical analysis of the finished project.

11-15. **Teaching Strategy**

Discuss with students why proper indentation is important in outline mechanics. Students may think you are nit-picking about form, when, actually, indentation is a helpful visual cue for a speaker. <u>Indentation indicates the importance of a point.</u> The farther toward the right margin, the less essential the idea. If a speech is running long, cut it by cutting outline items in reverse order of indentation. For example, II, A, 1, a. — speaker would cut the "a." statement first and the "1." statement next.

C. *Preparation and Delivery Outlines Yield the final Step: Speaker's Notes*

11-16. **Teaching Strategy**

Note cards or index cards can be purchased loose, or in a spiral-bound configuration. Students may prefer spiral-bound because if cards are dropped while speaking, they are still in order. Warn students who use loose, separate materials to number their pages or cards.

11-17. **Teaching Strategy**

Talk to students about the kinds of notes they plan to use for speeches. Ask them to reveal why they prefer note cards to sheets of paper. They may have funny stories about when they or another speaker had a fiasco with speaking notes. Remind students that they may alter their approach to speaking notes at any time in the course, especially if they find that one method doesn't work smoothly for them.

11-18. **Class Activity**

The purpose is to enhance students' listening, note-taking, and outlining skills. Show a videotaped speech to students, asking them to take notes on main points, subpoints, and supporting materials. The speech will go by quickly, so instruct students to write in phrases and key words to get as much information as they can. Independently or in small groups, have students transform their notes into delivery outlines. Working like this, in the reverse, from actual presentation to outlining stage will reinforce organization and outlining skills in students, and help them understand the transference from notes to live performance.

11-19. **Class Activity**

<u>This activity will help students preview or review the chapter information in a high-involvement instructor lecture.</u> A chapter on outlining is not usually one that elicits enthusiasm from students. But it is crucial information, so you may want to use a fun, involving way to teach outlining, like the "Candy Lecture." Before this lecture, buy candy bars and packs of gum, the names of which you will insert into the lecture. Keep items hidden so that students will be surprised. Emphasize the name of the candy or gum while you toss it to a class member and don't say the words in brackets in the script. Explain that students are welcome to enjoy the candy or gum while you speak.

SCRIPT FOR "CANDY LECTURE"

Today I plan to introduce Chapter 11 in a slightly different way. We've talked some about manuscript speaking; well today I am using a manuscript for my lecture. I'll be interested to know your reaction to this method. Have you all read Chapter 11? I understand that some of you might feel like a SLO POKE when it comes to the ideas in this chapter. No need to go to [REESE'S] PIECES over this material. Outlining is important and cannot be as exciting as HOT TAMALES! Chapter 11 is about the map to your speech, the outline. I know some of you think outlines are as out-of-date as [GUMMIES] DINOSAURS. But if you want to join the BIG LEAGUE [GUM] of public speakers, you'll need to prepare outlines.

Don't put off learning this information because it will help you NOW AND LATER. An outline allows you, the speaker, to accomplish many tasks that the manuscript of a speech does not. An outline will allow you to make minor and major alterations more easily than a manuscript (even if you're editing on a computer, all NESTLE[D] in your room). Although sometimes a speaker needs a manuscript — such as a political leader who must be really careful with word choices. But those manuscripts typically begin as outlines. An outline enables a speaker to easily check on major point development to see that all major ideas have been supported equally. An outline also enables you to quickly check whether a variety of supporting material has been incorporated as opposed to dependence on only one type. Plus, as speaking notes, you may use an outline style to adapt well to the audience. These benefits are evident in the two types of outlines speakers use. Both types can be a real BOUNTY for effective public speaking.

The first type discussed in your textbook is the preparation outline. This outline helps you plan the content of the speech, so you'll want to write it in full sentences so that your ideas are complete. Plus, use the language style you will eventually use in your speech. Don't SOUR[S] your planning! Use correct outline form, with standard numbering, at least two subdivisions per point, parallel structure, and proper indentation, punctuation, and capitalization. You'll want to label your specific purpose statement and central idea. Then you can add transitions, previews, summaries, introduction, and conclusion. Preparation outlines are essential to the best public speakers. Did I hear some CHUCKLES? Hey, this is serious stuff!

The other type of outline is called the delivery outline, which you may decide to use as speaking notes. This outline is not a WHOPPER[S]. Make your delivery outline as brief as possible, using only words and phrases. You'll need a shortened introduction and conclusion for your speaking notes. The delivery outline should include supporting materials and signposts. You only need your specific purpose or central idea if it is part of your introduction or conclusion. You can make GOOD AND PLENTY of sense by using standard outline form. Plus, the relationships will be clear and you won't feel like a NUT[RAGEOUS]. You may want to put the delivery outline on note cards or place the delivery outline on an attractive clipboard or in a folder you will use when giving the speech. You can RAZZLE[S] and dazzle the audience if you have easy-to-read notes — with any needed delivery reminders to yourself — prepared with an eye toward professionalism.

The PAYDAY and [ALMOND] JOY comes after using a preparation outline and a delivery outline to make your speech the most effective possible. Your actual delivery can be CAREFREE [GUM] when you know you have outlined effectively, when you know that your audience views you as a MR. GOODBAR, not as a BABY RUTH. This proven method of preparation gives you an EXTRA [GUM] edge over less-prepared speakers. Think, for example, of how useful that advantage can be in an employment situation. And, when you see the results of your efforts, you'll realize that outlines are LIFE SAVERS! Did I hear some SNICKERS?

ONLINE TEACHING PLAN

Preview activity: Go to the Virtual Presentation Assistant website at:
http://www.hamilton.edu/academics/rhetoric/intro_conclusion.pdf
This site has valuable information on how to construct a good speech, how to use introductions and conclusions. Encourage students to print it out and add it to their materials for preparing their next speech.

Teaching activity: Send students an e-mail containing a scrambled outline for a hypothetical speech. Tell them to unscramble the speech and send it back to you. You may choose to post responses on a class bulletin board to highlight the various ways students decoded the information. Include notes as to why the alternate organizational patterns are correct or incorrect.

Review activity: Students should use the sample delivery outline from the text to create a full sentence outline for submission to the instructor. This activity may be used in conjunction with an actual outline due as part of a speech assignment.

CHAPTER TWELVE: Using Words Well: Speaker Language and Style

Chapter-at-a-Glance

Detailed Outline	Instructor Resources	Supplements	Professor Notes
Oral versus Written Language Style (p. 255) • Oral more personal • Oral less formal • Oral more repetitious	**Learning Objective #1:** Describe differences between oral and written language **Annotated Chapter Outline (ACO):** 12-1, 12-5 through 12-7	**Style:** Allyn and Bacon Transparency #T-54	
Using Words Effectively (p. 256) • Concrete words • Specific words • Simple words • Correct words	**Learning Objective #2** List and explain ways of using words effectively **ACO:** 12-2, through 12-4, 12-8 **ACO:** 12-9 through 12-27	**Clarity:** Allyn and Bacon Transparency #T-55 **Rhythm:** Allyn and Bacon Transparency #T-56	
Adapting to diverse listeners (p. 259) • Understandable language • Appropriate language • Unbiased language	**Learning Objective #3:** Explain how to adapt style to diverse listeners **Learning Objective #4:** List and define common figures of speech	**Vivid language:** Allyn and Bacon Transparency #T-57	
Crafting Memorable Word Structures (p. 261) • Figurative images • Drama • Cadence	**Learning Objective # 5:** List techniques for creating drama and cadence **ACO:** 12-28 through 12-33	**Digital Media Archive for Communication** (DMAC) T14I04	
Speaker's Homepage (p. 265) **Tips for Using Language Effectively** (p. 267)	**Learning Objective #6:** Offer tips for using language effectively in public speeches **ACO** 12-34 through 12-36	**Find a Rhyming Word:** http://www.cs.cmu.edu/~dougb/rhyme.html	

LEARNING OBJECTIVES

1. Students will be able to describe three differences between oral and written language styles.

2. Students will be able to list and explain four ways to use words effectively.

3. Students will be able to adapt their language style to diverse listeners.

4. Students will be able to list and define three common types of figures of speech.

5. Students will be able to list and explain seven techniques for creating drama and cadence.

6. Students will be able to offer tips for using language effectively in public speeches.

CHAPTER OUTLINE

I. Oral language style differs in three major ways from written language style.

    A. Oral style is more *personal,* since speaker and audience can interact, sharing contact.

    B. Oral style is *less formal*, characterized by shorter words and phrases, and less complex sentence structures.

    C. Oral style is *more repetitive*, since, unlike reading, speakers must state, restate, provide examples, and summarize.

II. Speakers are challenged to use words effectively, specifically by use of four language techniques.

    A. Use specific rather than general words (e.g., "ball python" instead of "snake").

    B. Use *concrete* rather than abstract words (e.g., "fire and ashes" instead of "aftermath").

    C. Use *simple* words.

        1. The best language is often the simplest language.

        2. George Orwell lists words rules for utilizing simple words.

    D. Use words *correctly.*

        1. A public speech is not the time to demonstrate your lack of familiarity with English vocabulary and grammar.

        2. Be constantly aware that meaning in language has two dimensions: denotative and connotative; choose words carefully, especially with diverse audiences.

III.   Effective speakers adapt their language to diverse listeners.

    A.   Use language that your audience can understand.

        1.   Use the specific variety of English that fits your audience best.

        2.   If the audience is diverse, use standard U.S. English.

    B.   Use appropriate and unbiased language (avoid racist and sexist terms).

IV.   Effective speakers craft memorable word structures.

    A.   Memorable language creates *figurative images*, by means of two figures of speech.

        1.   <u>Metaphors and similes</u> create vivid comparisons.

            a.   <u>Metaphors</u> imply comparison, as in Jaime Escalante's "Education is the vaccine for violence."

            b.   <u>Similes</u> are more overt comparisons, as in Pope John Paul III's description of the Bosnian war as ". . .the shipwreck of the whole of Europe."

        2.   <u>Personification</u> is the attribution of human qualities to inanimate things or ideas (Franklin D. Roosevelt: "Nature still offers her bounty and human efforts have multiplied it. Plenty is at our doorstep.")

    B.   Memorable language creates *drama,* using, among others, four techniques.

        1.   Use a <u>short sentence</u> to express a vitally important thought. (Lincoln: "And the war came.")

        2.   Use deliberate <u>omission</u>, leaving out a word or phrase the audience expects to see (World War II: "Sighted sub — sank same").

        3.   Reverse normal word order, a technique called <u>inversion</u> (Russian president Boris Yeltsin, at the reintombment of Czar Nicholas II: "Guilty are those who committed this heinous crime").

        4.   At times, keep listeners guessing, called <u>suspension</u> ("What manner of men are these?").

    C.   Memorable language occasionally creates *cadence* through use of four language techniques.

        1.   Parallelism occurs when two or more clauses in close proximity have the same grammatical pattern.

        2.   In language style <u>antithesis</u> is a sentence having a parallel structure, but with two parts contrasting each other.

        a.   Franklin Roosevelt: "Our true destiny is not be ministered unto, but to minister to ourselves and to our fellow men."

        b.   John F. Kennedy: "Ask not what your country can do for you; ask what you can do for your country."

   3.   Repetition of a key word or phrase gives rhythm, power, and memorability to your message.

   4.   Alliteration is the repetition of a consonant sound (usually an initial consonant) several times in a phrase, clause, or sentence.

        a.   Franklin Delano Roosevelt, First Inaugural: "Discipline and Direction."

        b.   Winston Churchill, Address to the (U.S.) Congress: "virility, valor, and civic virtue."

V.   The Speaker's Homepage provides additional examples of memorable language style, including an observation that John F. Kennedy's "Ask not. . ." quotation uses all the stylistic devices of this textbook chapter.

VI.   Consider four tips for using memorable language effectively.

    A.   Do not overdo efforts to achieve vivid language.

    B.   Save use of stylistic devices for points where you really wish to score with an audience.

    C.   Short words are more forceful than long words (Sit! March! Stop!).

    D.   Recast too-long sentences as antitheses or suspensions.

REVIEW GUIDE

12-1.   In what three ways does oral language differ from written language?

12-2.   Illustrate these four language techniques: concrete words, specific words, simple words, and correct words.

12-3.   Illustrate metaphor and simile.

12-4.   Invent five personifications.

12-5.   Give an example of biased language and suggest ways of rephrasing it.

12-6.   From your own writing or speaking, recall the use of omission, inversion, and suspension.

12-7.   What are your favorite examples of cadence (parallelism, antithesis, repetition, and alliteration)?

12-8.   List and illustrate the textbook's four "Tips for Using Memorable Language Effectively."

12-9.   Why must oral style be more repetitious than written style?

12-10. Are abstract words (as opposed to concrete words) <u>always</u> out of line?

12-11. List any language "insults" you feel are still widespread.

ANNOTATED CHAPTER OUTLINE

A. *Oral and Written Language Styles have Significant Differences*

12-1. Teaching Strategy

Review the ways in which oral language style differs from written language style, using Outline, I, A-C as a guide.

12-2. Teaching Strategy

It doesn't get any better than this. Ask your students, "How can you tell when a public speaker is dead?" This author cannot predict for you exactly how students will respond, but it's going to be fun! What you are doing, of course, is introducing the concept of <u>vividness</u> in a speaker's style and use of language. Your point is going to be that a speaker who does not achieve memorable word structure might as well be "dead" (since his/her language already is). Remember the comedian who "died out there?" So it may be with speakers who neither know nor care about memorable style created by effective language.

12-3. Background Information

The videotape, "Great Moments from Great Speeches" provides thirty 3 minute speech clips from great speeches spanning sixty years of history. This tape is an excellent tool to supplement teaching of public speaking. It can also be effectively used for the strategy described in annotation 12.1. The total running time of the tape is 108 minutes; you can order it from The Educational Video Group, 291 Southwind Way, Greenwood, IN 46142.

12-4. Related Reading

A trend in public speaking courses is to show students examples of "great speeches," primarily made by men. For an excellent overview of female public speakers in U.S. history, see Kohrs Campbell, K. (1993). (Ed.). <u>Women public speakers in the United States, 1800-1925: A biocritical source.</u> Westport, CT: Greenwood.

12-5. **Teaching Strategy**

<u>This strategy reinforces text information on the differences between oral and written style, and helps students identify examples of effective language use by public speakers.</u> Try to locate a transcript and videotape of one of Ronald Reagan's speeches, as he was a master at using language to create a desired effect. Bill Clinton's inaugural address in 1993 also employed interesting uses of language. Or, you could ask students to compare the language usage of female and male speakers. Have students read the manuscript first, noting interesting or especially effective language. View the videotape, asking students to note any differences in the effects of language in a script and in an actual performance.

12-6. **Class Activity**

Ask four student volunteers to prepare written step-by-step directions from a location on campus to a well-known city landmark (city building, hospital, nightclub). When completed, collect them from students and convert them into projections. In a subsequent class ask four other volunteers to devise oral directions for the same trip. Give them a few minutes and then ask them to step outside. Arrange to show the projections behind students who will speak, where those students will not see the projections. Bring in the speakers one at a time to give their spiels. Audience will see the written and hear the oral directions. Discuss afterwards with students the differences they perceived in the oral and written directions.

12-7. **Background Information**

In the movie *Renaissance Man*, Danny DeVito is a teacher of less-than-brilliant military recruits. One session that evokes his students' interest pertains to uses of language, including metaphor, simile, and oxymoron. Show this excerpt as an introductory device for the use of language in speeches.

B. *By Use of Five Language Techniques Words May be Used More Effectively*

12-8. **Teaching Strategy**

Review for students Outline, II, A-E, the five language techniques. Prepare useful examples for the presentation.

12-9. **Class Activity**

Write noun sequences on chalkboard and ask students to arrange sequences from "Most Abstract" to "Least Abstract." Invite students to the chalkboard for the task. Scramble the sequences incorrectly.

- Athletic contests, football games, the playoffs, the Superbowl
- Transportation; vehicle, automobile, luxury car, Cadillac
- Reading material, book, novel, *Lonesome Dove*
- Celebrity, entertainer, comedian, Whoopi Goldberg

12-10. Teaching Strategy

Take up the subject of "concrete" versus "abstract" words. Share the general principle that concrete words are normally the "weapon of choice," but that at times abstract words simply must be employed. For example, in a speech on U.S. military interventions a speaker might wish to argue excessive cost. The speaker could use the word "overspending." A more powerful word would be more abstract: profligate. Abstraction, by nature, means more inclusive, wider in connotations. In that sense, abstract words are often more efficient, covering more ground in a single bound.

12-11. Teaching Strategy

When you discuss language usage in speeches, ask students to explain how they decide if a course lecturer's language is appropriate and effective. Does the teacher speak like a human being or like a book? Is her or his language easily understood, or would an encyclopedia be clearer? Responses will vary, but you hope that some students will mention aspects related to the language factors of concreteness, simplicity, vividness, correctness, and lack of bias. Getting students to talk about the language of someone local and familiar provides a smooth transition to talking about language in speeches.

12-12. Teaching Strategy

If you want to extend the textbook's discussion of unbiased language, strategically plan your approach to that discussion. Every time this author explores racial or ethnic slurs, sexist language, homophobic terminology, or hate speech with his students, he knows to be prepared for emotional reactions and resistance to change. He keeps hoping for better ways of teaching this subject to students, but does not back away. The mistakes of speakers who use biased language are long-lasting. Good luck. There is more to teaching than a paycheck and summer travel.

12-13. Teaching Strategy

Engage students in a discussion of politically correct language. Provide a list of politically correct terms, ranging from serious (African American, instead of Black) to humorous (follicularly challenged instead of bald, and vertically challenged instead of short). Which of the terms do students readily use, not realizing they are politically correct or incorrect? Which terms can students not imagine themselves using? Why? Discuss the goals of politically correct language, as well as the "backlash" against it. Why are people reluctant to change, to make their language more sensitive to diversity? Provide a handout for students that contains examples of biased, insensitive, and politically incorrect language. Ask students to isolate the problems and provide alternative language. Examples could include:
- "If a student wants a good grade he must study hard." (change to "she or he")
- "The black guy in my history class asked an interesting question today." (change to "This guy")
- "My dad has this great lady lawyer working on his malpractice suit." (change to "great lawyer")
- "Chang is very proud of being Oriental." (change to "being an Asian American")

12-14. **Related Reading**

For an excellent resource on unbiased language, see Maggio, R. (1988). *The Nonsexist Word Finder: A Dictionary of Gender-Free Usage.* (Boston: Beacon Press).

12-15. **Class Activity**

The Beebe textbook has, of course, twin key themes: audience-centered planning and delivery, which must, of necessity, involve speaker adaptation to diverse audiences. Your students may not yet be aware of the depth of sexism, racism, and, for that matter, <u>ageism</u>. You will do them a service, as well as your school and community, a service by reviewing some existing "horrible examples." Explore with your students extent of usage, depth of insult, and alternatives to the following words and phrases.

- Graybeards
- The weaker sex
- People of color
- He (as generic)
- He (as Deity)
- Old people
- My old lady
- Egghead
- Queer
- Nerd
- Oriental

12-16. **Teaching Strategy**

Trace usage of the word "vivid," using dictionaries. Find interesting synonyms in a thesaurus. Remind audience that in Spanish, the word "vivo" connotes <u>life</u> (I live). For word choice it indicates the obvious: some language LIVES AND MOVES; other language simply "is." Share with students that just as with art and literature, great speeches have been collected for centuries. Of many things the collected speeches have in common, the greatest similarity of all is the vividness of the speakers' language. Remind students that, believe it or not, great student speeches have been made, and they, like the immortal classics, share the characteristic of beautiful style and vivid language. Refer students to the Appendix D speech by Bradley student Karen Bowers, "Schadenfruede" (your author is a Bradley alum). Emote for your students her peroration, beginning with the words, "By focusing on improving our own behavior. . ." and continuing until the bittersweet end. Your students' appreciation will probably be greater if they read along silently.

12-17. Teaching Strategy

Discuss the power of language in the following partial quotations from speeches. What mental images are created? How does the choice of words add to the statement's impact?

1. Martin Luther King, Jr.: "When evil men burn and bomb, good men must build and bind."
2. Abraham Lincoln: "A house divided cannot stand."
3. John F. Kennedy: "Ask not what your country can do for you...ask what you can do for your country."
4. Malcolm X: "We declare our right on this earth...to be given the rights of a human being, in this society, on this earth, in this day, which we intend to bring into existence by any means necessary."
5. Franklin D. Roosevelt: "A day which will live in infamy"
6. Jesse Jackson: "The rainbow coalition"
7. Ann Richards: "George Bush was born with a silver foot in his mouth."

12-18. Class Activity

Instruct students to prepare a thirty-second oral essay on "My Favorite Place in All the World." Ask students to do their very best to use vivid language to develop forceful images. Hear speeches in a subsequent class. Ask audience to identify words, phrases, clauses, sentences that, for them, really "lit things up." Do tell students no notes are permitted, and to please not write and memorize.

12-19. Teaching Strategy

You may wish to prepare as projections the following examples of effective and ineffective language style. And, you'll get a chance to perform, emote.

- Blah: We should not be afraid of anything.

- The Real Thing: "We have nothing to fear but fear itself" (FDR).

- Blah: Don't be selfish; do something for your country.

- The Real Thing: "Ask not what your country can do for you; ask what you can do for your country" (JFK).

- Blah: We owe a lot to a small number of pilots.

- The Real Thing: "Never have so many owed so much to so few" (Winston Churchill).

- Blah: This country will be in trouble if it keeps human slavery.

- The Real Thing: "This country cannot long exist half-slave and half-free" (Abraham Lincoln).

- Blah: I see good things in the future.

- The Real Thing: "I have a dream that one day. . ." (Martin Luther King).

- Blah: The future will come quickly; be prepared.

- The Real Thing: "The future comes like a thief in the night, unobserved until the time for action has passed" (Charles Wise).

Lead students in a sharing of their most memorable phrases, clauses, and sentences.

12-20. Teaching Strategy

Place the acronym "K.I.S.S." on the chalkboard. Ask students what it stands for. Don't be surprised by anything you hear. You will probably hear two most popular interpretations — "Keep It Sweet and Simple," or (the author's choice) "Keep It Simple, Stupid!" Suggest to students that when speakers "KISS" they seldom make errors in grammar and meaning (denotation and connotation). However, when speakers, particularly inexperienced speakers, reach out for the stars in language style, they do run certain risks.

12-21. Class Activity

Generate a list of words and phrases that tend to evoke strong connotative meanings. Some examples are *freedom, faith, justice, fidelity.* As you write words on the chalkboard, solicit student connotative meanings. While the class discusses various meanings, ask several students to look up dictionary, "denotative" meanings. Discuss differences between both types of meaning. Emphasize that connotative meanings can evoke emotional responses in audience members. Ask when such responses are appropriate or inappropriate for the purpose of the speech.

12-22. Class Activity

For an interesting lesson in the power of language to influence attitudes, try this exercise. On the board, have students create a list of terms that reflect stereotypes about people. Encourage an open and honest exchange, because talking about stereotypical, even offensive language, can help to de-mystify it. After creating the list, ask students how the terms have led to the development of attitudes about certain groups of people. For example, professors are stereotyped as being "absent-minded." How has that stereotype affected students' perceptions of professors? Asian-American students are often called "brains" and expected to excel. What is the relationship between the labels a person uses and a person's attitudes?

12-23. Teaching Strategy

Define and discuss euphemisms and their accompanying substitution words or phrases. A few examples are: passed away (died); penal institution (jail or prison); reinforced protective reaction strike (military invasion). Should euphemisms be used in speeches? Why or why not?

12-24. Teaching Strategy

Review the concept of denotative and connotative meaning and what the concepts can do for a speaker's effectiveness, both positive and negative. Point the discussion especially to diverse audiences.

12-25. Background Information

Two educational films from Films for the Humanities and the Sciences (PO Box 2053, Princeton, NJ, 08543) illustrate to students the power of language. The first film, *Doublespeak*, explores ways in which English is distorted, manipulated, and inflated to confuse meaning (Color; 28 minutes). The second film, *Sexism in Language,* offers an excellent overview of the bias in language topic, including examples of sexist and nonsexist language in song lyrics, everyday conversation, and newspaper articles (Color: 52 minutes).

12-26. Class Activity

The purpose of this activity is to give students practice applying principles of effective language by rewriting speech segments. Give students sample speech segments that need rewriting. Students have to identify the mistakes or ineffective elements in the segments and rewrite them, demonstrating an appropriate use of language. Collect the writings and select some for class sharing.

Speech Segment #1: (Television Violence — rewrite statistical explanations and sexist language)
There is just too much violence on television these days. In fact, 70% of the public thinks there's too much violence on television. Although media violence is not the only contributing factor, research says that the media cause at least 10% of the violence in the U.S. Consider, for example, the typical viewing habits of an elementary school child. By the time the average kid finishes elementary school, he will have seen 8,000 television murders and over 100,000 acts of violence. This desensitization toward violence means that it is time for things to change.

Speech Segment #2: (Sweatshops — rewrite statistical explanations and sexist language)
Erik Ness of the Progressive Media Project reported that conditions for workers in Indonesia are pitiful. A workman making Nike sneakers averages ten hours a day; he works six days a week to bring home a measly fourteen cents an hour to his family; he gets two cents an hour for overtime. Of these workmen, 80% are female and 88% of those women are malnourished. Last year, Nike's net profits were $329 million.

Speech Segment #3: (Racial Discrimination — rewrite racist, outdated terms)
One national leader says that "the drug war is a war against minorities." According to last Sunday's *USA Today*, Negroes are four times more likely to be arrested than Caucasians. Now, I'm not talking about if two people are in a comparable situation. A black guy is in a suspicious situation in one place, and a white guy is in a suspicious situation in another place. We saw that last year when a local black minister was pulled over and beaten by police. Do you think that would have happened to a white minister?

12-27. **Class Activity**

The purpose is for students to consider the varied meanings of words, particularly regarding different age or cultural groups. Have students write a definition for each of the following words or phrases. Then use their responses to spark discussion on (a) which words have negative connotations; (b) which words have positive connotations; (c) which words reveal bias; and (d) how the meanings of words change over time.

Bad	Killer	Groovy
Frontin'	Rap	Momma
Ball	Gay	Funky
Chillin'	Square	Shootin' Hoop
Blast	Grass	Laid Back
Cool	Hairy	Old Fogey
Punk	Stud	Chick
Crash	Heavy	The 'Hood
Homey	Daisy Dukes	Perps
Baby Got Back	The Bomb	Blow
Nerd	Queer	Hangin'
Bread	Juice	Old Maid

C. *Effective Speakers Craft Memorable Word Structures*

12-28. **Teaching Strategy**

Share the Outline material from III, A, 1 through C, 4. Consider adding examples from your files and experience.

12-29. **Class Activity**

Ask students to find and list a minimum of ten common metaphors and similes. The newer the better, but older models are acceptable. Prime the pump for students with these examples:
- Working my fingers to the bone
- Wound tighter than a yo-yo
- Hitting the nail on the head
- Busy as a bee
- Crookeder than a dog's hind leg
- Caught between a rock and a hard place
- Mr. Clean
- Our teacher? A regular Simon Legree!
- It is easier for a camel to pass through the eye of a needle than it is for a rich man to enter the gates of Heaven.

In a subsequent class, divide into groups. Have students share all items. Ask each group to choose its "coolest" or "jazziest" example to share with entire class (funniest would be OK, too).

12-30. Teaching Strategy

To help explain how metaphor and simile can be effectively incorporated into a speech, ask students to complete the following sentence — either orally or in writing: "Giving a public speech is _____." Some common similes and metaphors might be: "pure hell," "like a trip to the dentist's office," "almost the same as breaking up — painful, but a lot sweatier." Discuss which examples are metaphors and which are similes.

12-31. Teaching Strategy

Review with students that "effective speakers craft memorable word structures." Recall that earlier in the class students were referred to the *Readers Digest* as a source of vivid language for possible quoting in speeches. Share with them "Until you become very good at inventing vivid language it's OK for you to borrow. After that, future students will begin borrowing from you!" To cement your referral to the *Digest*, share these items from May, 1999 issue:

- "If you have but one wish, let it be for an idea." Percy Sutton

- "Half the harm that is done in the world is due to people who want to feel important." T.S. Eliot

- "Beauty isn't worth thinking about; what's important is your mind. You don't want a fifty-dollar haircut on a fifty-cent head." Garrison Keillor

- "Nobody minds having what is too good for them." Jane Austen

- "Money brings some happiness. But, after a certain point, it just brings more money!" Neil Simon

- "Growth demands a temporary surrender of security." Peggy Noonan

- "When you don't know what you want, you often end up where you don't want to be." Bob Greene

- "The art of being wise is the art of knowing what to overlook." William James

12-32. **Class Activity**

Create a projection that shows on the left side the vivid language descriptors of this chapter, and on the right phrases, clauses, and sentences. Challenge students to match right to left. If students disagree, require them to argue their point of view. Use these sentences and others you create.

- His airplane flew with the grace of a dancer, maneuvering effortlessly as a champion slalom skier.
  <u>Personification</u>

- Religion is the opiate of the proletariat.
  <u>Metaphor</u>

- Is there no one who can rid me of this millstone about my neck<u>?</u>
  <u>Suspension</u>

- As a ship in a gale may founder, so may our ship of state in this crisis.
  <u>Simile</u>

- Heavy, heavy hangs over thy head.
  <u>Inversion</u>

- She sells sea shells by the sea shore.
  <u>Alliteration</u>

- Do not negotiate from fear, but never fear to negotiate.
  <u>Antithesis</u>

- We will fight them on the beach; we will fight them in the villages, and in the cities; we will fight them in the mountains, and if this war should last a thousand years men will still say this was their finest hour.
  <u>Repetition</u>

- The footbone connected to the anklebone; the anklebone connected to the kneebone; the kneebone connected to the thighbone. . .
  <u>Parallelism</u>

12-33. **Class Activity**

Have students write the names of three of their favorite songs on a blank piece of paper. Instruct them to write some of the most meaningful or significant lyrics for each. Remind the class that words have the power to create mental images and influence our attitudes and behavior. Ask for volunteers to read examples from their songs that fulfill each of these functions. As discussion ensues, look for opportunities to note agreement and disagreement among students' interpretations of lyrics.

D. *Four Tips for Using Language Effectively Guide Effective Speakers*

12-34. **Class Activity**

Advertisers use the stylistic techniques of omission and suspension frequently to promote products. Ask students to bring example advertisements from magazines or television that illustrate these techniques. Here are a few examples:

Omission: Nike ads that read "Just do it," "Pizza Hut...Making It Great!" "Diet Pepsi...Uh Huh!"

Suspension: "You're the heart of me, that's a part of me, Dr. Pepper you're a part of me," "It's a new generation of Olds," "Let it be Lowenbrau."

12-35. **Teaching Strategy**

A few "Tips for Using Memorable Language Effectively." Tip #1 — don't overdo it. The author previously referred to the movie *The Man Who Shot Liberty Valance*. If you acquired a video clip of John Carradine performing elocution, play it, Sam. The actor simply defines "overdoing it," in both language choices and delivery. Do remind students it was the way to go for most speakers and audiences of that age. Ask them how they would feel if they visited another country and found this speech style still in effect.

12-36. **Class Activity**

The purpose is to analyze how language is used in songs, to illustrate principles that apply to public speaking. For the purposes of playback in class, ask students to bring cassette tapes and CDs cued up to songs that employ interesting (and tasteful) uses of language. You may want to require students to produce written transcripts of the lyrics, especially by musicians who don't care about articulation! Have students play their selections while students note specific choices of words. Discuss the language use as it applies to the chapter information.

ONLINE TEACHING PLAN

Preview activity: Go to the website entitled *"Before you have that talk"* at:
http://www.fastcompany.com/online/09/beforetalk.html. Use this discussion about how to choose appropriate words for a conversation to begin discussing how to choose appropriate language for a speech. Students should write a brief response to the article that related the three questions posed in the article to their own upcoming speech.

Review activity: read the website entitled, *"Say it with style"* at:
http://www.abacon.com/pubspeak/organize/style.html
Students should write a brief summary of ways they might use concrete words, specific words, simple words, and correct words that are appropriate for their audience and speech topic.

CHAPTER THIRTEEN: Delivering Your Speech

Chapter-at-a-Glance

Detailed Outline	Instructor Resources	Supplements	Professor Notes
The Power of Speech Delivery (p. 274) • Good delivery is expected • Communicating emotions and attitudes • Audiences believe what they see	**Annotated Chapter Outline (ACO):** 13-1, 13-2, 13-3 **Learning Objective #1:** Identify three reasons delivery is important **ACO** 13-4, 13-5, 13-6 13-7, 13-8, 13-9 13-10	**Rehearse Your Speech:** Allyn and Bacon Transparency #T-46, T-47	
Methods of Delivery (p. 276) • Manuscript speaking • Memorized speaking • Impromptu speaking • Extemporaneous speaking	**Learning Objective #2:** Identify and describe four types of delivery **ACO:** 13-11 through 13-16 **ACO:** 13-17 through 13-20	**Methods of Delivery:** Allyn and Bacon Transparency #T-48	
Characteristics of Effective Delivery (p. 280) • Eye contact • Gestures • Movement • Posture • Facial expression • Vocal delivery • Personal appearance	**Learning Objective #3:** Identify physical characteristics of effective delivery **ACO:** 13-21, 13-22, 13-25 **ACO:** 13-23, 13-24, 13-26 through 13-32 **ACO:** 13-33 through 13-38	**Elements of Vocal Delivery:** Allyn and Bacon Transparency #T-51 **Elements of Physical Delivery:** Allyn and Bacon Transparency #T-52	
Speaker's Homepage (p. 292)	**ACO:** 13-39		
Audience Diversity and Delivery (p. 293)			
Rehearsing Your Speech (p. 294)	**Learning Objective #4:** Describe the steps in rehearsing a speech	**Digital Media Archive for Communication (DMAC)** T14I05	
Delivering Your Speech (p. 295) **Adapting Your Speech Delivery for Television** (p. 297)	**Learning Objective #5:** List four suggestions for delivery **ACO:** 13-40 through 13-42	**DMAC** T14I06	
Responding to Questions (p. 299)			

LEARNING OBJECTIVES

1. Students will be able to identify three reasons delivery is important to a public speaker.

2. Students will be able to identify and describe four types of delivery.

3. Students will be able to identify and illustrate physical characteristics of effective delivery.

4. Students will be able to describe the steps to follow when a speech is rehearsed.

5. Students will be able to list four suggestions for enhancing the final delivery of a speech.

CHAPTER OUTLINE

I. Effective nonverbal behavior is important to a speaker's delivery for three reasons.

   A. Listeners expect effective delivery (nonverbal expectancy theory).

   B. Listeners make emotional connections with the speaker through delivery.

   C. Listeners believe what they see, and what they see is nonverbal behavior.

II. Speakers may use one of four methods of delivery (which also influences audiences' perceptions of speaker nonverbal behavior).

   A. One method is *manuscript speaking,* presenting the speech word-for-word from prepared paper.

      1. Some speeches should be carefully prepared and read.

         a. The President of the United States can ill-afford a slip of the tongue.
         b. Corporation chief executives' addresses cannot often be informal.

      2. The goal of an effective manuscript speech is to sound as if you were not delivering from a manuscript.

   B. A second method of delivery is *memorized speaking.*

      1. If you are accepting an award, introducing a speaker, making announcements, or delivering other brief remarks, memorized delivery is sometimes acceptable.

      2. Most memorized speeches sound stiff, stilted, and over-rehearsed.

3. Speakers also run risks of forgetting parts of a speech, leading to awkward searches for words as the audience fidgets.

4. Speakers cannot adapt the speech if the situation changes.

C. The third method of speech delivery is *impromptu speaking* (aka "speaking off the cuff" and "thinking on your feet").

1. Impromptu speaking can result in informal delivery and direct eye contact.

2. However, impromptu speeches often lack thorough research and logical organization.

3. Consider five pieces of advice for effective impromptu speaking.

a. Analyze your audience.

b. Be brief.

c. Organize! (Try simple organizational patterns.)

d. Speak honestly, but with reserve, from personal experience and knowledge.

e. Be cautious.

D. The fourth and final method of speech delivery is *extemporaneous*.

1. When delivering a speech extemporaneously, you speak from a written or memorized general outline, without exact wording available to you.

2. An extemporaneous style is conversational, and appears spontaneous to audiences.

3. An extemporaneous style may be developed in four stages.

a. First, rehearse your speech using many notes, or looking at your full content outline.

b. Second, continue to rehearse, relying less on notes and not trying to memorize word-for-word.

c. Third, you find that you have internalized the overall speech structure, although the exact expression of your ideas is not "fixed."

d. Fourth, you rely less on notes, focusing on audience adaptation, and requiring only an abbreviated outline, key words, and essential facts.

III. Effective speech delivery rests on seven nonverbal behavior categories.

A.   For North Americans, at least, the most important speech delivery factor is *eye contact*.

1.   Eye contact with your audience opens communication, makes you more believable, and holds your audience interest.

2.   Listeners feel that good speaker eye contact means a speaker is capable and trustworthy.

3.   One study showed that audience recall is stronger when speakers have maintained good audience contact.

4.   Simple principles make for good eye contact.

   a.   Establish eye contact with audience even before beginning to speak.

   b.   Slowly, deliberately try to maintain eye contact with entire audience, not just a portion in front.

   c.   Look at individuals, establishing person-to-person contact.

   d.   Don't look over audience's heads.

B.   Effective delivery depends upon *gestures*.

1.   Gestures emphasize important points, as well as indicating places, enumerating items, and describing objects.

   a.   Gesture usage, types, and patterns vary with culture.

   b.   Gestures lend strength to messages in six ways: repeating, contradicting, substituting, complementing, emphasizing, and regulating.

   c.   Seven suggestions about using gestures are very helpful.

      (1) Stay natural.

      (2) Be definite.

      (3) Use gestures consistent with message.

      (4) Vary gestures.

      (5) Don't overdo it!

      (6) Coordinate gestures with message.

      (7) Make gestures appropriate to audience and situation.

C. Effective delivery requires effective *movement.*

   1. Make movement purposeful, consistent with verbal content of message.

   2. Use movement to reduce physical barriers between speaker and audience.

   3. Use movement to reinforce verbal transitions.

   4. Make movement logical to your listeners; avoid random pacing and overly dramatic gestures.

D. General *posture* of speakers appears to communicate significant information about speakers.

   1. While face and voice indicate <u>what</u> emotion, a speaker's posture apparently communicates the <u>intensity</u> of the emotion portrayed.

   2. Speech teachers today, in contrast to last century, believe that <u>stances</u> taken by speakers should reflect "doing what comes naturally."

   3. Posture recommendations: don't sit while speaking; avoid slouched shoulders, shifting from foot to foot, or drooping your head.

E. *Facial expression* play a key role in expressing your thoughts, especially emotions and attitudes.

   1. Your face sets the emotional tone of the speech before you open your mouth.

   2. Your facial expression should be consistent with the content of the message.

   3. Rehearse in front of the mirror to monitor clear communication of emotions.

F. *Vocal delivery* and vocal clues are an important part of speaker image created in an audience's mind.

   1. Vocal delivery includes variables such as pitch, rate, volume, pronunciation, articulation, pauses, and general variation of voice.

   2. A speaker has at least two key vocal obligations to audiences.

      a. A speaker must speak <u>to be understood.</u>

         (1) Control **volume,** speaking loudly enough to be heard.

         (2) Control **articulation,** producing speech sounds clearly and distinctly.

(3) Unless you are a newscaster required to use "standard American" pronunciation; **speak in your natural dialect.**

(4) Control your **rate** of speaking, especially if non-native to English.

(5) Control **pronunciation,** pronouncing words correctly, or as the audience pronounces them.

    i.   If English is not your native language, spend extra time working on pronunciation and articulation.

    ii. Practice by exaggerating and prolonging vowel sounds.

b.   A speaker must <u>speak with variety</u>.

(1) Use **pitch variety** to achieve vocal variety and to use **inflection** effectively.

(2) Select an **average rate** of speaking that fits your "speaking style" and the message content.

(3) An appropriate **pause** can often accent your message.

3. Speakers should take care to properly use microphones.

a.   If required to use a stationary "mike," remain behind it, maintaining the same mouth-to-mike distance.

b.   Mikes amplify; be especially careful with pronunciation and enunciation.

c.   Having found a proper amplification level, speak directly into the mike, maintaining your volume "level."

G.   Speakers should attempt to comply with researched suggestions about *personal appearance*, perhaps modified by audience expectations.

1. Evidence suggests that personal appearance affects audience responses.

2. In doubt? "If In Rome, Do As the Romans Do;" dress like the audience is expected to dress.

3. Still in doubt? Select something conservative.

IV.   What is the appropriate relationship between <u>diverse audiences</u> and delivery?

A.   Suggestions in this chapter have tended to be based on typical North American audiences.

B.   Consider four suggestions for adapting delivery to more diverse audiences.

    1. Avoid an ethnocentric mind set.

    2. Consider using a less dramatic delivery style for predominately high-context listeners (Chapter 5).

    3. If you know that you will be speaking to a group of people from a culture different from your own, try to observe other speakers presenting to that audience before you.

    4. Monitor your level of immediacy with your audience.

    5. Monitor your expression of emotion.

    6. Know the nonverbal "code" of your audience.

V.   Speaker's Homepage (p. 295)

VI.   Rehearse your speech: some final tips.

A.   Finish drafting outline at least two days before speaking.

B.   Rehearse aloud before deciding on final form for speaking notes.

C.   Revise the speech to meet the time limits.

D.   Prepare your speaking notes as "whatever works best for you." (Complete sentences, pictures or symbols, outline pattern words and phrases).

E.   Rehearse standing up; don't memorize text and gestures.
F.   Rehearse to somebody; practice eye contact and get feedback.

G.   Record during rehearsals; check out your vocal and physical mannerisms and make necessary changes.

H.   Rehearse all visual aids, as well as speech itself.

I.   Try to simulate the "real thing" as closely as possible — speaking area, seating arrangements.

J.   Don't practice mistakes; practice good delivery skills while rehearsing.

VII.   Four suggestions will maximize effective delivery in your speech.

A.   Get plenty of rest before speaking.

B.   Review the suggestions in Chapter 2 for becoming a confident speaker.

C.   Arrive early to speak, and check it all out (repeating your earlier reconnaissance, perhaps).

D.   Visualize success; review your excellent preparation.

VIII.   You may be required to adapt your delivery for television in at least seven ways.

A.   Consider toning down gestures.

B.   Dress for TV success.

C.   Monitor your facial expressions.

D.   Keep your target audience in mind.

E.   Keep it short.

F.   Choose your words with care and style.

G.   Become familiar with the technology before you speak.

IV.   Responding to Questions

A.   Prepare responses to questions in advance.

B.   Repeat or rephrase the question.

C.   Stay on message.

D.   Ask yourself the first question to get things started.

E.   Listen non-judgmentally to questions.

F.   Neutralize hostile questions.

G.   Admit you don't know when you don't know.

H.   Be brief.

I.   Use organizational signposts to respond.

J.   Indicate when the Q & A's are concluding.

REVIEW GUIDE

13-1.   List four reasons effective nonverbal behavior is important to speakers.

13-2.   Roughly, what percentage of all message meaning is conveyed by nonverbal speaker behavior?

13-3.   Do audiences respond more to speech content, or to speaker delivery?

13-4.   List and explain the four general methods of delivery.

13-5.   Why don't most speech teachers prefer manuscript and memorized methods of delivery?

13-6.   Explain the advantages and disadvantages of each delivery method.

13-7.   List five nonverbal behavior categories that affect effective speaker delivery.

13-8.   Which of the five categories in 13-7 seems to be the most important for North Americans?

13-9.   List the four Beebe principles for effective speaker-to-audience eye contact.

13-10. List seven variables of vocal delivery.

13-11. What are two speaker vocal obligations to audiences?

13-12. What suggestions to improve pronunciation are made for non-native English speakers?

13-13. What are the best three ways to achieve vocal variety?

13-14. What textbook advice is given for proper use of microphones?

13-15. List the "Do's," "Don'ts," and "Maybe's" of speech delivery and personal appearance.

13-16. What are four suggestions for adapting "North American" delivery to culturally diverse audiences?

13-17. Recall as many as you can of the tips for final speech rehearsals.

13-18. Just before speaking, what are common sense suggestions for maximizing delivery?

13-19. What are seven ways you might wish to modify your delivery for television speaking?

13-20. Briefly describe how to "dress for TV success."

13-21. List several techniques to effectively respond to questions.

ANNOTATED CHAPTER OUTLINE

A. *Delivery of a Well-Rehearsed Speech is Important for Three Reasons*

13-1. Background Information

The introductory material to this chapter refers to several interesting topics for possible research. Students interested in classical periods may want to investigate Aristotle, Quintilian, or Cicero. The elocutionary movement in England and America could also be a fascinating topic for a speech.

13-2. Teaching Strategy

Even though there are many parts to preparing a speech, we often judge speeches based solely on the delivery of the speaker. Lead a probing discussion of the relative importance of delivery and whether it should students should actually rank it as they do.

13-3. Teaching Strategy

Ask students to think of one great speaker they have heard live or seen on television. Ask them to brainstorm and write down elements of that speaker's delivery that were especially memorable. Ask students to share their notes; write on the board the textbook terms for these delivery elements.

13-4. Teaching Strategy

Comedians call it "Being on." Actors say it's "Being in character." It means, in the case of theatre, you don't wait until you get on stage to become your character. You do that before you enter the action. So it is with speakers. Alert students that movement *before* and *after* a speech can be as important as movement *during* a speech. As a speaker rises and approaches front of room or lectern, he or she should stay in control — bodily and vocally. Audiences quickly begin to assess speaker credibility, and a positive approach to speaking can lead audiences to a positive beginning evaluation.

13-5. Class Activity

Ask five students to pretend to approach the lectern to speak, coming from the classroom door. They are to demonstrate confidence and control. Then ask for five volunteers to demonstrate a lack of confidence or control on their way to the lectern. Lead a short critical analysis of the examples and offer strategies to overcome the negative characteristics demonstrated by students.

13-6. Class Activity

Do a takeoff on the old "Saturday Night Live" routine, "subliminal speaking." Ask a group to create a one-minute speech introduction, supposedly from a student speaker who really rather would not speak. Consider lines such as these, remembering that the skit involves confident statements expressed loudly and followed by sotto voce comedic asides:

Good evening; I am so glad to be here (no I'm not). You look like a wonderful audience (like knots on a log, actually). Tonight, I want to talk to you about three important ideas (what were they?).

You get the idea and so will your volunteers, quickly and joyfully. They'll make a hilarious and deeply teaching monologue. After, remind the audience about the importance of agreement between verbal and nonverbal messages.

13-7. Class Activity

Pair students. Ask each pair to prepare a short demonstration of "mixed messages" (delivery where words appear to communicate one meaning, while nonverbal activity denies the verbal meaning). Allow each pair to choose as they will from the following speech situations (one student will serve as creator and coach; the other as the actor and presenter of the skit):

• Speaker declares: "I stand firmly resolved that we shall never retreat."

Speaker, bodily, shows defeat.

• Speaker declares: "I have never been nervous when speaking in public."
Speaker, bodily, shows speech anxiety.

• Speaker declares: "I trust you 100%."
Speaker, bodily, shows distrust.

• Speaker declares: "I have never been more serious about anything in my whole life."
Speaker, bodily, can hardly contain laughter.

Begin this show and tell class with all in the hall. Invite the first pair to share with you, and be seated. In comes the second pair, presents and sits. When all pairs have completed their Oscar-winning performances, review the concept of mixed messages and the importance of speaker consistency with both words and nonverbal behaviors.

13-8. **Class Activity**

Ask students to select one of their other courses, and to observe the nonverbal behaviors of the course's instructor as she or he lectures. Ask them to take notes and briefly report (as many reports as practicable) their observations to the class, addressing such questions as:

- "How did you judge the credibility and competence of that instructor, based on nonverbal cues?"
- "What were the predominant nonverbal behaviors of the students during the lecture period?"
- Did the student nonverbal cues reveal their like or dislike for the class?"

If you have the *chutzpah* for it, ask several students, impromptu, to analyze your typical nonverbal habits when lecturing! Lead a summarizing discussion of the role of nonverbal communication in speech delivery.

13-9. **Class Activity**

If you have access to tapes of the presidential or vice-presidential debates from the 1992 election, you can offer students this guaranteed to please exercise. Show a segment of a tape to students without sound. Have them take notes on specific delivery elements such as body movement, gestures, eye contact, facial expressions, and physical appearance. Replay the same segment, this time with sound. Have students note vocal characteristics and whether the words complement or contradict the speaker's nonverbal communication. Finally, just listen to the segment. What kinds of emotions are evoked by the voices of Bush, Clinton, Perot, Gore, Quayle, and retired Admiral Stockdale?

13-10. **Related Reading**

Beginning speakers may not be aware of the nonverbal behaviors they exhibit while speaking. To procure an excellent exercise that helps students understand the negative impact of ineffective speech delivery, read Pamela Hayward's essay entitled "Delivery Cards" in the Spring, 1994 issue of *The Speech Communication Teacher,* page 3.

B. *Communication Teachers Identify Five Methods of Delivering a Speech*

13-11. **Class Activity**

Write the four delivery methods on the board and have students generate at least three advantages and three disadvantages of using each method. Engage the class in discussion about types of delivery they have tried in your class, in other classes in which they have made presentations, in high school speech classes, and in actual public speaking situations. Explain which methods you will accept, which ones you won't, and why.

13-12. **Teaching Strategy**

Mention to students that manuscript delivery is often helpful when strict time limits have to be maintained. This is especially true when buying media time. Manuscript delivery lends itself to the accurate control of time.

13-13. Teaching Strategy

Discuss specific ways that oral style differs from written style. For example, oral communication uses short words, contractions, simpler sentence structure, and repetition. Why must these differences be taken into account when using a manuscript delivery? If a speaker decides to use a manuscript format, what aspects of effective delivery must he/she work hardest to produce?

13-14. Teaching Strategy

Share with students that ever since Franklin D. Roosevelt, U.S. Presidents have had multiple-member speechwriting teams, normally with a head writer (for FDR, Robert Sherwood, playwright; for JFK, Theodore Sorenson). The team's main function is to prepare, with the president's final changes, carefully scripted speeches. The team's main "sweat," especially with FDR, was that he would depart the manuscript's wording at critical moments! Use the story to illustrate that sometimes manuscripted speeches are the way to go.

13-15. Class Activity

Select a manuscript, serious in nature, that requires about a minute to deliver. Ask for two student volunteers. Assign one student to deliver the manuscript "cold" (student will not see the script until five minutes before delivery). Ask the second student to memorize the manuscript and rehearse it. Practice the script yourself until you can do a really good job with it, i.e., it seems spontaneous to listeners. On the designated day call for the speakers in order. Should you get lucky, the first speaker will sound ill-prepared, the second "memorized," and you, spontaneous. Afterwards, lead a discussion of the places for, advantages of, and disadvantages of the manuscript reading delivery method. Thank the volunteers as if you were never going to quit thanking them. They will have done the class and you a valuable service.

13-16. Teaching Strategy

Warn students that rote memorization of a speech is no easy task. Since we are not accustomed to doing much memorization these days, it is a difficult, time-consuming project. In addition, a memorized speech does not give the speaker much opportunity for audience feedback. As with a manuscript, if the speaker has already determined exactly what to say, then he or she will also probably not be as sensitive to audience feedback.

13-17. Class Activity

For a quick but supportive exercise in impromptu speaking, divide students into groups and give these instructions. Each group will listen to their members speaking. Offer them a choice of location — whatever you think will facilitate and motivate the exercise. Student 1 gives student 2 a topic, and student 2 speaks a minimum of two minutes. Student 2, of course, gives student 3 the topic, who. . .and you see how it goes. Again, never mind the noise — it's all for a good cause. After, reinforce the advantages and disadvantages of the impromptu speaking method.

13-18. Teaching Strategy

Share with students an anecdote from the United States Senate, at the time of the debate on the Compromise of 1850 (concerning negotiations between North and South on the issue of slavery). John C. Calhoun, fiery southern orator, had delivered an acrimonious speech in favor of the Southern position, laying out a series of well-prepared arguments. When Calhoun desisted, Senator Daniel Webster, acknowledged orator supreme for the North, immediately arose and, apparently with little preparation, brilliantly demolished Calhoun's main points. Afterward, a colleague accompanied Webster into his Senate office. "How could you do that?" the colleague asked, "I've never heard such an impromptu retort in all my life." Without a word, the story goes, Webster reached into his desk drawer and displayed a healthy set of notes. "I've known what he was going to say for months," Webster acknowledged, "and worked out all my arguments, waiting for this day." Webster, of course, had spoken extemporaneously.

13-19. Teaching Strategy

Explain to students that every time an extemporaneous speech is rehearsed, it changes somewhat. Thus, one disadvantage of extemporaneous delivery is the difficulty in timing a speech accurately. Extemporaneous speakers also tend to be more sensitive to audience feedback. This sensitivity is generally a plus, unless it causes the message to lengthen when a speaker responds to audience confusion. Through adequate rehearsal and with experience, a speaker should be able to gauge the time of a message within 30-40 seconds. Helping students learn to match a body of information to time constraints is another goal of the public speaking course.

13-20. Class Activity

Ask for three student volunteers. Distribute a one-page, full-sentence outline of a speech to inform to each volunteer. Give the volunteers several class days to rehearse a short speech based strongly on the outline (they will be permitted only one note card while speaking). As students prepare to speak, project the original outline behind the speakers, so that audiences can see the outline and hear the speaker. Ask two students to wait outside, while the first speaks and then is seated. You know the drill...

After the speeches, discuss the differences which the speeches demonstrated. Lead a discussion of the advantages and disadvantages of the extemporaneous speech delivery method. Review all the speech delivery methods. Suggested is the Outline material, II, A-D.

C. *Communication Teachers Identify Eleven Characteristics of Effective Speech Delivery*

13-21. Teaching Strategy

Illustrate the six ways in which gestures strengthen verbal messages. You may choose to use the following illustrations.

Repeating

- One, two, buckle my shoe;
  Three, four, open the door;
  Five, six, pick up sticks.

Show: one finger on each hand then flash three, then four fingers; show five and one fingers.

Contradicting

- To those who oppose us, we say, "Live Long and Prosper."

Show: the classic "Cut Throat" gesture, slicing your own throat with index finger.

Substituting

- And why did we make this terrible mistake of judgment?

Show: arms outstretched, palms-up gesture of "Who Knows."

Complementing

- We pray to Almighty God that this day the final victory shall be ours.

Show: palms steepled under chin

Emphasizing

- Emote: Power to the People!

Show: the clenched fist salute

Regulating

- Now, just a moment, please; it's my turn to talk.

Show: arm up and extended, open palm toward person being interrupted (the classic "Stop" gesture).

13-22. Class Activity

Ask six volunteers to take speaker positions up front. Tell them it's going to be competition in producing effective gesturesAnnounce a needed gesture. On count of three all six will attempt the required gesture and <u>hold it</u>. Audience will be asked to pick a "winner" for each performance. Consider these and other gesture possibilities:

- "On the other hand"
- "Power to the People!"
- "God Only Knows"
- "My second point"
- "We scorn them"
- "I accuse you!"

13-23. Teaching Strategy

Demonstrate use of platform movement for two purposes.

- Show use of movement to "reduce physical barriers with audience": move across front of area with appropriate movements to get closer to more of audience; move down aisles, if possible and appropriate.

- Demonstrate use of movement to "reinforce verbal transitions": make appropriate movements side-to-side and forward-backward in sync with verbal point changes, telling students what you are doing, of course.

13-24. Class Activity

Ask three volunteers to be seated up front (except when they are demonstrating). They are to invent and display appropriate platform movement for a situation. Project the "script" for the exercise (for example, Lincoln's "Gettysburg Address"), and furnishing the volunteers with an enlarged hard copy. Allow them a few minutes to mark the script for movement. Tell them to share the performance of the planned movements. You emote the piece from the rear, <u>slowly</u>, for the "actors" sake.

13-25. Class Activity

Ask students to observe a favorite comedian, newscaster, or instructor, noting their use of gestures. During a subsequent roll call, ask for a quick report from each student, hopefully including some "show and tell."

13-26. Teaching Strategy

Dramatize the effects of common movement patterns on an audience. These can include restless, unrelenting pacing back and forth, and so on. Ask students for personal experience examples of this type of unproductive platform movement.

13-27. Teaching Strategy

Explore the effects of posture on messages. Ask students their interpretations of the speaking and associated postures you will display.

- Stand rigidly, the classical military attention posture.
  Say to the student audience, "I feel very relaxed when teaching."

- Stand apparently relaxed, but with arms tightly clasped behind your back.
  Say to students, "Students are very welcome in my office."

- Sit on the table, whatever, all slouched down.
  Say to students, "I absolutely need your undivided attention."

Ask students to share their own examples about use of posture to vivify messages, and to weaken messages.

13-28. Teaching Strategy

Ask students, "What do you suppose I mean when I say that people 'dim their lights?'" Let them think a bit. Unless they know from another class, they probably do not know the phrase refers to persons approaching each other with no intent of stopping for conversation. How do you indicate "No, No Contact, Please?" Answer: one or both look down and away about 25 degrees, hence, "Dimming the Lights" (eyes!) Review the use of the eyes for other clear messages. Don't neglect courtship; it's an attention-getter for students. Ask if students know the ancient Chinese proverb about eyes ("The eyes are the windows to the soul"). Use the saying, if you like, as a basis for review of the Outline V, D, 1-5, d.

13-29. Class Activity

Ask three volunteers to sit in a semicircle up front. They are to conduct a conversation on the topic "my hero." However, they must play "The Great Stone Face" — no facial expressions, no bodily movement, maintaining vocal monotone. Only the mouths move. Expect much audience mirth. After, explore the obvious: how much nonverbal behavior contributes to our communication, especially in public speaking.

13-30. Background Information

The feature film *Dave* has several excellent scenes involving public speaking. Kevin Kline's character is called on to impersonate an ailing president, and the scene in which he rehearses the president's gestures and voice inflection may be an effective supplement to the textbook's information on body language. Another appropriate scene for use in public speaking class depicts him impersonating the president at a press conference, making a brief speech announcing a national job works program.

13-31. **Class Activity**

Have students make tape recordings for self-analysis of vocal characteristics. Assign them to:

- Make a recording of a short piece of prose they especially like. Ask them for narrative prose, without characters and dialogue.

- Make a recording of brief spontaneous speaking on a topic chosen by the speaker.

Tell students to try to make their readings transmit the author's ideas; they should not try to sound like they are acting. After recording both the prose and their spontaneous speaking, they should listen to the tape several times, thinking about the vocal components explained in this chapter. Was you're the vocal delivery better in one of the recordings?. If so, why do they think that's the case?

13-32. **Class Activity**

Remind students of the importance of vocal inflection in a speaker's arsenal for creating meaning. Use this classic (you'll be glad you did): Write this phrase on chalkboard: I WOULD NOT SAY YOU LOST THE FIGHT. In turn, ask students to say the sentence placing emphasis on just one word. Begin with "I" and move through "fight," emphasizing one new word at a time. Students will do it well, and the lesson, which may not be necessary anyway, is certainly cast in cement. Ask students in their next speech to rehearse and then use occasional meaningful inflections.

13-33. **Teaching Strategy**

The issue of personal appearance, which mostly means clothing, is not simple. In this author's judgment (speech) communication teachers should raise this issue with students. Ask your students straight out: "Should people who speak in public dress formally and conservatively?" "Should students who speak in this class do the same?" "Do audiences respond to speakers and speeches on the basis of dress and other aspects of personal appearance?" Have your debating skills at the ready, provided, of course, that opinion is divided, yours included!

13-34. **Background Information**

If you have the film, show a portion of the first presidential debates (Richard M. Nixon and John F. Kennedy). The idea is to supplement the textbook on nonverbal behavior, speech delivery, and speaker credibility. Have students concentrate on nonverbal communication in terms of personal appearance, gestures, eye contact, facial expressions, and vocal pitch, volume, and rate variety. By way of reinforcing the importance of nonverbal communication, share with students an interesting study of audience reactions to the debates. Those who watched on TV overwhelmingly picked JFK as the "winner," while those who listened only (radio) picked RMN as the winner. Ask students to account for the different audience reactions. Probe. Make them tie their ideas to this chapter's theory and concepts.

13-35. Class Activity

Students know that such things as eye contact, movement, gestures, volume, and rate of speaking can detract from or enhance a message. But, they may be more able to recognize these attributes in other speakers than in themselves. If students are willing to talk about their delivery strengths and weaknesses, they can build common bonds with other class speakers, more fully realize their "pluses" as speakers, and begin to work on counteracting the "minuses" in their delivery.

13-36. Class Activity

The purpose of this activity is for students to express emotions through the use of face, voice, and body. Type the words below on slips of paper to distribute to students. Primary emotions that humans express are marked with an asterisk. Give students time between classes to practice. In a subsequent class, using the phrase "Testing 1, 2, 3...," have students portray the emotions on their slips of paper through voice, facial expressions, posture, gesture, and movement. To help students more readily identify the emotion a classmate conveys, display a poster or transparency containing all the words. You may need to add to this list or take only volunteers for this exercise, depending on the size of your class.

anger*	hatred	stress
fear*	happiness*	kindness
amusement	suspicion	apathy
sympathy	excitement	friendliness
love	impatience	joy
frustration	pain	disgust*
contemplation	surprise*	jealousy
grief	tolerance	self-pity
thoughtfulness	gratitude	sadness*

D. *Audience Diversities Can Affect a Speaker's Delivery Plan*

13-37. Teaching Strategy

Gestures rarely have universal meaning; most meanings are culturally determined. For example, our "OK" gesture is a phallic gesture in the Middle East. Lead the class in a discussion of gestures that are only understood by a particular group. If you have international students, students who have traveled extensively or lived overseas, or students from various regions of the U.S., a lively discussion should ensue. Make sure to relate the information to a speaker's task of being audience-centered.

13-38. **Class Activity**

Assign students to talk to members of different cultures (and subcultures). They are to compile a list of gestures which seem to have different meanings in different cultures. What is a speaker's responsibility to "different strokes for different folks" when it comes to cultural differences confronting a public speaker? How far must a speaker go in pursuing the prize: effective audience-centered speaking?

E. *Effective Delivery of a Speech Requires Effective Rehearsal*

13-39. **Teaching Strategy**

This author feels that a verbatim presentation of Outline, VI, through VIII, rehearsing a speech, is a quite practical training exercise for students.

13-40. **Class Activity**

If you have heard students speak several times, the students are quite ready and willing to discuss their delivery "problems" in small groups. Allow them to talk about their delivery difficulties in their own critical categories first. Suggest several ways of looking at delivery improvements needed. Do students feel that they have some, more, or too many of these problems?

- Being a "human statue," needing work on body movement
- The "whispering pines" syndrome, nervousness causing a soft tone and low volume
- The "glazed over" facial look, interfering with good eye contact
- The "speed demons," the desire to get it over with in a hurry

After, ask each group to brainstorm ideas for solving these delivery problems a little bit at a time.

13-41. **Class Activity**

Assign students a short speech on a topic of their choice. They are to prepare and make <u>very short</u> speaker notes. In a subsequent class divide into groups in different parts of the room. Each student is to deliver a speech to the two others. The element to be concentrated on is *eye contact*. Ask students to carefully and deliberately exaggerate eye contact (probably to the tune of giggles). Nonetheless, they are to use their notes and deliver the planned speech. The lesson will be clear without your help; go on to even bigger and better things.

13-42. **Class Activity**

Ask students to bring all their speaking note cards thus far accumulated. Divide into groups. Have students share their notes, asking questions that come to mind, including:

- How did you get your topic idea?
- What, where, and how did you do your research?
- Have you tried other stuff with your notes?
- Did you memorize the notes?
- Do you plan to improve your scheme? How?

ONLINE TEACHING PLAN

Preview activity: Students should visit the Allyn and bacon Public Speaking website at:
http://wps.ablongman.com/ab_public_speaking_2/0,9651,1593283-,00.html
Preview the concepts in this chapter and write a brief summary of the major ideas from the website.

Teaching activity: View a speech online at http://www.historychannel.com/speeches/archive.html. Write a brief critique of their delivery style using concepts from this chapter.

Review activity: Students should find a volunteer audience member to watch them practice a speech and give a brief critique of their delivery. The volunteer should write 3-5 suggestions for the speaker and submit them to the instructor.

CHAPTER FOURTEEN:
USING PRESENTATION AIDS

Chapter-at-a-Glance

Detailed Outline	Instructor Resources	Supplements	Professor Notes
The Value of Presentation aids (p. 306)	**Learning Objective #1:** Discuss how presentation aids help communicate ideas. **Annotated Chapter Outline (ACO):** 14-1 through 14-10	**Audience Memory and Impact of Visual Aids:** Allyn and Bacon Transparency #T-80	
Types of Presentation Aids- Three Dimensional (p. 308) <ul><li>Objects</li><li>Models</li><li>People</li></ul>	**Learning Objective #2:** Describe the use of three-dimensional aids.	**Digital Media Archive** (DMAC) T13I01, T13I06, T13I04, T13I05, T13I06 Preparing Presentation Aids for Presentation, ALL	
Types of Presentation Aids—Two Dimensional (p. 310) <ul><li>Drawings</li><li>Photographs</li><li>Slides</li><li>Maps</li><li>Graphs</li><li>Charts</li><li>Flip charts</li><li>Chalkboards/ whiteboard</li><li>Overhead transparencies</li><li>Computer-generated aids</li></ul>	**Learning Objective #3:** Identify ways of producing two-dimensional aids. ACO: 14-11,through 14-15 ACO: 14-16, 14-17 ACO: 14-22	**Types of visual aids:** Allyn and Bacon Transparencies #T-82, T-83 **DMAC** T13I11 **Using the Internet as A Presentation Aid** http://www.abacon.com/bebepub/homepage/shchapter14.htm **(In)effective graphs** Allyn and Bacon Transparencies #T-97, T-98, T-99, T-100 **DMAC** T13I02, T13I03, T13I07, T13I08, T13I09, T13I10, T13I09, T13I12	
Speaker's Homepage (p. 319) <ul><li>Audiovisual aids</li><li>Videotapes and movies</li><li>CD-ROM</li><li>DVD</li><li>Audio aids</li></ul>	**Learning Objective #4:** Discuss the uses of audiovisual aids	**Guidelines for selecting visual aids:** Allyn and Bacon Transparency #T-84	
Guidelines for Developing Presentation Aids (p. 322) <ul><li>Make them easy to see</li><li>Keep them simple</li><li>Select the right aids</li><li>Do not use dangerous or illegal presentation</li></ul>	**Learning Objective #5:** Identify the guidelines for developing presentation aids ACO 14-20	**Guidelines for preparing visual aids:** Allyn and Bacon Transparency #T-85	

Detailed Outline	Instructor Resources	Supplements	Professor Notes
aids		**Avoid distracting your audience:** Allyn and Bacon Transparency # T-86	
Guidelines for Using Presentation Aids (p. 324)	**Learning Objective #6:** Identify guidelines for using presentation aids.		
• Rehearse your presentation aids	**ACO** 14-23, 14-24, 14-25, 14-26	**Using storyboards:** Allyn and Bacon Transparencies #T-87, T-88	
• Have eye contact with audience, not presentation aids		**Design Rules for visual aids** Allyn and Bacon Transparencies #T-88; T-89; T-90; T-91; T-92	
• Explain your presentation aids			
• Do not pass objects among your audience			
• Use animals with caution	**ACO** 14-27, 14-28, 14-29, 14-30, 14-31		
• Use handouts effectively		**(In)effective clipart:** Allyn and Bacon Transparencies #T-93, T-94	
• Time your visuals to control your audience's attention			
• Use technology effectively		**Too much information:** Allyn and Bacon Transparency #T-95	
• Remember Murphy's Law!		**Enough information:** Allyn and Bacon Transparency # T-96	
		DMAC T13I13 T13I14 through T13I25	
		Using Visual Aids: Allyn and Bacon Transparency #T-81	

LEARNING OBJECTIVES

14-1.   Students will be able to discuss five ways in which presentation aids help communicate ideas to an audience.

14-2.   Students will be able to describe the use of three-dimensional presentation aids.

14-3.   Students will be able to identify ways of producing and using two-dimensional visual aids.

14-4.   Students will be able to discuss the uses of presentation aids.

14-5.   Students will able to identify guidelines for developing presentation aids.

14-6.   Students will be able to identify guidelines for using presentation aids.

CHAPTER OUTLINE

I.   As an audience-centered speaker, you will find presentation aids invaluable for five reasons.

    A.   Presentation aids enhance *understanding*.

        1. Of five senses, more is learned visually than with all other senses combined.

        2. Because of TV viewing habits, audiences are visually oriented.

    B.   Presentation aids enhance *memory*.

    C.   Presentation aids help listeners *organize ideas*.

    D.   Presentation aids help *gain and maintain attention*.

    E.   Presentation aids help *illustrate a sequence of events or procedures*.

II. Presentation aids are grouped in three broad categories.

    A.   A first category of presentation aid is *three-dimensional aids,* including three types.

        1. Actual <u>objects</u> add listener interest because they are tangible, real, and can be touched, smelled, and tasted as well as seen.

        2. If objects cannot be practicably brought to the speech, consider <u>models,</u> which can suggest the real thing nicely.

        3. <u>People</u> can serve as excellent presentation aids.

            a. The speaker is his or her own best presentation aid.

            b. Do choose a trusted friend or colleague and rehearse; don't try it "cold turkey!"

            c. Bring them on when needed, and retire them when finished with the demonstration.

    B.   A second category of presentation aid is *two-dimensional aids.*

        1. <u>Drawings</u> are common two-dimensional presentation aids.

        2. <u>Photographs</u> can be excellent presentation aids.

        3. <u>Slides</u> can serve a visual purpose well, provided you have projector and screen.

            a. Slide shows have inbuilt possible problems, including slide jams and bulb burnouts.

b. Know your equipment and be sure slides are in proper presentational order.

4. Maps, if enough magnification is possible, typically interest audiences.

5. In today's world of computer generation and enhancement graphs present useful statistical information in an easy-to-understand format.

a. Bar graphs and pie graphs are well-known to audiences and easy for them to grasp information from.

b. Line graphs and picture graphs often improve upon bar graphs.

6. Charts summarize and present a great deal of information in a small amount of space.

7. Flip Charts are commonly used in business presentations and training sessions.

8. For college people the chalkboard or whiteboard is still the most readily available visual, or presentational aid.

a. When using the chalkboard try not to talk with back to the audience.

b. Use chalkboard briefly; other aids are much better to prepare and use.

9. Overhead transparencies are popular.

a. Lights need not be dimmed to view the projection.

b. Speaker can maintain audience eye-contact.

c. Remember important advice when using overhead projection.

(1) If possible, practice use of aid in actual area to be used.

(2) Turn off projector when visual is not in use.

(3) Limit amount of information on a single transparency.

(4) Align projector; eliminate the annoying "Keystone Effect."

(5) Speak loudly enough to neutralize projector "hum."

(6) Consider using a larger font size on transparencies.

(7) Consider blocking portions of transparency not yet in use (use a piece of paper).

(8) If possible leave the bottom one-fourth blank (audiences may not see bottom portion, due to seating in the room).

(9) Colored transparencies are better; try using them.

(10)   For ease of handling, fix transparencies in a cardboard frame.

10. Computer-generated presentation aids offer professional looking illustrations to your speech.

    a.   Using presentation programs such as Microsoft PowerPoint you can design and create presentation aids on your computer.

    b.   After construction, your computer can be hooked up to a special large-screen projector.

    c.   Design features you may employ include outlines, graphs, charts, and drawings.

    d.   With the available equipment, images, video and audio clips may be inserted directly into your presentation (black/white and color "Clip Art" is now readily available, a sort of "image bank").

    e.   Tips for designing computer graphics:

        (1) Keep sights and sounds simple.

        (2) Repeat visual elements of your presentation.

        (3) Choose a typeface with care.

        (4) Make informed decisions about using color.

        (5) Allow plenty of time to prepare your presentation aids.

C.   The third broad category of presentation aid is *audio-visual.*

    1.   Audio-visual aids have graduated; in place of passively instructing or entertaining us, we may now use them to actively support ideas.

    2.   VCRs can be connected to regular TVs to show brief scenes from movies, training movie excerpts, or a self-made video.

3. CD-ROMs are particularly exciting, allowing instructor or trainer to instantaneously endlessly retrieve any type of information and add it to whatever else is going on in a projection.

4. DVDs are widely used as presentation aids.

    a. DVDs produce exceptional sound and picture quality.

    b. Players may be hooked up to TV sets or computers, and provide quick access to the necessary audio and video clips.

5. Tapes and compact audio discs can complement a visual display.

III. Observe five principles in designing and constructing presentation aids.

A. MAKE IT EASY TO SEE! MAKE IT BIG ENOUGH FOR EVERYBODY IN THE AUDIENCE TO SEE!

B. Keep it simple; complexity is not a virtue in presentation aids.

C. Select the right presentation aid, keeping these criteria in mind.

    1. Consider your audience, especially size.

    2. Think of your speech objective.

    3. Take into account your own skill and experience.

    4. Know the room in which you will speak.

D. Do not use dangerous or illegal presentation aids, that may shock or endanger an audience.

IV. Follow nine time-tested guidelines to effective presentation aid use.

A. Rehearse using your presentation aids just as you rehearse the speech or presentation itself.

B. Have eye contact with your audience, not your presentation aids.

C. Explain your presentation aids; audiences don't necessarily immediately grasp your visual point.

D. Do not pass objects among your audience; they'll not see it while you are talking (frustration), or they'll get it and stop listening while you are still talking.

E. Use animals with caution; they are unpredictable.

F. Use handouts effectively.

   1. Don't hand them out at all during the speech, unless it is an absolute must (they'll look and read, not listen).

   2. If they must look, or are looking when you don't want them to, at least direct them where to look in the handout.

   3. Tell the audience to keep the handouts face down until they need them.

   4. Prepare an overhead transparency for each page of the handout.

   5. Number the pages in your handout.

   6. Again, don't distribute unless necessary (distribute a handout summary of your ideas after the speech).

G. Time your visuals, showing when appropriate and stowing when no longer needed.

   1. Remove your presentation aid when no longer needed.

   2. Have visuals, especially overhead transparencies, already in place and ready for use.

   3. Consider an assistant to help handle the presentation aid setup and use.

H. Use technology effectively.

   1. Choose the technology that enables you to retain contact audiences.

   2. Do begin to learn and utilize new teaching and learning technology.

I. Remember "Murphy's Law" (If something can go wrong, it will!).

REVIEW GUIDE

14-1.   List five textbook reasons why presentation aids are invaluable to speakers.

14-2.   List three specific types of three-dimensional presentation aids.

14-3.   List ten types of two-dimensional presentation aids.

14-4.   List four textbook audio-visual presentational aids.

14-5.   List and explain with examples five principles in designing and constructing presentation aids.

14-6.   List and explain nine guidelines to effective use of presentation aids.

14-7.   What is the relationship between understanding and memory?

14-8.   What is the distinguishing difference between two-dimensional and three dimensional presentation aids?

14-9.   Why are objects desirable presentation aids?

14-10. Considering computer technology, why are overhead transparencies still popular?

14-11. List ten tips for effective use of overhead transparencies.

14-12. What excellent presentational aids can be generated with PowerPoint?

14-13. How does the concept KISS apply to this chapter?

14-14. What are the advantages and disadvantages of the traditional chalkboard as a presentation aid?

14-15. How have audio presentation aids evolved?

14-16. List four criteria to guide selection of the right presentation aids.

14-17. Which is more important: the presentation aid or the speaker/presenter?

14-18. Review reasons for not passing objects among the audience during a presentation.

14-19. What are three good rules for effective use of handouts?

14-20. Briefly describe "Murphy's Law." How does it apply to this chapter (list as many possibilities as you can)?

ANNOTATED CHAPTER OUTLINE

A. *Why Use Presentation Aids?*

14-1. **Related Reading**

To learn more about teaching students to use PowerPoint and other presentation aids, review the following article:

Downing, J. & Garmon, C. (2001) Teaching Students in the Basic Course How to Use Presentation Software. *Communication Education, 50,* 218-230.

14-2. **Background Information**

To introduce the chapter, show one or more of these films.

- *Aids to Speaking*, Coronet/MTI Films and Video. Color, 15 minutes.
- *Choosing the Audiovisual Dimension,* Films for the Humanities (1982). Color, 15 minutes.
- *How to Get Your Point Across in 30 Seconds or Less*, Coronet/MTI Films and Video. Color, 30 minutes.

14-3. **Teaching Strategy**

Briefly explain five reasons presentation aids are invaluable to speakers (use Outline, I, A-E).

14-4. **Teaching Strategy**

Are audio-visual aids really <u>necessary</u> in speeches? Don't provocative ideas, strong evidence, and appropriate language convey everything a speaker needs to convey? These are questions sometimes heard from students, although most students enjoy developing and using audio-visual aids in speeches (it reduces their nervousness). Lead a class discussion of the relationship of audio-visual aids to audience-centering and the usefulness of audio-visual aids to a speaker.

14-5. **Class Activity**

Your students may be involved in very large classes. If they are lucky, their classes are taught using state-of-the-art technology. Ask students who are in such classes to take notes on the visual aids used, remembering the rules and guidelines of this chapter. In subsequent classes, ask a few students for an informal oral report, based on their notes.

14-6. **Teaching Strategy**

Ask students to think of topics that involve a sequence of steps or events. How can presentation aids help demonstrate the process? Some examples are obvious, e.g., repotting a plant, buying materials, switching containers, and rejuvenating the soil. Other topics are more of a challenge, e.g., how HIV can spread from one set of partners to many people. Diagrams or cluster charts can help illustrate the progression of this chain reaction into an epidemic.

14-7. Teaching Strategy

Make students aware of campus regulations regarding animals, alcohol, firearms, and controlled substances. Having any of them on campus without permission is probably a violation of college policy.

14-8. Teaching Strategy

Bring in a friend or colleague to use as a live "presentation aid." Introduce them and ask them to give a brief account of their favorite memory or their most memorable vacation spot.

14-9. Class Activity

Publishing companies often provide videotaped samples of student speeches with their textbooks. In many of these speeches, students use audio-visual aids. Showing taped speeches like these is an effective supplement to this chapter. Students can critique the speaker's choice of aids and their effective or ineffective use of them. Student speeches are available from your textbook's publisher, as well as from Internet resources.

B. *Three Basic Types of Presentation Aids are Three Dimensional, Two Dimensional, and Audio Visual*

14-10. Teaching Strategy

Briefly explain all forms of presentation aids except computer-generated images, by use of Outline, II, A through C, 4, e. Caution students: "Never again completely believe what you see in images of any kind — pictures, movies, TV, computers." Through technology we have the capacity to present anything at all as "Reality." The film *The Matrix* makes this point agonizingly clear. Or did we really believe *Forest Gump*'s Lieutenant Dan had no legs? Lead a short discussion: is computer-generated "reality" necessary in our lives?

14-11. Teaching Strategy

<u>Demonstrate to students the wide range of audio-visual aids that can be used to enhance the delivery of a message.</u> Videotape one nightly network news broadcast for purposes of analyzing and evaluating with your class the myriad of audio-visual aids used. Any show chosen will probably have a nice mix of objects, models, drawings, charts, graphs, maps, and video clips.

14-12. Teaching Strategy

Using posters as an example, present these ideas about proper presentation aids use in a speech.

- Do not show the visual aid until logically and psychologically appropriate.
- Everybody in the room must be able to see the visual aid at all times.
- Talk to the audience, not to the presentation aid.
- Clearly direct audience attention to appropriate parts of presentation aid in sync with verbal analysis.
- "Stow" the presentation aid temporarily or permanently when use is suspended or complete ("show and stow").

14-13. Teaching Strategy

Bring personal snapshots. Demonstrate appropriate and inappropriate ways of using the shots as presentation aids. Enlarge a shot, to contrast it with using visuals too small for the audience. Not all students will know the developing technology of digital images. Talk that up a bit.

14-14. Teaching Strategy

Maps can be good news for speeches. If you cannot find an outline map with no detailed features, an overhead transparency may be a good alternative. Transparencies are easily made, but they can be ineffective if used poorly (see chapter guidelines, usage).

14-15. Class Activity

This activity will combine a review of demographic audience analysis with production of visuals. Give the necessary number of volunteers the results of the "Get Acquainted" questionnaire completed by students as part of the Chapter 1 exercises. Ask two students to prepare a *bar graph* of collective year in school of the class. Ask two more students to prepare a *pie graph* analyzing the ages of the class. Ask a third pair to construct a *line graph* of ethnic membership data. In the subsequent class, direct the volunteers to recreate their designs on chalkboards, allowing "process" to be demonstrated. Lead a critical discussion of (a) the visual techniques, (b) the proper graph mechanics, and (c) the use of the chalkboard in this instance. Thank the volunteers.

14-16. Teaching Strategy

Overhead transparencies can be effective mechanisms for using other types of presentation aids. Explain to students that drawings, for example, can be made onto transparencies. Basic graphs, diagrams, and charts can all be put onto transparencies and used with a projector. Also, some photocopy machines, possibly in the library or media center on your campus, will make transparencies if you insert a sheet of plastic instead of paper into the feed tray.

14-17. **Teaching Strategy**

Demonstrate the problems associated with overhead projectors. Cartoon panels might hold audience attention to the errors quite well.

- Place the projector where it cannot be plugged in. Ham it up. Advise students: practice deployment of presentation aids ahead of time if you can.
- Leave the projector running while you go on to a point not associated with the visual. Advise students: turn off their projector when not in use ("stow it").
- Show a really busy transparency. Advise students again: presentation aids should not be too busy.
- Demonstrate and eliminate the "keystone effect."
- Speak lower than classroom noises, especially the projector hum. Advise students the obvious: always adjust speaker volume as needed.
- With several transparencies, demonstrate the desirability at times of using larger fonts.
- Crowd a transparency bottom with important detail. Ask students in the rear what the transparency has on it. Advise students: try to leave the bottom fourth blank.
- Contrast two transparencies with same detail, one clear, with black text, the other colored, with black text. Advise students: color is easier on the eyes (and the audience's attention span).

14-18. **Teaching Strategy**

Use the chalkboard as sparingly as possible as a prime instructional or training device. Inappropriate uses may include:

- Inordinate amounts of instructor time spent on chalkboard inscribing.
- Poor use of chalkboard, in terms of preparing striking visual assists.
- Indirect evidence that instructor spends little time preparing a lesson (anything that goes on a chalkboard can go on any other type of visual assist).
- Poor vocal use of presentation aid (instructor tends to talk to the chalkboard).
- Instructors who reject presentation aids other than chalkboard also tend to scorn the idea that visual images convey more information than words (the chalkboard, after all, is seldom used by instructors to create artistic designs).

14-19. **Class Activity**

Divide into groups. Assign each group to pick a speech topic that would involve a series of steps to be explained. Ask them to meet outside class and create a list of necessary steps. Tell them also to think of appropriate presentation aids (a variety, please) for each step. Direct them to produce a poster-type presentation aid to display to the class at a subsequent time. Essentially, posters will contain (a) statement of the topic, (b) on one side a list of the steps, (c) on the other side a corresponding list of presentation aids. Lead class in a brief analysis of the posters, applying criteria for construction and design. If time permits, also analyze groups' choices of steps.

C. *Effective Speakers Should Observe Five Guidelines for Design and Construction Of Presentation Aids*

14-20. **Teaching Strategy**

A verbatim exposition of Outline material III, A-E, "Five principles in designing and constructing presentation aids" is suggested.

14-21. **Teaching Strategy**

Suggest to students that many presentation aids involve artistic composition, that is, the putting together of balanced visual elements on a surface, be it chalkboard, poster, computer image, or projection. Using a poster board as an example, provide these rules of composition. If you have a storehouse of poster presentation aids to display as models of the rules, so much the better.

- Everything on the poster must be big enough for everybody in the room to see.
- The poster cannot be too busy — do not include too much detail or too many items.
- The poster had best not be so flimsy as to fold over and fall off a podium or other display method.
- Use color — especially red, white, and black.

This author tends to use poster board-type presentation aids as his generic teaching device, postulating that principles of construction and use of poster boards tends to "transfer" strongly to many other types of presentation aids.

14-22. **Teaching Strategy**

If possible, in your classroom, or in a media center location, demonstrate the range of computer simulation and projection available to speakers. Include these elements:

- Using PowerPoint or persuasion to generate enhanced projections of this chapter's Outline (include a small amount of clip art).
- Adding images to the enhanced projections by scanning photographs appropriate to Outline text.
- Use an audio or video disc to provide background "mood music."
- Interfacing your voice-over presentation with the electronic visual assists in explanation of the chapter.

D. *Effective Speakers Should Follow Nine Time-Tested Principles For Using Presentation Aids*

14-23. Teaching Strategy

This strategy provides a creative approach to the discussion of do's and don'ts regarding the use of audio-visual aids in a speech. Any weeknight you can tune into *Late Night with David Letterman* and hear a hilarious "Top Ten List." A list like the one below can be an interesting, creative way to help students understand some basic principles related to audio-visual aids (especially if the list is delivered "Dave style"). Here's a humorous introduction to the list: "Ladies and gentlemen, from the home office in Boston, Massachusetts [the home of Allyn & Bacon publishers], the top ten things to remember about using audio-visual aids in a speech are . . ."

TOP TEN THINGS TO REMEMBER ABOUT USING AUDIO-VISUAL AIDS IN A SPEECH

Number 10: Procrastinate, so you can prepare your audio-visual aids in the 2:00am quiet of your home.

Number 9: They might be useful, but audiences don't flip over flip charts.

Number 8: Your speech will be more entertaining if you don't practice with your audio-visual aids. That way there's no telling what interesting things might happen.

Number 7: Don't allow your buddy to throw you when you demonstrate the wrestling hold that made you a champ.

Number 6: A photograph circulating around the room may be more fun for the audience than your speech is.

Number 5: Pie graphs are not available at your local bakery.

Number 4: In a boring round of speeches, the suspense of waiting for a poster to fall off the easel can stimulate an audience.

Number 3: Darken the room for videos and slide shows so your classmates can take a much-needed nap.

Number 2: Distribute handouts so the audience will have paper for doodling and spitball ammunition during your speech.

AND, Ladies and Gentlemen, the Number One most important thing to remember about using audio-visual aids in a speech is...(drum roll, please...) **Cows will go up stairs, but not down stairs.**

14-24. Teaching Strategy

Consider a verbatim review of Outline, IV, A-H, "Nine time-tested guidelines to effective visual aid use."

14-25. Class Activity

Ask students to watch a gourmet cooking show on TV. Alternatively, videotape a segment for classroom showing. Probe the class.

- What presentation aids does the chef use?
- Are the aids used effectively? Why or why not?
- Do the objects promote attention?
- Do you think the chef practiced the presentation aids before this show?

14-26. Background Information

Show a clip from the film *Nothing in Common*, in which Tom Hanks uses presentation aids. Hanks nicely illustrates our textbook's information about using videotapes and movies for supplementing speeches. His character's staff supplies the visual and audio effects for Hanks-as-David Bannister's presentation.

14-27. Class Activity

Organize a review quiz game using major concepts from the chapter.

14-28. Class Activity

In a written essay, ask students to respond to the following situation:

You enroll in an intercultural communication course. Your professor assigns final oral presentations to cultural groups, either international cultures (e.g., Japanese culture, New Zealander culture) or co-cultures within the United States (e.g., physically disabled individuals, gays and lesbians, Jewish Americans). What will you choose as the topic of this presentation?

First, students should select a cultural or co-cultural group as the focus of their hypothetical class assignment, offering a brief explanation of why they chose that particular group. Then, students should use the following items to structure the remainder of the essay:

(1) Discuss five ways in which audio-visual aids will help communicate your ideas to your intercultural communication class.
(2) Describe the use of one possible three-dimensional visual aid for this presentation.
(3) Identify ways of using two-dimensional presentation aids for this presentation.
(4) Discuss the uses of any audio-visual aids that could enhance this speech.
(5) Identify how you would apply the guidelines for using audio-visual aids in your speech.

If time permits, ask several students to share essays orally with the class.

14-29. Class Activity

The purpose of this activity is to provide students with ideas for audio-visual aids to use in upcoming speech assignments. During the time that students are developing speeches and getting prepared to deliver them, form triads of students for the purpose of brainstorming for audio-visual aid ideas. Each student shares her or his topic and main points with the other two classmates, then the group works to generate possibilities. For example, a group member may have just rented a movie on videotape that has a scene that would be highly effective to illustrate a point in someone's speech; a member has read something for another class that pertains to someone's topic; a classmate knows someone in town who is an authority on someone's topic.

14-30. Teaching Strategy repeated

Make students aware once again of campus regulations regarding animals, alcohol, firearms, and controlled substances. Having any of them on campus without permission is probably a violation of college policy.

14-31. Class Activity

Bring your "stockpile" of presentation aids. Ask students to rate them on a scale from 1 to 10 for their adherence to principles and effectiveness. Add the Ebert and Roper technique of "thumbs up" and "thumbs down" as a way of determining the "grand winner."

ONLINE TEACHING PLAN

Preview activity: Go to the website entitled, *When Your Presentation Crashes* at http://www.fastcompany.com/online/07/130crash.html.

This site offers valuable information about the dangers of using technology for visual aids when giving a speech. Students should review the information and write a brief retrospective about a time in the past when technology has failed them. Then ask them to post the responses to share with the class.

Teaching activity: Divide the class into online "groups." Assign each group to pick a speech topic that would involve a series of steps to be explained. Ask them to meet online or correspond using email, and create a list of necessary steps. Tell them also to think of appropriate presentation aids (a variety, please) for each step. Direct them to produce a PowerPoint presentation aid to submit for the class. Essentially, the PowerPoint visual aid should contain (a) a statement of the topic, (b) on one side a list of the steps, and (c) on the other side a corresponding list of presentation aids. Post the responses and ask for constructive feedback from class members. Lead class in a brief analysis of the posters, applying criteria for construction and design. If time permits, also analyze groups' choices of steps.

Review activity: After reading the information presented on the website entitled, *Using the Internet as a Presentation Aid* at http://www.abacon.com/beebepub/homepage/shchapter14.htm, ask students to write a brief response statement to describe their feelings about the usefulness and appropriateness of multimedia presentation aids. Students might create a website or slideshow that exemplifies concepts discussed in this chapter regarding guidelines for presentation aids. Run the slide show on the class bulletin board, or post links to the websites on the course website.

CHAPTER FIFTEEN: Speaking to Inform

Chapter-at-a-Glance

Detailed Outline	Instructor Resources	Supplements	Professor Notes
Goals of Informative Speaking (334) • Enhance understanding • Maintain interest • Be remembered	**Learning Objective #1:** Identify three goals of speaking to inform **Annotated Chapter Outline (ACO):** 15-1, through 15-14	**Purposes of Informative Speeches:** Allyn and Bacon Transparency #T-58 **Digital Media Archive for Communication** (DMAC) 12I01	
Types of Informative Speeches (p. 336) • Speeches about objects • Speeches about procedures • Speeches about people • Speeches about events • Speeches about ideas	**Learning Objective #2:** Describe five different types of informative speeches **ACO:** 15-8, 15-15, 15-16	**Types of Informative Speeches:** Allyn and Bacon Transparency #T-59	
Strategies to enhance audience understanding (p. 341) • Speak with clarity • Use principles of adult learning • Clarify complex processes • Use effective visual reinforcement	**Learning Objective #3:** Use four strategies to enhance audience understanding **ACO:** 15-9, 15-17, through 15-30	**Speech Preparation Workbook** (SPW) pp. 69-70	
Speaker's Homepage (p. 345)			
Strategies to maintain audience interest (p. 344) • Present information that relates to your listener • Establish a motive for your audience to listen to you • Tell a story	**Learning Objective #4** Use three strategies to enhance audience interest **ACO:** 15-31		
Strategies to enhance audience recall (p. 346) • Build in redundancy • Pace your information flow • Reinforce key ideas verbally • Reinforce key ideas nonverbally	**Learning Objective #5:** Use four strategies to enhance audience recall of information. **ACO:** 15-32		
Sample Informative Speech (p. 348)			

LEARNING OBJECTIVES

1.   Students will be able to identify three goals of speaking to inform.

2.   Students will be able to describe five different types of informative speeches.

3.   Students will be able to effectively and appropriately use four strategies to enhance audience understanding.

4.   Students will be able to effectively and appropriately use three strategies to enhance audience interest.

5.   Students will be able to effectively and appropriately use four strategies to enhance audience recall of information presented in an informative speech.

CHAPTER OUTLINE

I.   To inform is to share information with others to enhance their knowledge or understanding of the information, concepts, and ideas you present.

A.   To inform is to become a teacher inasmuch as you define, illustrate, clarify, and elaborate upon topics.

B.   Speech teachers and past public speaking students believe that speaking to inform is the single most important skill taught in public speaking classes.

II.   Effective speaking to inform presupposes three goals.

A.   Informative speaking should enhance understanding.

B.   Informative speaking should maintain interest.

C.   Informative speaking should be memorable.

III.   Informative speeches divide into five types.

A.   Informative speeches may be about *objects*.

B.   Informative speeches may concern *procedures*.

C.   Informative speeches may be about *people*.

D.   Informative speeches may deal with *events*.

E.   Informative speeches may explore *ideas*.

IV.   Effective speaking to inform requires four general strategies.

A.   Informative speakers need a strategy to *define ideas clearly.*

1. Speakers may find that less sophisticated listeners will need clear, easy-to-understand <u>definition by example</u>.

2. More sophisticated listeners may profit more from technical, or <u>operational definitions</u>.

B.   Informative speakers need to *use principles of adult learning.*

1. Adults like to be given information they can use immediately.

2. Adult learners like to be actively involved in the learning process.

3. Adult learners like to connect their life experiences with the new information they learn.

4. Adult learners like to know how the information is relevant to their needs and their busy lives.

C.   Informative speakers need a strategy to *clarify complex processes.*

1. By using <u>analogy</u>, informative speakers allow audiences to learn about the new by comparison with the old.

2. Informative speakers would do well to offer <u>models</u> or <u>pictures</u>, or other visual aids, to take advantage of the audience's strong visual sense (Chapter 14).

3. Informative speakers should <u>describe</u>, offering answers to who, what, when, where, and why of a process.

4. Informative speakers should provide strong <u>descriptions</u> (word pictures) through four descriptive tools.

a. Form a clear mental image of the person, place, or object before attempts to describe.

b. With lively language, lead listeners to see the appearance of person, place, or object.

c. With colorful, onomatopoetic words, tell your listeners what they will hear, smell, feel, and taste.

d. Describe smell, touch, and taste, if appropriate.

      e.   With specific adjectives, tell listeners what emotions they will feel when they experience the situation you are describing.

    D.   Effective informative speakers use *visual reinforcement*.

V.   Speaker's Homepage

VI.   Effective informative speakers use three strategies to *enhance audience interest*.

    A.   Establish a *motive for your audience to listen*.

        1. Audiences are not "waiting breathlessly for you to speak."

        2. Take advantage of built-in audience motivations, such as, "Listen to my lecture and do better on the next test."

    B.   *Tell a story.*

        1. A good story incorporates conflict.

        2. A good story includes action.

        3. A good story creates suspense.

        4. A good story may incorporate humor.

    C.   Present information that *relates to your listeners*.

VII.   Effective informative speakers use four strategies to *enhance audience recall*.

    A.   Build in *redundancy* (Chapter 4); remember the "Golden Rule."

        1. Repeat key points.

        2. Use previews and summaries (Chapter 9).

    B.   *Pace* your information *flow*.

        1. Be especially sensitive to flow if your topic is new and unfamiliar to audience.

        2. Adjust flow to audience capability, not speaker needs and desires.

    C.   Reinforce key ideas <u>verbally</u>.

    D.   Reinforce key ideas *nonverbally*.

1. Use gestures and pauses (Chapter 13).

2. Use platform movement to emphasize main ideas (Chapter 13).

REVIEW GUIDE

15-1.   List three general goals of speaking to inform.

15-2.   List four strategies to enhance audience understanding in informative speaking.

15-3.   List three strategies to enhance audience interest in informative speaking.

15-4.   List four strategies to enhance audience recall of information in informative speaking.

15-5.   List five relatively different types of speeches to inform.

15-6.   Give topic examples for each of the five types.

15-7.   Illustrate operational definition with four examples.

15-8.   Relate computer images to photographs with an analogy.

15-9.   Attempt to relate the topic of Social Security administration to your public speaking class.

ANNOTATED CHAPTER OUTLINE

A. *Effective Informative Speaking has Four Goals*

15-1. **Related Reading**

In a recent article, Katherine Rowan outlines methods of teaching explanatory speaking, a form of informative speaking. She traces this practice through its classical roots, suggesting that public speaking teachers should emphasize invention or the content of ideas, not just their arrangement. For an insightful discussion about teaching informative speaking, see Rowan, K. E. (1995). "A new pedagogy for explanatory public speaking: Why arrangement should not substitute for invention." Communication Education 44, 236-250.

15-2. Teaching Strategy

Invite an experienced salesperson or agency spokesperson to speak with your class on the techniques he or she uses to inform customers about a product or service. An insurance salesperson, for example, might emphasize definitions and descriptions because many people are unfamiliar with the types of policies and coverage and with the jargon of the insurance business. A rape crisis counselor might use more analogies and operational definitions in a presentation, due to the sensitive nature of the topic.

15-3. Class Activity

Divide into groups. Assign each to exhaustively define the verb, "to inform," concentrating on uses associated with writing and speaking. Without being specific, ask students to use as many defining methods as they know how. Collect papers and convert into transparencies or other projections. Share in subsequent class. Call attention to astounding number of synonyms for "inform."

15-4. Teaching Strategy

Students often struggle with the difference between informing and persuading. You will likely need to clarify for students that the main difference rests in the desired response from the audience. Also stress the importance of learning to present "just the facts" (informative speaking), versus offering one's evaluation of those facts (persuasive speaking). Share sample speech topics with the class and have students discuss how each topic could be used for an informative speech, and then turned into a persuasive speech.

15-5. Class Activity

This activity encourages students to practice creating different kinds of informative purpose statements. Below are several topics. Have students independently or in small groups narrow each topic and write specific behavioral purpose statements for a speech to inform.

Architecture	Russian Culture
Arkansas	Sports
Astronomy	Starving People Around the World
Caring for a Healthy Body	Streets
Donations to Favorite Charities	Stress Reduction
Fish	Technology
Oppression of Others	Teeth
Personal Spirituality	Theatre
Poet Maya Angelou	Weather

15-6. Class Activity

Assign students a written essay in which they must address five items in response to the following hypothetical speaking situation:

Imagine that you are a member of the city council. The council has just passed a new ordinance that mandates a curfew for persons under the age of 13. Your task is to explain the ordinance to the public and the media at a town hall meeting. You will first make a brief presentation on the curfew and its ramifications on local citizens, then engage in a question-and-answer period with the audience and reporters. Since this situation involves informative speaking, use the following five items to analyze this situation.

(1) Which of the goals of informative speaking apply in this situation?
(2) Describe five different types of informative speeches and indicate which is most appropriate for this situation.
(3) Provide a definition, a description, and an analogy that could be used in this presentation.
(4) Explain the four-part strategy to change common misconceptions that could arise about the ordinance.
(5) Of the nine ways to make an informative speech memorable, select four and explain how they would be of benefit in this case.

If time permits ask students to share their essays with the class.

15-7. Teaching Strategy

As an interest-promoting device, emphasize the importance of demonstrating to an audience how they will personally benefit from the speech in some way. Ask students how they could directly relate the following topics to an audience of college students:
1. the bleak future of Social Security — part-time and full-time workers pay into Social Security, but may not receive its benefits when they reach retirement age (practical); cuts in Social Security benefits cause problems for elderly family members (economic);
2. the origin of rap music (curiosity, entertainment, cultural awareness).

15-8. Class Activity

In triads, have students choose several news events that could be developed into an informative speech. Some examples include: the Littleton High School and other similar school tragedies, the booming U.S. economy, presidential integrity, and the U.S. military's role in NATO peace-keeping missions. Next, ask the triads to consider two questions: How can this topic be made relevant to our classroom audience? What organizational pattern would be most appropriate?

15-9. **Class Activity**

Ask students to design audience motivation statements to stimulate listener interest for these topics:
1. the effects of tourism on the preservation of national parks
2. health risks related to high-cholesterol intake
3. environmental racism
4. regular nursing/retirement home inspections

15-10. **Teaching Strategy**

Ask your students, "How many of you are planning to be teachers?" Students will interpret the question as "credentialed teachers," and just a few will raise their hands. Tell them they are all likely to play the role of teachers in our rapidly changing society: teacher, trainer, coach, mentor — call it what you will. Of all things teachers are called upon for, communicating, speaking to inform, is the most common and most valued. To teach is to aid and abet learning, and learning comes from information taken in, absorbed, and integrated. All must plan to inform and to teach within families, workplaces, communities, and the organizations to which all belong. It is not for nothing that public speaking teachers and past students call speaking to inform the highest skill to be learned in such classes. Learn and profit from this unit, speaking to inform.

15-11. **Teaching Strategy**

Ask students, "How many of you have pets? How many have dogs? How many have cats? How many have dogs and cats?" Your true point is this question: "What makes humans truly distinct from other animals?" You will receive a variety of answers, some off the wall, some humorous, and some really on target. One student, perhaps more, will make your point for you. Humans are distinguished by verbal communication ability. Ask students if their philosophical and religious beliefs suggest to them that verbal communication was granted to humans exclusively for a reason. If that be their belief (and it need not be), then perhaps humans have a sort of responsibility to use that gift well. And, if communicating to inform is the most special of all, then do we not have an obligation to learn well about it? Think about it, you say to them. To lightly close this rather heavy little bit, ask students: "With which other animal do we share 99% of our DNA?" Wild guesses, you bet, but one may know: we indeed are that similar to chimpanzees.

15-12. **Class Activity**

Ask students, "What is the purpose of hat racks, clothes hangers, and cup hooks?" Students will probably answer quickly, although puzzled about where you're going. Right. To hang things. Next, ask, "How can you think of things to say when you can't think of things to say?" That may be a puzzler for them. Finally, own up to where you're going: you want them to have some built-in "hooks" they can use to retrieve information regardless of the topic.

First, explain the concept of semantic differential and the "polar adjectives" used in semantic differentials. Give them examples of polar adjectives:

Tall – Short
Warm – Cold
Good – Bad
Workable – Unworkable
Ugly – Pretty
Quick – Slow

Divide in groups. Ask each group to list polar adjectives. Be sure each student copies the group list, as a personal possession for future use. Devise your own list, a list that students can readily use. Below is a suggested list.

Timely – Untimely
Advisable – Inadvisable
Warm - Cold
Short Run – Long Run
Pretty – Ugly
Cheap - Expensive
Quick – Slow
Old – New
Like – Dislike
Bright – Dim
Slim – Fat
Cool – Square

15-13. Class Activity

Ask students to compose their own "semantic differentials." In a subsequent class, divide into groups. Issue the same informative topic for all groups. Direct them to converse on that topic, generating a good discussion. Cruise the groups, motivating and assisting as needed. Students should see the practical application of the polar adjectives, and probably will view the exercise quite favorably. Tell students, of course, that the device is not limited to public speaking class.

15-14. Teaching Strategy

During a roll call ask four students in turn to list one of the four goals of speaking to inform. Follow up with this class question: "Are all four goals always looked for?" Lead a discussion of the interrelationships of the four goals. Ask students, "Think about my lectures; which goal do I pursue most strongly?" Don't let students off the hook easily on this one. The resulting discussion may be the clincher for getting students to remember the four goals.

15-15. **Class Activity**

Pair students and ask them to confer. Have each suggest to the other an informative topic they would like to know more about. Ask students to research topics briefly. In a subsequent class have each pair member explain for a minute or two why the other pair member should want to hear about their topic ("Giving the Audience a Reason to Listen"). Review with all students the four goals of informative speaking. How well do they feel they, themselves, provided partners with listening motivation? How well did their partners do? Retain pairs from above. Have each pair devise the general purpose and specific purpose statement for their two "speeches." Call for quick down-and-dirty oral reports to the entire class.

B. *Five Types of Informative Speeches are Distinguished*

15-16. **Class Activity**

Review operational definition (Chapter 8). Ask particular students to give one or more operational definitions of the five types of informative speeches: objects, procedures, people, events, ideas. The exercise also gives students practice in impromptu retrieval of speech topics. Extend exercise to other students as time permits.

C. *Strategies for Informing Your Listeners*

15-17. **Teaching Strategy**

Ask students if they have been to Las Vegas or other gambling places (quickly tell them they don't have to answer the question unless they want to). Ask those who say they have visited these places if they know the game of "craps." Well, you say, craps and other games are "games of chance;" that is, you take a chance of winning and accept a chance of losing. Believe it or not, planning a speech is a game of chance, depending on probabilities of being on target in your planning. Consider audience analysis for a speech to inform. Ask students to explore with you the word "sophistication." Hopefully, you have convinced a few students to carry and use dictionaries. Take your time. This word is important, as you recall, under the general speaking to inform strategy of "explaining new ideas." What are "less sophisticated" and "more sophisticated" listeners? Given a particular topic, how can a speaker tell the difference in advance of speech planning? Remember, tell the students, you truly don't have time for everything. Sometimes you have to roll the dice, hoping for a seven and not "snake eyes." You can be right, and you can be rather horribly wrong in your audience analysis and associated strategy planning. The audience may not be the enemy, but a campaign (the speech) must be planned and the opponent outmaneuvered.

15-18. Class Activity

Use this exercise to illustrate the concept of simplifying ideas to appeal to a given audience. Tell the class to imagine that they were asked to explain their college major to an audience of third graders. Have students role play this speech, including explanations of some concepts related to their majors. The simpler the explanations, the more comprehension and retention there will be among listeners. Finally, explain how this process is effective no matter the age or sophistication level of the audience.

15-19. Class Activity

For a list of sample speech topics, ask students to generate main or subpoints by using the informative speech strategies the text explains. For example, how could definitions (word definitions, definitions by example, and operational definitions) be used as points in a speech about changes in professional football as a result of the institution of the salary cap? How could an analogy, a description, or a word picture improve an informative speech about skin cancer? What are some common misconceptions about contraceptives?

15-20. Class Activity

Divide students into pairs, to play a mild game of "One Up." This game is simply trying to stay ahead of your partner by using good examples. In turn, one student offers a specific topic, or possible happening, and the other student must offer an <u>example pertinent to the suggested topic</u>. The more vivid the example is, the better.

15-21. Class Activity

Divide the class into small groups. Ask each group to find a recent article on a technical subject (e.g., health, science, medicine, economics) from a weekly news magazine (e.g., *Time, Newsweek, U.S. News and World Report*) or a major newspaper. Groups should analyze how the author of the article makes the subject matter clear for a lay audience. In addition, how does the author demonstrate accuracy?

15-22. Class Activity

Videotape an "infomercial" that demonstrates or explains a process or procedure and show it to students. How does the show's host verbally and non-verbally explain how something is done, how it is made, or how it works? Students might mention factors such as repetition, internal summaries, concrete definitions and explanations, use of models or visual aids, and incorporation of pauses. Granted, TV personalities have various cameras and editing to their advantage; however, what makes these individuals successful in this type of informative speaking? Why are infomercials such big money makers?

15-23. Teaching Strategy

Recall with students this old saw: "Sometimes you think you don't know, but that's because you don't know you know." Let that one sink in a bit, and be prepared to repeat it several times. Your point is that students do know what <u>analogy</u> is, and that they use it both consciously and unconsciously. However, in writing and speech classes, for whatever the reason, it is sometimes like pulling teeth to get students to produce analogies on demand. To promote free and easier student production of analogies, share analogies like those below as a way of priming this particular pump. Tell students that you are going through an outline of the chapter, main point by main point with analogies. Suggest that analogies be placed on transparencies, and used in a "strip tease" procedure (students need time with several of them).

Speaking to inform is like exploring an unknown territory, but with a workable map.

Effective speaking to inform is like playing basketball; there is a goal and the object is to hit it.

Just as there are different types of exercise, there are different types of speeches to inform.

A football coach always has a game plan, as does a smart speaker to inform.

New ideas can be like bad tasting medicine, easy to refuse.

Explaining complex procedures to audiences can be like running a maze — where do you go next?

A speaker's attempt to relate to an audience can be like asking for a date: you risk rejection.

An audience's motivation to listen is sometimes as fragile as crystal.

Speaker redundancy compares to a baseball runner tagging the stolen base twice, just to be sure.

A simple idea is to a complex idea as is playing hopscotch to playing chess.

Verbal reinforcement is to nonverbal reinforcement as is one Siamese twin to the other.

A babbling brook flows evenly but sparkling, as should information in an informative speech.

Older information is to newer information as a midwife is to birth.

Memorable visual aids strike us like lightning illuminating a dark cloud.

15-24. **Class Activity**

Divide the class into small groups. Furnish each group with a 100-piece jigsaw puzzle. Direct students to turn all pieces face down. Tell them the puzzle is a "complex process" (as is speaking to inform), and that a plan is necessary to put the puzzle together quickly. Ask each group to agree on a short series of steps that will effectively carry out the task. Flash your stopwatch; tell students they are being timed (in reality, they are not), and you're looking for a winner (you're not). After a time, or a "Bingo!" compare students' lists of steps to a list you previously prepared:

A. Elect a group coordinator (leader).

B. Turn the pieces face up.

C. Leader commands four groups of pieces arranged by general colors.

D. Four persons attempt to join only pieces in "their pile."

E. Leader coordinates final assembly.

Debrief the exercise by reminding that clarifying complex procedures is best accomplished by systematic preplanning. Also announce to students that in several ways the exercise also previewed Chapter 19: Speaking in Small Groups.

15-25. **Class Activity**

Bring to class two diverse pieces of literary description and ask a student to read each aloud. Analyze why each excerpt is effective and vivid. To what senses are the authors appealing? What emotions are evoked? Two excellent passages are the introductory paragraphs of Edgar Allan Poe's "The Fall of the House of Usher," and Flannery O'Connor's description of a doctor's waiting room in "Revelation." Ask students under what circumstances it would be appropriate to include a vivid word picture in an informative speech. Can speakers avoid becoming persuasive while using vivid description and word pictures?

15-26. **Class Activity**

Instruct students to think of two things between classes: (A) what is one of their very favorite things, or activities; and (B) what are some of the wild beliefs (misconceptions) that people have about their thing or activity? In a subsequent class, divide students into groups, asking each group to do two things: (A) thoroughly share with each other the misconceptions people have about their thing or activity; and (B) discuss how the group thinks these misconceptions could be addressed.

15-27. **Teaching Strategy**

Write a word picture of a vivid memory you have from your childhood. The word picture should include vivid, colorful language that appeals to its senses. Read your version to the class and ask students to write their own word pictures.

15-28. **Class Activity**

Pair students who do not yet know each other very well. Direct them to question each other. The questions should yield answers which each, if they were a speaker and the other were in the audience, could use for both preplanning and delivery to "relate" to the audience. Example: "What is your most important personal value? May I ask for other values you hold?"

15-29. **Class Activity**

Videotape a segment of an informative TV program that would interest your students. Programs on the Discovery Channel and Public Broadcast channels work well. Review the textbook's principles of effective informative speaking; then, have students note each principle the program employs, while viewing the tape. Discuss which principles were effective and why, which were not effective and why not, and which were not employed at all.

15-30. **Class Activity**

As a class, view and critique several videotaped student informative speeches (either from a publisher's tape or from past classes). Encourage positive comments by asking what worked well, what they liked, or what were the speaker's strengths. In pairs, students should practice an upcoming informative speech in a class workshop. The role of a student's partner is to provide positive feedback and constructive suggestions for improvement. Afterwards, the speaker can discuss things with which they are not satisfied with, and solicit suggestions and guidance from the partner.

D. *Nine Speaking To Inform Principles Produce Memorable Informative Speeches*

15-31. **Teaching Strategy**

<u>The purpose is to challenge students to make potentially boring informative speech topics interesting, through the application of information in the text chapter.</u> Come up with a list of the most boring, un-audience-centered informative speech topics you can think of (or maybe that you've heard!). As you reveal them to your class, ask students to generate angles on each topic and techniques or strategies to make each topic more engaging. Here are some potentially boring sample informative topics: "The Evolution of the TseTse Fly," "Little Known Facts About Ingrown Toenails," "My Last Trip to the Dentist," and "Calculating the Density of a Rock."

15-32. **Class Activity**

Give students the opportunity practice using strategies to make an informative speech memorable. Present the following information to students in a handout; then have them address the specific items listed below.

Fran is a Doctor of Veterinary Medicine. She travels with her wolf, Two Socks, to educate people about the ways of the wolf, as part of her responsibilities as a member of a group trying to reintroduce the wolf to Yellowstone National Park. Most often she gives informative speeches about wolves, but she also tries to motivate audiences to work to save wolves from extinction. Her audiences range from groups of schoolchildren to people who might drop by a pet store where she and Two Socks are appearing.

Fran is particularly impressive in her use of word pictures to create mental images for audiences. She appeals to many senses when she: (a) describes the appearance of wolves, (b) compares their characteristics to German Shepherds, (c) conveys an image of how wolves move and run, and (d) talks about the sound of their cries, the lack of smell of wolves (even when wet), and how the coat feels to the touch. Below are the suggestions from the textbook for making an informative speech memorable. Give an example from the description of Fran's approach to speechmaking, or that you imagine Fran would use in her speeches about wolves.

1. Presents information that relates to listeners.

2. Establishes a motive for your audience to listen.

3. Builds in redundancy.

4. Uses simple ideas rather than complex ones.

5. Reinforces key ideas verbally.

6. Reinforces key ideas nonverbally.

7. Paces information flow.

8. Relates new information to old.

9. Creates memorable visual aids.

ONLINE TEACHING PLAN

Preview activity: Review the website entitled, *"5W's and How for Informative Speeches"* at: http://www.abacon.com/pubspeak. Students should submit their responses to the interactive exercise to their instructor.

Teaching activity: Post teaching activity 15-32 on your class bulletin board or chat room. Students should complete the assignment online and submit their answers to the instructor.

Review activity: Students should view the information on finding late-breaking information for informative speaking at http://www.abacon.com/beebepub/homepage/shchapter15.htm Go through some of the links in class and discuss how they might be used.

CHAPTER SIXTEEN: Understanding Principles of Persuasive Speaking

Chapter-at-a-Glance

Detailed Outline	Instructor Resources	Supplements	Professor Notes
Persuasion Defined (p. 354) • The influencing of attitudes • The changing of beliefs • Changing or reinforcing values • Changing behavior	**Learning Objective #1:** Define Persuasion **Annotated Chapter Outline (ACO):** 16-1 through 16-4	**Types of Informative Speeches:** Allyn and Bacon Transparency #T-59	
How Persuasion Works (p. 356) • Elaboration likelihood model • Motivation		**Types of Persuasive Speeches:** Allyn and Bacon Transparency #T-60 **Digital Media Archive** (DMAC) T12I04, T12I05, T12I06, T12I07, T12I08, T12I09, T12I11	
How to Motivate Listeners (p. 357) • Using dissonance to motivate • Using listener needs to motivate • Using positive motivation • Using negative motivation	**Learning Objective #2:** Describe cognitive dissonance **ACO:** 16-5 through 16-11 **Learning Objective #3:** Identify five levels of needs	**Speech Preparation Workbook** (SPW) pp. 72-74 **Persuasion is more likely if….** Allyn and Bacon Transparency #T-61	
Developing Persuasive Speeches (p. 364) • Consider the audience • Choose a persuasive topic • Determine purpose • Develop your ideas	**ACO** 16-12, 16-13, 16-14, 16-15,16-16 16-17, 16-18	**Decide What Changes You Want to Effect:** Allyn and Bacon Transparency #T-62	
Putting Persuasive Principles into Practice (p. 370) • Goals consistent with listener attitudes, beliefs, values, and behaviors • Advantages seen to outweigh disadvantages • Proposal meets listener needs	**Learning Objective #4:** Select and develop an appropriate topic for a persuasive speech **ACO:** 16-19 through 16-24 **Learning Objective #5:** Identify three principles of persuasive speaking	**Speaker Ethos/ Credibility:** Allyn and Bacon Transparency #T-64 **Understand What Changes You Can Effect:** Allyn and Bacon Transparency #T-63 **Audience Resistance to Persuasion:** Allyn and Bacon Transparency #T-67	
Speaker's Homepage (p. 371)	**ACO:** 16-24		

LEARNING OBJECTIVES

16-1.   Students will be able define persuasion.

16-2.   Students will be able to describe cognitive dissonance.

16-3.   Students will be able to identify Maslow's five levels of needs, which explain how behavior is motivated.

16-4.   Students will be able to select and develop an appropriate topic for a persuasive speech.

16-5.   Students will be able to identify three principles of persuasive speaking.

CHAPTER OUTLINE

I.   Careful definition of "persuasion" is necessary for good understanding and effective practice.

   A.   Persuasion develops naturally from informing, since both informing and persuading require good organization, interesting supporting material, well-chosen language, smooth transitions, and fluent delivery.

   B.   Speech purpose graduates to target reinforcement or change in your audience's *attitudes, beliefs, values,* or *behavior.*

   C.   To achieve the further speech purpose of persuasion, *evidence* and *argument* must be added to information.

   D.   Speaker *credibility* is even more critical for persuasion than for informing.

II.   What is persuasion?

   A.   Persuasion attempts to reinforce, modify, or change <u>attitudes</u>, which are "learned dispositions to respond favorably or unfavorably toward people, places, events, or objects" (attitudes may be simplified as our "likes and dislikes").

   B.   A persuasive speech could also change or reinforce <u>beliefs</u>, which structure our perceptions of reality as either true or false.

   C.   A persuasive speech may also attempt to change or reinforce a *value*, a person's enduring conception of right or wrong, good or bad.

III.   Why is it useful to make distinctions among attitudes, beliefs, and values?

   A.   The three personal qualities persuasion seeks to reinforce, modify, or change are not equally susceptible to persuasive speaking.

286

B.   The order of change difficulty for a persuasive speaker is: Values>Beliefs>Attitudes.

C.   Persuasive messages may go beyond reinforcement, modification, or change: persuasion may seek <u>behavior change</u>.

D.   To make persuasive planning choices a persuasive speaker must know which personal quality is the "target" for the speech, with corresponding differences in planning and delivery.

E.   Since a speaker cannot reasonably expect to "reach" all the audience, a certain portion of the audience will be selected as the "target" audience.

IV.   Persuasive speaking has four general methods that are useful to motivate listeners to reinforcement, modification, change, or behavior change.

A.   Dissonance Theory (*cognitive dissonance*) is based on the principle that people attempt to act in ways consistent with their attitudes, beliefs, and values.

1. "Cognitive" refers to our thoughts, our mental processes; "dissonance" (lack of "harmony," in music) is a lack of agreement, an imbalance.

2. "Cognitive dissonance" means that audiences experience a set of thoughts that are inconsistent and uncomfortable; the audience "wants out" of the imbalance.

3. Speakers may deliberately induce dissonance in audiences, to win acceptance for persuasive messages.

a. A speaker favoring banning aerosol sprays portrays dire consequences, despite knowing the audience enjoys the utility and economy of the sprays.

b. A political candidate argues serious community problems, and then blames the incumbent mayor.

4. Audiences may react in one or more of five ways when experiencing cognitive dissonance, only the last favoring the speaker's message.

a. Listeners may discredit the source (the speaker), the famous remedy "Kill The Messenger!"

b. Listeners may reinterpret the message.

c. Listeners can seek out new information, to refute and negate the speaker's arguments.

d. Listeners may simply stop listening, diffusing dissonance.

e. Listeners, however, may go the speaker's way, adopting the speaker's calls for changes in audience attitudes, beliefs, values, or behaviors.

B. Speakers may adopt the strategy of "*creating audience needs and meeting them.*"

1. Abraham Maslow created a famous "pyramid of human needs."

2. Human needs range upward from physiological needs to self-actualization needs.

3. Speakers point out needs and suggest solutions that will meet these needs (the speaker's proposition, or message).

4. Speakers may "appeal" to any of the five levels of need.

a. Physiological needs: food, water, air.

b. Safety needs: when physiological needs are met, audiences are concerned about safety, security, protection for themselves and loved ones.

c. Social needs: with safety needs met, audiences become desirous of contact and reassurance from others, to be loved and valued.

d. Self-esteem needs: with the esteem of others audiences seek to think well of themselves, to feel "they are somebody."

e. Self-actualization: the highest level of need, to achieve our greatest potential, to "Be All That You Can Be."

C. Speakers may decide to utilize a strategy of *positive motivation.*

1. Speakers determine what an audience values most.

2. The persuasive message is then tailored to offer what audiences value.

a. A speaker who wants you to enroll in a language course will extol the positive benefits of enrollment.

b. Salespersons trumpet the desirability and utility of their product.

D. Persuasive speakers may choose to use *negative motivation:* using <u>fear appeals,</u> subtly threatening audiences with negative consequences if they do not adopt the speaker's proposition.

1. A strong threat to a loved one tends to be more successful than a fear appeal directed at the audience members themselves.

2. The more competent, trustworthy, or respected the speaker, the greater the likelihood that an appeal to fear will be successful.

3. Fear appeals are more successful if you can convince the audience that the threat is real and will probably occur unless they take action.

4. Increasing the intensity of a fear appeal usually makes it more effective.

V. Follow four stages in developing a persuasive speech:

A. Consider the audience.

B. Select and narrow your persuasive speech.

1. Speakers should choose topics they feel strongly about.

2. Controversial topics make excellent training topics.

3. Speakers should pay attention to the media to keep current on important issues.

C. Determine your persuasive purpose.

D. Develop your central idea and main ideas.

1. Speakers should develop purpose as a "proposition," a statement for audiences to agree with.

2. Propositions are of three types.

a. Proposition of Fact: "When women joined the military the quality of the military improved."

b. Proposition of Value: "It is wrong to turn away immigrants who want to come to the United States."

c. Proposition of Policy: "Each student at our school should receive a new personal computer."

E. The final stages in developing a persuasive speech are parallel to all speech preparation and fruition: develop central idea, identify main ideas, gather supporting material, organize, rehearse and deliver.

VI. Speakers need to follow three guidelines when putting the persuasive principles into practice:

A. Make your speech consistent with the audience's beliefs, attitudes and values.

B.   Make sure that the advantages of your proposition are greater than the disadvantages.

C.   Make sure that your proposal meets the audience's needs.

VII.   Speaker's Homepage

REVIEW GUIDE

16-1.   Define persuasion in the classical manner.

16-2.   Define and distinguish among *attitudes, beliefs, and values.* Use operational examples.

16-3.   Define *argument* and *evidence,* demonstrating their relationships.

16-4.   What is the order of difficulty in change among attitudes, beliefs, and values?

16-5.   What is a "target audience"?

16-6.   Describe the essence of "dissonance theory."

16-7.   List five ways in which listeners may attempt to escape, or neutralize dissonance created by speakers.

16-8.   Describe Abraham Maslow's contribution to the theory of human needs. Delineate his "Pyramid."

16-9.   How must a speaker adapt to the Maslow formulation?

16-10.   For a persuasive speaker, what are the advantages and disadvantages of "positive motivation" as a persuasive technique?

16-11.   For a persuasive speaker, what are the advantages and disadvantages of "negative motivation" as a persuasive technique?

16-12.   List the four stages in the development of a persuasive speech.

16-13.   Distinguish among propositions of fact, policy, and value, with operational examples.

16-14.   List the three principles that link persuasive practice to persuasive success?

ANNOTATED CHAPTER OUTLINE

A. *What is Persuasion?*

16-1. Teaching Strategy

"Persuasive speaking may be the most used and abused of all the forms of oral communication. It is an important part of our lives as both an assertive and defensive human activity.

"Effective persuasion requires knowledge of and respect for <u>valid evidence</u>, along with effective use of <u>logical reasoning</u> in its many forms and types. Valid evidence and logical reasoning establish a framework for ethical persuasion. When the framework is supplemented by appropriate 'motive appeals,' we have the complete (and beautiful) process.

"We use persuasion assertively to promote worthy ideals and causes, and to gain acceptance of our beliefs. We defend ourselves against the persuasion of others, ethical and not ethical. We must be good listeners capable of analyzing and evaluating the forces of evidence, reasoning and motive appeals which constantly confront us and our society.

"Yes, we are persuaders, and we are persuaded almost daily. A study of persuasion will assist in establishing ethical standards for ourselves and those whom we instruct. The ultimate result will be our own positive influence on the Twenty-First Century."

Lawrence E. Norton, Ph. D. (1906-   )
Professor Emeritus, Speech, Bradley University

16-2. Teaching Strategy

Begin the study of persuasion by exploring the differences between "propaganda" and "persuasion." Ask students to generate examples of propaganda that you can list on the board; then discuss differences and similarities between the two. Both attempt to change people's thoughts or behaviors, yet methodologies, strategies, tactics, and ethics are often quite different.

16-3. Teaching Strategy

Lead the class in a discussion on the role of persuasive speaking in a democratic society. You can begin this session by reading the First Amendment to the Constitution and asking students to interpret it. Which events in our nation's history have occurred as a result of persuasive rhetoric? Which persuasive speeches have motivated action?

B. *Effective Persuasive Speaking Has Four Main Goals, Related to Attitudes, Beliefs, Values, and Behavior*

16-4. Teaching Strategy

Remind students that speakers must try to find out important things about audiences. How shall those "things" be classified? For a long time theorists in persuasion have used the textbook terms of classification: attitudes, beliefs, values, and behaviors. Review these terms, perhaps taking somewhat of a different slant, to accrue the advantages of repetition and rephrasing.

16-5. Teaching Strategy

Some things change very little, hence the old saying, "The more things change the more they stay the same," eh? Aristotle wrote that assertions, arguments, and evidence (logos) are not enough. For persuasive success a speaker's audience must <u>want</u> to believe the speaker (ethos) and proposition (pathos). Logic + Emotion = Persuasion.

16-6. Class Activity

This exercise helps students to distinguish among persuasive messages based on attitudes, beliefs, and values. Bring to class several copies of the editorial/opinion pages from a *USA Today* newspaper. The "Debate" and "Face-Off" columns print opposing viewpoints about current topics. As a class, analyze each and determine what the authors' underlying attitudes, beliefs, and values are. Hint: Beliefs are often characterized by forms of the verb "to be." For example, "It's wrong to muzzle the pleas of beggars" (*USA Today*, February 7, 1990, p. 10A). Value statements are often characterized by the words *should* or *ought* or by such judgmental terms as *terrible, repugnant, good*, or *essential*. For example, "Reinstating the fired air traffic controllers...would be clearly in the best interest of the flying public" (same reference).

16-7. Teaching Strategy

ATTITUDES

Not only do we have individual attitudes, according to theory, we have attitudes that cluster, or form groups of related forces. For example, researchers suggest that positive attitudes on topics listed below are "close together in there" and reinforce each other: capital punishment; pro-life; respect for police; conservative voting; and support for strong classroom discipline. Theory, of course, is a beautiful game, and games are both won and lost. If theory is reasonably accurate in this case it means sampling an audience attitude or two may go a long way. If we tap into a cluster or two we could have excellent operational audience information. With attitudes defined as "tendencies to respond favorably or unfavorably," a speaker looking for action needs much information quickly. A suggested class exercise will introduce students directly to the cluster theory. By way of lighter stuff, ask students what the current expression, "with an attitude" refers to, as in, "A gorilla with an attitude." And, how did it develop? Has the expression anything to do with the way we're using the word?

BELIEFS

Our beliefs keep us sane and motivated. Of course, the sun will rise in the morning. Of course, God exists. Of course a college education will pay off. Beliefs can be very strongly held. Haven't you heard the expression, "Don't confuse me with the facts; my mind is made up"? To deliberately run counter to an audience's basic beliefs is probably to court disaster as a persuasive speaker. What will cause a listener to consciously entertain questions about a basic belief? Shall we try pessimism first? For a long time this author has posed this question to his public speaking and other students: Do most people automatically give positive or negative responses (when responses are sought)? His students have nearly unanimously replied "Negative," and looked more than a little cross-eyed at the occasional student who went the other way. "Why," says their instructor (who is positive first, negative reluctantly about life in general), "Why?" "Well," say the students, "it's just easier to be negative." "Is that so," retorts the instructor, "Or are you showing the results of a lifetime conditioning (by parents, peers, teachers, religious instructors) to be negative?"

Fascinating. What is the point? <u>Beliefs are probably established on a negative motivational basis.</u> Good grades are based on good study habits, and without good grades you will not succeed in life. Eat well if you want physical health. Republicans care nothing for the common man. All Democrats care about is elect and spend, spend and reelect. A persuasive speaker, at best, should plan on gradual modification of beliefs, as the textbook makes clear. We are told that "He who lives by the sword will die by the sword."

VALUES

The textbook definition of values is quite workable: concepts of intrinsic (built-in) good and bad, right and wrong. This is good; that is bad. These are right; those are wrong. Shall we go out on a limb? <u>Values for an individual person do not change until a vast number of persons with the values change them.</u> A persuasive speaker, for all intents and purposes, should concede that our values probably come with us from the womb. Is that strong enough for you? One close-to-home example should suffice. Do students value student honesty in the classroom? Will they, today, cheat on classroom exams? Will students inform on cheating peers? (Now might be the time to lead a good discussion of class ethics, but you probably already have.) Persuasive speakers: <u>Discover (or admit) the pertinent values of your listeners and adapt your message to those values.</u> "Adapting" means working within the framework of those values.

16-8. Teaching Strategy

For persuasive speeches, students tend to select topics that influence audience members' attitudes and beliefs. To make students more comfortable with persuading by appealing to values, ask students to discuss situations in which they have heard persuasive messages based on values. Patriotic speeches, inspirational speeches which rouse the spirits of the audience, and speeches which advocate one approach or plan of action over another are all examples of persuasive speeches based on values.

16-9. **Class Activity**

Have students volunteer slogans, mottoes, and pledges from schools they have attended or organizations they have joined. As a class, identify the attitudes, beliefs, and values implied or stated in each. Point out that "secret oaths" imply the value of exclusivity. Foreknowledge of this information can assist speakers in understanding specific audiences.

16-10. **Class Activity**

Place students in triads and give them three persuasive speech topics. Ask the triads to determine what audience attitudes a speaker should know in advance of speech preparation on the topics. A sample topic and some potential audience attitudes are as follows:

<u>To persuade an audience to donate blood for a community blood drive</u>
Audience apathy unless a friend or close relative needs blood
Audience misconception that donating blood runs the risk of HIV infection
Audience's general lackluster attitude about community involvement

16-11. **Teaching Strategy**

Much research fascinating to communication scholars has occurred in advertising and marketing. Some years ago the phenomenon of "Opinion Leader" was discovered. In many groups (and audiences) a few key individuals appear to "control" the opinions and actions of others. Persuasive speakers would do well to identify the opinion leaders and, perhaps, concentrate audience analysis on those few.

C. *Persuasive Speakers Have Access to Four Main Strategies of Persuasion*

16-12. **Teaching Strategy**

In his public speaking classes, this author makes cognitive dissonance the centerpiece strategy for his fledgling persuasive speakers. You might like to do the same. He typically begins in this fashion: "Well, let me tell you a recent experience a friend of mine had, and he won't mind my telling you. He has good luck with the girls, but even he was astonished at a party two weeks ago. In walked an absolutely gorgeous woman. Every guy in the place gravitated in her direction. But, at the end of the night my friend was the lucky one. What else is new, huh? After five straight date nights it was clear to the both of them; this was it. A few nights ago my friend determined to ask for a steady, permanent relationship. Near the end of a beautiful evening my friend prepared to speak. Realizing what was happening his beautiful lady touched his lips gently and said: 'I must tell you something. I am HIV-Positive.'" Silence. A lot of silence. A whole, whole lot of silence. Interrupted by the instructor, who says "I have just illustrated cognitive dissonance for you, have I not?" The instructor begins to comprehensively review the theory of cognitive. The dissonance in the example should be obvious: overwhelming desire for relationship with beautiful woman mentally clashes with the awful truths of HIV.

16-13. Class Activity

In a class subsequent to the one in which you explore 16-12, perhaps during roll call, ask students in sequence for the five ways listeners may try to get out of cognitive dissonance. Persist until all five are re-identified. Then, lead a discussion: "How do you suppose my friend escaped his cognitive dissonance with the beautiful lady?" Probe. This exercise, more than any other, will illuminate the concept and prepare them for speaker use of cognitive dissonance.

16-14. Teaching Strategy

Think of an example in which you experienced cognitive dissonance. It could be an example related to a difficult decision, a decision over which you agonized. Explain the personal example to your class and ask them to think of similar experiences in their own lives. Of those described in the text, which of the ways to restore cognitive balance did you use in your situation? Which ones did students use?

16-15. Class Activity

Ask each student to bring in one magazine or television advertisement that attempts to create cognitive dissonance in consumers' minds. Public service campaigns frequently use this technique to engender awareness of the seriousness of a problem. A few examples of dissonance-creating messages include: anti-smoking campaigns; weight control clinic advertisements; pro-life public service announcements; a speech opposed to cuts in Social Security funds for the elderly (presented to listeners who fear they may never see Social Security benefits).

16-16. Class Activity

Emphasize to students that all of us use the textbook-described five methods to resolve or reduce cognitive dissonance in our daily lives. Give the class the four scenarios below, each with a strong dilemma, and ask students which of the five options they would most likely use to restore balance.

1. You know and respect two married partners, but you see one of the partners in a romantic liaison with a third person, whom you also know and respect.

2. You are about to sign a contract for a new job when you read a newspaper article about sexual harassment suits leveled at a supervisor in your proposed new company (who would also be your supervisor).

3. You have always wanted to be an artist, despite your parents' objections. You read a recent survey on the high numbers of artists who have failed to make a living returned to college for second degrees.

4. You want to be a teacher, but are disillusioned by your perceptions of the bureaucracy and "red tape" in the educational system.

16-17. **Teaching Strategy**

Abraham Maslow's "Hierarchy of Needs" is taught in various disciplines. Your students may have been exposed to Maslow's *Motivation and Personality* in sociology, psychology, economics, marketing, or business courses. It is always a good idea to review this information because even if students have learned about it in other courses, they may not know how basic needs relate to persuasive speaking. Discuss each level of need and how each relates to the individual. Discuss why Maslow states that we generally move upwardly in the hierarchy, and that lower level needs must be satisfied before one can be motivated to achieve upper level needs.

16-18. **Teaching Strategy**

Lead students in a laughing repartee over these questions: How high is up? How long is long? How hot is hot? How smart is smart? How needy is needy? The latter question, of course, pinpoints the lesson of the day, the persuasive strategy called "meeting audience needs" (in exchange for their adoption of your proposition). Project or inscribe chalkboard with this idea: MOTIVATION + NEED = CHANGE (or reinforcement, or modification).

16-19. **Teaching Strategy**

Ask the students who was voted the MIP (Most Important Person) of the first fifty years of the 20th century. You'll get a lot of good guesses; compliment students for making good guesses. One student may stumble on it. If not, give them a succession of clues until answer cometh: Austrian; physician, died in the USA, had a famous daughter, first name began with "S." (It was Sigmund Freud, of course.) Review to your own delights and passions Freud's importance to human understanding of themselves and others. Freud postulated that when the "veneer of civilization" is stripped from humans, two overwhelming drives, or needs, are found. Again, see if you can draw from students these twin, powerful human motives. Be prepared to be proud of your students. They may or may not get the answers exactly so. But, they'll give some good answers and approximations of what you're looking for. Freud said that when facing imminent injury or death humans concentrate totally on two needs/motives/drives:

1. **To Survive**
2. **To Reproduce the Species**

This instructor typically asks his students how they feel about humans if this idea of "the two most basic drives" is true. Good discussion invariably arises — the kind of discussion you wish you had not started because you don't want it to end. But, then, "All good things must end." You will have laid the basis for a good review of the textbook's listing of "Physical Drives," and "Social Drives." If students really take issue with the Freudian thing, challenge them to read about lovely people, powerful and respected before entering forced confinement in Nazi concentration camps. Did inmates volunteer to assist executioners in order to buy a little additional time? Yes. Did young boys become sexual toys of jailers in order to survive? Yes. Did children inform on parents and parents on children? Yes. This instructor asks students: "Given the two most basic drives, survival and reproduction, what physical drives, in order of importance, do humans have?" There will be a good discussion, including some vigorous opposition to your order, which is:

1. AIR (three minutes, four, without serious brain damage?) (Watch out, though! A sharp student may know about the effects of body cooling on the need for oxygen.

2. SHELTER (means anything that regulates body temperature within survivable limits)

3. WATER (the body, which is almost all water, needs a lot of water to maintain body's efficiency and survival)

4. REST (body tissues begin to malfunction unless the body is given time to maintain them)

5. FOOD (which the students wanted much higher on the list) (Share with students some historical politically-motivated "fasts," aka "hunger strikes," in which humans went long periods without solid food. If an example is current, talk about it and the controversy provoking it.)

Students, by the way, will keep insisting that "sex" simply has to be on this list. Enjoy. Sharpen your retort skills. Then, go on to the point. Oversimplify the point. If a speaker knows, or can convince the audience, that the they are not meeting one of these needs satisfactorily, then a speaker can score by promising that the proposition, if accepted, would meet that need. For example:

I am told that the air in your Albuquerque valley is considered the most polluted air in any American city. Please listen to me. I carry with me great news of a revolutionary "air scrubber" that may restore to you the clean, healthy air we all want here in Albuquerque.

I know that many in our fine city are without adequate, affordable shelter. The Federal government has an excellent new program of "self-help" which will go a long way in solving our problem.

Potable, drinkable water will begin to run short in our beautiful city and valley in just ten short years. Let's vote now for the municipal water management proposal.

Have you lost a lot of sleep lately? Tossed and turned and made life miserable for yourself and loved one? Can't rest? What you need is our handy-dandy, whoop-de-do! Call this number now!!!

Are you as frightened as I am about these reports of sickness and death from contaminated supermarket foods? Let's do something about it now. Are you with me?

The second half of the textbook's discussion of needs focuses the complementing "social drives." Ask around the room for examples of social drives. Persist until you're convinced students have the idea, in which the process is identical to physical drives.

16-20. **Writing Suggestion**

This quick assignment will assist students' understanding of the different ways to persuade an audience. Ask students to generate three hypothetical persuasive topics for speeches that would appeal to attitudes, beliefs, values, and behavior. Also have students indicate which of the twelve topics they believe would make the most effective persuasive speech and why. If time permits, emote good papers.

16-21 **Teaching Strategy**

Select a videotaped sample speech to show students and generate class discussion. Which attitudes, beliefs, and values are overtly referenced by the speech? Which attitudes, beliefs, and values are implied? Did the speaker create cognitive dissonance? How? Did the speaker appeal to basic needs? Which needs?

16-22. **Writing Suggestion**

As a follow-up to class persuasive speeches, ask students to prepare essays on the following. Invite students to visit you and discuss the essay as part of your semester ending debriefings.

1. Audience Analysis: Report the results of your audience analysis. How did you use results of the analysis in preparing your persuasive speech?

2. Supporting Materials: Identify the major forms of supporting materials you selected. Why did you select them? How did your supporting materials help to (a) establish your credibility, (b) provide logical support for your ideas, and (c) provide motivational and emotional support?

3. Organization: Which organizational strategy did you choose? Why did you choose it? If you used the Motivated Sequence, what sections did you emphasize or de-emphasize? Why?

4. Obstacles: What do you think were the obstacles that could have prevented you from achieving your purpose (even if you did achieve your purpose)?

5. General Skills: Evaluate yourself as a persuasive public speaker. What are your strengths and weaknesses? How are you improving your skills? Which specific persuasive principles from Chapters 16 and 17 are you applying now in persuasive performances?

D. *Effective Persuasive Speakers Follow Four Principles in Seeking Change*

16-23. **Teaching Strategy**

The purpose of this strategy is to assist students in their selections of persuasive speech topics. Lead the class in a brainstorming activity. Ask students what topics they would like to hear and not like to hear in the upcoming round of persuasive speeches. These topics could range from highly controversial topics to ones that reinforce an existing belief. On the board, list suggested topics that almost everyone agrees upon. Ask students if anyone is already considering speaking on one of the topics. If so, encourage other students to take the opposing viewpoint on the topic. If someone's possible topic is one that classmates suggested they did not want to hear, ask dissenting students to explain their reactions. This approach could make for an engaging class discussion, as well as an exciting round of speeches.

16-24. **Class Activity**

The purpose is to give students practice in formulating specific purpose statements for persuasive topics geared toward behavioral changes. Using the following list of topics that could be used in persuasive speaking, students should generate specific behavioral objectives for each topic. For example, a persuasive speech on the Air Force might include such behavioral specific purpose statements as, "At the end of my speech, listeners will be able to explain three reasons why they should join the Air Force"; "At the end of my speech, the audience will be persuaded to write letters to congresspersons requesting the closure of several Air Force bases in the country"; or "At the end of my speech, listeners will be motivated to seek out and thank members of the U.S. Air Force for the excellent aerial bombardment in the current Iraqi war."

SPECIFIC PURPOSE STATEMENTS FOR PERSUASION AIMED AT BEHAVIORS

Instructions: Write a behavioral objective or specific purpose statement for each of the following potential speech topics.

Air Force	Insurance
Animals	Intelligence
Asbestos	Islam Religion
Asia	Latin America
Cajun Culture	Libraries
Canada	Lightning
Chinese Food	Milk
Education	Mississippi River
Ethics	Murder
Houston	National Healthcare

16-25. **Class Activity**

This activity will encourage students to generate examples of persuasive appeals in politics. Ask student volunteers to go to the local headquarters of political action groups or political parties and to obtain and read literature on politicians, issues, bills, legislation, and that particular group or party. Have students summarize some of the information for classmates; then analyze as a whole group the political strategies involved in the persuasive discourse.

ONLINE TEACHING PLAN

Preview activity: Assign the interactive exercise entitled, *"Persuasive speaking on legislative topics"* on the Allyn and Bacon website. The address is:
http://www.abacon.com/beebepub/homepage/shchapter16.htm
Students should print out a copy of their answers before submitting them, then send a copy to the instructor's e-mail address.

Teaching activity: Students should visit the Brookings Institute website at:
http://www.brook.edu/dybdocroot/
Each student should choose one current issue from the website and write a brief outline for a persuasive speech on that topic. The outlines might be for an upcoming speech, or simply an exercise to practice persuasive writing for speeches.

Review activity: Students should choose a persuasive topic and create arguments on that topic that exemplify using dissonance, using needs to motivate, using positive motivation, and using negative motivation. Submit responses to the instructor via e-mail.

CHAPTER SEVENTEEN:
Using Persuasive Strategies

Chapter-at-a-Glance

Detailed Outline	Instructor Resources	Supplements	Professor Notes
Establishing Credibility (p. 376) • Competence • Trustworthiness • Dynamism	**Annotated Chapter Outline (ACO):** 17-1 through 17-6	Speaker **Ethos/Credibility:** Allyn and Bacon Transparency #T-64	
Enhancing Your Credibility (p. 377) • Initial • Derived • Terminal	**Learning Objective #1:** Identify strategies to improve credibility	**Strategies for Persuasion:** Allyn and Bacon Transparencies #T-65, #T-66	
Using Logic and Evidence To Persuade (p. 379) Understanding Types Reasoning • Inductive • Analogy • Deductive • Causal	**Learning Objective #2:** Use principles of effective reasoning **ACO** 17-7 and 17-8, 17-10 through 17-12	**Audience Resistance to Persuasion:** Allyn and Bacon Transparency #T-67 **Integrate Support Material:** Allyn and Bacon Transparency #T-68	
Persuading the Diverse Audience (p. 382)			
Supporting Reasoning with Evidence (p. 385)		**Selecting Supporting Material:** Allyn and Bacon Transparencies #T-69, T-70	
Avoiding Faulty Reasoning: Ethical Issues (p. 386)			
Using Emotion to Persuade (p. 388)	**ACO:** 17-9, 17-13	**Types of Reasoning:** Allyn and Bacon Transparency #T-71	
Tips for Using Emotion to Persuade (p. 390) • Use concrete examples • Use emotion-arousing words • Use nonverbal behavior • Use visual images • Use metaphors and similes • Use fear appeals	**Learning Objective #3:** Employ effective techniques of using emotional appeal **ACO:** 17-14 through 17-20	**Testing a Claim:** Allyn and Bacon Transparency #T-73 **Steps in Refutation:** Allyn and Bacon Transparency #T-74	
Strategies for Adapting Ideas to People and People to Ideas (p. 393) • Persuading the Receptive Audience • Persuading the Neutral Audience • Persuading the Unreceptive Audience	**Learning Objective #4:** Adapt your messages to receptive, neutral, and unreceptive audiences **ACO:** 17-21		

Detailed Outline	Instructor Resources	Supplements	Professor Notes
Strategies of Organizing Persuasive Messages (p. 397) • Problem-solution • Refutation • Cause and effect • The motivated sequence	**ACO:** 17-25 **Learning Objective #5:** Identify strategies for effectively organizing a persuasive speech **ACO:** 17-22, through 17-31	**Digital Media Archive (DMAC)** T08I07, T08I08, T08I09, T08I10 **DMAC** T12I10	

LEARNING OBJECTIVES

17-1. Students will be able to identify strategies to improve initial, derived, and terminal credibility.

17-2. Students will be able to use principles of effective reasoning to develop a persuasive message.

17-3. Students will be able to employ effective techniques of using emotional appeal in a persuasive speech.

17-4. Students will be able to adapt persuasive messages to receptive, neutral, and unreceptive audiences.

17-5. Students will be able to identify strategies for effectively organizing a persuasive speech.

CHAPTER OUTLINE

I.   A primary speaker resource is speaker credibility, labeled by the Greek, Aristotle, as *ethos*.

   A.   Credibility is in the eyes of the audience.

   B.   A clear factor in speaker's credibility is the audience perception of speaker <u>competence</u>.

   C.   A second factor in speaker credibility is audience perception of speaker's <u>trustworthiness</u>.

   D.   A final factor in speaker credibility is audience perception of a speaker's <u>dynamism</u>, or energy. Charisma is a type of dynamism.

II.   Speakers build credibility in the minds of audiences in three stages.

   A.   Speakers come to a speech with a degree of credibility, called <u>initial credibility</u>.

       1. To enhance initial credibility be concerned with personal appearance.

       2. Furnish the person who introduces you with a good statement of your pertinent credentials and accomplishments.

   B.   <u>Derived credibility</u> is the perception of credibility your audience forms as you present yourself and your message.

       1. Early establishment of common ground with audience will increase derived credibility.

       2. Derived credibility can grow as speaker supports key argument with good evidence.

       3. Audience perception that message is well-organized can improve derived credibility.

   C.   <u>Terminal credibility</u> is credibility in the minds of an audience as speaker leaves the building, and may be enhanced in three ways.

       1. Continue good eye contact for moments after speech is complete.

       2. Don't rush away from the speaking area.

       3. Encourage questions from the audience; answer them to the best of your ability.

III. Since antiquity, persuasive speakers have known to use logic and evidence.

   A.   Speakers may utilize three types of reasoning.

1. A first type of reasoning is *inductive*; a conclusion is built from specific instances and meets three criteria.

   a. Are there enough specific instances to support the conclusion?

   b. Are the specific instances typical?

   c. Are the instances recent?

   d. A type of inductive reasoning is reasoning from *analogy*, or comparisons, which must also satisfy two criteria.

      (1) Do the ways the two things are alike outweigh the ways they are different?

      (2) Is the assertion true?

2. A second type of reasoning is *deductive* reasoning, the opposite of inductive reasoning.

   a. Deductive reasoning may proceed from <u>syllogisms</u>, a device from formal logic.

      (1) Syllogisms reach conclusions by means of three elements: Major Premise; Minor Premise; and Conclusion.

      (2) A typical syllogism takes this form: *Major Premise*: All gods are immortal; *Minor Premise*: Zeus is a god; therefore, *Conclusion*: Zeus is immortal.

   b. For validity of conclusions syllogisms require that major and minor premises be true, leading to twentieth century doubt of syllogisms.

3. A third type of reasoning is *causal* reasoning.

   a. Causal reasoning relates events as one event <u>causing</u> the other.

   b. This reasoning may proceed backward, so to speak, from effect to cause.

4. (An aside: Cultures respond somewhat differently to persuasion.)

B. Conclusions may not be accepted unless supported by adequate <u>evidence</u>.

   1. If *facts* are offered as evidence those facts must have been directly observed or otherwise proven to be true.

   2. *Examples* as evidence must be pertinent, valid, and true.

3. *Opinions* can serve as evidence if made by an expert, and the expert is known to be unbiased, fair, and accurate.

4. *Statistics* may be used properly or improperly as evidence.

5. If an *inductive conclusion* is offered as evidence, that conclusion must be based on sufficient facts, examples, statistics, and credible opinions to support the conclusion.

6. If a *deductive conclusion* is made to be evidence, the premises must be proven to be true.

IV. Persuasive speakers must avoid eight types of faulty reasoning ("fallacies"), to prevent damage to logical conclusions, and to satisfy ethical needs in argument.

A. Speakers must avoid <u>causal fallacy</u>.

1. One event following another does not necessarily indicate cause.

2. To be a cause an event must be logically and powerfully connected to the supposed effect.

B. Speakers should not use the "<u>bandwagon fallacy</u>."

1. This fallacy occurs when speakers argue that "everybody's doing it."

2. This fallacy calls upon audiences to accept unsupported generalizations.

C. The <u>either-or fallacy</u> is committed by speakers who oversimplify complex issues, arguing that only two actions are possible.

D. <u>Hasty generalization fallacies</u> occur when speakers conclude with insufficient evidence.

E. Speakers all too often utilize "ad hominem" (<u>attacking the person fallacy</u>),concentrating on supposed faults of the speaker, as opposed to the speaker's argument, logic, and evidence.

F. The <u>red herring fallacy</u> consists of raising supposedly valid but actually irrelevant issues to divert audience attention from a damaging conclusion.

G. The <u>appeal to misplaced authority fallacy</u> uses irrelevant (but popular) "experts" to validate conclusions, as in use of TV and sports heroes to extol breakfast cereals.

H. <u>Non-sequitur fallacies</u>, or, literally, "it does not follow," attempt to support conclusions with unrelated other conclusions or evidence.

V.   In addition to argument, reasoning, and evidence, persuasive speakers must use *emotion*, rousing passion and feelings in audiences.

    A.   Although listings of specific emotions are lengthy, all emotions may be classified as coming from three broad sources.

        1. A first source of emotion is the dimension of <u>pleasure or displeasure</u>.

        2. A second dimension is <u>arousal-non arousal</u>.

        3. Thirdly, emotions come from the <u>power or powerless</u> dimension.

    B.   Theory suggests that if an audience member is aroused and caused to feel pleasure and power that audience member is open to speaker conclusions.

        1. Emotion is a powerful way to move an audience and support your persuasive purpose.

        2. A public speaker trying to sway listeners to a viewpoint must use emotional appeals to achieve the goal.

        3. Public speaking theory offers six tips for using emotion to persuade.

            a. Use concrete examples to help your listeners visualize what you describe.

            b. Use emotion-arousing words.

            c. Use nonverbal behavior (Chapter 13) to communicate emotional response.

            d. Use visual images to evoke emotions.

            e. Use appropriate fear appeals.

            f. Consider simultaneous appeals to several emotions.

                (1) Appeal to "hope."

                (2) Appeal to "pride."

                (3) Appeal to "courage."

                (4) Appeal to "reverence."

            g. Tap audience members' beliefs in shared myths.

VI.   Persuasive speakers adapt their persuasive strategies to *diverse audiences.*

    A.   Different cultures have different perceptions about effective persuasive speaking.

        1.   North American audiences prefer a direct, linear, methodical approach to supporting ideas.

        2.   Russians tend to explain the current situation by connecting it to the past.

        3.   Middle Easterners prefer narratives to inductive or deductive reasoning.

    B.   Speakers addressing diverse audiences need to give attention to three issues:

        1.   Ideas about validity and reliable *evidence* differ from culture to culture.

        2.   In high-context cultures, appeals to action should be stated more indirectly.

        3.   Audiences differ in their expectations about *message structure* and its formality.

        4.   In some cultures, the preferred *persuasive communication style* is centered around emotion rather than logic.

VII.   Persuasive speakers must be *ethical* in use of emotional appeals.

    A.   Avoid <u>demagoguery</u>, or substituting speaker popularity for adequate evidence.

    B.   Trumped up, scanty evidence and unethical use of fear appeals mark the demagogue.

VIII. In order to "adjust people to ideas, and ideas to people," a persuasive speaker must deal with three possible audiences: *receptive, neutral,* and *unreceptive.*

    A.   A persuasive speaker needs strategies for <u>receptive audiences</u>.

        1.   Identify with your audience.

        2.   Clearly state your speaking objective.

        3.   Tell your audience exactly what you want them to do.

        4.   Ask listeners for an immediate show of support.

        5.   Use emotional appeals effectively.

        6.   Make it easy for your audiences to act.

B. Persuasive speakers should consider somewhat different strategies for <u>neutral audiences.</u>

    1. Capture audience attention early in the speech.

    2. Refer to beliefs that many listeners share.

    3. Relate your topic not only to your listeners but also to their families, friends, and loved ones.

    4. Be realistic in what you can accomplish.

C. The really tough persuasive speaker audience is the <u>unreceptive audience</u>, requiring different and careful strategies.

    1. Don't immediately announce your plan to change their minds.

    2. Begin your speech by noting areas of agreement before you discuss areas of disagreement.

    3. Don't expect a major change in attitude from a hostile audience.

    4. Acknowledge the opposing points of view your audience may hold.

    5. Establish your credibility strongly.

    6. Consider making understanding rather than advocacy your goal.

IX. Research suggests five general strategies for *organizing* persuasive speeches.

A. If you feel that audience may be hostile to your point of view, advance your strongest argument first.

B. Do not bury key arguments and evidence in the middle of your message.

C. If you want your listeners to take some action, it is best to tell them what you want them to do at the end of your speech.

D. When you think your listeners are well-informed and are familiar with the disadvantages of your proposal, it is usually better to present both sides of an issue, rather than just the advantages of the position you advocate.

E. Make some references to the counter-arguments and then refute them with evidence and logic.

F. Four specific patterns of organizing persuasive speeches can be useful.

1. Problem–Solution: State and develop the problem; state and develop the solution.

2. Organization by Refutation: State objections clearly; refute the objections.

3. Cause and Effect organization: Typically begin with undesirable effects and then attempt to logically connect effects to the cause to be eliminated.

4. The classical Motivated Sequence will serve persuasive speaking organizational needs well.

    a. Get listeners' attention.

    b. Establish why your audience should listen.

    c. Show how your plan meets audience need.

    d. Visualize problem and solution strongly for your audience.

    e. Ask your audience for action.

REVIEW GUIDE

17-1. List three factors in the process of "speaker credibility."

17-2. In the minds of audiences, what are three stages of speaker credibility?

17-3. How can the speaker credibility initial stage be enhanced?

17-4. How can a speaker cause growth in audience perception of the second stage of speaker credibility?

17-5. How can a speaker maximize and preserve final audience perceptions of speaker credibility?

17-6. List and discuss critical tests of each reasoning form: inductive, analogy, deductive, causal.

17-7. List and discuss critical tests of each evidence category: facts; examples; opinions, statistics, inductive conclusion, deductive conclusion.

17-8. Explain in simple terms eight fallacies of reasoning, with historical and other examples for each fallacy.

17-9. Human emotions may be classified as arising from three dimensions of human feeling. List the three sources.

17-10. Explain how speaker arousal of human emotional states leads to acceptance of a speaker's proposition.

17-11. List six steps in the effective speaker use of emotional appeals.

17-12. What four emotions do Beebe and Beebe especially recommend a speaker arouse?

17-13. Define *demagoguery*. What are the unethical speaker signs of demagoguery?

17-14. Distinguish between receptive audiences, neutral audiences, and unreceptive audiences.

17-15. List six suggested persuasive speaker strategies for receptive audiences.

17-16. List four suggested persuasive speaker strategies for neutral audiences.

17-17. List six suggested persuasive speaker strategies for unreceptive audiences.

17-18. List five general Beebe and Beebe suggestions for organizing persuasive speeches.

17-19. List four specific organizational forms recommended for persuasive speeches.

17-20. List the steps in Monroe's classic "Motivated Sequence" form of organizing persuasive speeches.

ANNOTATED CHAPTER OUTLINE

A. *Establishing Credibility*

17-1. Teaching Strategy

For an excellent example of a persuasive speech that employs strategies found in this chapter, show the videotaped lecture, "Democracy in a Different Voice," by Lani Guinier, controversial Clinton nominee for assistant attorney general in 1993. Media Education Foundation, 26 Center Street, Northhampton, MA 01060. Color, 37 minutes.

17-2. Teaching Strategy

By now your students will have had multiple interactions, as speakers and audiences, as small group exercises participants, as pre-class and post-class chatters and, perhaps, even in newly formed social relationships. They are ripe for a good discussion of speaker credibility. In fact, they probably have good estimates of each other's credibility within the class. Begin your discussion with Aristotle's famous dictum that speakers must ". . .find all the available means of persuasion." Expose students to the classical trio of persuasive means, albeit using slightly more modern language: *Ethos* — the audience-perceived competency and trustworthiness of a speaker; *Logos* — how the audience perceives the speaker's skill in using argument, logic, and evidence; and *Pathos* — how effectively the audience feels the speaker has aroused their emotions. Tell them they evaluated, before each classmate spoke, the <u>initial</u> credibility of that classmate; that they have now listened several times to each classmate and formed ideas about the <u>derived credibility</u> of each classmate; and, after all that, each student now has a feeling, an actual comparative estimate, of the <u>terminal credibility</u> of his and her classmates. Just to be on the safe side, undertake a bit of review. Ask students in turn to explain speaker credibility. Persist until you feel everybody is with it. Ask more students in turn to explain the ideas of initial, derived, and terminal credibility. Again, keep it up until everybody is a happy camper on speaker credibility.

Now for the fun part. Ask students to look at the student on their left (some can't, of course). Monitor them. Be firm. They are to look. Next, ask them to look at the student on their right. Insist. Next and next, ask them to look at the student in front of them and the student behind them. Ignore the titters and groans. When students have finished their oglings, say to them in all seriousness: "You are not to answer my next question out loud. Please close your eyes and think a moment. Which of the students you looked at has, to you, the greatest class speaker credibility? Think about it. Why?"

17-3. Class Activity

Place students into small groups and give each group a handout that contains headings for possible combinations of the three types of credibility: Initial, Derived, Terminal. For instance, one heading might read "High Initial–Low Terminal"; another could be "Low Initial–High Derived." Groups' tasks are to provide hypothetical persuasive speaking situations in which the speaker experienced the various types of credibility. As an example, for the "High Initial–High Terminal" heading, students might describe a speaker who had done very well on previous class speeches. In her or his final persuasive speech, this speaker discussed a topic about which he or she had personal experience and provided supporting research. Thus, the speaker sustained that high level of credibility all the way to the end of the speech.

17-4. Class Activity

Students are to mentally list their recollections of class interactions and speeches, specifically those recollections the students feel contribute to their estimates of speaker credibility among their classmates. From those remembrances students are to rank their "top five" classmates (excluding selves) according to perceived speaker credibility. In a subsequent class, divide into groups, and ask students to share their thoughts about classmates and credibility. Specifically, each group is to develop a list of things that appear to affect public speaking students' credibility estimates of each other. After group oral reports to class, the instructor should gather reports, synthesize the reports into a workable number of items, and subsequently share with students. If time permits, lead a discussion of the data accumulated and its seeming impact on credibility theory presented in the textbook.

17-5. **Teaching Strategy**

Lead a discussion of political figures and speaker credibility. What are student perceptions of George W. Bush, John Kerry, Al Sharpton, Al Gore, and Jesse Jackson? How about Bill Clinton? Others students would like to list and consider? Ask students to comment on perceptions of the President's competence, trustworthiness, and dynamism.

17-6. **Class Activity**

The purpose of this activity is to develop students' ability to judge a person's credibility as a speaker. Videotape television personalities who are perceived as having moderate to high credibility. Show segments of the tape to the class; then have students identify the methods and strategies the communicator uses to establish her or his credibility. Some television figures to videotape for this exercise might include: Peter Jennings, Oprah Winfrey, Larry King, Ted Koppell, Katie Couric, or Brian Williams.

B. *Using Logic and Evidence to Persuade*

17-7. **Teaching Strategy**

Define "reasoning." Explain it as a process of getting to a conclusion in a way that listeners can accept and approve. For example, cause-to-effect reasoning is in everybody's bag of tricks, and audiences will buy at least the <u>way</u> you are thinking. If you assert, "Students with poor study habits will probably get poor grades," your students can dig that — probably both the form of the reasoning, as well as the conclusion. Tell them you're going to give examples of all four forms of reasoning in Chapter 17. Please feel free to either improve upon the samples below, or to use them. Do tell students something is seriously wrong with each example, and that they can really impress you by nailing the errors in reasoning.

<u>Reasoning Inductively (reasoning from specifics to the general)</u>

A teacher examined demographic data from students and noted that the first eight of twenty-four students reported themselves as married. The instructor concluded: all students in this class are married.

<u>Reasoning from Analogy (noting similarities; concluding that two things are similar in vital respects and may well share the same future)</u>

Airplane A and B are very similar. Each airplane has wings, tail, elevators, rudders, fuselage, and engine(s). Airplane A has a bit of nasty history; every now and then its elevator goes into intense fibrillation (flutter) and separates from the aircraft. And so, we expect Aircraft B to soon start having the same deadly problem.

<u>Deductive Reasoning (the opposite of inductive reasoning — reasoning from the general to the specific)</u>

I have had ten super teachers in college. The eleventh will be just as great.

As an addition, ask students to digest and criticize the "syllogism" below (use by name two agreeable and previously-alerted students)

Major Premise: All good students flatter their instructors.

Minor Premise: _____ and _____ are good students.

Conclusion: _____ and _____ flatter their instructor.

<u>Causal Reasoning (asserting a producing relationship between one thing and what it produces — the effect)</u>

The Marine Corps makes men.

17-8. **Teaching Strategy**

Ask students to examine the dictionary and common meanings for the word "fact." Push hard. Students know more than they think they do about this word and its synonyms. Share with students a discussion of "observed facts." What does that mean? Do all "observers" see, feel, taste, hear, and smell alike? Do all college educated people observe alike? Do facts mean the same to all jury members? Continue until students have let go a bit of a rather smug preconception of what facts are. Review with students the role of examples in evidence. Go over "real" examples (they have happened); "hypothetical" examples (they surely could happen); and "figurative" examples (haven't and won't happen, but do help in understanding something). Remind students that examples must be pertinent to what is exemplified, valid, and true (at least the real examples). Remind students that expert "opinions" must be unbiased, fair, and accurate. Explore with them dictionary and common sense meanings for "unbiased" and "fair." Refer students to the grand little book, *How to Lie with Statistics*. Tell them they'll love it, even if they don't read it (see how that flies!). Share some of your favorite anecdotes from that famous old tell-all. Do refer to Chapter 8 and quickly review proper speaker use of statistics.

Share with students the following:

Facts: Two plus two is four

Examples: Ricardo Montalban is a fine example of the talents of Spanish actors (Hint: Señor Montalban was born in Mexico).

Opinions: According to Paul Newman, most salad dressings today leave a lot to be desired (Hint: Newman is a very successful businessman in the salad dressing business).

Statistics: Professional golfer Tiger Woods breaks par in tournament golf 8 out of 10 rounds, for an .800 average. Sammy Sosa, Chicago Cubs outfielder, gets a hit three times in 10, or .300. Obviously, Woods is a much better professional athlete than Sosa.

As a summary, suggest to students they are a lot smarter than when they first came to class today (but that they came pretty smart to begin with).

17-9. Teaching Strategy

The Beebes have exemplified well in the textbook the eight classical logical "fallacies." In addition to clarifying fallacies, the examples shed light on almost all other persuasive speakers' logical problems. A review of the Beebe examples of each fallacy should boost your students' critical thinking skills gratifyingly. Computer-enhanced projections are probably advisable (for impact).

17-10. Class Activity

Students are to choose one of the forms of reasoning: inductive, deductive, analogy, or causal. They are expected to write five examples of persuasive propositions cast in the reasoning form they have selected. The written work will be turned in for evaluation. However, students will place one example each on chalkboard and defend it against colleagues' criticisms. Urge uncertain students to visit you. Assign this topic (or another of your choice) to students: President Clinton did not lie when he denied a sexual relationship with Monica Lewinsky. Students are to find and write valid instances of each type of evidence which could be offered in support of the persuasive assertion: facts, examples, expert opinions, and statistics. By this time, students will have developed the necessary research skills to find and apply the evidence. But several will be somewhat confused. Be kind.

17-11. Teaching Strategy

After discussing analogy as a form of inductive reasoning, ask the class what problems exist, if any, with the assertions below:

A.   Canada has the most efficient, cost-effective system of health care in the world; thus, the United States should adopt the Canadian system.

B.   My sister lost twenty pounds in three weeks using diet pills; therefore, I am going on the same diet for three weeks.

C.   Reinstating the death penalty in New York has led to a significant decrease in violent crime; thus, other states should follow suit.

17-12. Class Activity

Ask each student to procure a "letter to the editor" from a local newspaper. (Would you believe you will have to show more than a few students where the editorial pages are in a daily newspaper?) The letter is to be chosen because the writer used "inductive reasoning" in supporting claims. In a subsequent class, have students share their letters for collective criticism of the writer's use of inductive reasoning. Guide the fledgling critics with these questions: Are sufficient examples given or implied? Are the examples typical of the alleged problem? Are examples recent?

17-13. Class Activity

Ask students to bring one or more examples of magazine advertisements that appear to be based on one or more logical fallacies. In a subsequent class collect the examples. Between classes make projections of good ones. Lead discussion of the projections vis a vis Chapter 17.

C. *Using Emotion to Persuade*

17-14. Class Activity

The Beebes identify correctly four emotions very arousing to Americans of all persuasions: hope, pride, courage, and reverence. Assign students, for practice in using persuasive emotional appeal, to choose one of the emotions. They are to also choose a current event. Using the current event as a vehicle, students are to prepare a one-two minute speech intended to arouse the chosen emotion in listeners.

17-15. Teaching Strategy

Procure a copy of that beautiful film *All the King's Men,* wherein Broderick Crawford turns in an Oscar-winning performance in a thinly-disguised portrayal of the "Kingfish" (Governor Huey Long, later an assassinated public figure). Show excerpts from the Crawford film showcasing the use of demagoguery, guided by the Beebe definition: speakers' use of "trumped up scanty evidence," and the "unethical use of fear appeals." Assign a review of the concept of demagoguery, including dictionaries, encyclopedias, and the textbook. Students should take notes. If they access cable TV, have them tune in to early episodes of two older series: "All in the Family," and "The Jeffersons." The latter assignment demonstrates demagoguery in comedic fashion. In a subsequent class, divide into groups and share viewing results in a free-wheeling discussion without any conscious structure (although you should probably cruise the groups, prodding and probing).

17-16. Class Activity

Ask students to bring newspaper or magazine advertisements that employ emotional appeals. In a subsequent class, match the examples to the "Six tips for using emotion to persuade" in this chapter. Ask a few students to argue why their advertisement is the class's best example of using of emotional appeals.

17-17. **Teaching Strategy**

Advertising campaigns often use emotional appeals to promote a product or service. Invite an advertising major or practitioner to speak to your class about the importance of emotional persuasion in marketing. Lead a class discussion of ethics in the use of emotional appeals to sell goods and services.

17-18. **Related Reading**

For strategies that teach students how to develop appeals in a persuasive speech, read and summarize to students Joan M. Yamasaki's essay entitled, "Teaching the Recognition and Development of Appeals." It can be found in the Spring, 1994 issue of *The Speech Communication Teacher,* pp.12-13.

17-19. **Class Activity**

Ask students in groups to develop moderate fear appeals for the following topics:

A.   Nuclear arms threats from countries such as North Korea and Iran.

B.   Cutbacks in school lunch programs (as part of welfare cuts).

C.   Routine physical exams to reduce threat of disease.

D.   Health risks associated with tattoos.

17-20. **Class Activity**

Hand out the scenarios below. Ask each student to write a short but emotional paragraph for one of the scenarios, utilizing powerful words and vivid imagery. In a subsequent class, students are to emote their paragraphs.

A.   The scene of a domestic dispute being mediated by police officers (writer is doing volunteer work at a women's shelter).

B.   The scene of a head-on collision killing three teenagers and injuring others (alcohol is involved).

C.   The side of a hill covered with tsunami refugees, including many orphans (the writer contributes to relief funds).

D.   The awards assembly for a Special Olympics track and field competition (writer is impressed by courage and dignity of contestants).

E.   A funeral procession for an officer killed in the line of duty (argue for gun control legislation).

D. *Strategies for Adapting Ideas to People and People to Ideas*

17-21. Teaching Strategy

Point out to students that the scheme of dividing audiences into receptive, neutral, and unreceptive members using available methods of classification is a workable approach. "However," you say, "Don't forget the idea of 'Opinion Leaders.' If an audience just happened to be 'under the influence' of its opinion leaders) the speaker should adopt persuasive strategies consonant with the leader's needs.'" At this time, insufficient rhetorical theory has developed around the opinion leader as audience. Accordingly, a solid verbatim use of the Outline, VI, A-C, 1-5 will serve students well for beginning analyses of their classroom audiences.

E. *Strategies for Organizing Persuasive Messages*

17-22. Teaching Strategy

Elaborate two general strategies for organizing persuasive messages (Outline, VII, A-E). Below are two situations that result in the need for the strategies, and, opposite, examples of historical speeches you might wish to analyze and present to your students.

A. Audience hostile to point of view; advance strongest argument first	Henry Ward Beecher, *Liverpool Address*
B. Audience well-informed on topic, especially disadvantages of your proposal; present both sides of proposal	Henry Grady, *The New South*

17-23. Teaching Strategy

Demonstrate three patterns of persuasive speech organization by showing differences in central ideas for each pattern, given the same persuasive purpose.

<u>Persuasive Purpose</u>: I want my audience to take a second course in public speaking.

Organizational Pattern	*Central Idea*
Problem–Solution	A second course in public speaking adds needed skills not possible in a single course.
Refutation	Opponents of a second public speaking course offer irrelevant reasons.
Cause and Effect	A second course in public speaking will lead to highly marketable skills.

17-24. Teaching Strategy

Share with students that Alan Monroe's "Motivated Sequence" is a truly significant 20th century contribution to rhetorical (communication) theory. The Beebes have analyzed and exemplified motivated sequence as both the process of a speech and of the speech organizer.

17-25. Class Activity

Pair students and ask them to pick one topic from those listed below. It must be one on which they have opposing views. If that doesn't happen with the provided topics, ask them to come up with their own. Allow at least one class to intervene. Students should think and prepare enough to allow (with one little old note card) 1-2 minute speeches. The exercise is intended to permit practice in approaching hostile audiences. Remind students to review and try to build into speeches five textbook suggestions for handling unreceptive audiences.

    A.   Increasing their school's tuition and fees in order to renovate campus facilities.

    B.   Mandatory military draft for women and men in peacetime.

    C.   Legalization of currently illegal drugs.

    D.   Mandatory HIV screenings as a college admissions requirement.

    E.   All first and second year college students to live in dormitories.

17-26. Class Activity

Explain to students that developing the Monroe need step is not difficult when the problem is already quite evident (the plight of the homeless, for example). However, for many topics, the speaker must create a dissatisfaction with the status quo, illustrating that a serious problem does exist. Ask students in groups to develop need in the topics below.

    A.   Campus day care facilities.

    B.   Reform in Catholic church because of diminishing supply of priests.

    C.   Privately managed prisons to control overcrowding and violence.

17-27. Class Activity

In small groups, role-play advertising agencies. Each group has fifteen minutes to create and present a 2-5 minute skit commercial selling a product or service. Catch: the presentation must be an organized "Motivated Sequence." Have the students critically analyze the use of Monroe's Sequence. Class should pick a "winner" and briefly justify the choice.

17-28. **Class Activity**

Ask students to respond to the following situation by using the items below to structure written essays:

You have problems "beyond your control" with your car and are unable to get to your public speaking class to make a presentation. When you argue that the instructor should make an exception to rules about absences and make-up work, the instructor responds, "Ethically, to show fairness to <u>all</u> students I cannot change my policy this late in the semester. I recommend you withdraw from the course to avoid an 'F'." When you continue to argue your case, the response is: "No, I will not change my policy, but I will allow you to present your case to the entire class. If the majority of students agree with your argument, I'll go along. But you must convince them for me to be satisfied with the fairness of the situation."

1. Identify strategies to improve your initial, derived, and terminal credibility in this instance.
2. Use principles of effective reasoning to develop a persuasive message.
3. Describe effective techniques of using emotional appeals in this situation.
4. Adapt your persuasive message to the receptivity of this particular audience.
5. Identify strategies for effectively organizing this persuasive speech.

Allow time for writings between classes. In subsequent class, divide the class into groups of three. Each student will read their essay to the other two. The group will vote which essay the entire class should hear. If groups do not vote for one essay, they will not be heard. Remind students that in Chapter 17 the authors discuss supporting materials as evidence. A speaker's evidence should support conclusions, contentions, and claims. Review the various types of evidence with students. Lead discussion of the essays presented to the class. Compliment and thank all for writing.

17-29. **Class Activity**

<u>The purpose of this activity is to expose students to an outside speaker, to advance their understanding of persuasive strategies in public speaking.</u> Invite a local politician to speak with your class about persuasive strategies employed effectively or ineffectively in his or her most recent campaign. If such a person is not available, a campaign manager, campaign volunteer, or political science professor might be a good substitute. These questions can be asked to stimulate discussion: What were the objectives in your most recent campaign? Were there any problems related to persuasion in the campaign? If so, what strategies were used to overcome them? Your guest speaker might also have interesting information on how she or he improved or enhanced personal credibility during the campaign.

17-30. **Class Activity**

Divide students into groups of five. Ask groups to develop a persuasive speech topic and central idea. Then, each student, with the assistance of the group, should develop one step for the speech, following the structure of the Motivated Sequence. Allow time for the five-part development; at the end of the planning time, ask groups to present their drafted speeches to the class. Classmates can then determine how well the Motivated Sequence was utilized. What were the strengths and weaknesses in each group's persuasive message?

17-31. **Class Activity**

Students should practice creating effective persuasive strategies that they can later incorporate into their speeches. Ask students to imagine that they are listening to persuasive speeches on the topics that follow. Students should identify two persuasive strategies that could help speakers change the attitudes or behaviors of their audiences. Students should be prepared to discuss their responses with the class during the next session.

PLANNING PERSUASIVE STRATEGIES

Instructions: Imagine that you are listening to persuasive speeches on the following topics:

1. Taking a polygraph (lie detector) test before starting a new job

2. Signing a petition to remove Native American burial remains from museums and return them to their homelands

3. Anti-terrorist legislation

4. Changing to a vegetarian diet

5. Joining an abortion rights protest

ONLINE TEACHING PLAN

Preview activity: Review the website entitled *Stephens Guide to Logical fallacies* at:
http://www.intrepidsoftware.com/fallacy/welcome.php
After reading the information presented, students should write a brief response about their own perceptions of the importance of logic in public speaking.

Teaching activity: Students should submit a one-page opinion essay via email on the importance of credibility in public speaking. What factors are the most crucial to either establishing or ruining credibility? Why?

Review activity: Using the topic of an upcoming speech, create one deductive argument and one inductive argument that might be used to persuade an audience. Submit responses to the instructor via e-mail.

Chapter-at-a-Glance

Detailed Outline	Instructor Resources	Supplements	Professor Notes
Public Speaking in the Workplace (p. 412) • Reports • Public-Relations speeches	**Learning Objective #1:** Identify and explain the requirements for types of speaking common in the workplace	**Ceremonial Speaking:** Allyn and Bacon Transparency #T-75	
	Annotated Chapter Outline (ACO): 18-1 through 18-5	**Digital Media Archive (DMAC)** T12I12, T12I13	
Ceremonial Speaking (p. 414) • Introductions • Toasts • Award presentations • Nominations • Acceptances • Keynote addresses • Commencement addresses • Commemorative addresses and tributes • Eulogies	**Learning Objective #2:** List and describe nine types of ceremonial speeches **ACO:** 18-6 through 18-17		
After-Dinner Speaking: Using Humor Effectively (p. 421) • Humorous Stories • Humorous Verbal Strategies • Humorous Nonverbal Strategies	**Learning Objective #3:** Explain the purpose and characteristics of after-dinner speech **ACO** 18-18, 18-19, 18-20 **Learning Objective #4:** List and Explain strategies for humor in a speech		

LEARNING OBJECTIVES

17-1.   Students will be able to identify and explain the requirements for two types of speaking situations likely to arise in the workplace.

17-2.   Students will be able to list and describe nine types of ceremonial speeches.

17-3.   Students will be able to explain the purpose and characteristics of an after-dinner speech.

CHAPTER OUTLINE

I.   Two types of public speaking are common in the workplace.

    A.   Reports communicate information or policy, and can end with persuasive appeals.

        1. Follow three simple rules when planning and delivering reports.

            a. Your audience is there to hear you address a particular problem, so be sure to acknowledge it.

            b. Explain your research group's decisions; then explain how the information was gathered.

            c. Present the possible solutions, telling your audience what's in it for them.

        2. Expect to provide written copies of the report.

    B.   Public-relations speeches are often volunteered or assigned.

        1. Public-relations speeches are expected to inform the public and improve relations with the public.

        2. Public-relations speeches normally deal with problems, solutions, and questions.

            a. The speech may be to explain that the company or organization does not feel a suggested problem is a problem and, of course, why or why not.

            b. The speech may be to acknowledge a problem and how the company or organization is working to solve the problem.

            c. Anticipate objections and do your best to answer to questioner's satisfaction.

II.   People who speak in public will be called on for nine different types of *ceremonial* speeches.

    A.   An <u>introductory</u> speech is much like an informative speech, as one speaker provides audience with information about the main speaker.

        1. As an introducing speaker, be brief; they came to hear the main speaker.

        2. Be accurate; the main speaker should not have to waste time correcting the introduction and introducer.

        3. Keep audience needs in mind at all times.

B.   A <u>toast</u> is a brief salute to a special occasion or person, usually with the clinking of glasses (and perhaps "drinking the toast").

    1.   Toasts are normally quite short: "Salud!" is not uncommon.

    2.   Be sincere; sincerity is more valued than wit.

C.   Presenting an <u>award</u> is frequent and important.

    1.   First, refer to the occasion.

    2.   Next, describe the history and significance of the award.

    3.   Finally, name and glowingly describe the accomplishments of the award recipient.

D.   <u>Nomination</u> speeches are similar to award speeches.

    1.   Note the occasion; describe the purpose and significance of the office to be filled.

    2.   Explain clearly why the nominee's skills, talents, and past achievements qualify her for the position.

    3.   Propose the actual nomination at end of the speech; welcome the nominee forward if appropriate.

E.   Awards and nomination speeches provoke <u>acceptance</u> speeches.

    1.   BE SINCERE AND SHORT!

    2.   Thank the person making the presentation and the organization that is represented.

    3.   Comment on the meaning or significance of the presentation to you.

    4.   Reflect briefly on the larger significance of the presentation to people and ideas honored.

    5.   Find meaning, if possible, for your audience.

F.   <u>Keynote</u> addresses deal with the importance of topics, purposes of meetings, and motivations for audiences to learn more and work harder: set a theme.

    1.   Face the task of being specific enough to arouse interest and inspire audiences.

    2.   Be very sure to include many examples and illustrations to which audience can easily relate and respond.

      G.   <u>Commencement</u> addresses come to many who study public speaking.

           1. First, praise the graduating class, with specific achievements when possible.

           2. Turn graduates' attention to their futures, offering new bright goals and inspiration to reach out for those goals.

      H.   <u>Commemorative</u> and <u>tribute</u> addresses are delivered on special occasions.

           1. Present facts about the event commemorated or the people receiving tribute (both may happen in the same time frame).

           2. Build on the facts, to increase the depth of commemoration and the tribute offered.

           3. If felt appropriate, challenge the audience to respond even more strongly to the future of the event commemorated, and encourage self and others to qualify for similar tribute.

      I.   <u>Eulogies</u> are a special form of tribute speech--to those who have died.

           1. List, and linger over, the unique achievements of the person eulogized.

           2. Include personal, even humorous recollections of the departed.

           3. Finally, turn to the living; encourage them to transcend loss and give thanks that the eulogized lived among them, even if only briefly.

III.   <u>After-dinner</u> speeches (may not be after-dinner; may not be after anything) are very frequently given, due to popularity with business, professional, and service organizations).

      A.   After-dinner speeches may present information or attempt to persuade, but a primary purpose is <u>to entertain</u>.

      B.   Humor is the challenge of the after-dinner speaker.

           1. Humorous speech content can include both verbal and nonverbal strategies.

REVIEW GUIDE

18-1. What two types of speech purposes are typical in the workplace?

18-2. List the textbook's three rules for planning and delivering reports.

18-3. What are two expectations for the results of public-relations speeches?

18-4. With what three situations do public relations speeches typically deal?

18-5. List nine types of ceremonial speeches.

18-6. Lay out the suggestions for effective ceremonial speeches of the various types.

18-7. What is the primary purpose of after-dinner speeches?

18-8. Must an after-dinner speaker be a master of comedy?

18-9. What is the place of written reports in a group's final actions?

18-10. Can you give an example from personal experience of each type of ceremonial speech?

18-11. What is the cardinal rule of acceptance speeches?

18-12. What are some verbal and nonverbal strategies for using humor in after-dinner speaking?

ANNOTATED CHAPTER OUTLINE

A. *You Will Be Required to Speak in Public in the Workplace*

18-1. Class Activity

Review the qualities of effective employment interviews with your class. Form triads and engage in mock employment interviews, rotating so that each student plays, in succession, the roles of employer, applicant, and an observer/critic who takes notes on the conduct of the interviews. Afterwards, have groups evaluate themselves as applicants and employers.

18-2. Class Activity

You may well have working students in your class whose job responsibilities extend to oral and written reports. Ask for volunteers to share short reports they may have submitted to superiors and colleagues.

18-3. **Writing Suggestion**

Have students write a report of the kind they might make and present in a future position. Students are to explain the type of work done, the purpose of their hypothetical report, time parameters for the report, and so on. Finally, direct students to attempt a description of the perceived differences between this oral report and other speech situations already studied and practiced.

18-4. **Teaching Strategy**

Share rudimentary information about workplace reports and public relations speeches from the Outline (I, A through B, 1-2, c). If time permits, follow with verbatim presentation of the Beebes' textbook explication and examples of reports and public relations speaking.

18-5. **Class Activity**

Ask students to report on any jobs they may hold that require them to present reports at work or to make public relation speeches. Ask students to describe any experiences they have had with either of these forms of special-occasion speeches, in or out of the workplace. Divide into groups. Ask students to predict to the other members of their groups when and where they might volunteer or be required to give each of the following special-occasion speeches: speech of introduction, award presentation, nomination speech, acceptance speech, keynote address, commencement address, commemorative address, eulogy.

B. *Public Speaking Teachers Distinguish Nine Types of Ceremonial Speaking*

18-6. **Teaching Strategy**

Ask your class, "If I were to speak at an occasion next week, and I wanted one of you to introduce me, who would the class select to do it?" Ask a volunteer to introduce you.

18-7. **Class Activity**

Ask students to look about the room and decide on a student to whom they would like to drink a mock toast. They are to conceal their choice of "Toastee" until the day of the exercise. Students will create a toast, one line, perhaps two — and, yes, they can steal a line from the library if they must. The toasts are to be sincere, even if humorous (which is certainly permissible). In subsequent class provide plastic toast glasses and a two- or three-liter bottle or more of your choice of fake liqueur. Let students volunteer according to their perceptions of when their toast will be most appropriate. Get ready for superior learning in a most delightful context, although you may have to kick start initial interactions with each toast ("Hear, hear!" "Right on!" and the like). At the end lead a sprightly chorus of "For He's a Jolly Good Fellow" (if the ladies and your local political correctness commissar will let you get away with it).

18-8. Teaching Strategy

Review the rules for Award and Acceptance Speaking (Outline, I, C, 1-3 and I, E, 1-5. As reinforcement, share selected clips from an unbeatable lecture visual aid, the videotape, *Oscar's Greatest Moments: 1971-1991*. The tape contains some of the most memorable moments from the annual Academy Awards ceremony. In sometimes <u>excruciating</u> detail, the clips show students what to do and <u>what not to do</u> when presenting and accepting awards. If unable to access this film, tape <u>any</u> annual broadcast of the ceremony.

18-9. Related Reading

One way to examine both nominating speeches and acceptance speeches is to read examples from the national nominating convention of a political party. Many are printed and readily available in *Vital Speeches of the Day* and *The New York Times*. Recommend readings to students apparently interested in politics, parties, pressure groups, and these special speeches.

18-10. Teaching Strategy

Review textbook suggestions for three of the remaining ceremonial speeches:

Speeches of Nomination	Outline, II, D, 1-3
Keynote Addresses	Outline II, F, 1-2
Commencement Addresses	Outline, II, G, 1-2.

As students to share their experiences, whether as speaker or audience, in each of the three speech situations. Probe strongly about students' experiences with commencement addresses. Encourage students to share the good, bad, and ugly about those experiences; some of these students will give commencement addresses — save their future audiences now!

18-11. Teaching Strategy

If you have students of non-traditional college ages in your class, ask them if they have recently attended a commencement ceremony at either a high school or a college. Was the commencement speech very different than the one they heard at their own graduation ceremony? In what ways was it similar or different? Then ask younger students to share any interesting or humorous experiences they had in listening to commencement addresses.

18-12. Teaching Strategy

Ask students this hypothetical question: "If you could go to a convention and hear any keynote speaker in the world, living or dead, who would it be? Why?"

Ask students to imagine they have been selected to keynote a student government association conference. What topic would they choose? Will they choose to inform, or to persuade? How would they attempt to maximize initial credibility and derived credibility? Will humor play an important role?

18-13. Teaching Strategy

Access any of the keynote speeches from the 2004 presidential conventions on the Internet. Review how the keynote speeches used techniques learned in this book. What made the keynote address effective or ineffective?

18-14. Class Activity

Pair students. Ask them to share with each other their "greatest triumphs." Each student is then to create a two-minute speech of tribute, which is accompanied by an actual award. In a subsequent session, each student gives tribute and an award to the other student. The actual awards are chosen by each student and are to be concealed until presentation (this part will vary from deeply serious to outrageously funny).

8-15. Class Activity

Ask students if they viewed the original version of the initial film in the series generally referred to as *Planet of the Apes*. All or most will have. Review the Beebes' suggestions for eulogy speaking — in this case eulogies for the dead: (a) list, and linger over the unique achievements of the person eulogized; (b) include personal, even humorous recollections of the departed; and finally (c) turn to the living, encouraging them to transcend loss and give thanks for the departed's brief sojourn among the living. From your procured and cued copy of the film, show the right-on funeral eulogy Charlton Heston interrupts as he escapes from the apes. Each Beebe principle is exemplified in just brief moments of the dominant ape's eulogy for a departed outstanding ape citizen. You might choose to project the three "rules" for eulogies as you show the film clip.

18-16. Class Activity

Ask students to write a brief speech they would like someone to say at their own funeral.

18-17. Class Activity

This activity will expand students' thinking on the purposes of eulogies, while also providing practice in this important kind of special-occasion speaking. It may sound irreverent to you, but there are many other uses for eulogies than just paying tribute to dead persons. When you assign this activity, explore those other uses with students. For example, a speech can eulogize one's lost youth, the ending of a long and intense project (like completing a college degree), a relationship that has dissolved, a car that has been totaled in a car wreck, and so on. Ask students to prepare brief (two-minute) eulogies on these topics or others. Make sure students understand that this activity is designed in no way to ridicule or make light of the primary purpose of eulogies.

C. *After-Dinner Speaking is Pervasive in Our Society*

18-18. Teaching Strategy

Although after-dinner speeches do not require the services of a professional comedian, humor is the sine qua non of these speeches. In fact, the actual "shtick" of many professionals takes the form of after-dinner speaking. Examples include George Carlin, Dr. Bill Cosby, and Lily Tomlin. Videotape a stand-up comedian of your choice in a segment where a serious subject is treated with light, but constant, humor. Show the segment to your classes (indeed, teaching can be fun), directing them to look for these elements in an effective after-dinner speech: timing, facial expressions, humorous transitions, double takes, slow burns, and the beat goes on.

18-19. Class Activity

Assign students to select a short persuasive topic related to campus life. Students will simply "state their case and prove it," which is what Aristotle said a speaker ought not have to exceed. Proof, in this case, is humorous. Students receive practice in the basic elements of after-dinner speaking: state point; laugh it in; or laugh it off. Now is a good time to remind students of the *Reader's Digest* humor sections:

> Point: "The war between the sexes is not over."

> Support by anecdote: Connie was very supportive of her husband's campaign to be elected vice-president of the teacher's credit union. She missed seeing him off for work the day of the election. Since she would also be late arriving home that day, she left a special message for him on their home answering machine: "Good luck, honey, and don't worry. No matter how the election turns out, YOU'LL ALWAYS BE VICE-PRESIDENT IN OUR HOUSE."

18-20. Class Activity

The purpose of this activity is to help students become more comfortable with microphones. Ask media services or a radio/TV/film department to loan you a stationary or lavaliere microphone for in-class practice. Experiment with the mike in class, giving each student an opportunity to speak through it. If possible, try to borrow both types of mikes, because a speaker's delivery is often greatly affected by the intervention of a microphone. Review the textbook's tips for effective microphone use.

ONLINE TEACHING PLAN

Preview activity: Review the website entitled, *"20 Tips for super speeches"* at:
http://www.confetti.co.uk/weddings/advice_ideas/speeches/speech_tips.asp. Keep these tips in mind as you work through chapter 18 of the text. Are there any differences between the website and the text? What are they?

Teaching activity: Go to the website entitled *"Eulogies: Guide Picks"* at:
http://dying.about.com/cs/eulogies. After reviewing the information, students should write a brief eulogy for a famous figure in history. Create a bulletin board of the students' submissions, and use it to comment on concepts from the text.

Review activity: Go to the website entitled, *"Wedding Toasts"* at:
http://quotations.about.com/cs/weddingtoasts/a/bls_wed_toasts.htm
After reviewing the sample toasts on the web site, students should write their own fictitious toast for a famous couple. Submitted toasts can be posted on the class bulletin board or Blackboard/WebCT site and the instructor can provide general feedback based on concepts from the text.

CHAPTER NINETEEN: Speaking in Small Groups

Chapter-at-a-Glance

Detailed Outline	Instructor Resources	Supplements	Professor Notes
Small Group Communication: Definition (p. 430) **Solving Problems in Groups and Teams** (p. 431) • Identify and define the problem • Analyze the problem • Generate possible solutions • Select best solution • Test and implement solution **Participating in Small Groups** (p. 434) • Come prepared • Analyze problems before suggesting solutions • Evaluate evidence • Help summarize group progress • Listen and respond courteously • Help manage conflict **Leading Small Groups** (p. 436) • Responsibilities • Styles **Managing Meetings** (p. 438) • How to Give Meetings Structure • How to Foster Group Interaction	**Learning Objective #1** Define small group communication **Annotated Chapter Outline (ACO):** 19-1 through 19-4 **Learning Objective #2** Organize group problem solving, using the steps of reflective thinking **ACO:** 19-5 through 19-10 **Learning Objective #3** Participate effectively in a small group as a member or a leader. **ACO:** 19-12 through 19-15 **Learning Objective #4:** Contribute effectively to a group meeting **ACO:** 19-11 **Learning Objective #5:** Develop a plan for coordinating a group project **ACO:** 19-16 through 19-24	**Types of Group Speeches:** Allyn and Bacon Transparency #T-77 **Digital Media Archive** (DMAC) T07I09 **Preparing for Group Presentations:** Allyn and Bacon Transparencies #T-78, T-79	

Detailed Outline	Instructor Resources	Supplements	Professor Notes
Presenting Group Recommendations • Symposium • Forum • Panel • Written **Planning Group Presentations** (p. 443) **Making Group Presentations** (p. 444)	**Learning Objective #6:** Present group conclusions in a symposium, forum, panel presentation, or written report **ACO:** 19-25		

LEARNING OBJECTIVES

19-1.   Students will be able to define small group communication.

19-2.   Students will be able to organize group problem solving, using the steps of reflective thinking.

19-3.   Students will be able to participate effectively in small groups as member or leader.

19-4.   Students will be able to contribute effectively to a group meeting.

19-5.   Students will be able to develop a plan for coordinating a group project.

19-6.   Students will be able to present group conclusions in a symposium, forum, panel presentation, or written report.

CHAPTER OUTLINE

I.   As in ancient Athens we still "Search For Truth in Groups," requiring skill-building in small group communication.

    A.   Employees spend much time in work groups; ranging up to 60% of work time for senior managers.

    B.   Building skills in group communication reduces uncertainty and anxiety about group processes.

    C.   Small group communication is defined as "Interaction among three to around a dozen people who share a common purpose, feel a sense of belonging to the group, and influence one another."

    D.   Teams are special kinds of groups that emphasize coordinating activity with more clearly defined structure of who does what.

II.   The central purpose of many groups is solving problems; most groups follow a version of John Dewey's "Steps in Reflective Thinking."

    A.   The first step in reflective thinking is to *identify and define the problem,* seeking answers to four general questions.

        1. What is the specific problem that concerns (and confronts) us?

        2. What terms, concepts, or ideas do we need to understand in order to solve the problem?

        3. Who is harmed by the problem?

        4. When do the harmful effects occur?

        5. It might be helpful to phrase the problem as a proposition of policy as in: "What should be done to improve security on our campus?"

    B.   The second step in reflective thinking is to *analyze the problem,* considering at least seven general questions.

        1. What is the history of the problem?

        2. How extensive is the problem?

        3. What are the causes, effects, and symptoms of the problem?

        4. Can the problem be subdivided for further definition and analysis?

5. What methods do we already have for solving the problem, and what are the limitations of those methods?

6. What new methods can we devise to solve the problem?

7. What obstacles might keep us from reaching a solution?

8. Before proceeding to the next step, identify <u>criteria,</u> or standards for identifying acceptable solutions. For example, "A suggested solution must not exceed our funding decision."

C.   Third in reflective thinking is *generating possible solutions*, following five facilitative guidelines.

1. Set aside judgment and criticism while suggesting solutions.

2. Think of as many possible solutions to the problem as you can.

3. Have a group member record all ideas mentioned.

4. After a set time elapses, evaluate ideas, using the criteria established.

D.   The reflective thinking fourth step is to *select the best solution,* measuring each solution against five questions.

1. Which of the suggested solutions deals best with the obstacles?

2. Does the suggestion solve the problem in both short and long runs?

3. What are the advantages and disadvantages of the suggested solution?

4. Does the solution meet the established criteria?

5. Should the group revise its criteria?

6. What is required to implement the solution?

7. When can the group implement the solution?

8. What results will indicate success?

E. The final stage, or step in reflective thinking is to *test and implement the best solution*, involving at least three actions.

    1. Develop a step-by-step plan of implementation.

    2. Set time frames.

    3. Assign responsibilities.

III. Beebe and Beebe offer six suggestions for effective participation in small groups.

A. Come prepared for group discussions.

B. Do not suggest solutions before analyzing the problem.

C. Evaluate evidence.

D. Help summarize the group's progress.

E. Listen and respond courteously to others.

F. Help manage conflict, with one or more of six techniques.
    1. Keep the discussion focused on issues, not personalities.

    2. Rely on facts, rather than personal opinions, for evidence.

    3. Seek ways to compromise; don't assume there must be a winner and loser.

    4. Try to clarify misunderstandings in meaning.

    5. Be descriptive rather than evaluative and judgmental.

    6. KEEP EMOTIONS IN CHECK!

IV. Instead of holding face-to-face meetings, many organizations are turning to "Virtual" meetings, utilizing the power of technology.

A. E-mail, special software programs, and video conferences permit group members to work together when not physically present.

B. A growing body of research suggests conclusions about virtual meetings held with assistance from "GDSS" (Group Decision Support Systems).

    1. GDSS appears to lead to increases in ideas generated, as compared to face-to-face brainstorming.

2. Virtual meeting methods appear to work best when tasks are structured step-by-step.

3. Some group members find managing conflict and negotiating relationship issues more difficult than in face-to-face meetings.

4. E-mail for give and take messages may contribute to greater polarization of opinions, and group members may take more extreme positions in writing as compared to oral communication.

5. Electronic meetings will be smoother with the services of a technical expert to manage inevitable hardware and software glitches associated with new technology.

V. Small groups require leadership, even when leadership is shared; important issues in group leadership are *leadership responsibilities* and *leadership style.*

A. Leadership, however and whoever, involves leadership <u>roles</u> and leadership <u>functions</u>, often viewed as "task" and "maintenance" functions.

1. Task leadership roles include at least agenda setter, information and opinion seeker, elaborator, and energizer.

2. Maintenance roles encompass encourager, harmonizer, compromiser, and gatekeeper.

B. Leadership styles are historically divided in three styles.

1. *Authoritarian* leaders assume positions of superiority, giving orders and assuming control of the group's activity.

2. *Democratic* leaders involve their groups more in the decision-making process, rather than dictating what should be done.

3. *Laissez-faire* leaders allow a group complete freedom in all aspects of the decision-making process, and do little to help achieve group goals (often leaving groups frustrated).

C. Research suggests that no single leadership style is most effective in all group situations.

VI. To manage common complaints about meetings, *structure* and *interaction* must be properly balanced.

A. According to research and simple observation, many people have many complaints about typical meetings.

1. Getting off the subject, lacking goals or agenda.

2. Running long, with poor or inadequate preparation.

3. Inconclusive and disorganized, with ineffective leadership and control.

4. Starting late, wasting time on irrelevant information.

5. Allowing interruptions within and without, restricting decision-making.

6. Certain individuals dominating discussion, or leader permitting rambling, redundant, digressive discussion.

7. No published results or follow-up actions.

B. Give meetings sufficient structure.

1. Develop and pursue a chronological agenda, with important items listed first.

2. Share information early; make decisions later.

3. Meeting leader must keep an eye on: THE AGENDA and THE CLOCK.

C. Leaders may foster more effective and satisfying group interaction by asking participants to observe four patterns of interaction.

1. Organize your contributions and make one point at a time.

2. Speak only if your contribution is relevant, and support your ideas with evidence.

3. Listen actively and monitor (control) your nonverbal activity.

4. Agree to Parliamentary Procedure as a method of organizing the meeting, remembering the degree of formality may vary (see Speaker's Homepage for guidance and tips).

VII. Groups may present their recommendations in at least four different ways, and should be guided by eight tips for the presentations.

A. Groups may decide on a *symposium*, a series of short public speeches to an audience.

B. The choice might be a *forum*, with audiences directing comments and questions to group members, who respond with short impromptu speeches.

C. A *panel discussion* is an informative give-and-take discussion, with an appointed chairperson, or moderator.

D. *Written reports* summarize a group's key deliberations and final recommendations, and may substitute for or accompany other forms of group reporting.

E. Eight tips will assist in planning effective group presentations:

1. Make sure each group member understands the task or assignment, and that members work together to identify a topic.

2. If your group assignment is to solve a problem or to inform the audience about a specific issue, try brainstorming to develop a topic or problem question (Chapter 6).

3. Give group members individual tasks.

4. Develop a group outline and decide on an approach.

5. Decide on your presentation approach.

6. Rehearse the presentation.

7. Incorporate principles and skills of effective audience-centered public speaking when giving group presentation.

8. Armed with a well-planned outline, present findings to your audience, incorporating the skills and principles of effective public speaking.

F. Four tips will assist in making more effective group presentations:

1. Clarify your purpose

2. Use presentation aids effectively

3. Assign someone to serve as a coordinator or moderator

4. Be ready to answer questions

REVIEW GUIDE

19-1   Describe the average percentages of time spent in group communication for: line employees, lower level managers, senior managers.

19-2.   What are two advantages of building group communication skills?

19-3.   Repeat the Beebes' definition of small group communication.

19-4.   List Dr. John Dewey's "Steps in Reflective Thinking."

19-5.   List four questions used to develop the first Dewey step.

19-6.   List seven questions used to develop the second Dewey step.

19-7.   List five questions used to develop the third Dewey step.

19-8.   List eight questions used to develop the fourth Dewey step.

19-9.   List three stages of carrying out the final Dewey step.

19-10.   List and elaborate on the first five tips given by the Beebes for effective participation in small groups.

19-11.   The sixth tip, or suggestion, is to "Help manage conflict." The Beebes offer five techniques for helping manage conflict; list and elaborate upon each technique.

19-12.   In the Outline, this author printed the sixth technique, "Help manage conflict," in all caps. Speculate why this was done.

19-13.   List apparent advantages and disadvantages of "virtual" meetings, as compared to and contrasted with traditional meetings.

19-14.   List as many leader task leadership responsibilities as you can.

19-15.   List as many leader maintenance responsibilities as you can.

19-16.   Recall the three traditional classifications of leadership styles. Compare and contrast the advantages and disadvantages of each style with the other styles.

19-17.   The Beebes list seven common complaints meeting participants eagerly voice. List all seven.

19-18.   According to the Beebes, three cautions will give meetings more structure. List and elaborate.

19-19.   Group interaction will improve if four suggestions are followed. The first is to "organize your contributions and make one point at a time." What are the other three suggestions?

19-20. List and briefly describe the four ways in which groups may choose to present results.

19-21. List the eight Beebe tips for preparing effective group presentations.

19-22. List the four Beebe tips for making effective group presentations.

ANNOTATED CHAPTER OUTLINE

A. *Solving Problems in Groups is Pervasive and Increasing in our Society*

19-1. Background Information

Group members talk to each other; group members *must* talk to each other. We are not alone; we cannot escape. Nor, for that matter, should we wish to. Just as you urged upon your students a paramount need to build platform speaking skills, so you must urge them, this author thinks, to amass group communication skills. Share with them two observations: (a) our society gives evidence that problem-solving and decision-sharing in groups will only increase; and (b) just as skill building in public speaking reduced uncertainty and anxiety about public speaking, so will skill building in group communication reduce the same factors there. The Beebes' definition of small group communication, it seems to this author, is quite workable and easy to communicate to students. Examples could be very helpful. The definition, you recall, is "Interaction among three to around a dozen people who share a common purpose, feel a sense of belonging to the group, and who influence each other." The examples following should be useful, and you will easily think of many others.

Example #1: a competitive bowling team, unisex or mixed; five to seven members; primary group purpose to win the league while having fun; often with social life organized around the team and its many activities; showing clear distribution of roles and status

Example #2: a community college teaching discipline, mixed genders; eight members; primary group purpose of showing preeminence among the college's teaching disciplines; may use group as dominant social organizer, including mixed gender recreational sports, professional recitals, and social outings which become traditional; status often clear and enforced; roles often informally developed.

Example #3: a school "clique," often, but not always single sex; five-seven members; two primary purposes (1) show superiority to other similar groups and individuals, (2) organizer for traditional rebellious feelings toward family and school, (3) leader–follower status clearly established

19-2. Class Activity

To increase student awareness of group membership pervasiveness, lead discussion centering on student memberships in small groups. Students often do not remember to mention their families, or partners in current living arrangements. Share that families are a <u>primary</u> group, often exerting influence on other group memberships and activities. Ask students to think of informal as well as formal group memberships, such as committees and staffs, friendship circles, and athletic teams. Give this example of a college student's memberships in small groups:

Family; church; class, or age group; recreational sports team; departmental workforce team on part-time job; study group in a class; friendship circle as social organizing vehicle; college newspaper staff; college social, political, or ethnic organization; political candidate campaign staff volunteers.

Considering that group memberships can be very real to students, with short and long run life implications, students will profit from greater knowledge of small group processes and communication theory.

19-3. Class Activity

Instruct students to list any small groups in which they are members. Remind them to include both formal and informal group memberships. In a subsequent class, divide into small groups and have each student report memberships. After, reinforce the obvious conclusions: in our society, small group memberships are common for all, and it behooves us to learn about small group processes and communication.

19-4. Class Activity

Discuss the important role that small groups play in the world of work. Ask if students believe that the majority of the work accomplished in the world gets done in small groups. Is this a good thing or a bad thing? What are the advantages and the pitfalls to working with colleagues in a small group or team? Ask students with work experience to describe the role of small groups in their workplaces.

19-5. Teaching Strategy

Prepare strong projections of the Dewey steps, accompanied verbatim, perhaps, with Outline, II, A-E, 3.

19-6. Class Activity

Lead a discussion of the characteristics of effective small group members and effective small group leaders. Then ask students to remember an earlier time in the course when they accomplished a public speaking task, assignment, or activity in a small group. Did group members display effective behaviors? Did group leaders emerge? If so, did they display effective leadership behaviors? How can the behaviors of members and leaders complement each other? What negative member and leader behaviors can tear a group apart?

19-7. Teaching Strategy

Consider a group problem-solving discussion as the last major performance of the semester. Students will be asked to meet on their project both inside and outside of class. Students report this kind of group presentation is not uncommon in other classes and workplaces. Hence, the exercise would seem to be excellent practice for both your class, other classes, and the students' welfare in the "real world." Assign students in groups, or post topics on chalkboards to see if students will group themselves satisfactorily by topic. Six-person groups are an ideal size to aim for. If deemed necessary, review again the steps in reflective thinking, encouraging students to use this process and organization in their discussions. The assignment is for groups to plan, research, organize, and present a group panel discussion. In presentation, they are to propose a policy and course of action pertinent to a significant school, community, or national issue/problem. Allow as many weeks as possible for groups to meet and plan their presentations. On presentation days, groups should turn in typed outlines and bibliographies of sources. After each presentation, discuss the speech in terms of group process, use of reflective thinking, trouble spots in either planning or presenting, and individual participant positive highlights.

B. *Six Tips Assist Participating in Small Groups*

19-8. Teaching Strategy

Impress upon students the importance of coming to group meetings *punctually* and *prepared.* "Wheel spinning" occurs when group members give no thought to group tasks between meetings, and actual meeting time is not used efficiently. Suggestions for preparation, you tell them, include reviewing notes from last meeting, reading background material on essential topics for the groups to tackle, and interviewing outside the group for peoples' opinions on relevant group issues. Talk informally to group members; write down ideas for the next meeting.

19-9. Teaching Strategy

By way of opening discussion of problem solving through reflective thinking, share with students common problems among those untrained in group interaction and problem-solving.

A. Severity of problems tends to be assumed, since "Everybody's talking about it."
B. Many people want to begin talking about solutions much too soon in the reflective process.
C. Participants are all too often unaware of necessary roles and patterns of interaction required for effective group problem-solving.
D. Untrained participants often lack research and support for conclusions.
E. Few have been trained in formal and informal leadership skills.
F. Few understand the importance of establishing guiding and evaluative criteria, especially for solutions and implementation of solutions.
G. Few have received guided practice in managing small group conflict.

Inform students that businesses, institutions, and organizations pay well to find people with good training in group process and interaction, and especially those with group leadership skills. You might wish to tell students the emphasis on experiential learning in your class has side benefits — informal but profitable group process training.

19-10. **Teaching Strategy**

Consider, as a clincher for the tips for effective small group participation, showing videotape of the film, *Twelve Angry Men,* the defining film of court jury as small group. Prepare a series of overhead projections to accompany the tape. Projections might be in this order:

JURY COMES TOGETHER AS POSSIBLE GROUP

FORMAL AND INFORMAL LEADERSHIP EMERGES

ROLES BEGIN TO DEVELOP AND SOLIDIFY

INDIVIDUAL ATTITUDES AND VALUES SURFACE

CRITICAL THINKING ABOUT EVIDENCE DEEPENS

LEADERSHIP ROLE SHIFTS TO EMERGING OPINION LEADER

JURY BEGINS TO IGNORE CONFLICT MANAGEMENT:

a. *personalities, not issues, dominate discussion*
b. *personal opinions are submitted as evidence*
c. *in place of seeking compromises, group polarizes*
d. *attempted clarifications founder on personal needs*
e. *evaluative and judgmental assertions substitute for description*
f. *emotions run riot in early and middle stages of decision making*

INDIVIDUALISM SHIFTS TO TEMPORARY ALLIANCES

LOGIC, ARGUMENT, AND EVIDENCE BUILD A CONSENSUS

FORMAL LEADER YIELDS LEADERSHIP TO OPINION LEADER

GROUP PRESSURE CREATES BANDWAGON EFFECT

Students may respond intensely to this film, and quickly grasp the principles being taught. Fifteen minutes of brief previewing of the projections is time normally well-spent, allowing the instructor to merely point to the projections as examples of each projection's point take place. Students will be eager to discuss the film and will not object as instructor melds their points into the group process theory being explored.

19-11. **Class Activity**

Have students take the "Six tips for managing conflict" and change them into reworded negative statements instead of positive. For example, "Keep discussions focused on personal opinion, not facts."

C. *Leadership in Small Groups: Responsibilities, Styles, Structure, Interaction*

19-12. **Teaching Strategy**

Review the three classic styles of leadership: authoritarian, democratic, and laissez faire. Although oversimplified, these conclusions from 1940s research still make sense to students:

Authoritarian Leaders: groups tend to be more accurate and swifter in task completions than with other leaders; group members may report low satisfaction with group process and leader

Democratic Leaders: slower in task completion than with authoritarian leaders; group members usually report much higher satisfaction with tasks and leadership

Laissez Faire Leaders: general dissatisfaction with leadership; disorganized approach to tasks; low group morale

Project the "Leadership Roles in Groups and Tasks" summary as you describe leadership styles; it is an excellent group process teaching device (textbook, page 638). Briefly explain the categories, speculating how the three leaders above might vary in their approaches to and coverage of each category.

19-13. **Class Activity**

Ask students to review the "three leaders' styles" and to think about persons they figure fit one of the leadership styles (parent, teacher, boss, friends, Hollywood characters in type, others). In a subsequent class, divide the class into small groups and ask them share their examples with one another. Lead a class-wide discussion of these questions, encouraging widespread responses: How do you feel about authoritarian leaders? Democratic leaders? Laissez faire leaders? Think of one of the leaders you named who led you in a group — how satisfied were you with that leader and the group results? Were you glad to have been part of the group? How strong, on average, was the motivation of members? If you have been with different style leaders in several important group projects, which style did you prefer? Why? Is a particular style best for all projects and situations? Why or why not? What kind of leader are you?

19-14. Teaching Strategy

Discuss some leaders throughout history, as well as current leaders. This list of names might include Indira Gandhi, Adolph Hitler, Dr. Martin Luther King, Jr., Ann Richards, John F. Kennedy, Jesse Jackson, Elizabeth Dole, and the president of your college or university. Ask students what makes or made these individuals effective or ineffective leaders. What leadership qualities did or do these people possess? Do students think these leaders were "born" or "made"?

19-15. Class Activity

Ask each student to fantasize about being president of these United States. What kind of general leadership style would each student prefer in themselves? How would the desired leadership style manifest itself in cabinet meetings? How would problems get solved, tasks accomplished, conflict be managed at this level of decision making, etc., with this leadership style? How do students perceive the general leadership style of the current president?

19-16. Class Activity

Procure enough index cards to ensure that you can give one to each class member. From page 638 of the textbook, select and type a "task leadership role" on one side of the card. On the other side of each card type one "group maintenance leadership role." When the time arrives shuffle the "cards." Lay the cards down. Instruct students that they are to come forward and select a card, but that they may not show or describe the card to anyone. After cards are drawn, tell students what is on the cards. Instruct students to study their two leadership roles carefully. What does a person in a group say and do when they are playing these roles? In a subsequent class, divide students into five- or six-person groups. Tell them to start a problem-solving discussion on this topic (or, another topic of your choice):

"How can the United States best reduce the yearly number of murders?"

For the first fifteen minutes (or until you call time), each student is to role-play the task leadership role. Ask each to orally list the roles they saw being played. Resume the discussion with each student now role-playing the maintenance leadership social role. Cruise the groups jibing and jabbing. Call time. Have groups orally list the roles they felt were being played. Have each group award one Oscar for best role-player. Consider a pop quiz on the task leadership/ social leadership roles.

19-17. Teaching Strategy

Assign a class "leader for the day," who will have these responsibilities: taking roll; orally summarizing key ideas from the last class; summarizing key ideas in the assigned reading for today's class; providing significant leadership in daily class discussions; and announcing assignments, readings, or upcoming events. Students, of course, take their turns as "leader for the day." Near the end of the course, particularly when this chapter is under study, ask students to reflect on their experiences as class leader. How did it feel to manage a class meeting? What kind of training or experience would have helped them to become a more effective leader? With which kind of leadership style do they most identify? Is it good or bad they feel as they do?

19-18. **Teaching Strategy**

Presentation of material from Outline, VI, A-C, 4 will be quite useful as review and preview.

19-19. **Class Activity**

Direct students to prepare a hypothetical agenda for a short meeting of one of their more formal groups. In a subsequent class, divide into triads and share pertinent information: What kind of group? What kind of meetings are usually held? Is an agenda typically prepared? What are your typical responsibilities in the group? Students should speculate how they would keep their group focused on the supposed agenda.

19-20. **Teaching Strategy**

Most everyone has participated in a nightmare meeting — poorly organized and led, straying from the agenda (if there was one at all), rife with interpersonal conflict, frozen with inability to make decisions, and on and on and on. Who did students think was responsible for the nightmare? Were the students part of the problem? What suggestions does the textbook offer that might have helped that atrocious meeting?

19-21. **Class Activity**

The purpose of this activity (Group Snoop?) is to provide students with the experience of observing problem-solving groups in action. Have students observe a small group meeting, such as a weekly staff meeting, officers' planning session, or committee gathering. Ask students to specifically look for member behaviors that can be categorized as task roles and maintenance roles. (They may have to take notes quickly because the interaction may speed past them.) What were the primary group decisions? If there were no decisions, explain why not. What was the process used for decision making? Did it resemble Dewey's reflective thinking process? How did the leader(s) of the group function? What task roles did the leader assume? Was the leadership effective or lacking? Also ask students to rate the overall quality and effectiveness of the group members. Students should justify their ratings.

19-22. **Class Activity**

The purpose of this activity is to help students identify steps within the problem solving process, as well as to recognize task and maintenance roles of group members. Stage a group problem-solving session using four student volunteers (two women and two men) from your class. Set up the exercise and give time between for preparation. Group members are executives in a major corporation; the group has come together for their monthly meeting. The main task for this meeting is to decide upon a course of action against a high-ranking employee who has sexually harassed female colleagues and subordinates. Assign student volunteers the following roles:

Dominant Dave: Corporate Vice President. Dave is a successful vice president, but is overbearing in his leadership and communicator style. He dominates meetings and openly communicates the fact that he is the immediate supervisor of the other three people in the group. People do not generally "warm" to Dave.

Efficient Emily: National Director of Marketing and Research. Emily is well-organized and comes prepared to make reports and offer suggestions at meetings. However, while Emily is efficient, she is shy and unassertive in her communication with colleagues.

Brown-Nose Bob: National Director of Corporate Expansion. Bob is the perpetual "yes" man to the boss; he is talkative, pleasant, and friendly, but lacks discipline and is averse to hard work. He likes to bluff his way through meetings. His style makes him fairly likeable, but not trustworthy.

Radical Rita: Corporate Director of Human Resources. Rita is a known feminist and civil rights activist within the organization. She voices opinions assertively, but often without tact or consideration for the listener. She is a valued employee, recognized for her accomplishments, but is generally viewed as "pushy" and as having a "chip on her shoulder." As Human Resources Director, she is the most knowledgeable of the group about the sexual harassment case.

As this role-played group meeting ensues, have other class members view the meeting, noting the portrayal of roles in the discussion. Who played what task roles? Who played what maintenance roles? Did the group's problem solving discussion stay on track, following Dewey's process of reflective thinking? If it did not, what or who caused it to stray? Did the group successfully solve its problem or merely table it until another meeting?

D. *Reporting Group Recommendations is Accomplished in One or More of Four Methods*

19-23. Class Activity

This activity will expose students to the various formats available for presenting group recommendations to an audience. Assign students to three large groups. If you have large classes, you may need six groups (i.e., the number reflects the types of group presentation formats provided in the text). Give one topic to the whole class, but request that certain groups use certain formats to structure their group presentations. Students don't have to actually conduct research for this activity; they merely craft points for a hypothetical group speech. The main purpose is to experience differing formats of group presentations. On a designated day, have groups role play a symposium, a forum, and a panel discussion, all focused on the same topic. Decide as a class which format seemed to fit the topic and the group members better than others.

19-24. **Class Activity**

Assign students roles in the scenario below, asking them to read it. Then they should respond to it in a class discussion based on the five questions below.

Sonja, Karen, Marsha, and Chris are assigned to a group project in their English class. Their objectives include: (a) to select a type of literature to study, (b) to research and study the literature, and (c) to make an informative group presentation to the class.

1. How does this group fit the definition of small group communication?
2. What are the advantages and disadvantages of working with a group in this situation?
3. What is the problem or task before the group?
4. What kinds of participants and leaders does this group need?
5. How should the group organize and make an effective presentation to the class? Which format is preferable? Why?

E. *Eight Tips Will Assist Planning an Effective Group Presentation*

19-25. **Teaching Strategy**

Suggest materials from Outline, VII, E, 1-8. Since students will have worked in small groups quite a bit by this time, consider working their experiences into your presentation, as in:

(*specify a particular, recent class small group activity*) "_____, how did your group ensure that each group member understood their part of the group task?"

ONLINE TEACHING PLAN

Preview activity: Go to the Allyn and Bacon website about participation in small groups. The address is http://www.abacon.com/commstudies/groups/group.html. Preview major concepts from this chapter, including group development, conflict, leadership, and types of groups.

Teaching activity: Being a leader in a small group can be a challenge. Put students into "virtual groups" and ask them to complete a task of their choice using online communication only. After they complete their task, ask them to dissect their interactions to uncover how their leader(s) emerged, how they decided on roles and rules, and how they managed (potential) conflict. Write a brief summary.

Review activity: Review class activity number 19-22, as described above. Students should conduct an online role-play using the descriptions for the characters from the activity. In the online role-play, students should try to give examples of concepts from this chapter in the text of their script/messages. After the online role-playing, the instructor should comment on aspects of the script that present relevant chapter concepts.

Teaching Tips for First-time Instructors and Adjunct Professors

Teaching Tips Contents

1   How to be an Effective Teacher

(Adapted from Royse, *Teaching Tips for College and University Instructors: A Practical Guide*, published by Allyn & Bacon, Boston, MA, ©2001, by Pearson Education)

A look at 50 years of research "on the way teachers teach and learners learn" reveals seven broad principles of good teaching practice (Chickering and Gamson, 1987).

1. Frequent student-faculty contact: Faculty who are concerned about their students and their progress and who are perceived to be easy to talk to, serve to motivate and keep students involved. Things you can do to apply this principle:

    ✓ Attend events sponsored by students.
    ✓ Serve as a mentor or advisor to students.
    ✓ Keep "open" or "drop-in" office hours.

2. The encouragement of cooperation among students: There is a wealth of research indicating that students benefit from the use of small group and peer learning instructional approaches. Things you can do to apply this principle:

    ✓ Have students share in class their interests and backgrounds.
    ✓ Create small groups to work on projects together.
    ✓ Encourage students to study together.

3. Active learning techniques: Students don't learn much by sitting in the classroom listening; they must talk about what they are learning, write about it, relate to it, and apply it to their lives. Things you can do to apply this principle:

    ✓ Give students actual problems or situations to analyze.
    ✓ Use role-playing, simulations or hands-on experiments.
    ✓ Encourage students to challenge ideas brought into class.

4. Prompt feedback: Learning theory research has consistently shown that the quicker the feedback, the greater the learning. Things you can do to apply this principle:

    ✓ Return quizzes and exams by the next class meeting.
    ✓ Return homework within one week.
    ✓ Provide students with detailed comments on their written papers.

5. Emphasize time on task: This principle refers to the amount of actual involvement with the material being studied and applies, obviously, to the way the instructor uses classroom instructional time. Faculty need good time-management skills. Things you can do to apply this principle:

    ✓ Require students who miss classes to make up lost work.
    ✓ Require students to rehearse before making oral presentations.
    ✓ Don't let class breaks stretch out too long.

6. Communicating high expectations: The key here is not to make the course impossibly difficult, but to have goals that can be attained as long as individual learners stretch and work hard, going beyond what they already know. Things you can do to apply this principle:

    ✓ Communicate your expectations orally and in writing at the beginning of the course.
    ✓ Explain the penalties for students who turn work in late.
    ✓ Identify excellent work by students; display exemplars if possible.

7. Respecting diverse talents and ways of learning: Within any classroom there will be students who have latent talents and some with skills and abilities far beyond any that you might imagine. Understanding your students as individuals and showing regard for their unique talents is "likely to facilitate student growth and development in every sphere – academic, social, personal, and vocational" (Sorcinelli, 1991, p.21). Things you can do to apply this principle:

- ✓ Use diverse teaching approaches.
- ✓ Allow students some choice of readings and assignments.
- ✓ Try to find out students' backgrounds and interests.

✓ Tips for Thriving: Creating an Inclusive Classroom

How do you model an open, accepting attitude within your classroom where students will feel it is safe to engage in give-and-take discussions? Firstly, view students as individuals instead of representatives of separate and distinct groups. Cultivate a climate that is respectful of diverse viewpoints, and don't allow ridicule, defamatory or hurtful remarks. Try to encourage everyone in the class to participate, and be alert to showing favoritism.

---

2   Today's Undergraduate Students

(Adapted from: Lyons et al, *The Adjunct Professor's Guide to Success*, published by Allyn & Bacon, Boston, MA, ©1999, by Pearson Education)

Total enrollment in all forms of higher education has increased over 65% in the last thirty years. Much of this increase was among part-time students who now comprise over 70% of total college enrollment. The number of "nontraditional" students, typically defined as 25 years of age or older, has been growing more rapidly than the number of "traditional" students, those under 25 years of age. Though there is a great deal of common ground between students of any age, there are some key differences between younger and older students.

Traditional students: Much more than in previous generations, traditional students are the products of dysfunctional families and have had a less effective primary and secondary education. Traditional students have been conditioned by the aftermath of high-profile ethical scandals (such as Watergate), creating a mindset of cynicism and lack of respect for authority figures – including college professors. Students of this generation are quick to proclaim their "rights". Many of today's students perceive professors as service providers, class attendance as a matter of individual choice, and grades as "pay" to which they are entitled for meeting standards they perceive as reasonable.

Nontraditional students: Many older students are attending college after a long lay-off, frequently doubting their ability to succeed. The other time-consuming challenges in their lives – children, work, caring for aging parents – often prevent adequate preparation for class or contribute to frequent absences. While traditional students demand their "rights," many older students won't ask for the smallest extra consideration (e.g., to turn a project in a few days late). Most older students learn best by doing, by applying the theory of the textbook to the rich set of experiences they have accumulated over the years.

Emerging influences: Today, a fourth of all undergraduate students are members of minority groups. Obviously, ethnicity, language, religion, culture, and sexual orientation are each significant issues to which a professor should be sensitive. The successful professor sees these differences as an opportunity rather than a threat to learning.

✓ Tips for Thriving: Be a "Facilitator of Learning"

Be energized by students who "don't get it" rather than judgmental of their shortcomings. View yourself as a "facilitator of learning" rather than a "sage on a stage."

What students want from college professors: While each student subgroup has particular characteristics that affect the dynamics of a college learning environment, students consistently need the following from their college instructors:

- ✓ Consistently communicated expectations of student performance that are reasonable in quantity and quality
- ✓ Sensitivity to the diverse demands on students and reasonable flexibility in accommodating them
- ✓ Effective use of classroom time
- ✓ A classroom environment that includes humor and spontaneity
- ✓ Examinations that address issues properly covered in class and are appropriate to the level of the majority of the students in the class
- ✓ Consistently positive treatment of individual students

The new paradigm of "colleges and universities as service providers to consumer-oriented students" is now firmly entrenched. The successful professor will do well to embrace it.

3   Planning Your Course

(Adapted from Royse, *Teaching Tips for College and University Instructors: A Practical Guide*, published by Allyn & Bacon, Boston, MA, ©2001, by Pearson Education)

Constructing the syllabus: The syllabus should clearly communicate course objectives, assignments, required readings, and grading policies. Think of the syllabus as a stand-alone document. Those students who miss the first or second meeting of a class should be able to learn most of what they need to know about the requirements of the course from reading the syllabus. Start by collecting syllabi from colleagues who have recently taught the course you will be teaching and look for common threads and themes.

Problems to avoid: One mistake commonly made by educators teaching a course for the first time is that they may have rich and intricate visions of how they want students to demonstrate comprehension and synthesis of the material, but they somehow fail to convey this information to those enrolled. Check your syllabus to make sure your expectations have been fully articulated. Be very specific. Avoid vaguely worded instructions:

Instruction	Students may interpret as:
"Write a short paper."	Write a paragraph.
	Write half a page.
	Type a two-page paper.
"Keep a log of your experiences."	Make daily entries.
	Make an entry when the spirit moves me.
	At the end of term, record what I recall.
"Obtain an article from the library."	Any magazine article.
	An article from a professional journal.
	A column from a newsletter.

☑ **Tips for Thriving: Visual Quality**

Students today are highly visual learners, so you should give special emphasis to the visual quality of the materials you provide to students. Incorporate graphics into your syllabus and other handouts. Color-code your materials so material for different sections of the course are on different colored papers. Such visuals are likely to create a perception among students that you are contemporary.

(Adapted from: Lyons et al, *The Adjunct Professor's Guide to Success*, published by Allyn & Bacon, Boston, MA, ©1999, by Pearson Education)

Success in achieving a great start is almost always directly attributable to the quality and quantity of planning that has been invested by the course professor. If the first meeting of your class is to be successful, you should strive to achieve seven distinct goals.

Create a Positive First Impression: Renowned communications consultant Roger Ailes (1996) claims you have fewer than 10 seconds to create a positive image of yourself. Students are greatly influenced by the visual component; therefore you must look the part of the professional professor. Dress as you would for a professional job interview. Greet each student entering the room. Be approachable and genuine.

Introduce Yourself Effectively: Communicate to students who you are and why you are credible as the teacher of the course. Seek to establish your approachability by "building common ground," such as stating your understanding of students' hectic lifestyles or their common preconceptions toward the subject matter.

Clarify the Goals and Expectations: Make an acetate transparency of each page of the syllabus for display on an overhead projector and using a cover sheet, expose each section as you explain it. Provide clarification and elicit questions.

Conduct an Activity that Introduces Students to Each Other: Students' chances of being able to complete a course effectively is enhanced if each comes to perceive the classmates as a "support network." The small amount of time you invest in an icebreaker will help create a positive classroom atmosphere and pay additional dividends throughout the term.

✔ **Tips for Thriving: Icebreaker**

The following activity allows students to get acquainted, exchange opinions, and consider new ideas, values or solutions to problems. It's a great way to promote self-disclosure or an active exchange of viewpoints.

Procedure

1. Give students one or more Post-it™ notes
2. Ask them to write on their note(s) one of the following:
    a. A *value* they hold
    b. An *experience* they have had recently
    c. A *creative idea* or solution to a problem you have posed
    d. A *question* they have about the subject matter of the class
    e. An *opinion* they hold about a topic of your choosing
    f. A *fact* about themselves or the subject matter of the class
3. Ask students to stick the note(s) on their clothing and circulate around the room reading each other's notes.
4. Next, have students mingle once again and negotiate a trade of Post-it™ notes with one another. The trade should be based on a desire to possess a particular value, experience, idea, question, opinion or fact for a short period of time. Set the rule that all trades have to be two-way. Encourage students to make as many trades as they like.
5. Reconvene the class and ask students to share what trades they made and why. (e.g., "I traded for a note that Sally had stating that she has traveled to Eastern Europe. I would really like to travel there because I have ancestors from Hungary and the Ukraine.")

(Adapted from: Silverman, *Active Learning: 101 Strategies to Teach Any Subject*, published by Allyn & Bacon, Boston, MA, ©1996, by Pearson Education).

Learn Students' Names: A student who is regularly addressed by name feels more valued, is invested more effectively in classroom discussion, and will approach the professor with questions and concerns.

Whet Students' Appetite for the Course Material: The textbook adopted for the course is critical to your success. Your first meeting should include a review of its approach, features, and sequencing. Explain to students what percentage of class tests will be derived from material from the textbook.

Reassure Students of the Value of the Course: At the close of your first meeting reassure students that the course will be a valuable learning experience and a wise investment of their time. Review the reasons why the course is a good investment: important and relevant content, interesting classmates, and a dynamic classroom environment.

5   Strategies for Teaching and Learning

(Adapted from: Silverman, *Active Learning: 101 Strategies to Teach Any Subject*, published by Allyn & Bacon, Boston, MA, ©1996, by Pearson Education)

Getting participation through active learning: To learn something well, it helps to hear it, see it, ask questions about it, and discuss it with others. What makes learning "active"? When learning is active, students do most of the work: they use their brains to study ideas, solve problems, and apply what they learn. Active learning is fast-paced, fun, supportive, and personally engaging. Active learning cannot occur without student participation, so there are various ways to structure discussion and obtain responses from students at any time during a class. Here are ten methods to get participation at any time:

1. **Open discussion**. Ask a question and open it up to the entire class without further structuring.
2. **Response cards**. Pass out index cards and request anonymous answers to your questions.
3. **Polling**. Design a short survey that is filled out and tallied on the spot.
4. **Subgroup discussion**. Break students into subgroups of three or more to share and record information.
5. **Learning partners**. Have students work on tasks with the student sitting next to them.
6. **Whips**. Go around the group and obtain short responses to key questions – invite students to pass if they wish.
7. **Panels**. Invite a small number of students to present their views in front of the class.
8. **Fishbowl**. Ask a portion of the class to form a discussion circle and have the remaining students form a listening circle around them. Bring new groups into the inner circle to continue the discussion.
9. **Games**. Use a fun exercise or quiz game to elicit students' ideas, knowledge, or skill.
10. **Calling on the next speaker**. Ask students to raise their hands when they want to share their views and ask the current speaker to choose the next speaker.

(Adapted from Royse, *Teaching Tips for College and University Instructors: A Practical Guide*, published by Allyn & Bacon, Boston, MA, ©2001, by Pearson Education)

Team learning: The essential features of this small group learning approach, developed originally for use in large college classrooms are (1) relatively permanent heterogeneous task groups; (2) grading based on a combination of individual performance, group performance, and peer evaluation; (3) organization of the course so that the majority of class time is spent on small group activities; (4) a six-step instructional process similar to the following model:

1. Individual study of material outside of the class is assigned.
2. Individual testing is used (multiple choice questions over homework at the beginning of class)
3. Groups discuss their answers and then are given a group test of the same items. They then get immediate feedback (answers).
4. Groups may prepare written appeals of items.

5. Feedback is given from instructor.
6. An application-oriented activity is assigned (e.g. a problem to be solved requiring input from all group members).

If you plan to use team learning in your class, inform students at the beginning of the course of your intentions to do so and explain the benefits of small group learning. Foster group cohesion by sitting groups together and letting them choose "identities" such as a team name or slogan. You will need to structure and supervise the groups and ensure that the projects build on newly acquired learning. Make the projects realistic and interesting and ensure that they are adequately structured so that each member's contribution is 25 percent. Students should be given criteria by which they can assess and evaluate the contributions of their peers on a project-by-project basis (Michaelsen, 1994).

✔ Tips for Thriving: Active Learning and Lecturing

Lecturing is one of the most time-honored teaching methods, but does it have a place in an active learning environment? There are times when lecturing can be effective. Think about the following when planning a lecture:

Build Interest: Capture your students' attention by leading off with an anecdote or cartoon.
Maximize Understanding and Retention: Use brief handouts and demonstrations as a visual backup to enable your students to see as well as hear.
Involve Students during the Lecture: Interrupt the lecture occasionally to challenge students to answer spot quiz questions.
Reinforce the Lecture: Give students a self-scoring review test at the end of the lecture.

---

6   Grading and Assessment Techniques

(Adapted from Wankat, *The Effective, Efficient Professor: Teaching, Scholarship and Service*, published by Allyn & Bacon, Boston, MA, ©2002, by Pearson Education)

Philosophy of grading: Develop your own philosophy of grading by picturing in your mind the performance of typical A students, B students and so on. Try different grading methods until you find one that fits your philosophy and is reasonably fair. Always look closely at students on grade borders – take into account personal factors if the group is small. Be consistent with or slightly more generous than the procedure outlined in your syllabus.

Criterion grading: Professor Philip Wankat writes: "I currently use a form of criterion grading for my sophomore and junior courses. I list the scores in the syllabus that will guarantee the students As, Bs and so forth. For example, a score of 85 to 100 guarantees an A; 75 to 85, a B; 65 to 75, a C; and 55 to 65, a D. If half the class gets above 85% they all get an A. This reduces competition and allows students to work together and help each other. The standard grade gives students something to aim for and tells them exactly what their grade is at any time. For students whose net scores are close to the borders at the end of the course, I look at other factors before deciding a final grade such as attendance."

✔ Tips for Thriving: Result Feedback

As stated earlier, feedback on results is the most effective of motivating factors. Anxious students are especially hungry for positive feedback. You can quickly and easily provide it by simply writing "Great job!" on the answer sheets or tests. For students who didn't perform well, a brief note such as "I'd love to talk with you at the end of class" can be especially reassuring. The key is to be proactive and maintain high standards, while requiring students to retain ownership of their success.

7 Using Technology

(Adapted from: Sanders, *Creating Learning-Centered Courses for the World Wide Web*, published by Allyn & Bacon, Boston, MA, ©2001, by Pearson Education)

The Web as a source of teaching and learning has generated a great deal of excitement and hyperbole. The Web is neither a panacea nor a demon, but it can be a valuable tool. Among the many misunderstandings about the use of Web pages for teaching and learning is a view that such efforts must encompass an entire course. Like any other tool in a course (e.g. lectures, discussions, films, or field trips) online material can be incorporated to enhance the learning experience.

The best way to start using the Web in a course is with small steps. Developing a single lesson or assignment, a syllabus, or a few well-chosen links makes more sense than trying to develop a whole course without sufficient support or experience. Testing Web materials with a class that regularly meets face-to-face helps a faculty member gauge how well a lesson using the Web works. Making adjustments within the context of a traditional class helps fine-tune Web lessons that may be offered in distance education without face-to-face interaction.

✔ Tips for Thriving: Using Videos

Generally a videotape should not exceed half and hour in length. Always preview a video before showing it to ensure the content, language, and complexity are appropriate for your students. Include major videos on your syllabus to encourage attendance and integrate them into the context of the course. Plan to evaluate students' retention of the concepts on exams or through reports. Avoid reinforcing the common student perception that watching a video is a time-filler.

By beginning with good practices in learning, we ask not how the new technology can help us do a better job of getting students to learn, but rather we ask how good pedagogy be better implemented with the new technology.

8 Managing Problem Situations

(Adapted from Wankat, *The Effective, Efficient Professor: Teaching, Scholarship and Service*, published by Allyn & Bacon, Boston, MA, ©2002, by Pearson Education)

Cheating: Cheating is one behavior that should not be tolerated. Tolerating cheating tends to make it worse. Prevention of cheating is much more effective than trying to cure it once it has occurred. A professor can prevent cheating by:

- Creating rapport with students
- Gaining a reputation for giving fair tests
- Giving clear instructions and guidelines before, during, and after tests
- Educating students on the ethics of plagiarism
- Requiring periodic progress reports and outlines before a paper is due

Try to develop exams that are perceived as fair and secure by students. Often, the accusation that certain questions were tricky is valid as it relates to ambiguous language and trivial material. Ask your mentor or an experienced instructor to closely review the final draft of your first few exams for these factors.

✓ Tips for Thriving: Discipline

One effective method for dealing with some discipline problems is to ask the class for feedback (Angelo & Cross, 1993) In a one-minute quiz, ask the students, "What can I do to help you learn?" Collate the responses and present them to the class. If behavior such as excessive talking appears in some responses (e.g. "Tell people to shut up") this gives you the backing to ask students to be quiet. Use of properly channeled peer pressure is often effective in controlling undesired behavior

---

(Adapted from Royse, *Teaching Tips for College and University Instructors: A Practical Guide*, published by Allyn & Bacon, Boston, MA, ©2001, by Pearson Education)

Unmotivated Students: There are numerous reasons why students may not be motivated. The "required course" scenario is a likely explanation – although politics in colonial America is your life's work, it is safe to assume that not everyone will share your enthusiasm. There are also personal reasons such as a death of a loved one or depression. Whenever you detect a pattern that you assume to be due to lack of motivation (e.g. missing classes, not handing assignments in on time, non-participation in class), arrange a time to have the student meet with you outside the classroom. Candidly express your concerns and then listen.

Motivating students is part of the faculty members' job. To increase motivation professors should: show enthusiasm for the topic; use various media and methods to present material; use humor in the classroom; employ activities that encourage active learning; and give frequent, positive feedback.

(Adapted from Baiocco/Waters, *Successful College Teaching*, published by Allyn & Bacon, Boston, MA, ©1998, by Pearson Education)

Credibility Problems. If you are an inexperienced instructor you may have problems with students not taking you seriously. At the first class meeting articulate clear rules of classroom decorum and comport yourself with dignity and respect for students. Try to exude that you are in charge and are the "authority" and avoid trying to pose as the students' friend.

9   Surviving When You're Not Prepared

(Adapted from: Lyons et al, *The Adjunct Professor's Guide to Success*, published by Allyn & Bacon, Boston, MA, ©1999, by Pearson Education)

Despite your thorough course planning, your concern for students, and commitment to the institution, situations will arise – illness, family emergencies – that prevent you from being fully prepared for every class meeting. Most students will excuse one flawed performance during a term, but try to develop contingency plans you can employ on short notice. These might include:

- Recruiting a guest speaker from your circle of colleagues to deliver a presentation that might interest your students.
- Conducting a carousel brainstorming activity, in which a course issue is examined from several perspectives. Divide the students in to groups to identify facts appropriate to each perspective. For example, you might want to do a SWOT analysis (Strengths, Weaknesses, Opportunities, Threats) on a particular organization or public figure.
- Dividing the class into groups of three or four and asking them to develop several questions that would be appropriate for inclusion on your next exam.
- Identify a video at your local rental store that embellishes material from the course.
- Assign students roles (e.g. press, governmental figures, etc.), and conduct a focused analysis of a late-breaking news story related to your course.
- Divide students into groups to work on an assigned course project or upcoming exam.
- As a last resort, admit your inability to prepare a class and allow students input into formulating a strategy for best utilizing class time.

In each case, the key is to shift the initial attention away from yourself (to permit you to gather your thoughts) and onto an activity that engages students in a new and significant way.

10   Improving Your Performance

(Adapted from: Lyons et al, *The Adjunct Professor's Guide to Success*, published by Allyn & Bacon, Boston, MA, ©1999, by Pearson Education)

The instructor who regularly engages in systematic self-evaluation will unquestionably derive greater reward from the formal methods of evaluation commonly employed by colleges and universities. One method for providing structure to an ongoing system of self-evaluation is to keep a journal of reflections on your teaching experiences. Regularly invest 15 or 20 introspective minutes following each class meeting to focus especially on the strategies and events in class that you feel could be improved. Committing your thoughts and emotions enables you to develop more effective habits, build confidence in your teaching performance, and make more effective comparisons later. The following questions will help guide self-assessment:

> *How do I typically begin the class?*
> *Where/How do I position myself in the class?*
> *How do I move in the classroom?*
> *Where are my eyes usually focused?*
> *Do I facilitate students' visual processing of course material?*
> *Do I change the speed, volume, energy, and tone of my voice?*
> *How do I ask questions of students?*
> *How often, and when, do I smile or laugh in class?*
> *How do I react when students are inattentive?*
> *How do I react when students disagree or challenge what I say?*
> *How do I typically end a class?*

✓ Tips for Thriving: Video-Recording Your Class

In recent years a wide range if professionals have markedly improved their job performance by employing video recorders in their preparation efforts. As an instructor, an effective method might be to ask your mentor or another colleague to tape a 10 to 15 minute mini-lesson then to debrief it using the assessment questions above. Critiquing a videotaped session provides objectivity and is therefore more likely to effect change. Involving a colleague as an informal coach will enable you to gain from their experience and perspective and will reduce the chances of your engaging in self-depreciation.

References

Ailes, R. (1996) *You are the message: Getting what you want by being who you are.* New York: Doubleday.

Chickering, A.W., & Gamson, Z.F. (1987) Seven principles for good practice in undergraduate education. AAHE Bulletin, 39, 3-7.

Michaelson, L.K. (1994). Team Learning: Making a case for the small-group option. In K.W. Prichard & R.M. Sawyer (Eds.), *Handbook of college teaching.* Westport, CT: Greenwood Press.

Sorcinelli, M.D. (1991). Research findings on the seven principles. In A.W. Chickering & Z. Gamson (eds.), *Applying the seven principles of good practice in undergraduate education.* New Directions for Teaching and Learning #47. San Francisco: Jossey-Bass.